W9-BGO-401

The
Corporate
Planet

SANDRA:
OTRO INGREDIENTE
de la LIBERTAD
es el "SABER"
La VERDAD, y las
posibilidad para
ACTUAR. TE
Queremos Mucho
TU MAMÁ

The Corporate Planet

Ecology and Politics in

the Age of Globalization

Joshua Karliner

Sierra Club Books – San Francisco

The Sierra Club, founded in 1892 by John Muir, has devoted itself to the study and protection of the earth's scenic and ecological resources—mountains, wetlands, woodlands, wild shores and rivers, deserts and plains. The publishing program of the Sierra Club offers books to the public as a non-profit educational service in the hope that they may enlarge the public's understanding of the Club's basic concerns. The point of view expressed in each book, however, does not necessarily represent that of the Club. The Sierra Club has some sixty chapters coast to coast, in Canada, Hawaii, and Alaska. For information about how you may participate in its programs to preserve wilderness and the quality of life, please address inquiries to Sierra Club, 85 Second Street, San Francisco, CA 94105.

www.sierraclub.org/books

Copyright © 1997 by Joshua Karliner

The publisher thanks Milton Nascimento and Fernando Brandt for permission to reprint an excerpt from *Planeta Blue*, words and music by Milton Nascimento and Fernando Brandt. © Copyright 1987 Nascimento Edicoes Musicais Ltda. and Tres Pontas Edicoes Musicais Ltda. All rights controlled and administered in the United States and Canada by EMI April Music, Inc. All rights reserved. International Copyright Secured. Used by permission.

All rights reserved under International and Pan-American Copyright Conventions. No part of this book may be reproduced in any form or by any electronic or mechanical means, including information storage and retrieval systems, without permission in writing from the publisher.

Library of Congress Cataloging-in-Publication Data
Karliner, Joshua
    The corporate planet: ecology and politics in the age of globalization/by Joshua Karliner.
       p. cm.
    Includes bibliographical references and index.
    ISBN 0-87156-434-3 (alk. paper)
    1. International business enterprises—Environmental aspects.
    2. Environmental policy. I. Title.
HD2755.5.K375   1997
658.4'08—dc21   97-8088

Production by Susan Ristow
Cover and book design by Amy Evans

Printed in the United States of America on acid-free paper containing a minimum of 50% recovered waste paper of which at least 10% of the fiber content is post-consumer waste.

10 9 8 7 6 5 4 3 2

For my parents, Joel and Adela,
who, in a great number of ways,
made this book possible

This first impression of

The Blue Planet

Is not the truest vision

Beyond the color, blue is also very sad

There can be a naked side, a raw side

A dark side of blue

Milton Nascimento
& Fernando Bradt,
"O Planeta Blue"

Contents

Preface

The idea for this book emerged from my experience helping to coordinate Greenpeace International's work for the United Nations Earth Summit in Rio de Janeiro. It was 1992 and the world was changing rapidly. The Cold War had ended and economic globalization seemed to be the watchword of the day. Quickly leading the march were a few hundred transnational corporations—some of the most powerful economic forces in the history of civilization. At the Earth Summit these giant energy, chemical, forest products and food corporations claimed that they were the ones with the solutions to the world's environmental and social problems. Greenpeace and a number of other environment and development groups disagreed.

In Rio's aftermath I decided to take the time to study this issue further. The ensuing process consumed me for nearly four years. It has been a multifaceted adventure. My research took me across the southwestern United States, down into Mexico, farther south to Argentina, Uruguay and Chile and back to Brazil. I also visited Asia, spending time in Japan, Hong Kong, China, Vietnam, Malaysia, Papua New Guinea and India. Ideally I would have personally visited Europe and Africa as well, rounding out worldwide research on a global topic. Unfortunately, time and money ran short, and I decided to complete the project before all my hair either turned gray or fell out.

What I found over this time and during my journeys is that, despite having made some minor modifications, transnational corporations continue to speed the planet full throttle down a socially and ecologically unsustainable course while whistling a tune of change. The following chapters describe this phenomenon, detailing how self-defined "corporate environmentalists" have fabricated an elaborate series of green veils through which they obfuscate their responsibility for some of the most destructive activity ever unleashed upon the world.

As I researched and wrote I also discovered many sources of hope. Everywhere I went, people were not only friendly, open and supportive, but many also shared a set of values that were diametrically opposed to the most destructive aspects of corporate globalization. Not a small number of these individuals, communities, organizations and networks were engaged in ongoing battles with individual corporations that were attempting to usurp their resources or dump a load of toxic waste in their backyards. Some groups were trying to build or maintain alternative, locally based economies, and a growing number were working together with their counterparts across the planet to develop democratic methods and mechanisms for holding transnational corporations accountable on the local, national and international levels. When taken together, all these efforts form a vibrant web of activism for social, economic and environmental justice that I like to call *grassroots globalization*. This phenomenon forms the basis of my environmental optimism.

This book is divided into seven interrelated chapters. Each is designed to explore various aspects of corporate globalization while highlighting those who are resisting its mal-effects. Chapter One, "The Corporate Planet," offers an overview of the role that transnational corporations are playing as the "engines" of economic globalization. It then presents an analysis of their far-reaching ecological and social impacts. Chapter Two, "The Greening of Global Reach," uses the Earth Summit experience and a number of other examples to explore the phenomenon of corporate environmentalism, documenting how many transnational corporations and industry associations have begun to play a leading role in defining ecological problems and "solutions" on a worldwide scale. These first two chapters serve as an introduction that sets the stage for a series of case studies which demonstrate in more detail how ecology and politics are interacting in this, the age of globalization.

Chapter Three, "Surfing the Pipeline," traces the Chevron Corporation's history as a classic U.S. transnational, following it from its days as a California oil company that was swallowed up by the Rockefeller Standard Oil Trust at the turn of the century, up to present-day battles concerning the global oil industry's environmental impacts. The fourth chapter, "Island of Dreams," examines the Mitsubishi Group of corporations, whose history is emblematic of the rise, worldwide growth and environmental impacts of Japanese corporate power.

Chapter Five, "Toxic Empire," examines the role that the World Bank and various free trade agreements play in promoting the spread of environmentally destructive modes of production. It also looks in depth at the three major paths hazardous industry follows when it migrates from the North to the South and from the West to the East. Chapter Six, "The Emerald City," takes a broad look at the role that advertising, public relations and media corporations are playing in environmental politics. It examines how these transnationals drive the consumerism responsible for many environmental and social problems, how they paint green images for polluting companies and how they have contributed to a strategy aimed at co-opting mainstream green groups.

Finally, Chapter Seven, "Grassroots Globalization," seeks to bring to light a dispersed but determined worldwide movement that is confronting the mal-effects of corporate globalization.

In the course of this book I use a number of key terms repeatedly. In the interests of clarity, I want to define them at the outset, although no attempt at definitions is without qualifications and contradictions.

The word *corporation* is found throughout these pages. You probably already know what one is, but just for the record, corporations are legal fictions, first created by the British Crown in the sixteenth century. The Crown perceived a need to encourage people to take the economic risk of investing in colonial adventures and therefore chartered corporations in order to limit an investor's liability for losses to the amount of his or her investment—a privilege not enjoyed by individual citizens. Today, corporations are still chartered by state or national governments, which also reserve the right to revoke such charters.[1]

More than 40,000 modern-day descendants of the original corporations operate internationally.[2] These *transnational corporations* were defined back in the 1970s by the United Nations Economic and Social Council as "all enterprises which control assets—factories, mines, sales offices and the like—in two or more countries."[3] The vast majority of transnational corporations are relatively small and carry out business in only a few countries at a time. Many medium-size corporations function regionally (e.g., in the Americas, Europe or Asia). Most of the few hundred largest corporations—in which the greatest economic and political power is concentrated—operate on a worldwide basis. These are known as *global corporations*. Throughout this book, the terms *transnational* and *global corporations* are sometimes used interchangeably.

Due to the tumultuous transformations of recent decades, accurate geopolitical and economic definitions are tough to come by. I use the

terms *North* and *South* throughout the book. The *North* distinguishes the
twenty-odd wealthy industrialized nations, most of which are located in
the northern regions of the planet and consume most of the world's
resources, serve as home base for the vast majority of transnational corporations and maintain the bulk of the world's political, economic and
military power. The rest of the world, which is less industrialized, has
more people, is by most measures poorer, and is less politically powerful, generally is located in the physical *South*. Of course, this is an inadequate definition, because aside from purely geographical inconsisten-
cies, there are elements of the wealthy industrialized North in the
impoverished South, and there is a growing South in the North as well.
What's more, levels of economic development within the South range
greatly, from newly industrializing countries (NICs) such as Taiwan and
South Korea to deeply impoverished countries such as the Congo and
Chad.[4] I also find it useful to occasionally make reference to the "East"
and "West," so as to distinguish the former communist countries of
Eastern Europe—which in many respects increasingly resemble Third
World countries—from the Western industrialized nations.

But other definitions are even less satisfactory. For instance, the commonly used parlance of "developed" and "developing" nations implies
that the "developed" have arrived at some predefined, desirable goal,
whereas the "developing" are still striving to get there. These terms
ignore the huge environmental and social problems of the North, as
well as the fact that if the rest of the world were to achieve such "development" it would trigger a global ecological collapse. Furthermore, the
end of the Cold War, as well as the emergence of the NICs, has made the
categories of "First," "Second" and "Third" Worlds virtually obsolete.
However, many of my colleagues from the *Third World* still find the term
useful and proudly employ it. I, too, often use it when referring to the
countries of the South.

Finally, there are three interrelated principles that run to the core of
the popular response to corporations described in this book. One can
find them imbedded in the demands of a broad spectrum of environmental activists who are waging battles against corporate polluters,
World Bank structural adjustment projects, free trade agreements and a
host of other socially and environmentally destructive activities. All, in
one way or another, base their theory and the practical alternatives they
propose on the principles of ecological sustainability, social justice and
democratic participation.

Ecological sustainability can perhaps be best defined as the long-term viability of local, regional and global ecosystems and the maintenance of the biological and genetic integrity of those ecosystems.[5] Of course, such environmental protection cannot be achieved without the inclusion of a strong social dimension. Indeed, some measures, if decided upon and taken up solely in the name of the environment, can lead to negative and undesirable social and political repercussions.

Thus the second principle of *social justice* (often referred to as social equity or economic justice) comes into play. In this book, social justice is taken to mean empowering the world's impoverished majority so that they can meet their basic needs. It also requires protecting basic human rights, as well as racial, ethnic and cultural diversity. It signifies supporting labor rights and gender equality. Moreover, it means providing for a more just and equal access to resources within and between nations—something that, adhering to the principle of ecological sustainability, will require the reduction of consumption in the industrialized North and the concomitant rise of basic consumption in the South.

The third principle, *democratic participation* (also referred to as popular participation or popular democracy), is an essential vehicle for achieving ecological sustainability and social justice. This principle was perhaps best defined by the United Nations Research Institute on Social Development, which described it as "organised efforts to increase control over resources and regulative institutions in given social situations, on the part of groups and movements of those hitherto excluded from such control."[6]

So much for definitions. Now I must attempt to acknowledge the vast support, encouragement and generosity I received while working on this project. So many people did so much to make this book happen. I beg the forgiveness of those whose names I will inevitably leave out. First, I must thank my agent, Joe Spieler, who believed in this project enough to make it happen, and who went to bat for it in the most crucial moment. My editor, Danny Moses, also deserves my sincerest gratitude for laying a strong yet calm hand on what came to him as a somewhat unwieldy manuscript. I also must thank Linda Gunnarson for her sharp copyediting, as well as Erik Migdail, Jim Cohee, Sharon Donovan, Nick Setka, Peter Beren and the other fine folks at Sierra Club Books who put time and energy into this project.

A number of people spent a good amount of their valuable time reviewing drafts. I have them to thank for making this a much better, more accurate work than it would otherwise have been. Special gratitude goes to Michael Robins, Michele Perrault, Vandana Shiva and Joel Karliner, who read the entire manuscript and made some very helpful suggestions. Tani Adams, China Brotsky, Kenny Bruno, John Cavanagh, Jack Doyle, Danny Faber, Harris Gleckman, Dave Henson, Adela Karliner, Greg Karras, Yoichi Kuroda, Ralph Lewin, Jerry Mander, Michael Marx, Steven McKay, Maria Rogers, Dan Seligman, John Stauber, Kay Treakle, Victor Wallis and Larry Williams each critiqued at least one chapter.

This book would not have been possible without the generous financial support that a number of institutions and individuals provided for TRAC—the Transnational Resource and Action Center—the organization that I direct and that helped provide a context for this book. These philanthropists include Lucy Miller and the Lawson–Valentine Foundation, Al and Don Lippincott at the Lippincott Foundation, the Rockwood Foundation, the late W. H. Ferry, Carol Bernstein Ferry, Joel and Adela Karliner, Harriet Barlow, the Burr Oak Fund, and the V Fund. Thank you, all.

In addition to various employees of a number of corporations who wish to remain anonymous, many other people provided buckets of help along the way, letting me stay in their homes, passing along ideas, contacts, information and reports, helping with fact checking, and generally encouraging me as I slogged through the sometimes torturous writing process. They include Paulo Adario, Tom Athanasiou, Manuel Baquedano, Nikki Fortunato Bas, Joanne Bauer, Fernando Bejarano, Walden Bello, Pablo Bergel, Jose Bravo, China Brotsky, Brian and Richard Brunton, Andre Carothers, Chee Yoke Ling, the people of Chevron Niugini, Lafcadio Cortesi, Charlie Cray, Clif Curtis, E. Deenadayalan, Antonio Diaz, Mark Dowie, Brad Erickson, Ana Feage, Grant Ferrier, Jeanne Gauna, Paul Gonsalves, Jed Greer, Richard Grossman, Matt Hale, Nicholas Hildyard, Lisa Hoyos, Allan Hunt-Badiner, Vincent Idemyor, Joe Kane, Danny Kennedy, Martin Khor, Yoriko Kishimoto, Sara Larrain, Ann Leonard, Kate Mailer, Francesco Martone, Jane McAlevey, Victor Menotti, Richard Moore, Ward Morehouse, Nick Morgan, Cindy Nolan, Pratap Parameswaran and the folks at Third World Network–Penang, Simon Pasingan, Michele Perrault, Ruben Prieto, Silvia Ribeiro and Comunidad del Sur/REDES in Uruguay, Marcia Rivera and the people at CLACSO in Buenos Aires, Maria Luisa Robleto, Kirby Rogers, Atila Roque, Satinath Sarangi, Kavaljit Singh, Teruko Sugimoto, Ana Toni, Ryusoke Ugo, Miriam Ursua,

Jim Vallette, David Weir, Rob Weissman, Sara Wood, and Ariadne and Palmer Wright.

Finally, I must thank my partner, Maria Rogers, who has celebrated this project with me on many occasions, whose love and support helped me make it through the most trying of times, and who carried Sofia into this world in the middle of the book process, bringing many people much joy.

Of course, despite all the incredible support and help everyone has given me, I am responsible for any unintentional errors and for the entire content of this work from cover to cover.

The
Corporate
Planet

Chapter One

The Corporate Planet

Environment and the Crisis of Globalization

The global corporation is the most powerful human organization yet devised for colonizing the future. By scanning the entire planet for opportunities, by shifting its resources from industry to industry and country to country, and by keeping its overriding goal simple—worldwide profit maximization—it has become an institution of unique power. . . . In making business decisions today they are creating a politics for the next generation.

> Richard J. Barnet and Ronald E. Muller,
> *Global Reach*, 1974

While the 1990s were supposed to be the environmental decade, very few people realized that the most visible and aggressive ecological protagonists at the end of the twentieth century would be the global corporations. Yet there they are, waving the Earth flag as they march triumphantly across the map. For the most part, we just look up from our televisions, computers and gas-guzzling automobiles, whip out our credit cards and wave back.

A generation ago, when astronauts first beamed pictures of the Earth back home, the image of a life-sustaining Blue Planet floating in infinite space helped inspire social movements to work to save the world from the depredations of industrialism. Yet today, while still motivating billions of people toward a planetary consciousness—toward action based on a profound love and respect for the interconnectedness of all life—the Earth's image has been co-opted into a corporate logo. It can be found in advertisements for enterprises ranging from communications companies to fast food dealers to chemical giants. What's more, transnational corporations now hold up the Blue Planet as an object whose pressing problems of ecological decay and pervasive poverty can be solved only by the technological, economic and managerial prowess at their command—a capacity unmatched in human history.[1]

The stunning portrait of the Earth has also become the icon for a millennial version of manifest destiny known as economic globalization. We are told that this corporate encirclement of the planet will bring with it greater prosperity, peace and ecological balance. Certainly, it is difficult to resist embracing such an enticing vision, especially when there is no clear counterbalance or alternative on the horizon. Soviet and Eastern European communism has left little but a legacy of ruin, including ecological devastation. In many respects numerous traditional nation-states, including both high-tech industrial democracies and a multitude of Third World governments, are growing weaker and less relevant by the day. At the same time, a growing number of countries are plagued by escalating nationalism and ethnic divisions within their borders, leading to xenophobia, fundamentalism, fascist tendencies and war. This leaves the corporate capitalists and the leaders of the industrialized democracies to present their neoliberal* brand of globalization as an historical inevitability and themselves as healers of the world's ills.

In the absence of a coherent alternative, the transnational corporations carry on inexorably. Increasingly flagless and stateless, they weave global webs of production, commerce, culture and finance virtually unopposed.[2] They expand, invest and grow, concentrating ever more wealth in a limited number of hands. They work in coalition to influence local, national and international institutions and laws. And together with the governments of their home countries in the European Union, North America and Japan, as well as international institutions such as the World Trade Organization, the World Bank, the International Monetary Fund and, increasingly, the United Nations, they are molding an international system in which they can trade and invest even more freely—a world where they are less and less account-

---

*As opposed to political liberalism—a term commonly used in the United States to define the philosophy of those who favor government intervention for the social good—the term *neoliberalism*, which is regularly employed in much of the world, should be understood to refer to a set of economic policies rooted in the old free-market economic liberalism epitomized by Adam Smith's *Wealth of Nations*. Today's neoliberalism can be defined as including the following components: the primacy of the market, the reduction in public expenditure for social services, the reduction of government regulation and the privatization of state-owned enterprises. (See Elizabeth Martinez and Arnoldo Garcia, "What Is 'Neo-Liberalism?'" found on the Internet at www.corpwatch.org/trac/corner/glob.

able to the cultures, communities and nation-states in which they operate. Underpinning this effort is not the historical inevitability of an
evolving, enlightened civilization, but rather the unavoidable reality of
the overriding corporate purpose: the maximization of profits.

One consequence of this predominant trend is that our Blue Planet—
home to untold cultural and biological diversity, to clear, raging rivers
and majestic, ancient forests, to a plethora of civilizations, nations,
tribes and idiosyncratic communities—is being held hostage to the
tyranny of the bottom line. It is falling increasingly under the dominion of those who rule from on high, those who are deciding much of
the world's fate from the sanctuary of their executive suites and board
rooms. Indeed, the Corporate Planet is encroaching upon the Blue
Planet, commodifying it, homogenizing it and enclosing it with its
predatory global reach. Dismembered parts of it are for sale, wrapped up
with pretty green bows, in the shopping mall nearest you.

Of course, despite the recent hype, these dynamics aren't all that new.
Christianity went global in the fifteenth century, as its missionaries
began working hand in hand with the governments of Spain, Portugal,
England and the Netherlands to colonize much of the planet. This
process imposed a homogeneous ideology on a diversity of cultures
located across a vast geographical spread. It also engendered horrendous
activities such as the global slave trade. Newly formed corporations such
as the British East India Company helped lead the colonial charge into
the "New World," coining the term *global reach* to describe their economic scope. Succeeding generations saw the far corners of the Earth
become increasingly intertwined.

By the first half of the twentieth century, many U.S., Japanese and
European corporations had become major international players. The
world's economies, meanwhile, became still more interconnected. This
growing political, economic and social integration reached an inauspi-
cious zenith at the time of the Great Depression and with the outbreak
of the global military conflicts known as the First and Second World
Wars. In the post–World War II era, political, economic, social and cultural processes, while still diverse, and at times polarized, converged
even more.

The "globalization" we are witnessing in the 1990s is in fact an accel-
eration of historical dynamics, hastened by the advent of increasingly
sophisticated and rapid communications and transportation technologies, the decline of the nation-state, the absence or ineffectiveness of

democratic systems of global governance and the rise of neoliberal economic ideology. Its primary beneficiaries are both the transnational corporations and the privileged consumer classes in the North and, to a growing degree, in the industrializing nations of the South.

Certainly, some aspects of growing international political, economic, social and cultural interconnection are quite positive. As University of Sao Paulo professor Henrique Rattner observes, there is an aspect of globalization that has "awakened humanity's consciousness of its common destiny."[3] Such planetary awareness has led to worldwide efforts for peace, human rights and ecological sustainability. Many of these initiatives have been taken up by the United Nations over the past fifty years.[4] Meanwhile, the worldwide proliferation of some technologies, while not nearly meeting their promise to end disease, starvation and poverty, has helped bring essential services such as clean drinking water and basic health care to more of the world's peoples. However, this beneficial side of globalization is not necessarily linked to the workings of transnational corporations and is, in fact, often limited by their prerogatives.[5] Indeed, it is highly unlikely that *corporate globalization* (or, perhaps better said, global corporatization) will foster a world based on democratic participation, social justice, nonviolence and ecological sustainability.

In almost every country, however, there are broad and diverse movements that are playing a key role in promoting alternative visions, pressing in an assortment of ways for a balancing of power away from corporations toward a new, more democratic and accountable political process. These movements are made up of labor unionists and scientists, peasants and small farmers, community leaders, lawyers and politicians, student activists, parents and teachers, religious leaders, small business owners, environmentalists and more. As numerous examples offered in the following chapters demonstrate, they are organizing locally, nationally and increasingly on an international level. Although these incipient forces of grassroots globalization are not yet nearly strong enough to check corporate globalization head on, they have triggered many important changes and set forth a series of challenges that contain the seeds of an effort that could reverse the negative trends of globalization and reclaim the Blue Planet.

Corporate Globalization

As the world sails into the new millennium, there is no doubt that transnational corporations are at the helm, piloting and propelling global geopolitics and the process of economic globalization. Indeed, many corporations have more political and economic power than the nation-states across whose borders they operate. One simple indicator of the comparative might of corporations and governments is the economic wealth each generates, measured by corporate sales and a country's gross domestic product (GDP). Using this benchmark, it turns out that the combined revenues of just General Motors and Ford—the two largest automobile corporations in the world—exceed the combined GDP for all of sub-Saharan Africa.[7] Similarly, the combined sales of Mitsubishi, Mitsui, ITOCHU, Sumitomo, Marubeni and Nissho Iwai, Japan's top six *sogo shosha*, or trading companies, are nearly equivalent to the combined GDP of all of South America.[8] Overall, fifty-one of the largest one hundred economies in the world are corporations.[9]

Just as GDP does not tell the whole story about a country or region, using sales alone to measure corporate power also comes up short.[10] Consider the following: the number of transnational corporations in the world has jumped from 7,000 in 1970 to 40,000 in 1995. Described by the United Nations as "the productive core of the globalizing world economy," these corporations and their 250,000 foreign affiliates account for most of the world's industrial capacity, technological knowledge and international financial transactions.[11] They mine, refine and distribute most of the world's oil, gasoline, diesel and jet fuel. They build most of the world's oil, coal, gas, hydroelectric and nuclear power plants. They extract most of the world's minerals from the ground. They manufacture and sell most of the world's automobiles, airplanes, communications satellites, computers, home electronics, chemicals, medicines and biotechnology products. They harvest much of the world's wood and make most of its paper. They grow many of the world's agricultural crops, while processing and distributing much of its food. All told, the transnationals hold 90 percent of all technology and product patents worldwide and are involved in 70 percent of world trade.[12] More than 30 percent of this trade is "intrafirm"; in other words, it occurs between units of the same corporation. Meanwhile, sales made by transnational corporations' foreign affiliates—worth more than $5 trillion—exceed total international trade.[13] And while the world economy is growing by 2 or 3 percent every year, the biggest transnationals are, as a group, growing at a rate of 8 to 10 percent.[14] Indeed, by most measures, transnational corporations are playing a more important role in world politics, economics and culture than they have in the past.[15]

While ever more global in reach, these corporations' home bases are quite geographically concentrated. Despite the emergence of a number of transnationals from Brazil, Taiwan, Australia, South Africa and other Southern nations, power is centered in the industrialized countries of the North, where 90 percent of all transnationals are based—the so-called Triad of the United States, the European Union and Japan. More than half come from just five nations: France, Germany, the Netherlands, Japan and the United States.[16] Moreover, despite the growing numbers of transnationals, power is concentrated at the top. For instance, *The Economist* estimates that the world's top 300 firms account for one-quarter of the world's productive assets.[17]

This clustering of clout in the hands of a very few entities has given the corporate world a case of myopia. As Richard Barnet and John Cavanagh write in their book *Global Dreams*, "The interests and self-defined responsibilities of corporate leaders are global but parochial; their eyes are on the global market, but most of the world's people remain invisible."[18] Or as Indian scientist and activist Dr. Vandana Shiva puts it, the transnationals do "not represent the universal human interest" but rather "a particular local and parochial interest which has been globalised through its reach and control."[19] It can also be argued that up until recently, when they became a serious public relations problem, the Earth's ecosystems existed beyond the blinders of the corporations' narrow, profit-driven vision.

Global corporations also exert significant influence over the domestic and foreign policies of the Northern industrialized governments that host them. Indeed, the interests of the most powerful governments in the world are often intimately intertwined with the expanding pursuits of the transnationals they charter. To a large degree, the Triad of Japan, the European Union and the United States can be seen as three large corporate states, at times cooperating, at times competing with one another to promote the interests of their rival transnationals across the globe.

At the same time, transnational corporations are moving to circumvent national governments. The borders and regulatory agencies of most governments are caving in to the New World Order of globalization, allowing corporations to assume an ever more stateless quality, leaving them less and less accountable to any government anywhere. This combination of stateless corporations and corporate states appears contradictory on the surface, but in effect it allows a large transnational to hide behind the protection of a national flag when convenient, and to eschew it when it's not. Let us examine each of these two interrelated dynamics in turn.

Reciprocal relationships between governments and corporations have existed for centuries. These tight links began when European governments created state-chartered corporations as vehicles for the colonization of Asia, Africa and the Americas. Together with Europe's imperial navies, these first transnational corporations achieved an early version of global reach, exploiting the people and natural riches of their new-found territories, obliterating indigenous nations and accumulating the wealth that fueled the industrial revolution back home.[20] Indeed, most of the original American colonies were created by chartered British corporations whose business was to turn a profit for European investors.[21] After the colonies rebelled against British rule and became an independent nation, the newly formed states began chartering their own corporations. Despite a series of provisions in the states' charters aimed at preventing corporate dominance of the public sphere, U.S. corporations used their wealth and power to gain an increasing stranglehold on the country's political and economic life in the ensuing century.[22] Meanwhile, across the Pacific, Japanese corporations emerged roughly a hundred years later, springing from the country's samurai families and quickly becoming intertwined with the Japanese state in the early part of the twentieth century.

Despite numerous attempts by local and national governments, spurred by citizens' movements, to limit corporations' power and increase their accountability to the public, today these economic power-houses maintain a firm grip on many key aspects of political life in their home countries, corrupting the democratic process. Nowhere is this clearer than in the United States.

The political power of U.S. corporations is derived from their economic power. In 1994, for instance, the revenues of the top 500 corporations in the United States equaled 63 percent of the country's gross domestic product.[23] As analysts such as William Greider and as recent election campaigns have shown, the transnationals use this substantial wealth to exert a significant influence over both the legislative and executive branches of government through campaign financing and other forms of patronage.[24] The large percentage of representatives from the corporate world who sit in every U.S. president's Cabinet reflects this influence.[25] So does the more than $30 billion of subsidies and $4.5 billion in tax breaks that Congress annually appropriates and legislates for ecologically damaging corporate activities—part of a broader "corporate welfare" program that totals more than $85 billion annually in government subsidies for corporations.[26]

Meanwhile, U.S. foreign policy has consistently reflected corporate concerns. For instance, the military invasions of Central America in the late nineteenth and early twentieth centuries, as well as the CIA-backed coups that overthrew democratically elected presidents in Guatemala (1954) and Chile (1972), were undertaken, in large part, to protect U.S. business interests.[27] U.S. military operations such as the Persian Gulf War continue to serve corporate interests, but economic combat is preferred. As President Bill Clinton put it in 1993, "our place in the world will be determined as much by the skills of our workers as by the strength of our weapons, as much by our ability to pull down foreign trade barriers as our ability to breach distant ramparts."[28] Thus intervention today takes place more often through the economic strategies devised by the Department of Commerce's Advocacy Center. Literally an economic "war room" that coordinates efforts among government agencies from the EPA to the CIA, the Advocacy Center works through U.S. embassies to support United States–based corporations vying for contracts in countries such as Indonesia, China and Brazil.[29] Meanwhile, the United States Trade Representative's office and its Japanese and European counterparts represent the interests and rely heavily on the input of big business to develop their positions vis-à-vis international accords such as the General Agreement on Tariffs and Trade (GATT).[30]

The permeation of corporate power in the political life of the most polluting nation on Earth makes reform toward environmental sustainability difficult. A look at the obstacles faced by the Clinton Administration—initially hailed as the "greenest" presidency ever—is telling. When they began to attempt to implement new environmental policies, the more liberal members of the Clinton White House found that although they were supposedly at the pinnacle of power, they were still restrained by undue corporate influence. Clinton officials were forced to retreat on a series of initiatives.

Almost immediately after assuming office in 1993, Vice-President Al Gore was obliged to bow to political pressure from an array of business interests and renege on a campaign pledge to review an incinerator project located next to an elementary school in East Liverpool, Ohio.[31] Similarly, mining and ranching interests in the western states easily countered attempts by Interior Secretary Bruce Babbitt to end ecologically destructive government subsidies that virtually give away public resources. Administration efforts to institute a "BTU tax" on ecologically unsound energy consumption were swatted down by the oil companies and a number of other interests.[32] And former Labor Secretary

Robert Reich found little support forthcoming from his colleagues in the government when he spoke up during the 1995 debate on balancing the federal budget, calling for an end to corporate welfare.[33] Reich soon fell silent on the issue, and the national debate continued to focus largely on cutting social welfare, health, education, housing and environmental programs.

Although U.S. corporations have profound political influence, Japan is perhaps the most classic example of the traditional corporate state. *Sei-kan-zai ittaikiko,* the Japanese amalgamation of politics, bureaucracy and big business, has come to be known in the West as "Japan Inc." This fusing of elements is reinforced by a series of interfamily ties that link the government and corporate leadership of the country (*kei batsu*), by "old boy" university networks (*gaku batsu*), by a powerful corporate lobby and by the system of *amakudari* (descent from heaven), which resembles the "revolving door" of the Western nations, where high-ranking government officials slip right into corporate boards of directors upon retirement.[34] Such tight relationships, combined with a foreign aid program that subsidizes investment abroad, provide a solid base from which Japan's corporations project themselves into the world economy.

While the transnationals maintain a strong grip on the domestic and foreign policies of their home countries, they are also using the accelerating process of globalization to gain an increasing degree of independence from governments. In many respects they are relegating national governments to supporting roles on the world stage. Takuya Negami, a senior executive in charge of international operations at the Kobe Steel Corporation and chair for the Environmental Cooperation Task Force of Keidanran (Japan's powerful Chamber of Commerce), puts it kindly when he says, "the nation-state is not really dead, but it's being quickly retired."

Sitting behind a luxurious desk at his $13-billion-a-year company's otherwise spartan Tokyo offices, Negami, a well-traveled, highly cultured man, elaborates on his perspective. Facing the increasingly global nature of the world economy and growing corporate mobility, he suggests, the industrialized nation-states are seeking to redefine themselves. "Governments have had to change their function. I think that's the reason for the EC or NAFTA. They wanted to expand their borders to have a much wider reach. Otherwise the current nation-state is getting meaningless as an authority. So people are adjusting. Government is adjusting. Bureaucrats are adjusting. Of course, the corporations adjusted first."[35]

With help from the World Bank and International Monetary Fund's "structural adjustment" policies—a series of economic strictures that have pried open previously protected economies in the South and the East to foreign investment—the transnationals "adjusted first" by framing a succession of intergovernmental trade and investment accords. These treaties serve as the frameworks within which economic globalization is evolving, allowing international corporate investment and trade to flourish across the Earth, while undermining sovereignty, self-determination and democracy at the local and national levels everywhere. The most powerful and important among these agreements is the Uruguay Round of the General Agreement on Tariffs and Trade (GATT), dubbed by many activists "a corporate bill of rights" for the global freedom to trade and invest it bestows upon the transnationals. The new World Trade Organization (WTO) was created to enforce GATT rules. Taking the GATT/WTO several steps further is the proposed Multilateral Agreement on Investment (MAI), negotiated in secret by the world's industrialized nations and slated to be imposed on the rest of the world. According to an analysis of the draft text—which was leaked to the organization Public Citizen in early 1997—the MAI would accelerate economic globalization by severely restricting the ability of national and local governments to regulate corporate investment—including for social, economic, and environmental goals. The MAI would also give investors and corporations unprecedented legal standing to directly sue governments in international tribunals for breaking the agreement's rules.

Parallel yet somewhat contradictory to the GATT/WTO and MAI are a series of regional accords that were fostered by corporate collaboration with the governments of their respective legs of the Triad. These include the North American Free Trade Agreement (NAFTA), the European Union (EU), and an informal Asian trading bloc led by Japan. While GATT/WTO and MAI provide a worldwide regulatory framework, the regional economic blocs aim to strengthen the global competitiveness of each part of the Triad vis-à-vis one another. These agreements also aim to help transnational corporations build integrated regional production, distribution and service networks.[36]

Most advanced of these regional networks is the European Union, in which national regulations designed to protect local industries have been replaced by Europe-wide rules that protect companies with "European" reach. This has served to promote greater trade and investment, based on economies of scale, within the region.[37] As a result, reports the British publication *The Ecologist,* "the nation state has been pushed into the background as the unit of economic administration: sovereignty has shifted to pan-European factions within government and business, operating through the institutions that make up the EU." The region's large multinationals have been able "to boost profits at the expense of product quality; to drive smaller companies out of business; and to undermine (or block) environmental and public health measures deemed onerous to business." In essence, *The Ecologist* points out, the EU does not serve its stated objective to be a "union of the peoples of Europe," but rather functions as "a union of multinational business interests" that facilitates the free movement of European corporations across the region's national boundaries, while bolstering their competitiveness globally.[38]

The traditional sovereignty of the nation-state has been further eroded by the increasingly global nature of the international financial system. Huge sums of money move electronically from computer to computer, bank to bank, and country to country—billions of dollars per minute, twenty-four hours a day.[39] The volatile nature of the international financial system—which sends money into orbit, scouring the world's markets for the best return on an investment—makes it extremely difficult for governments to formulate and follow through on national economic strategies. As was clearly illustrated by Mexico's 1995 financial crisis, Third World governments that have opened up their financial services and created securities markets linked to the global economy are particularly vulnerable to investors' whims. Similarly, as former Harvard Business School professor David Korten explains in his book *When Corporations Rule the World:*

> If the speculators that are shuffling hundreds of billions of dollars around the world decide that the policies of a government give preference to . . . environmentalists, working people or the poor—over the[ir] interests . . . they take their money elsewhere, creating economic havoc in the process. In their minds, the resulting economic disruption only confirms their thesis that the policies of the offending government were unsound.[40]

Korten argues that publicly traded corporations themselves are also locked into this dynamic, which is driven by a focus on short-term return. Thus companies committed to investing in the future, to providing employees with job security, to furnishing solid retirement funds, to paying their share of local taxes and to managing environmental resources sustainably, are seen as "weaker market players." As a result, "a predatory financial system teams up with a predatory market to declare responsible managers 'inefficient' and purge them from the system" with either the threat of a hostile takeover or, if a company resists, a takeover in the name of shareholders' "rights" to maximize their profits.[41]

Although they are often still dependent on the nation whose flag they fly for markets and political support—and therefore subject to some regulatory control—the transnationals are less and less accountable everywhere. They are increasingly mobile, maneuvering technology, finance, information, goods and services throughout vast regions and across the globe, seeking to exploit the optimum combination of low wages, skilled nonunion workers, burgeoning markets, abundant natural resources and lax environmental regulations. National and local governments, in turn, are seeking, sometimes desperately, to accommodate the corporations, offering tax breaks, subsidies, lax environmental regulation, laws (and enforcement) that get tough on organized labor, military protection and other incentives. This competition among governments to provide the "best" conditions for investment has set off a "race to the bottom" in terms of wages, worker health and safety, and environmental standards.

In the Triad nations this race can be witnessed as wages become depressed, unions grow weaker and some environmental protection laws fall. In the United States, corporations regularly play state and local governments against each other, seeking to leverage optimum investment conditions. And within the EU, European corporations can now play nations against each other, moving from Germany to lower-wage Portugal, for example.[42] This dynamic is replicated on a global level as international competition, enhanced by trade agreements such as GATT, encourages corporations to relocate from the Triad to the South and the East. This, in turn, pressures Northern nations to further undercut wages and standards in order to compete. It's a win-win situation for the transnationals, while workers and the environment lose out across the map.[43]

In sum, what has occurred is nothing less than a profound shift in the role of many nation-states vis-à-vis corporations. As one United Nations agency has noted, whereas many governments once served to control and contain the activities of transnational corporations while encouraging some limited investment, their function has shifted to one of competing for ever more investment by minimizing such controls.[44] Such a shift clearly signals the ascendancy of the global corporate imperative over that of national interests.

Globalization of the Ecological Crisis

Given their penetrating reach as well as their penchant to dominate economics, politics and technology, it is not surprising to find the big transnationals deeply involved in most of the world's serious environmental crises. These corporations effectively play the role of Earth brokers in the global economy—buying and selling the planet's resources and goods, as well as deciding what technologies will be developed and used, where factories will be built and which forests will be cut, minerals extracted, crops harvested and rivers dammed. Their inordinate power puts them in the position of mediating the future of local, regional and global ecosystems in the interests of their own bottom lines and an antiquated version of economic growth that is wreaking havoc on the world's ecology.

Of course, during the Cold War, the communist bloc's military and industrial complexes created their own environmental atrocities. But with the fall of communism in Europe and the ascendancy of free market capitalism as the dominant force on the world stage, the transnationals are left as the greatest perpetrators of these problems. While governments, private national companies and small businesses also employ many environmentally destructive practices, the transnational corporations often control and disseminate the technologies used by these entities. And, in many cases, large corporations subcontract some of their most environmentally hazardous activities to small companies, thus avoiding direct responsibility.[45]

Businessman-environmentalist Paul Hawken sums up the situation in his book *The Ecology of Commerce* when he writes, "given current corporate practices, not one wildlife reserve, wilderness, or indigenous culture will survive the global economy. We know that every natural system on the planet is disintegrating. The land, water, air, and sea have been functionally transformed from life-supporting systems into repositories for waste. There is no polite way to say that business is destroying the world."[46]

Yet many large corporations claim that such talk of an environmental crisis is green fear mongering and exaggeration. In an effort to respond to the negative environmental impression they give, not a few have become involved in a series of endeavors that Ken Derr, Chairman and CEO of transnational oil giant Chevron, describes as "a world-class job of bringing the facts before the public."[47] In addition to environmental advertising campaigns and other public relations strategies (see Chapter Six), many transnationals support their version of the truth by publicizing the views of a relatively small cadre of scientists (a number of whom are either directly or indirectly supported by industry funding) who tend to put forth an alluring array of doubts about the environmental crisis.[48] Their views, similar to those offered by tobacco corporations claiming that there is no "proof" that cigarettes cause cancer, are swallowed, digested and regurgitated by media demagogues such as talk show host Rush Limbaugh and congressmen closely allied with corporate America.[49] Journalists sympathetic to the corporate cause have also taken the bait. One, Gregg Easterbrook, produced a 700-page paen to the "coming age of environmental optimism," arguing that the industrialized world is well on its way to solving its environmental problems.[50] This "world-class" education job has contributed to an anti-environmental backlash led, in part, by corporations seeking freedom from "burdensome" regulations.

Of course, there are needles of truth in this public relations haystack. Various initiatives have in fact resolved, reduced or displaced a number of ecological problems; the air is cleaner in some places than it was thirty years ago; and some water is more drinkable. Yet overwhelming evidence points to a multitude of serious environmental problems that continue to expand throughout the world in tandem with economic globalization, threatening the sustainability of both local and global ecosystems.* Or, as the UN Environment Program put it in 1997, despite progress on several fronts, "from a global perspective the environment has continued to degrade during the past decade, and significant environmental problems remain deeply embedded in the socio-economic fabric of nations in all regions." At the root of many of these problems are a few hundred transnational corporations.

For instance, chlorofluorocarbons (CFCs) and their substitutes con-

---

* It would take an entire book to explore the scientific basis of the various environmental problems confronting humanity. The interested reader is encouraged to check this chapter's "Notes," which cite the strong scientific documentation on such issues as climate change, ozone depletion, dwindling forests and fisheries and the effects of dioxin on humans.

tinue to steadily deteriorate the protective ozone layers over both the Southern and Northern Hemispheres. They are projected to do so for decades to come, despite an international agreement to phase them out.[51] Companies such as DuPont, Imperial Chemical Industries (ICI) and Hoechst share most of the blame for this ecological disaster. Indeed, during the years that it questioned, resisted and attempted to discredit growing scientific proof that CFCs destroy the ozone, DuPont alone accounted for 25 percent of world production of this hazardous chemical; today it is a leading producer of "CFC-lite" substitutes—HCFCs and HFCs—two chemical replacements that are either harmful to the ozone or potent global warming gases.[52]

Global warming has become another prime target for those seeking to cast doubt on the scientific underpinnings of the environmental crisis.[53] Indeed, the attacks have intensified as scientific proof of the inevitability of climate change becomes increasingly incontrovertible.[54] In 1989, in 1990 and again in 1995, a United Nations–appointed group of more than 2,500 of the world's leading climate scientists—the Intergovernmental Panel on Climate Change (IPCC)—concluded with increasing certainty that without a serious reduction in carbon dioxide emissions (created by the burning of oil, coal and wood), global warming looms on the horizon. The IPCC predicts that human-induced climate change threatens to unleash more frequent and more powerful storms, melt polar ice caps and thus cause sea levels to rise, increase the occurrence of floods and drought, expand desertification, and augment extremes in temperature. All of these imply potentially catastrophic consequences for human populations around the world.[55]

The corporate role in this, the potentially most severe and all encompassing of environmental disasters, is quite clear. For instance, a 1992 report by the now defunct United Nations Centre on Transnational Corporations documents how "the influence of transnational corporations extends over roughly 50 percent of all emissions of greenhouse gases. This includes about half of the oil production business, virtually all of the production of road vehicles . . . most chlorofluorocarbon production, and significant portions of electricity generation and use."[56] It is from these corporate sectors that the greatest "doubt" and "uncertainty" about climate change are raised and where the most obstinate resistance to reducing emissions originates.

Meanwhile, annual world production of synthetic organic chemicals has skyrocketed from 1 million tons in 1930 to 7 million tons in 1950 to 63 million tons in 1970 to 500 million tons in 1990. At current rates, by the turn of the century, the world's industries will create more than a billion tons of synthetic organic chemicals every year.[57] The production of these chemicals, which are used to create pesticides, synthetic fibers, plastics, pulp and paper, also makes tremendous amounts of waste. For instance, roughly two-thirds of all hazardous waste produced in the United States comes from chemical manufacturing.[58] In fact, conservative estimates show that in the 1980s the United States generated more than one ton of such toxics for every man, woman and child.[59] What's more, despite the impression given by some corporate executives and pundits that industry has cleaned up its act in recent years, hazardous waste production actually increased in the 1990s.[60]

Indeed, despite improvements in efficiency in recent decades, the chemical industry still produces more waste than product. Dr. Barry Commoner notes, for example, that chemical production generates two barrels of waste for every barrel of product. A review of the German chemical industry shows that in the manufacture of plastics, every unit of product is accompanied by four units of waste. For pesticides the ratio is three units of waste to one unit of product. For synthetic dyes it is eight to one.[61]

Not surprisingly, parallel to this rise in toxic chemical production and its burgeoning byproduct of waste is a significant growth in cancer rates. For instance, a white male in the United States today is about twice as likely to get cancer as his grandfather was.[62] While the scientific links between growing industrial production of chemicals and increasing cancer rates are difficult to establish, there is a growing body of evidence in some areas. Chlorine, for example, is an elemental input into literally tens of thousands of industrial products, including polyvinyl chloride (PVC), a number of pesticides (such as DDT), pulp and paper, solvents, lubricants, soaps, shampoos, deodorants and cosmetics. During the manufacture, use and disposal of these products, large numbers of unwanted organochlorine byproducts are created, including some of the most biologically persistent and toxicologically potent chemicals known—dioxins. Dioxins have been found to accumulate in fatty tissue and are suspected to be major contributors to worldwide increases in breast cancer, immunological deficiencies and birth defects.[63] Such scientific evidence has moved a number of intergovernmental bodies to propose bans on chlorine production.[64] Yet corporate resistance is fierce, for mandating the elimination of chlorine production and replacing it with more benign industrial processes would go directly against the immediate interests of powerful transnationals such as Dow Chemical, ICI, Solvay and Mitsubishi Group member Asahi Glass, which dominate global chlorine production.

Nor are chlorine and the companies that produce it the only toxic culprits. A vast array of corporations—including the chemical, automobile, oil, high-tech, nuclear power and waste management industries—are responsible for myriad toxic and radioactive emissions, spills, leaks and explosions that regularly contaminate the workplaces, air, soil and water of communities and ecosystems around the globe. Corporations servicing the military-industrial complex, for instance, especially nuclear weapons contractors such as Westinghouse and General Electric, together with the world's military establishments, have created some of the worst toxic problems the planet has ever seen.[65] Global corporations such as Rio Tinto Zinc, Kobe Steel and Broken Hill Properties dominate the pollution-intensive mining, refining and smelting of metals such as platinum, aluminum and copper.[66] And, it turns out that the production of computers, still widely seen by the public as a "clean" industry, carries with it a set of negative ecological and social impacts. The Albuquerque-based Southwest Organizing Project points out that when the Intel Corporation produces just one six-inch silicon wafer from which its Pentium chip is cut, it also creates byproducts that include 25 pounds of sodium hydroxide, 2,840 gallons of waste water and 7 pounds of hazardous waste.[67] Meanwhile, California's Silicon Valley is host to thirty federal Superfund sites, more than any other region of its size.[68] As the world's economy becomes increasingly computer-driven and launches into cyberspace, high-tech corporations are dumping tons of toxic waste on Earth.

The corporate role in agriculture is no less striking. Just twenty chemical companies account for the sales of more than 90 percent of all the world's pesticides.[69] These agricultural chemicals are responsible for tens of thousands of deaths and at least a million more farmworker poisonings every year.[70] Chemical giants such as Shell, Monsanto, Mitsubishi and Sandoz now control much of the world's genetic seed stock, as well as much of the agricultural biotechnology industry, which presents a new group of potential environmental problems.[71] And global giants such as Phillip Morris, United Fruit, Pepsico, Cargill, Unilever and Nestlé oversee vast portions of international agricultural production and trade. In fact, transnationals either directly or indirectly command 80 percent of the land around the world that is cultivated for export crops such as bananas, tobacco and cotton.[72] Such agro-export "development" patterns regularly displace farmers producing food for local consumption, pushing them into situations where they must overexploit the environment to survive.[73]

On top of all this, the world's ancient tropical and temperate forests are quickly vanishing, and with them, a treasure house of biological and cultural diversity, including the lives of 50 million tribal people who still live in the tropical rainforests. At current deforestation rates, nearly all the world's tropical rainforests will be gone midway into the twenty-first century. What's more, the taiga, the last great temperate old-growth forest, spanning the U.S. Pacific Northwest, Western Canada and Siberia, is being voraciously logged.[74] While a number of factors contribute to deforestation, timber transnationals such as MacMillan Bloedel, Sumitomo and Georgia-Pacific play a central role. Indeed, overall commercial timber harvests have increased by 50 percent between 1965 and 1990.[75]

Overfishing is also undermining biological and cultural diversity. Once a way of life for millions of families and coastal communities, fishing has become big business. Highly mobile, high-tech, large-scale factory fishing fleets owned by corporations such as Spain's Pescanova, Japan's Taiyo, South Korea's Dong Won and the United States' Arctic Alaska/Tyson Foods roam the world's oceans, indiscriminately plundering the biological diversity of the seas, overstepping the limits of marine ecosystems and wiping out traditional fishing communities.[76] According to United Nations Food and Agriculture Organization (FAO) figures, nearly 70 percent of the world's conventional fish stocks are either fully exploited, severely overtaxed, declining or recovering. "This situation," says the FAO, "is globally nonsustainable and major ecological and economic damage is already visible."[77]

The sum of these corporate-driven problems, as well as others not mentioned here, prompted a group of nearly 1,600 scientists—99 of them Nobel Prize winners—from sixty-nine countries to issue a statement to the world's governments in 1992 titled "World Scientists' Warning to Humanity." In it they cautioned that "a great change in our stewardship of the earth and the life on it is required, if vast human misery is to be avoided and our global home on this planet is not to be irretrievably mutilated." Declaring that "uncertainty over the extent of these effects cannot excuse complacency or delay in facing the threats," this prominent group called for strong and immediate action.[78] Unfortunately, most of the "action" seems to be moving in the opposite direction.

As economic globalization continues apace, transnational corporations are further expanding their reach, investing in strategic economic sectors in the South and the East. They are snapping up privatized mines, fisheries and forests, along with formerly state-owned oil, chemical and other companies around the world. Thus the responsibility for an ever-growing portion of the world's most environmentally destructive enterprises is being transferred from nation-states and local corporations to the transnationals. This situation is compounded by the parallel phenomenon of expanding corporate investment in new power plants, refineries, factories and resource extraction projects in many parts of the world.[79] Much of this is generating new environmental problems; the United Nations estimates that between 20 and 50 percent of all the foreign direct investment in "developing countries" can be found in what it narrowly defines as "pollution-intensive industries."[80]

The underlying premise of ecological science—the fundamental interdependence of things, both in the smallest niche and in the planetary ecosystem—is antithetical to political boundaries. Yet while the world economy is increasingly transcending national borders, it does not operate within this dominant natural law. Indeed, by ignoring it, corporate globalization is augmenting the globalization of ecological crisis. For instance, the permeation of carcinogenic chlorine compounds in the world's ecosystems—they have already been found in the tissue of animals living on the high seas and in some of the most remote places in the world, such as Antarctica—is increasing as economic globalization helps chemical corporations expand chlorine production into markets such as India, China and Brazil.[81] Meanwhile, the potential severity of climate change is growing as automobile sales and profligate energy consumption fuel rapid industrial expansion across the South and the East (see Chapter Five).

Moreover, what were once local crises are being transformed into planetary ones as economic globalization taxes the limits of some of the Earth's most biologically diverse ecosystems, such as the forests and the oceans. What have traditionally been local struggles around forest resources, for example, are increasingly linked to worldwide economic and ecological dynamics. While big wood-consuming countries have traditionally gotten their timber imports from regional sources (e.g., the United States from Canada, Europe from Africa, Japan from Southeast Asia, and Russia from Siberia), the market is becoming ever more global as consumption grows and the supply diminishes.[82] The EU, for example, now imports plywood from a Mitsubishi subsidiary in the

Amazon, Eidai do Brasil, the largest foreign-owned timber concern in that country, rounding out a global timber circuit wherein the Latin American operations of a Japanese corporation supply wood to the European market.[83] Similarly, taking advantage of the opening of vast forest reserves in the former Soviet Union, the U.S. logging transnational Weyerhaeuser has begun to clear-cut and export Siberia's forests to Japan, China and the United States.[84] In fact, the globalization of the timber trade has reached the point where a price change, a logging ban or the depletion of resources in Southeast Asia will affect harvesting plans in Canada and South America.[85] Thus local forest issues are increasingly linked to and leveraged by a world timber trade that is fast devouring some of the last remaining stands of ancient forests on Earth, thereby deepening a planetary crisis of habitat destruction and biodiversity loss.

The plight of the world's fisheries is another example of how economic globalization is linking otherwise local environmental problems. Having totally depleted huge areas such as Canada's Grand Banks, the global fish corporations are moving on, seeking out recently opened frontiers such as those off the coasts of India and Chile. In the short term they are expanding the world seafood trade along with their profits. Yet by circumnavigating the planet's fishing grounds with devastating industrial harvest technologies, they are depleting one fishery after another. This has transformed a succession of local overfishing problems into a global crisis of the world's ocean ecosystems.[86]

Finally, globalization of the production and distribution of goods, in the name of efficiency and economies of scale, is in many instances leading to highly unsustainable development patterns. This is particularly clear in the case of food production. For example, in the 1980s, U.S. free market farm policies lowered price supports for the small farmer. As a result, a large number of family farms went into bankruptcy, while major food corporations enjoyed record profits. At the same time, Mexico, in preparation for NAFTA, wiped out important protections for its small, food-producing farmers. Consequently, U.S. agribusiness transnationals moved into the lucrative Mexican market. They effectively took over land dedicated to subsistence agriculture there, converting it to pesticide-intensive crops such as strawberries, broccoli, cauliflower and cantaloupes for export to the U.S. market. They then turned around and began selling Mexican farmers corn and beans grown in the Midwest.[87]

In theory this is a more "efficient" economic system, with large corporations growing the most productive crops on both sides of the border and distributing them in a businesslike way. However, such efficiency not only undermines Mexico's food security, increases the use of pesticides and threatens the viability of organic agriculture, but it has also caused thousands of farm families in both the United States and Mexico to lose their land. In Mexico, many of these people have migrated to the forest's edge, to the large cities or to the United States in search of sustenance.[88] This socially and ecologically unsound trend extends far beyond NAFTA and United States–Mexico relations. As Richard Barnet and John Cavanagh observe, "millions of acres once used to feed poor families in poor countries are now used to grow kiwis, asparagus, strawberries, and baby carrots for upper-middle-class consumers who can now eat what was once the fare of kings—365 days a year."[89]

The Globalization of Poverty

Interwoven with the globalization of the ecological crisis is the global crisis of poverty. Proponents of corporate globalization argue that it will bring greater economic growth and prosperity across the globe. Yet while fostering an expanding international system of production and distribution of goods, the world economy leaves more than half of the Earth's population out of the loop. These more than 3.5 billion people have, in the words of Barnet and Cavanagh, "neither the cash nor credit to buy much of anything." Moreover, they are "not needed or wanted to make the goods or to provide the services that the paying customers of the world can afford."[90] This means that more than half of the world's population lives in either a subsistence or an informal economy. Others work producing goods for the global economy—sewing trendy athletic shoes and assembling computer components—but they receive such meager wages that they cannot participate in it as consumers.

The dual nature of the world economy, where one side thrives while the other suffers, is well documented by the *1994 United Nations Human Development Report*. Looking back at the fifty years since the United Nations was created, the report finds that "what emerges is an arresting picture of unprecedented human progress and unspeakable human misery, of humanity's advances on several fronts mixed with humanity's retreat on several others, of a breath-taking globalization of prosperity side by side with a depressing globalization of poverty."[91]

The transnationals and other proponents of globalization argue that expanding investment will drive the economic growth necessary to create sustainable human and ecological development. Yet, in many respects, the world is moving toward deeper divisions. To be sure, advances have been made. Technology, most often developed and sold by the transnationals, has given us wings, allowing us to fly and drive across the Earth and to communicate by telephone, television, computer and fax. Medical advances have cured diseases previously thought to be incurable. In many places in the Third World, life expectancy rates have risen, infant mortality has dropped, nutrition has improved, fertility rates have fallen (in every region but Africa) and education has become more widespread. Indeed, while nearly 70 percent of the world's population lived in what the UN describes as "abysmal conditions" in 1960, only 32 percent suffered such ignoble circumstances in 1992.[92]

While significant, such achievements should not obscure the perpetuation of widespread poverty as well as deepening inequality occurring across the globe. The persistence of such vast numbers of poor is inexcusable, given the knowledge and resources at the world's command. While the technological potential to eliminate the worst problems of poverty certainly exists, this has been neither the goal nor the achievement of the forces driving the world economy. Rather, the progress that has occurred has emerged as an insufficient byproduct of the ever advancing bottom line. As a result, poverty is still pervasive throughout the South, and it is increasing in the East, where former Communist nations are removing social safety nets as they venture out onto the high wire of neoliberal economics. Again, the UN describes the overall situation: "Despite all our technological breakthroughs, we still live in a world where a fifth of the developing world's population goes hungry every night, a quarter lacks access to even a basic necessity like safe drinking water and a third lives in a state of abject poverty—at such a margin of human existence that words simply fail to describe it."[93] Overall, there are more than 1 billion people living in absolute poverty in the world today—70 percent of whom are women.[94] Indigenous tribes, and with them entire cultures and languages, continue to disappear. New diseases are on the rise, while ones supposedly cured are resurging. And although it has decreased somewhat, annual global military spending (much of which is captured by a handful of weapons-manufacturing corporations) still equals the combined income of one-half the world's population. Overall, the gap between rich and poor, which doubled worldwide between 1960 and 1991, continues to grow, as the benefits of corporate globalization fall into the hands of an elite group of recipients.[95]

Indeed the process of globalization is steamrolling social and financial support for the basic rights of the poor, increasingly shunting the disenfranchised off to the side, where they must fend for themselves in the brutally competitive "market." Growing numbers of people are becoming victims of globalization, as the forces of corporate expansion move into farmlands, deserts, oceans and river systems they previously ignored. Already poor, but largely self-sufficient, communities across the Earth are being cast into deeper social and ecological poverty, as well as cultural dislocation, as their resources are appropriated for the seemingly insatiable demands of the world's ever growing consumer societies.[96]

The heavily skewed nature of the world economy underlines the fundamental unsustainability of corporate globalization. For if the world economy's driving forces continue to exclude more than 50 percent of the Earth's population—and indeed are widening the gap between rich and poor—then this system, which is both failing to meet the needs of the present generation and compromising those of future generations, simply cannot be a recipe for sustainability and equity, as its advocates claim it is.

As the industrialized nations increasingly integrate themselves into the neoliberal world economy—cutting social services and allowing their industries to become "hollowed out" by corporations that evade local accountability and relocate to the Third World in search of greater "competitiveness"—poverty in the North is also on the rise. The United States, supposedly the wealthiest nation on Earth, now has the widest gap between rich and poor of any industrialized nation, and disparities continue to grow.[97] Poverty is also increasing in Europe, where 15 percent of the population already lives below the poverty line.[98] Of course, Northern corporations are not only seeking low wages and lax regulations when they invest and expand into the Third World. They are also taking advantage of huge, recently opened and rapidly growing consumer markets in such places as Brazil, India and China. In the process, a world middle class is emerging as the new consumer beneficiaries of globalization.[99]

While large in numbers, these consumers are not representative of overall conditions in their societies. For instance, while 100 million Indians are becoming world consumers, 800 million are left out of or pushed aside by the globalization process. "They're selling us TVs and washing machines while most people are trying to feed themselves," remarks Anthony Simoes, an analyst with the Goa Foundation in

Southern India.[100] Similarly, long-time Member of Parliament George Fernandes sees globalization as ignoring his country's most pressing needs. "The problems my country has cannot be solved by GATT and such other global ideas. . . ," he says. "The world may be a 'global village,' but there are 650,000 villages in India, most of which do not have drinking water, electricity or roads. . . . So I have different types of problems that the Americans are not going to help me solve, not the Germans, not the Japanese, not the rest of the world."[101]

There is a strong argument to be made that, far from helping to resolve these problems, the governments and corporations of the North are, in many ways, exacerbating them. Despite the very real dynamics of growing Northern poverty and increasing Southern affluence, there is no doubt that, overall, economic globalization generally serves the Northern economies at the South's expense. The bulk of resources and products continues to flow from the South to the transnationals' home countries in the North. This feeds profligate patterns of consumption in the North that augment the world's environmental and social crises in a multiplicity of ways.

For instance, the seven largest economies of the industrialized North—the United States, Japan, Germany, Canada, France, Italy and the United Kingdom—which make up less than 12 percent of the world's population, consume 43 percent of the world's fossil fuel production, 64 percent of the world's paper and from 55 to 60 percent of all the aluminum, copper, lead, nickel and tin.[102] The United States—the largest economy in the world—manages, with less than 5 percent of the planet's population, to consume nearly 25 percent of all fossil fuels and more than 30 percent of all paper, while creating 50 percent of the world's solid waste.[103]

Mirroring patterns begun in the colonial era, this resource flow furthers the social and ecological impoverishment of the South. Northern biotechnology corporations—leaders in one of the world's newest industries are deepening this already well-worn path. Seeking to corner the market for the Third World's biodiversity, they are extracting genetic resources from tropical rainforests, altering them with biotechnology, patenting them under GATT's rules and then selling them both in the North and back to the South, usually without compensating the local people who have served as stewards of these resources for generations.[104]

In addition to these ecologically and socially destabilizing resource flows and consumption patterns, constantly growing debt burdens continue to channel financial resources out of the South's coffers and into the Northern economies. In 1992, for example, just the interest that developing countries paid on their debt totaled $160 billion. This amount was more than two-and-one-half times the size of all the foreign aid and one-third again as much as all private investment these nations received in the same year.[105] Such debt burdens—the legacy of large banks flooding the South with cheap "petrodollars" in the 1970s—divert money that could otherwise be used for social and environmental programs, making it nearly impossible for the Third World to escape poverty's grip. Many of the poorer countries are also compelled to heighten the rate at which they exploit their natural resources in order to service their debts.[106] Moreover, the World Bank and the International Monetary Fund have used the Third World's debt burdens as leverage to implement structural adjustment programs. These programs have opened up huge sectors of the Southern economies to transnational corporate investment, accelerating the flow of resources to the North and exacerbating environmental destruction (see Chapter Five). This entire process, which is being institutionalized by international trade agreements such as GATT/WTO, lies at the core of corporate globalization or, as the venerable and vitriolic Indian journalist Chakravarthi Rhagavan has labeled it, "recolonization."[107]

The few nations that make up the North will continue to consume the lion's share of the world's resources for the foreseeable future, maintaining this neocolonial pattern of global inequity. The United Nations estimates, for instance, that the industrialized North will benefit from two-thirds of the $275 billion in expanded trade that the Uruguay Round of GATT is expected to generate. The other one-third will be divided up among the more than 100 poorer nations of the South.[108] More specifically, for example, while the UN predicts that world consumption of paper and paperboard will nearly double by the year 2010—greatly augmenting pressure on dwindling forest resources—it calculates that the consumer societies in the EC, North America and Japan will be responsible for more than 60 percent of the increase.[109]

Ironically, despite (or perhaps because of) the overwhelming evidence pointing to them as the principal protagonists in the environmental crisis, a number of corporate leaders blame the poor for many of the planet's environmental problems. For instance, under fire for its role in destroying the world's forests, Mitsubishi has pointed to "poverty and local needs" as the "principal causes of deforestation."[110] And Frank Popoff, chairman of the board of the Dow Corporation, one of the

largest chemical and pesticide manufacturers and the largest producer
of chlorine on the planet, stole a line from Indira Gandhi and told a
national television and radio audience in the United States that "poverty is the ultimate polluter."[111] It would be more accurate, however, to
say that rather than being the perpetrators of environmental destruction, the poor are most often its victims. Or as Japanese environmental
scholar Jun Ui puts it, when an environment is destroyed by industrial
forces "and thereby loses its productive viability, the economically,
socially, and politically weakest members of society are the ones who
suffer most radically from the destruction. Once there is a loss of environmental viability, a new round of poverty and related suffering is generated."[112]

The poor are certainly not the principal cause of global climate
change or other planet-wide environmental problems. Indeed, transnational corporations—especially the global oil giants—are primarily
responsible for this looming crisis. But while the entire world will be
affected as climate change scenarios begin to play themselves out, it will
be the coastal peoples of the most impoverished nations of the world—
countries such as Bangladesh, El Salvador and Tanzania, as well as small
island states such as Fiji, Jamaica and the Maldives—peoples who are
relatively marginal to the global economy and who contribute little to
the greenhouse effect, who will suffer the brunt of the predicted high-
intensity storms, rising sea levels, floods, drought and disease.

In the case of tropical deforestation, there is no doubt that timber
corporations such as Mitsubishi are responsible for devastating vast
areas of ancient rainforest and the myriad indigenous cultures that live
in places such as Sarawak, Malaysia and Papua New Guinea. Yet it is also
true that many tropical forests in other areas, such as Central America
or the Amazon Basin, are felled by impoverished peasants who practice
slash-and-burn agriculture to survive. A vast number of these people,
however, are merely what one analyst has referred to as "pawns in a
general's game."[113] Many have arrived at the agricultural frontiers of
Nicaragua or Brazil, for instance, after having been displaced from rich
land by large-scale agribusiness. They have often followed roads (funded by multilateral lending institutions such as the World Bank) designed
to open vast areas of tropical forest land for cattle ranching, mining and
industrial forestry projects. These projects, of course, benefit local elites
and frequently the transnationals, while pushing the marginalized into
deeper social and ecological poverty.[114]

Meanwhile, Dow's Popoff is certainly not alone in turning the issues on their head and describing poverty as the "ultimate polluter." Recently, immigrants to the United States, especially in the state of California, have been scapegoated for pollution problems and for overburdening the carrying capacity of the land.[115] Yet many of these impoverished people are bearing the brunt of pollution rather than creating it. For instance, migrant farmworkers from Mexico (some of whom have recently become disenfranchised as a result of the globalization process) receive extremely low wages for the grueling work of harvesting the rich yield of California's agricultural crops, risking potentially fatal exposure to hazardous pesticides.[116]

Not surprisingly, the poor in the United States—both recent immigrants and those who have been in the country for generations—are exposed to a much higher degree of pollution and unhealthy products than the wealthier segments of the population. Factors of race and class often combine to have a disproportionate impact on poor African, Latino, Asian and Native Americans, forming a pattern of what has been labeled "environmental racism." Corporations and the U.S. government have consistently followed the path of least resistance and sited hazardous waste facilities, factories, freeways and railroads in poor communities of color. This has occurred primarily because these communities, facing institutionalized economic and racial barriers, have traditionally lacked the political and economic power to resist such intrusions.

This was clearly the case when the global waste management transnational WMX Technologies attempted to locate a hazardous waste incinerator in the tiny central California town of Kettleman City, overwhelmingly populated by Latino farmworkers. "The company came here because it is a poor area where there isn't any political power," remarks local resident Ausencio Avila. "We are a poor area of *campesinos* —field workers. We don't have time to go to meetings because we're so tired every day. They never thought we'd be a problem here."[117] While Avila and the rest of Kettleman surprised WMX, organizing to successfully beat back the corporation's proposal, the town is still host to the largest hazardous waste dump in the western United States and the fifth-largest in the country.[118] What's more, the other two hazardous waste dumps in California, located in the towns of Buttonwillow and Westmoreland, both owned by the Laidlaw Corporation, are also located in poor rural communities overwhelmingly populated by Mexicans and Mexican-Americans.[119]

The above scenario mirrors a situation in the southern United States, where all three commercial hazardous waste facilities are located in communities composed of a majority of people of color. Nationally, three of the five largest commercial hazardous waste facilities are in African-American or Latino communities.[120] Waste companies have also made hundreds of proposals—some successful—to site various kinds of facilities on sovereign Native American lands.[121] Past government enforcement policies have only encouraged this inequity. The EPA has imposed penalties at hazardous waste sites that average 500 percent higher for areas most heavily populated by white people than the fines imposed in communities of color.[122]

Beyond waste disposal, an alarmingly high number of toxics-producing facilities—ranging from the chemical industry to the high-tech industry to oil refining and storage—are located in poor neighborhoods, many of which are populated heavily by people of color. These communities line the chemical corridor near New Orleans known as "Cancer Alley," live downwind from petrochemical complexes in both Carson and Richmond, California, and have their water supplies polluted by high-tech factories in the Southwest. Such inequity can be further found in the distribution of air pollution, lead poisoning, pesticides, occupational hazards and noise pollution.[123]

These situations have drawn fiery responses from long-time community civil rights activists, who correctly point to environmental discrimination as part of a deep and entrenched pattern of racism in the United States. These organizers are also part of a broader national movement that is calling for environmental justice—a broad vision of social justice that includes the right of all people to live in a clean and healthy environment and to participate equally in the decisions that affect their lives.[124]

While environmental racism casts an ugly shadow on the American landscape, it has an international dimension as well. As a number of chapters in this book document, transnational corporations are responding to the combination of tight environmental regulations in the North and the opportunities of globalization to move some of their most hazardous operations down the path of least resistance. This brings them to impoverished domestic zones frequently inhabited by people of color, and to the politically weak, often repressive, investment-hungry countries of the South, also populated primarily by people of color. This constitutes a global version of environmental racism, or as Vandana Shiva has called it, a structure of "environmental apartheid in which the North grows richer and cleaner and the South grows poorer and more polluted." [125] Of course, the cases of Eastern Europe and Japan, as well as internal class structures in many countries such as Nigeria, speak to a more complex reality wherein political and economic factors emerge as more important than race. However, this metaphor is still generally useful for understanding global political ecology. [126]

Chapter Two

The Greening of Global Reach

Corporate Environmentalism Comes of Age

The environment is not going to be saved by environmentalists. Environmentalists do not hold the levers of economic power.

> Maurice Strong, defending the central role transnational corporations were playing in the 1992 United Nations Earth Summit, of which he was secretary-general

Reliance on "market forces" and the failure of self-regulation are responsible, in large part, for the world environmental crisis. The time has come for greater and more effective monitoring and regulation of transnationals, the economic agents whose present and future behavior will determine the fate of the earth.

> Martin Khor, director, Third World Network

Plunging into Rio de Janeiro's tropical blue sea are emerald-colored hills studded with a mosaic of brown *favelas,* the city's ocean-view shantytowns. A jumble of wood and brick shacks, the *favelas* are so precariously perched on Rio's precipices that it looks as if at any minute they will tumble down onto the spectacular beachfront, where surfers, fast cars and luxury hotels show another face of Brazil. The two worlds remain virtually isolated from each other, polarized on either side of what seems to be an ever deepening gulf between wealth and misery, a microcosm of the profound divisions plaguing the planet. Bridging this chasm—between rich and poor, over- and underdevelopment, North and South—is the key to resolving the twin global crises of environment and poverty.

In 1992, the world paused for a brief moment to witness an attempt to build such a bridge. Billed as the "last chance to save the Earth," the United Nations Conference on Environment and Development

(UNCED) played host to more than a hundred presidents, prime minis-ters and dictators who arrived in Rio to shake hands, sign documents, create photo opportunities and deliver green speeches tailored to audi-ences back home. While UNCED, better known as the Earth Summit, was a media hit—its images beamed to the far corners of the world—the meeting failed to fulfill its promise of mandating fundamental changes to save the planet.[1] The Rio summit did, however, mark a turning point in international environmental politics for a number of reasons. Not the least of these was the transnational corporations' grand entrance on the world stage as self-proclaimed environmentalists.[2] Happenings such as Earth Day 1990 might have provided a forum in the United States for big business there to launch a "green" publicity blitz, but Rio was a glob-al event fitted to the scope and reach of the global corporations.

The Earth Summit marked the coming of age of corporate environ-mentalism—the melding of ecological and economic globalization into a coherent ideology that has paved the way for the transnationals to reconcile, in theory and rhetoric, their ubiquitous hunger for profits and growth with the stark realities of poverty and environmental destruction. In the aftermath of Rio, global corporate environmentalism has helped institutionalize ecological concerns as agenda items in the executive suites and board rooms of some of the world's largest busi-nesses. It has built a public image of transnational corporations as responsible global "citizens." It has also, to a certain degree, begun to set the terms of the debate along lines favorable to the transnationals. In the process, corporate environmentalism has partially neutralized efforts—ranging from popular environmental movements to intergov-ernmental treaties and conventions—that pose a threat to their bottom lines.

Indeed, by focusing a relatively small portion of their vast resources on environmental issues, the global corporations have, in many respects, reframed much of the environmental discussion. Livio De-Simone, chairman of the World Business Council for Sustainable Development (WBCSD), a coalition of senior executives and board chairs of 120 of the largest transnationals in the world, which emerged from the Rio process, explained the achievement on the eve of the five-year anniversary of the Earth Summit: "A paradigm shift has clearly taken place. Business . . . used to be depicted as a primary source of the world's environmental problems. Today it is increasingly viewed as a vital contributor to solving those problems and securing a sustainable future for the planet." Ricardo Carrerre, a forest activist with the Third

World Institute in Montevideo, Uruguay, puts it a bit differently: "Before Rio the environmental movement used the system to advance its goals. Now the system has appropriated the environmental discourse and is using the environmental movement."[4]

The emergence of corporate environmentalism as a force that is in some ways superseding the prerogative of the traditional environmental movement is a complex phenomenon. On the one hand, under pressure from community organizing and/or government regulation, the transnationals are instituting a number of real changes in their technologies and practices that are leading to cleaner production and less resource destruction in some locales. On the other hand, they have appropriated the language and images of ecology and sustainability in an effort to ward off the threat that the environmental movement might convince the world's governments to force them to make much more far-reaching changes. Self-proclaimed corporate environmentalists have achieved this by absorbing the question of ecological sustainability into their overriding agenda of economic globalization. Suddenly, they have made the worldwide expansion of resource extraction, production, marketing and consumption synonymous with sustainable development. This deft maneuver has twisted the imperative to solve the environmental crisis into a justification for maintaining the status quo.

Such a masterful co-optation of ecology, suggests Indian scientist and activist Dr. Vandana Shiva, should come as no surprise. "Over the past 500 years of colonialism," she writes, whenever the global reach of governments, corporations and international institutions "has been threatened by resistance, the language of resistance has been coopted, redefined and used to legitimate future control." Today, remarks Shiva, we are witnessing "the greening of global reach."[5]

Countering this argument are people such as Maurice Strong, the corporate executive-diplomat who was UNCED's secretary-general. He insists that business must redefine environmentalism in its own way if the world is to resolve the immense problems it faces. Strong, who is quoted at the beginning of this chapter, is partially correct. He is right when he says that CEOs, presidents, finance ministers and World Bank officers must help move the levers of power to achieve environmental change. But by advocating a top-down, technocratic, managerial solution to the problem while minimizing the role of "environmentalists," he is rendering the vast majority of the world's population marginal to the solution. At its core, Strong's assertion is profoundly antidemocratic, defying a long history of peoples' movements for social change and dismissing the pressure brought by the world's environmental movements, which forced the issue of sustainability to near the top of the international diplomatic and corporate agenda in the first place.

The Environment Industry

The role that organized communities, environmental groups and others have played in compelling the transnationals to change their behavior is an achievement that most corporate environmentalists fail to recognize. This is particularly true in their public pronouncements and advertisements for themselves, which frequently make it appear that they are ecological leaders and visionaries, while what they are usually doing is merely complying with a law, relenting after a protracted campaign against them or simply seeking profit. Of course, the leaders of many of the world's great corporations have publicly recognized that it is in their own interests to overcome the challenges posed by the global crises of environment and poverty. But pressure from below has played a major role in forcing this reality upon them.

Indeed, the contemporary environmental movements in the United States, Europe and Japan, which emerged in the 1960s, have had a powerful influence on corporate behavior. Their sway, which has forced many corporations to substantially alter the way they do business, can be compared to the leverage exerted by the turn-of-the-century "trust busters" in the United States or the labor movements of later years. Environmental movements composed of consumers, urban victims of industrialism and rural residents have carried out specific campaigns that have succeeded in forcing individual corporations as well as entire industrial sectors to change how they produce, and sometimes even what they produce. These social movements, emerging from quagmires such as Love Canal in the United States, Minamata in Japan and Sveso in Europe, have also pressed governments to enact legislation and regulations aimed at curbing some of the deleterious impacts of modern industrialism. Consequently, laws to clean up and safeguard the air, water and land have been enacted and enforced in many countries.

The Japanese government, for example, responding to growing popular protest and media coverage of a series of corporate-driven environmental disasters (see Chapter Four), enacted comprehensive legislation—the Basic Law for Pollution Control—in 1967 and created its environmental agency in 1971. With these tools in place, Japan began implementing a series of controls aimed at containing pollution.[6] Similar environmental legislation also proliferated at that time throughout Western Europe. In the United States, conservationists forced the passage of laws regulating air, water and soil pollution, including the Resource Conservation and Recovery Act (RCRA) and the Toxic Substances Control Act (TSCA) in 1976, and then CERCLA—commonly known as the Superfund—in 1980.[7]

Such regulation has resulted in a significant decrease of some pollution over the last thirty years in the Triad of the European Union, the United States and Japan. By forcing polluters to invest large sums of money in pollution control technology, it has also given rise to a multi-billion-dollar "environment industry" dominated by some of the world's largest corporations. Indeed, it has come to pass that environmental problems are also blossoming into big business for many capitalists as the system attempts to adapt to its own shortcomings.[8]

The environment industry is lauded by government leaders and corporate chiefs in the industrialized world as a way to combine profitability with sustainability. Yet the environment industry has generated its own set of environmental problems. This apparent irony originates in big business's initial efforts to resist, avoid or water down regulatory controls. For instance, when the bulk of U.S. environmental legislation was under discussion in the 1970s, polluting corporations conceded that regulation was inevitable, but opposed government control over the production process. In the debate over RCRA, for example, Dow Chemical, the second largest producer of hazardous wastes in the United States, argued that granting the government "authority to control production, composition, and distribution of products . . . would be devastating to free enterprise commerce." Instead, suggested DuPont, the leading private producer of toxic waste in the United States, "we believe that the *disposal* [emphasis added] of wastes ought to be regulated instead of regulating the nature and use of the product or the type of manufacturing process used."[9]

Such arguments were successful. Thus, instead of zeroing in on the source of the problems—regulating *what* the corporations produced and *how* they produced it, forcing industry to begin a fundamental transformation to clean production—legislatures in the Northern industrialized countries bowed to pressure from the corporate world and instituted a series of "end of the pipe" and "downstream" disposal-oriented solutions. These legislative responses—akin to mandating filters on carcinogenic cigarettes—preserved the production status quo while simultaneously creating the conditions for a new industry to emerge.

Today, the so-called environment industry, a group of toxics-hauling, wastewater-cleaning, air pollution–scrubbing corporations, is a global giant in its own right and a bastion of corporate environmentalism. While the industry itself is difficult to define, a study prepared by the Organization for Economic Cooperation and Development (the OECD is made up of the industrialized nations) placed the global market for environmental equipment and services at about $200 billion in 1990 and forecast growth to $300 billion by the year 2000.[10] The International Finance Corporation (IFC), an arm of the World Bank, used a broader definition that included "other" technologies, such as "clean" coal, and came up with a 1990 figure of $300 billion, estimating that the industry would double to a whopping $600 billion by the turn of the century.[11] By means of comparison, the aerospace industry's annual market is about $180 billion, while chemical products are estimated at $500 billion.[12] By any measure, such income makes the environment one of the fastest growing businesses on the planet.

In 1992 the United States environment industry, which accounts for about 40 percent of the world market, brought in revenues of about $86 billion, amounting to nearly 2 percent of the country's GNP and employing close to 200,000 people. Roughly half of this market was made up of 60,000 or so small firms.[13] The other half was made up of a very few large firms, big polluters all.[14] General Electric, for example, whose environmental abuses are widespread throughout the world and four of whose U.S. factories were on the EPA's list of the most dangerous sources of air pollution, has added air pollution control equipment to its balance sheet, becoming the top manufacturer in the United States and sixth in the world.[15] DuPont, which still produces more hazardous waste than any other U.S. corporation, has developed its own "environmental" services, including waste incineration and deep well injection.[16] K. D. Sadhle, a resident of Goa, India, who was actively involved in opposing DuPont's plans to site a nylon plant there, grasped the irony of this dual role. Commenting on the U.S. chemical giant's claims of eco-technological leadership, he observed, "You are selling poison on one counter, and you are selling the cure on the other counter. For both your motive is the same: making money."[17]

With the end of the Cold War, the military-industrial complex has switched gears. Defense contractors such as Westinghouse, which for years profited from lucrative nuclear weapons contracts, compete for the billions of dollars that the Department of Energy is doling out to clean up the tremendous radioactive mess they made. Companies such as Raytheon, the maker of the Patriot missile, have also added environmental segments to their business with the hope of altering their post–Cold War image while cashing in on the burgeoning new market. "You may think of Raytheon as a defense company," says Martin Cohn, PR flack for the Environmental Business Council of the United States, an industry association, "but really they're an environmental company." The *Raytheon 1992 Annual Report*'s list of "environmental" activities includes building and maintaining nuclear, chemical, pharmaceutical, biotechnology and gas-fired cogeneration power plants in less polluting ways. One such natural gas project in the Nevada desert just north of Las Vegas will furnish forty-six megawatts of energy to light up the roulette wheels and the flashing neon landscape of this gambler's mecca, while simultaneously cogenerating hot water to heat a twelve-acre greenhouse that will produce vegetables next to the power plant. This way, says Raytheon Vice-President Ed Woolen, "you get not only energy but tomatoes out of a barrel of fuel." [18]

The environment industry has also produced a few transnationals of its own. WMX Technologies, a company dedicated exclusively to waste, has evolved into one of the top 500 corporations in the world with annual revenues exceeding $10 billion and operations in more than twenty countries. [19] The world's leading "environmental services" company, WMX's network of dumps and incinerators alone accounts for more than 10 percent of the entire U.S. environment industry's revenues. Such stature has prompted *Forbes* magazine to dub the company a "green machine." [20]

Today, the vast majority of so-called environmental companies are not creating and selling clean technologies and products. They are not building or investing in emission-free hydrogen-powered cars, nonpolluting closed-system industrial factories or solar and wind energy plants. The environment industry spends billions on smokestack scrubbers instead of replacing the smokestack with a clean technology. It profits from hazardous waste dumps and incinerators rather than the reduction of toxic waste production. In fact, the environment industry is concentrated almost exclusively in what Grant Ferrier, editor-in-chief of the *Environmental Business Journal*, describes as the "brown" end-of-the-pipe sector of clean-up and control, rather than the "green" sector of pollution prevention. The latter, says Ferrier, makes up less than 1 percent of the entire industry. [21] Ferrier writes that polluters "increasingly pay lip service to proactive environmental management and pollution prevention, but most have yet to put their money where their mouth is in terms of active programs." If such changes were to occur, they would "only serve to preempt the environmental industry as we know it today."[22] Indeed, the environment industry is similar to the health care industry. It is an ever growing, moneymaking giant, but it is only treating the symptoms and not investing in prevention.

What's more, end-of-the-pipe strategies to contain hazardous waste in dumps or burn it in incinerators have served not to eliminate the problem but rather to displace it, rendering "green machines" such as WMX leading polluters—the sources of a steady stream of serious ecological, health, legal and technological problems.[23] These translate into health and environmental problems for neighboring communities. For instance, inherently unsafe and accident-prone, hazardous waste dumps are slow-trigger underground time bombs. Sooner or later, the landfills leak, leaching toxic substances into the groundwater. Dumping industry's hazardous waste into high-tech holes in the ground with sealers and liners only displaces, delays, and perhaps softens the toxic impacts of deadly chemicals, but it does not eliminate them. In fact, at least seven scientific studies have reported unusually high numbers of birth defects in children born to parents residing near such dumps.[24]

Incineration, another favorite technology of the environment industry, takes this process one step further, transforming hazardous chemicals from tangible waste that must be monitored in perpetuity to invisible chemicals that are spewed into the air. This makes the waste's impacts much more difficult to pin down, allowing corporations to literally burn their potential liability away. But the displaced waste is no less dangerous. Incineration, often called a "state of the art" technology, isn't as safe or reliable as its advocates maintain. Dioxin and other dioxinlike chemicals such as furans and PCBs are unwanted byproducts of burning chlorine-based chemicals in incinerators. It is well documented that these toxins lead to high rates of cancer, as well as problems in fetal development and harm to the immune system (see Chapter One). Indeed, incinerator emissions have been clearly linked to increased rates of cancer and neurologic disease, such as seizures, tremors, tingling, blackouts and incoordination. Nearly half of the workers at one incinerator in Arkansas were found to have elevated levels of PCBs in their blood. People living downwind from incinerators have been found much more likely to have emphysema, pneumonia, sinus trouble, asthma and allergies.[25]

Earth in the Balance Sheet

An authentic environment industry would focus on pollution prevention and the development of clean, environmentally sustainable production technologies. But it seems that unless a transition is forced upon them, the transnationals will continue molding the definition of what is environmentally sound to their bottom line. As the OECD explains, transformation "will be hastened to the extent that government regulations ensure" that industry is pushed in that direction.[26] Yet such a challenge is complicated by the tremendous economic and political power that the transnationals wield.

Paradoxically, the global corporations, responsible for such a large number of environmental problems around the world, are extremely well situated to help resolve the planet's environmental problems—were they actually committed or compelled to do so. They have the financial and human resources to create, invest in, produce and distribute new technologies and production processes. Yet their political and economic interests in maintaining a status quo that is most profitable to them has stifled such change.[27]

Conversely, if political and economic systems were transformed to promote ecological sustainability, rather than profitability as it is currently defined, then corporations as we know them might well cease to exist. If any were to survive, they might do so by building cars that get hundreds of miles to the gallon, or even ones that run on nonpolluting hydrogen. Their energies and know-how could help create public transport systems that reduce traffic congestion, air pollution and the "need" for cars in the first place. They would be compelled to dedicate their resources to replacing entire classes of chemicals such as those based on chlorine. The surviving paper companies, for example, would be the ones that produced chlorine-free, tree-free paper. Ancient forests might revert to serving as productive, sustainably harvested ecosystems that support local economies. Polluters would be forced out of business, and surviving corporations would be those that succeed in eliminating waste from their industrial production processes, creating closed-loop systems that effectively recycle the inputs. Corporations might still reap profits, but they would do so by sowing seeds of sustainability. Accompanying such a transformation would be prosperity and a better quality of life for all. This is a glimpse of a vision of a different reality—one in which economics serves the interests of ecological sustainability and social equity, and one in which corporations are forced to meet the

world's needs, rather than the world being obliged to meet their requirements.[28] It is a reality that is technologically possible today, if the political will exists to create it.

In recent years leaders of some of the world's most powerful corporations have begun calling for environmental change, but their kind of
change does not measure up to this vision of a sustainable world. The
pace and extent of the corporate reforms occurring today simply pale
before the fundamental challenge of reversing the world's most pressing
environmental and social problems. In sum, today's corporate environmentalism is to the ecological and social crises of globalization what a
band-aid is to a gaping wound.

Despite the inadequacy of today's corporate environmentalism, and
while it is difficult to separate public relations initiatives from real transformations, it is important to recognize that *some* change is beginning
to take place that goes beyond the end-of-the-pipe approach of the environment industry. Some corporations have sought to control the damage to the people and ecosystems they affect, and in this way to
improve their public images and bottom lines. Some have done so not
only by complying with legislation, but by going beyond it to address
the environmental ills they cause. And a few have begun to seriously
rethink how they function, strategizing about transforming their production processes and product lines. Some corporations, especially in
Western Europe and Japan, are beginning to implement these strategies.[29] What's more, there are many socially and ecologically conscien-
tious individuals who work for these companies. Many of them are
working to alter the corporations that employ them on every level, from
the shop floor right on up to the board room.

These innovations and reforms have manifested themselves in a
number of concrete ways. For instance, while the environment was a
topic rarely taken seriously in the business world just a decade ago, in
the last ten years a plethora of corporate environmental departments
and policies have emerged to set internal standards, rules, guidelines
and long-term goals. Japanese corporations created more than 300 environmental affairs departments in the early 1990s alone.[30] It is also not
uncommon today to encounter people in charge of environmental
issues among the ranks of senior executives and members of the board
of directors of a transnational. Moreover, global environmental management has become a respected profession, while environmental self-
audits and environmental impact assessments have become a common
tool for many transnational corporations.[31] Industry-wide voluntary

codes of conduct have also proliferated in the past decade or so. A number of corporations are beginning to explore how to account for environmental costs in their economic calculations.[32] And a plethora of positive case studies can be found in various books, touting changes in corporate management as well as technological innovations that are reducing waste, minimizing the impact of destructive production processes and making companies more environmentally sound in general.[33]

These various initiatives have evolved, however, within the context of economic globalization, which is promoting accelerated environmental destruction along with social dislocation. In an attempt to reconcile this inherent contradiction, the disparate strands of emergent corporate environmentalism have been consolidated under an ideological framework that seeks to merge the concepts of global capitalist enterprise and ecological sustainability.

While the doctrine had been incubating for quite some time in individual corporations, it began to gain prominence with the work of the 1987 Brundtland Commission, which produced a widely hailed global agenda for change.[34] It then gathered momentum when the UN General Assembly conceived of UNCED in 1989.[35] In the years leading up to the Rio Earth Summit, global corporate environmentalism became increasingly refined through a series of strategy meetings, forums and conferences such as the International Chamber of Commerce's (ICC) Second World Industry Conference on Environmental Management (organized in conjunction with the United Nations Environment Programme and the UNCED Secretariat) in Rotterdam, the Netherlands, where a "Business Charter for Sustainable Development" was promulgated in 1991. More than a thousand corporations signed the nonbinding charter, which urges that environmental management in a free market setting be recognized "as among the highest corporate priorities."[36]

This ideology of free market, corporate environmentalism was taken to a new level with the creation of the Business Council for Sustainable Development (BCSD), a group of forty-eight CEOs of some of the world's largest corporations, organized by Swiss billionaire Stephan Schmidheiny for the Earth Summit.* Schmidheiny and the BCSD issued a forward-looking book called *Changing Course* just before the Earth Summit began. This effort represented the culmination of not only the

---

* In 1995 the BCSD and the ICC's environmental arm, the World Industry Council for the Environment, merged to form the World Business Council for Sustainable Development (WBCSD).

BCSD's nearly two years of work, but also a highly evolved rendition of corporate positioning on issues of environment and development in general.[37]

Changing Course articulates a vision of "sustainable development" that, endorsed as it is by the CEOs of corporations such as Royal Dutch Shell, Volkswagen, Mitsubishi, Chevron, Dow and DuPont, has since been adopted by much of the corporate world. Reverberations of its declarations can be found today in the words and deeds of corporate leaders across the globe. This corporate environmentalism is based on four fundamental pillars. First, it contends that unleashing market forces to promote ongoing economic growth through open and competitive trade is the fundamental prerequisite for sustainable development. Second, it calls for pricing mechanisms to correct distortions in the world economy and reflect environmental costs. Third, it argues that self-regulation is the best, most preferable and most efficient method for transforming business practices. And fourth, the BCSD calls for further changes in technology and managerial practices in order to promote cleaner production and the more efficient use of resources.[38] These pillars, erected in 1992, continue to serve as the fundamental framework for corporate environmentalism today.

This approach to solving the world's social and environmental problems envisions a rosy scenario of more growth through globalization, more profits and a healthy Corporate Planet. Yet it is problematic for a number of reasons. First, its technocratic, top-down approach tends to undermine democracy and community environmental rights. Noting that "the world is moving toward deregulation, private initiatives and global markets," *Changing Course* asserts that this situation "requires corporations to assume more social, economic and environmental responsibility in defining their roles."[39] Under any circumstances, corporations could certainly assume far greater responsibility for their actions than they have to date. Yet, as discussed in Chapter One, global corporations are molding a world in which they are less and less accountable to the laws of nations or cultures or communities. In place of these traditional institutions, transnationals are creating methods of self-governance and auto-accountability designed to guide their interactions with the people they affect.

In this new pseudosystem of corporate governance, such people are envisioned as "stakeholders" in a corporate enterprise. Stakeholders range from first-class shareholders, customers and employees to second-

or third-class advocacy groups and communities who might live, for example, next to a polluting factory. The designation of "stakeholder" tends to remove citizens from the realm of political power achieved through participation in democratic institutions (if their society has such institutions). It also overrides any traditional community decision-making process and resource-use patterns. In place of these conventions, it redefines citizens and their communities as constituencies of transnational corporations in the world economy, virtually defining them as residents in a global version of the "company town."

In another blow to community control, corporations and some environmental organizations, such as the United States–based Environmental Defense Fund, have successfully encouraged national governments to adopt a new wave of "free market" environmental policies. For instance, free trade in "pollution credits" among corporations was enshrined in the U.S. Clean Air Act of 1990. This measure, in effect, allows a company to buy credits that enable it to continue to pollute beyond what is legally permissible in one area. The credits are bought from other corporations, which have earned them by reducing their own pollution below what is required by law. The result may be the decline of overall pollution levels in the country, but a community that continues to get dumped upon may lose its right to a clean and healthy environment.[40] In this version of free market environmentalism, corporate rights win out over people's rights.

On a global level, corporate environmentalism strongly endorses international economic agreements such as NAFTA, GATT/WTO and the proposed MAI as essential to addressing ecological questions. Indeed, it is virtually a mantra of corporate environmentalism that "open trade is a key requirement for sustainable development."[41] But as former Harvard Business School professor David Korten argues, by playing an integral role in drafting and supporting the passage of these agreements, the transnationals are "actively rewriting the rules of the market to assure their own rights and freedoms take precedence over the rights and freedoms of the world's citizens."[42] The environmental implications of these agreements are serious. Obscure bureaucratic decision-making panels are empowered to overturn local and national laws protecting the environment as well as consumers' and workers' rights. For instance, the GATT/WTO has ruled that a Canadian fisheries conservation measure, a Thai law limiting cigarette imports and U.S. laws that tax oil and chemical feedstocks to pay for hazardous waste clean-up are unfair barriers to trade.[43] These agreements are also having a chilling effect on governments formulating future environmental and other policies by limiting them to approaches that are consistent with GATT/WTO rules.[44] Meanwhile, mechanisms in international environmental agreements such as the Montreal Protocol to Protect the Ozone Layer, which provides for the transfer of ozone-friendly technologies to the Third World, are also potentially in conflict with the GATT/WTO, which may view such measures as unfair subsidies.[45]

Furthermore, these agreements are almost pushing the United Nations out of the picture when it comes to global governance, replacing the principle of "one country, one vote" with a world system dominated by the Triad. Indeed, the GATT text that establishes the World Trade Organization makes no mention of the United Nations, but rather calls for cooperation with the "Bretton Woods Institutions"—the World Bank and the International Monetary Fund—in the realm of economic policy making. "By excluding the General Assembly and other United Nations bodies from global economic policy making," argue former UN officials Harris Gleckman and Riva Krut, "GATT ensures that international economic policy and regulations will not be decided in a democratic multilateral arena, but on the basis of trading power."[46] This does not bode well for the multitude of environmental questions that are intimately intertwined with the economic realm.

In fact, there are efforts under way to empower these economic institutions to decide on environmental matters. If the GATT/WTO obtains dominion over ecological issues, it hands responsibility for global environmental management over to entities whose top priority is trade liberalization—entities that are virtually dominated by the industrialized nations and that are heavily influenced by the global corporations.[47]

Using international trade agreements such as the GATT/WTO as the regulatory superstructure to which environmental issues are subordinated makes sense to the global corporations. They base their approach to the environment and development on the firm belief that the general direction in which the world economy is sailing—toward increasing globalization of production and consumption, accelerating privatization, the lowering of national barriers to trade and investment, and the expansion of corporate markets and investment opportunities—will create both greater economic prosperity and ecological sustainability. Such continued growth, the corporate environmentalists argue, will bring ecologically sound technology to the Third World and alleviate poverty while simultaneously producing ever larger corporate profits. Or as the International Chamber of Commerce puts it, "Economic growth, open markets and environmental protection are complementary and compatible objectives. There can be no sustainable development without real economic growth; only such growth can create the capacity to solve environmental problems."[48]

Growth, in fact, has become an end in itself.[49] But the model of growth currently in force in the world economy is creating, not alleviating, poverty and environmental destruction. More important than the rate of growth is the nature of this economic activity—what kind of growth it is, who it benefits and who or what it harms. As the United Nations Development Programme professes, "much depends on how the fruits of economic growth are shared—particularly on what the poor get—and how much the additional resources are used to support public services—particularly primary health care and basic education."[50] In our increasingly globalized economy, fewer and fewer fruits of growth are channeled through government to meet people's basic needs. Instead, while corporate profits soar, ever weaker governments have less and less resources to devote to social issues such as health, education and environment, relegating them to the brutal whims of the "free market."[51]

While cutting back on social supports, many Third World countries are following an economic growth path based on increasing their exports of agricultural and industrial products. This tends to create new wealth by replacing old, less quantifiable riches of community economies based on common property resources such as agricultural and forest land. As Indian scholar Rajni Kothari observes, "The modernist thinking that economic growth will create wealth and this will in turn 'trickle down' does not take account of the wealth that had already existed through long periods of history and that is now being destroyed in the process of creating new wealth."[52] Indeed, many people in the world might be much better off without such economic growth.

Furthermore, the economic growth that has increased global output fivefold since 1950 is driven to a large degree by the petroleum, petrochemical, agribusiness, energy generation, transportation, mining and metal industries. These economic activities, dominated by a handful of transnational corporations, are precisely the ones responsible for a great number of the world's dire ecological problems. On top of this, relates David Korten, is the difficult reality that "the more environmentally burdensome ways of meeting a given need are generally those that contribute most to the gross national product (GNP)." He notes, for example, that consuming foods produced, processed and packaged by agribusiness adds more to GNP than buying natural foods in bulk, and that producing hazardous waste and then paying a corporation such as WMX to dispose of it contributes more to GNP (and is thus counted as greater economic growth) than not producing the waste in the first place.[53]

Certainly one point that most corporate environmentalists seem to hold as non-negotiable in their "growth equals sustainable development" scenario is that consumerism and consumption should continue to expand around the world. For all their talk of sustainable development, it is extremely rare to hear the leaders of transnational corporations speak of the need for anyone, anywhere, to consume less. Rather, they have embarked on a series of "green" marketing campaigns tailored to reassure the public that it can keep consuming with a clear ecological conscience. But this simply isn't the case. Globalized patterns of growth, geared to extending stratified consumption patterns, are diametrically opposed to ecological sustainability and social equity.[54]

The more sophisticated corporate environmentalists have answered the critique of the growth ideology by declaring that the reform of market mechanisms is the compass that will lead them to change the destructive course they are charting. *Changing Course,* for instance, argues that national and international economic systems must be transformed so that they can continue to grow while taking environmental costs into account.[55] Similar arguments are made by environmental economists such as Herman Daly and green business leaders such as Paul Hawken, who contend that markets and economics can work in favor of the environment and social equity if the price of natural resources and the costs of pollution are accurately reflected in accounting systems.[56] To convert the market system into a force that promotes—rather than undermines—ecological sustainability would require profound changes. Yet without integrating the Earth into the balance sheet, it will be virtually impossible to build ecologically sound, socially just societies. Despite some rhetoric, this is precisely the change that transnational corporations seem unwilling to accept.

It is important that many global corporations are calling for environmental pricing. Yet it must be recognized that, so far, they are promoting such a transformation almost exclusively in theory, while simultaneously promoting economic globalization and all of its destructive

manifestations as a full-fledged practice. If a transformation in economic accounting is to be the compass that guides global corporations
away from the unsustainable status quo, then self-proclaimed corporate
environmentalists must alter not only their words, but also their
actions.

In the United States, for example, less than a year after the Earth
Summit, the Clinton Administration proposed a relatively small BTU
energy tax that would have had its greatest impact on petroleum corporations. While not nearly a perfect application of full-cost accounting, the BTU tax was designed in part to force the price of oil in the
United States to begin reflecting its significant ecological costs. In
response, some of the same corporate CEOs, such as Chevron's Ken
Derr, who had endorsed *Changing Course*'s environmental accounting
proposals, as well as modest measures to address the possibility of global warming, changed their tune rather than changing course. According
to Derr, Chevron and its oil industry cohorts "gathered partners and
allies, and prevailed in efforts to head off that ill-conceived tax."[57]

Additionally, while environmental accounting systems—if they were
actually implemented—could push industry in a much more ecologically sound direction, the world can hardly afford, even then, to leave
questions of sustainability and equity completely in the hands of the
market.[58] This is so because internalizing environmental costs itself can
become a very subjective endeavor that pits different visions of economic well-being against one another. As Vandana Shiva argues in a critique of the World Bank's efforts to develop a system of environmental
accounting, "it uses economic logic to 'internalise' people's resources
into the market rather than internalising the social and ecological costs
of commerce . . . thus alienating even further the rights of local communities and removing all remaining ecological and social limits on
resource use." Furthermore, some things are priceless or intangible or
quite unpredictable. As Dr. Shiva observes, "resources can often have
very high value while having no price. Sacred sites like sacred forests
and rivers are examples" of such resources.[59] Nor can the market put an
adequate price on potentially catastrophic climate change until it has
already happened and is thus too late; it cannot fully anticipate and
integrate the impacts of unpredictable droughts, storms, floods and disease on billions of people's lives into an economic formula; it cannot
account for scientific modeling, endorsed by nearly all the world's top
climate scientists, that suggests we must reduce our carbon dioxide
emissions by 60 percent to avoid the deleterious impacts of climate

change. Pricing climate change also raises a series of other troubling questions, such as how one values human life in such a scenario or whether a Third World life should be valued as much as a Northern industrialized life.[60]

Preventing situations such as global warming requires more than market mechanisms that simply assign economic value to intangibles, or those which promote the international trade in pollution permits. Rather, it necessitates a different focus—one that, instead of concentrating on promoting a greened-over version of economic growth, makes its central priority that of eliminating poverty, fostering ecological sustainability and allowing for community control over production and resource decisions. By taking this approach, a new kind of regulated market would serve the interests of social, environmental and economic justice.

Rather than rolling over and allowing such a transformation, however, many transnationals advocate self-regulation as an alternative. While books such as *Changing Course* tip their hats to some limited government controls, self-regulation has become the watchword of corporate environmentalism. Stephan Schmidheiny, the former BCSD chairman, who sits on the boards of directors of both the Nestlé corporation and Asea Brown and Boveri, the engineering giant that is promoting coal and nuclear power in Eastern Europe, sums up the argument for corporate self-regulation. He suggests that instead of directly resisting change, corporations must go on the offensive and take control of the environmental issue before it takes further control of them. "We have two options," he asserts. "Either we resist and we will suffer, or we anticipate the changes and we will have more profits and more personal satisfaction." Such an offensive, says Schmidheiny, will allow the transnationals the opportunity to "promote self-regulation, provided we do it in time, we do it convincingly and in a transparent way. If we fail to do it in time, we face government regulations under pressure from the public."[61]

Yet, one must seriously question whether the transnationals, the biggest polluters in the world, are really capable of independently reforming and restructuring themselves so profoundly that it will fundamentally alter what they do. As former UN officials Harris Gleckman and Riva Krut point out, "'self-regulation' is really an oxymoron. Potential polluters cannot make 'laws' (i.e., regulate) and order 'sanctions' (i.e., authorize penalties and fines) that are against self-interest."[62]

Of course, there are times when self-regulation plays a constructive role. As a report by the former United Nations Centre on Transnational Corporations points out, "In some cases, self-regulation may be more effective than national regulations themselves, especially in those countries in which enforcement mechanisms are weak." But, noting that "there are many reasons why industry engages in self-regulation," the report goes on to observe that "self-regulation may be used to shape or avoid future legislation. . . . Self-policing by firms can also be an effective public-relations technique, especially at a time when consumers increasingly scrutinize industry performance before making purchasing decisions. For business generally, self-regulation of that kind is a preferable alternative to codes of conduct developed by international organizations" such as the United Nations.[63]

Self-regulation serves to stave off the efforts of governments and citizens' groups to impose tougher controls on the transnationals.[64] Corporate self-audits and environmental reports, for instance, effectively serve to preempt pressure on companies to open their facilities and books to independent inspectors who could more objectively assess the environmental impacts of their operations. What's more, U.S. corporations have lobbied hard to pass state laws that would prevent information generated through a self-audit from being used against them in a court of law. Industry codes and initiatives such as the U.S. Chemical Manufacturers Association's (CMA) "Responsible Care" program, along with the International Standards Organization's green-labeling initiatives, are vehicles that the transnationals use to define environmental issues on their terms. In Europe, for example, the CMA's counterpart, the Conseil Européen des Federations de l'Industrie Chimique, has created a set of voluntary rules intended, as *The Economist* reports, "to discourage the EC from inventing a European equivalent" of the Toxic Release Inventory, a law passed in the United States in the aftermath of the Bhopal gas disaster that requires corporations to report their chemical releases to the public.[65]

Perhaps the most striking indictment of corporate environmentalism can be found in comparing the transnationals' words with their actions.

---

* The PCSD was created by the Clinton Administration in the aftermath of the Earth Summit to bring industry and environmental leaders to the table with high-ranking government officials to work out a long-range plan that would move the United States toward greater ecological sustainability (see Chapter Six).

These contradictions were perhaps most apparent when the Republican Party swept into control of the 104th U.S. Congress in 1995. Suddenly, "environmentalist" companies such as Chevron, Dow Chemical and the timber transnational Georgia-Pacific, all of whom sat on the Clinton Administration's President's Council on Sustainable Development (PCSD),* showed their true colors by participating in an all-out assault to paralyze and gut U.S. environmental regulations.[66]

Together with their Republican allies in the House and Senate, for example, U.S. corporations opened up ancient forests on federal lands to clear-cutting, passing a law (signed by President Clinton) that overrode environmental protections already in place.[67] And while many of their initiatives were stymied in the legislative process or by presidential veto, the scope of the attempted rollback effort was truly stunning. They worked to slash the budgets for enforcing agencies such as the EPA and the Interior Department.[68] As they continued to deny the scientific basis of many environmental problems, they set their sights on making significant cuts in nearly all federal environmental science programs that provide crucial data on problems such as global warming.[69] They attempted to undermine laws mandating clean air and water, as well as those protecting endangered species and wilderness.[70] They moved to delay the phase-out of ozone-depleting chemicals.[71] They sabotaged food safety laws.[72] And they attempted to undermine laws that make them liable for defective products, as well as those that force them to pay for pollution crimes.[73]

U.S. corporations also helped write and promote laws that use a "risk assessment" formula to make economic considerations the determining factor over health protection when setting environmental standards, thus undermining government's ability to regulate corporate activities in the public interest. Implementation of risk assessment also promised to tie up the government's enforcement of environmental regulations. These corporations also helped offer up a "takings" law that inverts the burden of compensation, requiring that government reimburse landowners (often corporations) if a law lowers their property values. For instance, the federal government would be required to compensate a landowning corporation for "taking" its property if the government denied it a permit to build a hazardous waste dump over a shallow aquifer. Meanwhile, the landowner might not be forced to compensate the community whose aquifer it poisons if risk assessment determined that the economic value of the operation was greater than the cost of loss of human health.[74]

"The Congress has passed anti-environmental bills before," said Sierra Club Executive Director Carl Pope in response to these draconian measures, "but never before has it been so clear that a House of Congress is completely controlled by the special interests that pollute America."[75] Indeed, as the CEOs of some of the most polluting companies in the United States blithely mouthed tributes to the concept of sustainable development while sitting around the president's environmental table, their lobbyists were working overtime on Capitol Hill, taking advantage of an extraordinary political climate to undermine twenty-five years of environmental legislation. Even Jay Hair, then-president of the conservative environmental group the National Wildlife Federation was chagrined. "It's very duplicitous," commented Hair, a PCSD member and for years a booster of corporate environmentalism. "On the one hand, some of these folks want the good, positive public image of being on a President's Council. . . . On the other hand, when they, with all their wealth and minions, are back in Washington undermining the things that we're trying to achieve—that's very frustrating."[76]

Corporate Diplomacy

Some of the greatest potential to combat the growing globalization of the environmental crisis lies in international treaties and conventions, such as the Montreal Protocol for the Protection of the Ozone Layer, and the variety of agreements reached at the Earth Summit in Rio de Janeiro, including the Climate Convention, the Biodiversity Convention, and the 900-page Agenda 21. In the age of globalization, such agreements, arrived at by consensus among the governments of the world, serve as some of the best tools available to counter the global reach, control and environmental abuse of the transnationals. As such, these international regulatory mechanisms have posed formidable challenges to the global corporations. Indeed, global treaties and conventions have become a key battlefield for the future of the planet.

Of course, it is important to recognize that these international negotiations have become increasingly skewed in favor of the global corporations. As Vandana Shiva argues, the manner in which international environmental agreements are currently negotiated and structured gives the transnationals' interests a leg up on the interests of environmental and social justice. "The life of all people, including the poor of the Third

World, or the life of the planet are not at the center of concern in international negotiations on environmental issues," she writes.[77]

A prime example of this dynamic is the Montreal Protocol. For years, the big chlorofluorocarbon (CFC) producers resisted calls to phase them out; they disputed ozone science, called for more studies and predicted that dire economic consequences would ensue if CFCs were banned. But when the ozone hole actually appeared over Antarctica in the mid-1980s, the public's indignation rose and the world's governments moved to ban CFCs through the Protocol. It was then that the same transnational giants responsible for the ozone hole—DuPont, ICI, the Mitsubishi Group's Asahi Glass, Hoechst and others—saw the writing on the wall and moved to co-opt the issue and the Protocol itself. In the late 1980s and early 1990s, many of them developed and began marketing replacements for CFCs ahead of the Protocol's schedule, hailing themselves as environmental leaders. Forsaking the opportunity to shift to environmentally healthy alternatives, these chemical corporations decided instead to develop the most profitable, not the most ecologically sound, replacements. Thus, the same entities responsible for the ozone crisis now dominate a CFC-alternative market that consists primarily of HCFCs—an ozone-depleting chemical less virulent than CFCs—and HFCs, a gas with potent global-warming properties. These products were accepted by the world's governments negotiating the Protocol as substitutes for CFCs.[78]

What's more, some of these same corporations have played a key role in the Ozone Operations Resource Group, the panel that advises the World Bank on how to manage the 80 percent of the Protocol funds that it controls. A large portion of these funds, which are earmarked for disseminating CFC substitutes to the Third World, wind up in the pockets of the very corporations that created the problem in the first place and that are now marketing hazardous HFC and HCFC alternatives.[79] Thus, argues Shiva, "the financial resources that go into the Montreal Protocol Fund for transfer of technology are in effect subsidies for DuPont [and the others] and not for the Third World."[80]

The Montreal Protocol is still a ground-breaking international convention, one of the only global agreements with any "teeth" in the form of powerful economic enforcement mechanisms. The Protocol has also succeeded in banning CFCs and forcing the transformation of a multibillion-dollar industrial activity. Yet, in a master stroke of corporate diplomacy, the transnationals were able to shift the focus of the

Protocol away from ecological sustainability and toward the corporate bottom line. The situation was inadvertently summed up by one top U.S. representative to a 1994 Montreal Protocol meeting, who declared that the ozone issue was no longer "an environmental issue. It's an economic issue."[81]

Similarly, the petroleum corporations have sought to turn the focus of the Climate Convention negotiations away from the potential human and ecological consequences of global climate change and toward the purported economic implications of moving away from fossil fuels as the world's primary energy source. As Chevron CEO Ken Derr told a friendly audience of his peers in 1994, "a crash course to try to reduce CO_2 emissions could bring on a very genuine crisis in the global economy."[82] Armed with this self-serving argument, a scientific posture of questioning, and delaying tactics that resemble the stance of the CFC producers and the tobacco corporations over recent decades, the oil companies, as well as industry associations such as the Global Climate Coalition, vigorously and quite successfully lobbied the world's governments to minimize the reach and scope of the agreement.[83] Their aggressive actions prompted even Timothy Wirth, Clinton Administration undersecretary of State for Global Affairs, to accuse global warming's corporate critics of being "bent upon destroying" the Climate Convention.[84]

Although most of the world's attention has long since drifted from the Earth Summit, the corporate role in it deserves revisiting. For in addition to the consolidation of corporate environmentalism as a global ideology and practice, the transnationals' other major achievement at UNCED was their agile and successful endeavor to virtually silence all discussion among governments about the need for international regulation and control of global corporations in the name of sustainable development.

One of the first obstacles that the corporate diplomats from the ICC and the BCSD had to overcome was a branch of the United Nations itself—the United Nations Centre on Transnational Corporations (UNCTC). Created in the 1970s at the behest of Third World governments that expressed the need for systematized information on foreign corporations investing in their countries, the UNCTC had produced a series of reports and recommendations on labor, environmental and other issues. It had also been long at work on a nonbinding Code of Conduct for transnationals. Its stances had never been very radical (in fact, they became increasingly watered down over the years), but its efforts were still seen as a potential threat to the ideology of corporate self-regulation espoused by many corporations and governments, such as the United States, which regularly scorned its existence.

For the Earth Summit negotiations, the UNCTC was asked by the United Nations Economic and Social Council to prepare a set of recommendations on transnationals and other large industrial enterprises that governments might use when drafting the Earth Summit's central document, called Agenda 21.[85] But when it came time to present these recommendations in March 1992 at the UNCED preparatory meeting in New York, the UNCTC found itself marginalized.

First, in February, as part of his program to restructure and streamline the UN, then Secretary-General Boutros Boutros Ghali announced that the UNCTC would be eliminated as an independent entity. This move in effect gutted the agency of what little power it might have had.[86] But it still had the report commissioned by ECOSOC to deliver to Maurice Strong and his UNCED Secretariat. Try as it might, however, the UNCTC couldn't get the Secretariat to accept its report. Meanwhile, Strong had appointed Stephan Schmidheiny as his senior industry advisor. Schmidheiny proceeded to form the BCSD and prepare *Changing Course* as an official industry submission to UNCED.

At the same time, according to former UNCTC Environment Unit Director Harris Gleckman, the European Community, Japan and the United States launched a frontal assault "to avoid any reference to transnational corporations" in Agenda 21. And in the most stunning example of government-corporate collusion, the Canadian government hosted a series of meetings to coordinate the corporate lobbying of the Earth Summit negotiations.[87]

The BCSD and ICC, which, despite some friction, for the most part closely coordinated policies, proceeded to demonstrate what self-regulation meant: making the chapter of Agenda 21 on business and industry compatible with their positions; lobbying, most often successfully, for the elimination of references to transnational corporations wherever possible throughout Agenda 21; and making sure the idea of even a minimal system of international regulations never gained public acceptance.

In general, instead of mandating far-reaching change, the Earth Summit documents speak to the logic that the global fox must guard the planetary hen house. The World Bank, an institution that continues to receive widespread criticism for its environmentally destructive policies, was effectively put in charge of managing all of the funds generated by UNCED and its conventions, providing corporations with similar opportunities to distort and profit from these agreements, as they have from the Montreal Protocol. Free trade was enshrined as the sacred icon of sustainable development, subordinating the Earth Summit to the globalization framework created by international trade agreements. And the call from the South, as well as from many environmental groups, for a reduction in consumption by the Northern countries was rejected by the North.

The manner in which other aspects of Agenda 21 speak to the corporate agenda is equally striking. Agenda 21 proposes that "forest cover" be increased through the expansion of plantation forests, which would provide cheap raw materials for pulp, paper and timber companies, while failing to recognize and support the land and cultural rights of indigenous peoples and traditional forest dwellers. It assumes that biotechnology is a key component of sustainable development and offers only a lenient voluntary international code of conduct rather than calling for regulation. It fails to address the rampant expansion and industrialization of the world's fisheries. UNCED omitted any discussion of nuclear power and failed to recognize that there are no safe storage and disposal solutions to the world's growing radioactive waste problem. Discussion of the environmental impacts of the military, including the nuclear and toxic contamination caused by military activities around the world, are inexplicably excluded from the Earth Summit texts.[88]

Although a number of stray references to transnationals did sneak into Agenda 21, the corporations more or less ignored them. For instance, former UNCTC official Harris Gleckman observes that in the various meetings of corporate executives held in Rio, there was very little discussion of these references. Instead, these meetings focused on "further expansion of transnational investment and trade on their definition of environmental protection."[89]

Ultimately, the transnationals were extremely pleased with the results of the Earth Summit. As Jan-Olaf Willums and Ulrich Goluke write in the ICC's 1992 book *From Ideas to Action*:

> In general, the feeling among business participants was that the substantive output of UNCED was positive. It could have taken a negative stance on *market forces* and the role of business, and there was at one time the real possibility that the conference might be pushed to lay

down detailed guidelines for the operations of transnational corporations. Instead, it acknowledged the important role of business. . . .

National governments have now begun to formulate their own policies and programs in accordance with commitments given in Brazil. We
expect that these national laws and regulations will not be as stringent,
bureaucratic and "anti-business" as some feared before UNCED.[90]

The saga of the Biodiversity Convention, which first came to prominence at the UNCED event and which has continued ever since, also
illuminates the role that corporations play in the global diplomatic
arena. In Rio, the U.S. biotechnology industry and the U.S. government
teamed up at the last minute to oppose the convention and throw the
Earth Summit into some political disarray. While the United States originally supported the negotiation of this agreement, which was aimed at
preserving fast-disappearing genetic stocks of plant and animal species,
it began watering down the convention during the years that it was
negotiated. Then, in what the U.S. delegation chief and then–EPA
Administrator William Reilly called "a perverse twist," the U.S. government discovered that it had such fundamental objections to the agreement that it was compelled to reject it.[91] President George Bush justified
his 180-degree turn by explaining that "in biodiversity it is important to
protect our rights, our business rights."[92]

After the Earth Summit, the U.S. Council on International Business
(UCIB) elaborated on the theme in Congressional testimony. UCIB representative Jonathan Plaut explained that U.S. business opposed the
Biodiversity Convention because it called into question intellectual
property laws that allow the biotechnology industry to patent and
exclusively profit from genetic organisms often gathered in Third World
countries. The convention's provisions on subsidies for the "transfer" of
this biotechnology back to the Third World, from whence the original
resources came, ran counter to U.S. corporate and, not coincidentally,
U.S. government stances in GATT. According to Plaut, it threatened to
"undermine the U.S. negotiating position" in the Uruguay Round,
which was not yet complete at the time. Finally, Plaut noted that
American corporations were opposed to language in the treaty that
called for regulation of the biotechnology industry.[93]

William Reilly, toeing the Bush line, concurred in Congressional testimony, noting that the treaty singled out "the biotechnology industry
as inherently risky, unsafe and worthy of special attention and regulation." This threatened "an industry fraught with economic potential,

but also environmental opportunity to solve real and important environmental problems. We could not, therefore, agree to that." With this twisted logic of "environmental opportunity," Reilly justified U.S. opposition to the Biodiversity Convention. In a bold move, he actually argued that biotechnology corporations such as Genentech (a subsidiary of the Swiss firm Hoffman-La Roche) have the potential to generate so many environmental *benefits* that their economic growth shouldn't be stunted by environmental regulation[94]—this, despite the fact that leading scientists argue that the potential hazards to human and environmental health caused by biotechnology merit some sort of precautionary, regulatory control.[95]

The debate over the Biodiversity Convention has raged on through the mid-1990s. With the election of Bill Clinton it appeared that U.S. policy would substantially change. Once in office, however, the Clinton Administration only created a more sophisticated approach to protecting U.S. corporate interests. The administration agreed to sign the convention, thus appearing to support the international environmental cause of biodiversity protection, but at the same time it moved to attach a letter of interpretation to the convention. The letter, drafts of which were written by U.S. biotechnology corporations, reportedly turned on their heads some of the convention's regulatory and intellectual property provisions about which Bush had expressed so much concern. Given the power and reach of the U.S. government and the biotechnology industry, this statement had the impact of undermining much of the potential effectiveness of the agreement.[96]

The U.S. government has continued lobbying for the biotechnology industry during ongoing Biodiversity Convention negotiations, as well as in the United Nations Commission on Sustainable Development (CSD), the official follow-up body to UNCED. It has done so by opposing a biosafety protocol to the convention and by attempting to suppress discussion in the CSD of any internationally agreed-upon framework for the safe handling and transfer of biotechnology.[97] Its influence in the CSD was apparent when, in 1995, a group of scientists and activists issued a statement accusing the CSD of taking an approach to the biotechnology issue that was "akin to a public relations exercise for the industry."[98]

The Earth Summit came at a time when the world was entering the greatest political and economic transformation it has seen since World War II. When the United Nations General Assembly conceived of

UNCED in 1989, two-and-a-half years before the final event in Rio, the pattern of world events suggested that UNCED could play a key role in guiding global politics into the twenty-first century. The end of the Cold War and the triumph of capitalism were clearly running headlong into a new global dynamic characterized by increasing North-South tension, ethnic nationalism, global economic restructuring and spiraling ecological destruction. UNCED was strategically positioned to catalyze a major effort to address a number of these trends. Instead, the largest conference of heads of state in history was satisfied to cast a thin green veil over the ever more globalized world economy.

If nothing else, the Earth Summit clarified the fact that global corporations have the power and capacity to seriously influence the focus and trajectory of international agreements on environment and development. It also served as a forum through which they were able to consolidate their ideology of corporate environmentalism. Indeed, at UNCED the world witnessed the emergence of a mature and sophisticated corporate strategy vis-à-vis the environmental challenge.

Yet more than five years after the Earth Summit, the international diplomatic realm remains a key battlefield, one through which significant controls have been and continue to be placed on the operations of transnational corporations. Driven by pressure from below, for example, the parties to the Montreal Protocol are now attempting to phase out HCFCs, while HFCs are probably not far behind. Parties to the Protocol are also moving to phase out the ozone-depleting pesticide methyl bromide, despite a relentless lobbying effort orchestrated by a handful of chemical corporations.[99] Similarly, the Climate Convention looms as a serious problem for the petroleum giants; indeed, the powerful lobbying effort they have launched to stymie this agreement is indicative of the threat it poses to their nearly unrestricted production of fossil fuels. And the Biodiversity Convention continues as a viable vehicle for placing safety restrictions on the global biotechnology corporations, while also guaranteeing a modicum of equity for the stewards of biological resources—mostly Third World farmers and indigenous people who have developed and catalogued a vast array of plants over many generations. Thus, while the transnationals are doing their best to undermine them, these agreements do provide a forum in which national governments can agree on enforcing internationally coordinated actions which have the potential to rein in the destructive global reach of stateless corporations.

Chapter Three

Surfing the Pipeline

The Chevron Corporation
and the Environmental Impacts of Oil

It will not last forever. . . . But this day still belongs to petroleum.
Ken Derr, chairman and CEO, Chevron Corporation

Just south of Los Angeles, near the seaside town of Manhattan Beach, where luxury homes overlook a blue Santa Monica Bay, surfers ride the waves, capturing the ocean's energy and speed as it thunders onto the shore. When swell, wind and tide are just right, this surfbreak, known as El Porto, can resemble a small version of the Banzai Pipeline, that famous Hawaiian wave which forms perfect, reeling cylinders. But there is another sort of pipeline running through the sea here. Right in front of the surfers, easily visible to the traveler landing at Los Angeles International Airport (LAX), flanked by a massive sewage treatment plant and two oil-fired power plants, is Chevron Corporation's El Segundo refinery. The factory is a giant, two-square-mile labyrinth of conduits, ducts, ponds, tubes, flame-belching smokestacks and storage tanks. Its underwater oil pipelines take in wave after wave of crude oil from tankers that anchor more than a mile offshore.

Los Angeles is the largest gasoline market in the world. Chevron's El Segundo plant, the largest refinery on the West Coast of the United States, is one of this market's top suppliers. It provides the fuel for many of the nearly 8 million automobiles that careen daily through LA's maze of freeways, as well as for jets that whisk tens of thousands more in and out of LAX every day.[1] On this count, the plant plays an indirect but important role in Los Angeles's considerable air pollution problems, which are the worst in the United States.[2] What's more, the El Segundo refinery itself is one of the largest overall toxic air polluters in Los Angeles County.[3] And underneath it sits a massive lake of leaked oil.[4]

The refinery also spews thousands of gallons of effluent into the ocean on a daily basis. When its air, water and land emissions are taken together, Chevron's El Segundo refinery is one of the largest single sources of pollution in the greater Los Angeles area.[5]

Yet, in the neighborhood that borders the refinery, the American Dream reels onward, nearly oblivious to the nightmare that has infiltrated its core. Oil odors waft through Manhattan Beach's million-dollar oceanside homes. Many of these dwellings come equipped with hydrocarbon sensors designed to detect leaks, fires, explosions or other volatile situations that the refinery next door may generate.[6] Down on the sand, children play along the reeking shoreline, sunbathers soak up the rays and surfers—latter-day mutations of Tom Wolfe's Pump House Gang—ride the tide in the shadow of smokestacks and storage tanks. "It's real impactful," says Young Hutchinson, a local surfrider. "When you swim in the water, you come out of it smelling like diesel."[7]

While not on LA's list of top tourist attractions, El Segundo is an historical landmark of sorts. Built in 1911 by Standard Oil of California (now Chevron), the refinery fueled the transformation of Los Angeles from a sleepy seaside town of orange groves to the cosmopolitan, automobile-based megalopolis that it is today. While it is only one of two hundred oil refineries in the United States, one of a network of thousands spread out across the planet and one of twenty-six refineries that Chevron and its affiliates own around the world, the relevance of El Segundo reaches far beyond the Los Angeles Basin. Indeed, this case study of the Chevron Corporation, one of a handful of global oil giants that dominate the petroleum industry, traces the company's evolution by often returning to El Segundo as a point of reference precisely because, in many ways, the histories of El Segundo and Chevron mirror much of the history of oil in the twentieth century. This is no small distinction, given that petroleum has in many ways powered the past hundred years of civilization.

Building the Pipeline

Today, on the doorstep of the twenty-first century, civilization is more ensconced than ever in a hydrocarbon society. Countless products, from plastics, household detergents, tires, batteries and lubricants to industrial chemicals, fertilizers and pesticides, cosmetics and even surfboards, are derived from oil. Transportation and travel are based on it. Governments rise and fall because of it. As many analysts and historians have extensively documented, oil not only helped determine the outcomes of the First and Second World Wars, but revolutions, civil wars and global conflicts have also been fought and millions of lives lost over control of and access to oil. Entire cultures have been and continue to be transformed or destroyed by crude. New cultures—car cultures and plastic cultures—have emerged. The American Dream, aspired to by much of the world, is built on a lake of oil. In the age of globalization, oil remains the lifeblood of the world economy.[8]

Perhaps the most deleterious effect of the twentieth-century's fossil fuel revolution has been its environmental impact. As Pulitzer Prize–winning author Daniel Yergin writes, "oil, which is so central a feature of the world as we know it, is now accused of fueling environmental degradation; and the oil industry, proud of its technological prowess and its contribution to shaping the modern world, finds itself on the defensive, charged with being a threat to present and future generations."[9]

It is essential to understand the rise of oil power in the United States and around the world in order to begin to comprehend the sheer strength, the global reach and the political influence that Chevron and the other oil majors continue to hold today. This historical knowledge is also essential to meet the tremendous challenge posed by the ecological imperative of moving away from a fossil fuel–based economy and toward more environmentally sustainable forms of energy development.

Today, Chevron is one of the top-ten oil corporations in the world. The company is not nearly as large as global leaders Shell and Exxon, yet its size and clout are still formidable. In 1995 it ranked as the sixty-eighth-largest corporation on the planet, the eighteenth-largest U.S. company and the biggest corporation headquartered in the state of California.[10] In a good year, 1996, Chevron recorded more than $42 billion in revenues and cleared more than $2.6 billion in net profits.[11] Its total assets, valued at nearly $35 billion, are invested in a plethora of mostly petroleum-based activities carried out by more than 500 subsidiaries, divisions, branches, partnerships and affiliates in nearly 100 countries.[12] In terms of comparable companies, it is about the same size as its oil industry counterpart Texaco or the U.S. chemical giant DuPont.[13] Its revenues are about equal to the gross domestic product of Egypt and greater than those of Nigeria and Kazakhstan, both countries where Chevron has significant operations.[14]

The Chevron Corporation dates back to relatively modest beginnings more than a century ago. It was in 1879 that a group of investors put together $1 million to create the Pacific Coast Oil Company in San Francisco. Coincidentally, this was the same year that patents were granted for the electric light bulb and the internal combustion engine, two products that were destined to consume tremendous quantities of the oil that Chevron and its cousins would produce.[15] Pacific Coast Oil quickly grew to be the largest, most integrated petroleum concern in California. But by the turn of the century, when California really began to boom as an oil state, John D. Rockefeller's Standard Oil Trust, which was selling kerosene in the Golden State, bought out Pacific Coast Oil. By pouring millions of dollars into this already prosperous company, Standard moved into producing, transporting and refining in California. Rockefeller soon renamed Pacific Coast Oil the Standard Oil Company (California). Later, in 1926, the company reincorporated in the state of Delaware as the Standard Oil Company of California (SoCal), the name by which it was known until the late 1970s, when it became known as Chevron.[16] (For purposes of simplicity and clarity, the company, in its various incarnations, will be uniformly referred to as Chevron throughout the rest of this chapter.)

As part of Rockefeller's Standard Oil, Chevron was a wholly owned subsidiary of one of the very first and largest modern multinational corporations. Standard Oil, in its quest for total dominance over the world oil trade, evolved into a complex global enterprise that delivered its products—fuel oil, lubricants, and kerosene for cheap illumination—to the far corners of the Earth. While the founders of Standard's main international competitors, Royal Dutch and Shell (later to merge into one company), played significant roles in oil's formative years, Daniel Yergin credits Rockefeller not only as "the single most important figure in shaping the oil industry," but also arguably as the leading player in setting the course for the United States' industrial development path and in casting the mold of the modern corporation.[17] Rockefeller, for instance, conceived of and implemented the principle of vertical integration, whereby Standard Oil centrally controlled every step in the oil process, from exploration to production to transport to refining to distribution. "In every dimension," writes Yergin, "Standard's operation was awesome, overwhelming competitors." By the first decade of the twentieth century, Standard Oil dominated upward of 85 percent of the U.S. oil market and a great deal of the global trade.[18]

Rockefeller gained an iron grip on the oil industry. But as his conglomerate grew by either buying out or steamrolling over any competition, and by eviscerating state charters designed to control corporate abuse, it inspired the ire of small business owners, entrepreneurs and local as well as national government officials, including then-President Theodore Roosevelt, who called Standard Oil's executives "the biggest criminals in the country."[19] As the reach and grasp of its quasimonopolistic tentacles were unveiled by a succession of muckraking reporters, Standard Oil came to be seen as a heinous and immoral "octopus" that had the country in its grip. At the head of the monster, Rockefeller was reviled by the public.[20]

Indeed, Rockefeller's achievement of fashioning one of the first modern industrial multinational corporations provoked a backlash in the form of growing antitrust and anticorporate sentiment in the general public as well as in some of the upper echelons of government. This translated into the creation of federal regulatory and oversight machinery that was charged with monitoring and controlling the behavior of corporations in the United States. While the new laws did provide for a modicum of government jurisdiction, they were not nearly sufficient to ensure adequate democratic control over burgeoning corporate America. For instance, successive efforts by Presidents Roosevelt, Taft and Wilson to institute federal chartering for large corporations, so as to prevent companies from avoiding accountability by fleeing to states such as New Jersey and Delaware, which instituted lenient chartering regulations—a trend started by Rockefeller himself—failed.[21]

It was one of the new laws, the Sherman Antitrust Act, that the U.S. attorney general used to bring suit against Standard Oil. A special prosecutor assembled detailed evidence of the corporation's monopoly and what at the time was the exorbitant figure of nearly $1 billion in profits Standard had reaped in a twenty-five-year period. In May 1911 the U.S. Supreme Court mandated the dissolution of Standard Oil.[22]

The Standard Oil Trust was split into a number of separate entities. The largest, the former holding company, became Standard Oil of New Jersey and later Exxon; today Exxon is still the largest oil corporation in the United States, and the second-largest in the world. There was also Standard Oil of New York, which eventually became Mobil, and Standard Oil of Ohio, which ultimately wound up as the U.S. arm of British Petroleum. Standard Oil of Indiana became Amoco, and Continental Oil became Conoco (now owned by DuPont). Another entity was Atlantic, which became part of ARCO, and of course there was Standard Oil of California—Chevron.[23] In other words, with a few notable exceptions, such as Texaco and Unocal, almost every major U.S.

oil company is a direct descendant of John D. Rockefeller's corporate empire. Once cut off, each tentacle of the octopus grew back to become like its progenitor.

Even before the breakup, Chevron was emerging as a dynamic, highly integrated operation. The California economy grew and prospered into the first decade of the twentieth century; by 1910 the state was producing more oil than any foreign nation and was responsible for 22 percent of all world production.[24] Chevron had the largest share of California's black gold rush. The company expanded its activities, drilling for oil throughout the state and operating a refinery at Point Richmond, on San Francisco Bay, that opened in 1902.[25]

As Chevron continued to expand, it drew up plans to build a second refinery to complement Richmond. Located in the sand dunes on the shore of Santa Monica Bay, south of Los Angeles, the El Segundo refinery, which was planned to be the largest in the world, was hailed by the *Los Angeles Times* as "one of the greatest of all Southern California industrial enterprises."[26] Meaning "the second" in Spanish, El Segundo was completed and went into operation in November 1911, coinciding with the breakup of the Standard Oil Trust. Soon El Segundo was processing more crude than its sister plant in Richmond, servicing the southwestern United States, customers in Asia and Latin America, and, of course, Los Angeles with its growing population of 300,000 inhabitants. Overall, the expanding Chevron empire was providing 26 percent of all U.S. oil production.[27]

The nature of the oil business was also changing rapidly. While one of the El Segundo refinery's first sales consisted of several hundred tank cars of oil for southern California orange growers to burn in smudge pots to protect their crops against frost, most of those orange groves were destined to disappear in the following decades, as they were replaced with freeways and subdivisions.[28] The advent of the automobile industry was transforming the United States' landscape. While only 22,000 automobiles were manufactured in the United States in 1904, a decade later car registration totaled more than 1 million. Gasoline, once a useless byproduct of refining, quickly became oil's *raison d'être*.[29] Indeed, one cannot tell the story of the oil companies without venturing into the story of their symbiotic relationship with the automobile corporations and the environmental problems their partnership has engendered. The relationship between Chevron and General Motors is a fine example.

By the mid-1920s the automobile market in the United States had become saturated; those who wanted cars already had them, while a large portion of the U.S. urban population still rode the extensive public transport networks of electric trolleys and trains. In response, General Motors, the largest automobile corporation in the country, diversified into other transportation markets, including buses and rail passenger services. Soon GM gained a quasimonopoly in all sectors of the transportation business. Yet because automobiles were more profitable than either rail transport or buses, it was in GM's interests to see public transport phased out; the fewer trains and buses there were, the more consumers of automobiles there would be. Obviously, this was also advantageous to the other big automakers—Ford and Chrysler. Similarly, for oil companies such as Chevron, the more cars there were on the road, the more gasoline they would sell.[30]

Aided by economic dynamics that made some electric trolleys and trains less and less financially viable, General Motors' sales of both buses that ran on diesel fuel and of automobiles began to grow again.[31] But the transformation was not large or fast enough for GM and its partners. In 1936 General Motors, together with Chevron, Firestone Tire and two other smaller companies, allocated $9 million (a major sum at the time) to a holding company called National City Lines (NCL) for the purpose, in the words of Bradford C. Snell, a staff counsel to the U.S. Senate Subcommittee on Antitrust and Monopoly, "of converting electric transit systems in 16 states to GM bus operations." As buses proved a less efficient and less desirable form of transport than electric rail had been, more travelers gravitated toward the automobile. "The National City Lines campaign," according to Snell, "had a devastating impact on the quality of urban transportation and urban living in America."[32]

Nowhere was this impact more severely felt than in the Los Angeles Basin, which enjoyed a sophisticated, clean, relatively nonpolluting electric transit system up through the 1930s. As Snell writes, NCL "purchased the local system, scrapped its electric transit cars, tore down its power transmission lines, ripped up the tracks, and placed GM diesel buses fueled by Standard Oil [Chevron] on Los Angeles' crowded streets. In sum, GM and its auto-industrial allies severed Los Angeles' regional rail links and then motorized its downtown heart."[33] This allowed Chevron's El Segundo refinery to pump increasing quantities of gasoline into an increasingly motorized, smoggy and gridlocked Los Angeles market.

In April 1949 a federal jury in Chicago convicted GM, Chevron,

Firestone and others of criminally conspiring to replace electric transportation with gas- or diesel-powered buses and to monopolize the sale of buses.[34] But the court fined the conspirators a paltry $5,000, while an NCL official who the jury convicted for having played a central role in the motorization campaigns was fined merely one dollar.[35] After the convictions, General Motors marched onward, buying up public transport systems and ultimately engendering an American society almost wholly dependent on automobiles and therefore on vast quantities of oil.[36] As Snell relates, GM, along with Chevron, Firestone and others, had "reshaped American ground transportation to serve corporate wants instead of social needs."[37]

While the United States was undergoing motorization in the 1930s, the transnational auto and oil corporations were becoming increasingly influential global entities. General Motors, for example, established and expanded operations throughout Asia and Europe, including Adolf Hitler's Germany.[38] Meanwhile, Chevron was cornering the market for asphalt—key for building roads—in seventy-five countries and promoting the development of the aviation industry.[39] Chevron also unsuccessfully prospected for oil in Mexico, Central America and Southeast Asia. Its luck changed, however, when it struck oil on the tiny Persian Gulf island of Bahrain in the early 1930s and then in neighboring Saudi Arabia in 1938.

This latter discovery was to alter the prevailing global geopolitical balance, and for that matter the course of world history. The Saudis, along with Chevron as the sole concessionaire, were sitting on top of one of the world's greatest supplies of oil. Lacking outlets in Europe, Africa and Asia to refine and sell Saudi Arabia's bounty, Chevron formed a joint venture with Texaco, which did have the distribution network. Texaco received half of the Bahraini and Saudi concessions in exchange for giving Chevron a half interest in its extensive marketing apparatus in the Eastern Hemisphere. Thus the California Texas Oil Company (Caltex), a 50-50 Chevron-Texaco joint venture, which exists to this day, was formed. Still, the Saudi discovery proved to be so large that a need for more capital and greater distribution networks required that the two partners bring in two more U.S. oil giants, Exxon and Mobil. In 1948 these four corporations teamed up to form Aramco (the Arabian American Oil Company), a consortium designed exclusively to extract Saudi oil.[40] As American demand for oil grew, Aramco's interests in Saudi Arabia quickly became synonymous with the definition of U.S. national security in the region.[41] Thus Chevron's discovery of Saudi crude and its subsequent founding of Aramco, combined with another significant find in Indonesia, assured it of a solid position as one of the most powerful oil corporations in the post–World War II era.

After the war, the company continued to expand, participating in a number of big discoveries in locations ranging from the Gulf of Mexico to Australia to the North Sea. The company also engaged in a series of major acquisitions, including the purchase of the Gulf Oil Corporation in 1984 for $13.3 billion. This gave Chevron control over more oil reserves in the Gulf of Mexico and Africa, as well as refineries, distribution networks and other infrastructure in the United States. In 1988 Chevron bought Tenneco's oil and gas properties in the Gulf of Mexico, making it the second-largest natural gas producer in the United States at the dawn of a decade—the 1990s—when natural gas began to increase in importance and value.[42]

The People of Chevron

In many ways Chevron is virtually a state unto itself. Its revenues are larger than those of many countries where it operates. Its fleet of tankers is bigger than most navies. The corporation wields considerable clout over governments, its nearly 48,000 employees and the daily lives of millions more people who, in the contemporary corporate vernacular, are considered "stakeholders." The corporation frequently refers to actions that it has undertaken as being carried out by "the people of Chevron," almost the way a government acts and speaks in the name of "the people." Thus plaques that mark the corporation's philanthropy to charitable organizations read that the donations were "made possible by the people of Chevron" and its environmental advertisements drive home the slogan "People Do."

However, the people of Chevron who have ruled the corporation from the executive suites of the company's downtown San Francisco headquarters for more than a century are not the liberal environmentalists they make themselves out to be. Rather, the company, like many U.S. transnationals, is a conservative bastion, providing generous support for organizations such as the Heritage Foundation, a right-wing think tank.[43] The company has also been plagued by a number of accusations of racial and sexual discrimination. For instance, in May 1991, Chevron settled a class action discrimination lawsuit filed by African-American and Latino-American oil workers. While paying out $1.5 million, Chevron refused to admit to discrimination, prompting more than half the plaintiffs to object to the settlement.[44] And in 1995 it settled with four women employees for $2.2 million in one of the largest sexual harassment suits in U.S. history.[45] On an international scale, anti-apartheid activists long denounced Caltex for owning and operating an oil refinery in South Africa, despite calls for divestment by the African National Congress.[46]

To better understand the company, it is worthwhile to follow briefly the flow of oil through Chevron's pipeline. It explores for crude, extracts it from the far corners of the Earth, transports it around the world, refines it and then sells it to retail customers, all under the red-white-and-blue military-style standard from which it derives its name. Chevron produces more than one million barrels of oil and equivalent gas every day in twenty-two countries.[47] It is extracting both oil and gas from California, the Rocky Mountains, Texas and the Gulf of Mexico—where it is the largest producer. It also extracts oil and gas from Canada, China, the Republic of Congo, Kuwait, Indonesia, Papua New Guinea, Namibia, Nigeria and Venezuela, among others.[48] In Angola, Chevron is the leading petroleum corporation, and according to local Universidade del Cabo economist José Goncalves, its clout in the country, which depends on oil for roughly 80 percent of its foreign exchange, is such that "only the Catholic Church has more influence in Angola than Chevron."[49] The company's burgeoning new joint venture with the government of the former Soviet Republic of Kazakhstan is exploiting Tengiz, one of the largest new oil fields in the world. Among the largest projects in Chevron's history, Tengizchevoil, as it is known, has more than doubled the company's proved oil reserves, which are now brimming above 6 billion barrels.[50] Chevron is also exploring for more oil in the Republic of Congo, Albania, Azerbaijan, Yemen, Vietnam, Colombia, Bolivia, Trinidad and Tobago, Peru and Argentina.[51]

Once Chevron pumps the oil out of the Earth's crust, most of the crude enters the 13,064 miles of pipeline that the company either owns or has equity in around the world. Or it ends up on one of the forty-two tanker ships, with a total capacity of 37 million barrels, that Chevron either owns or controls. Much of the oil is then brought to one of twenty-six refineries around the world that are either owned and operated in part or full by Chevron or its joint venture with Texaco—Caltex. In addition to Chevron being one of the largest refiners in the United States, its Caltex refineries in South Korea, Singapore, the Philippines and Thailand place it at the center of East Asia's fast-growing energy markets.[52]

Once refined, Chevron's petroleum products reenter its vast network of pipelines, tanker ships and tanker trucks, to be distributed around the world. Some of the product, known as petrochemical feedstock, is fed into Chevron's $3-billion-a-year chemical subsidiary, whose plants operate in ten U.S. states as well as in France, Brazil, Japan, China and Saudi Arabia. The chemicals these plants produce, including benzene, polystyrene and polyethylene, are then marketed in more than eighty countries.[53] Back in the United States, Chevron is a leading marketer of refined products. It is the largest jet fuel vendor in the country, while its nearly 8,000 service stations hold a sizable chunk of the gasoline market share throughout the western and southern United States. Chevron sells many of its oil, gas, jet fuel and lubricant products under the brand name Gulf in the United Kingdom, and through Caltex, which, with its 17,500 retail outlets in twenty-nine countries, is the leading transnational corporate marketer of refined products in the Asia-Pacific region.[54] More than half of Caltex's outlets are located in Japan, where it has collaborated with Nippon Oil, the country's largest petroleum corporation, since the end of World War II.[55] Caltex is also moving aggressively to extend its distribution pipeline to capture market shares in the vast economic frontiers of China, India and Vietnam.[56]

Add Chevron's empire to those of the nine other oil majors that are either comparable in size, or, as in the cases of Exxon and Shell, more than twice the size, and one begins to get an idea of the contemporary scope and power of the oil majors and the global oil pipeline. Moreover, the relationships among the corporations that control the pipeline are complex and labyrinthine. For while there continues to be intense competition among them, each global oil giant is also linked to the other through a web of concessions and joint ventures that reaches around the world. The majors also have a history of colluding to control production levels and fix world oil prices, while participating in transfer pricing schemes to avoid paying taxes.[57] What's more, through industry organizations such as the American Petroleum Institute, they have developed coordinated responses to debacles such as the *Exxon Valdez* spill.[58]

A Crude Awakening

In building their global empires, Chevron and its corporate brethren have passed through numerous crises, ranging from the breakup of the

Standard Oil Trust, to the nationalization of their assets in Mexico, Venezuela, the Middle East and elsewhere, to the advent of the Organization of Petroleum Exporting Countries (OPEC) and the series of oil shocks that wrested, for a time, some control from the global corporations and put power in the hands of the Third World producers. But one of the greatest challenges to the oil corporations has come from the end of the global pipeline where toxic effluents flow, fires rage, smoke pours and leaks spurt forth. As the environmental impacts of oil have accumulated and grown during the twentieth century, so with them has the general public's environmental consciousness. And as the environmental movement has became more powerful and vocal in the industrialized nations, the oil giants, Chevron included, have faced an aroused public demanding corporate accountability for a healthy environment. The emergence of this issue has forced some fundamental changes in the oil industry, while continuing to torment it.

Listen to William Mulligan, manager of federal relations and former manager of environmental affairs for Chevron, a man who since the 1980s has been intimately involved at the highest levels of his corporation in dealing with environmental problems and the development of Chevron's environmental policies, programs and image. "The most fundamental change when you reflect back over the last roughly twenty years," muses Mulligan in an interview, "has probably been the growth of the environmental legislation and regulation that basically governs and kind of dominates the corporate existence." The environmental movement, he explains, has had a "huge impact on corporations as the environmental statutes have unfolded and regulations sort of descended on us. We've obviously had to shift our thinking over the last twenty to twenty-five years to essentially cope with a whole new reality." [59]

The reams of environmental legislation, most of it passed in the 1970s, to which Mulligan is referring include the Toxic Substances Control Act (TSCA), the Resource Conservation and Recovery Act (RCRA), the Superfund (CERCLA), the Clean Water Act and the Clean Air Act. The combined impacts of these rules and regulations sent corporate America reeling, while similarly dramatic developments were taking place in Western Europe and Japan. The oil companies, which had operated with virtual impunity, were suddenly subject to close public and governmental scrutiny in the industrialized North. Chevron and its cohorts, says Mulligan, "went into a period of shock and disbelief that all of this had been kind of unleashed on us." [60]

The oil industry, as well as much of corporate America, fought back, taking on the environmentalists and the barriers they had placed on the road to greater profits. With Ronald Reagan becoming president in 1980, they had their champion. Reagan sponsored a series of efforts to roll back environmental provisions, opening pristine lands to resource extraction and neglecting to enforce many environmental statutes.[61] Still, the oil corporations faced a dizzying array of problems as the new laws took hold and as their aging wells, storage tanks, refineries, tankers, drilling rigs and pipelines became increasingly rickety and pollution-prone. For Chevron, El Segundo was once again in the spotlight.

Claiming in 1985 that Chevron was illegally spewing thousands of pounds of oil, grease, ammonia, cadmium and cyanide into Santa Monica Bay, a recreation area to 14 million people in Los Angeles and once a rich source of fish, the Sierra Club filed a $2.3 million suit to stop the dumping.[62] Meanwhile, Greenpeace divers attempted to plug the refinery's effluent pipes, which sat just 500 feet offshore.[63] The next year the federal government got into the act in an effort "to get tough on those companies," charging, in an $8.8 million lawsuit, that Chevron had violated the Clean Water Act 880 times in only five years.[64] Chevron waxed indignant. "We really don't understand why the EPA has filed a lawsuit at all since we've dramatically improved our compliance record over recent years," said one representative.[65] By 1988 the company had settled with the U.S. government, making changes in the refinery to comply with the law and paying a $1.5 million fine.[66]

Despite the fines that the company had to pay (relatively small compared to its net profits, which were in the hundreds of millions), the settlement was laden with irony. The law that public pressure prompted the government to force Chevron to comply with—one in a series of regulations that corporate America claims are an overwhelming burden on the ability to operate—still allowed the company to discharge nearly 8 million gallons of wastewater a day into Santa Monica Bay. This hazardous waste, which was being spewed just beyond the surf zone of a beach that half a million people throng to every year, is laden with potential carcinogens.[67] Thus while Chevron complied with the law and the environmental groups backed off, the ocean and its recreational users continued to be poisoned.

Its pollution of Santa Monica Bay was only one of the problems that Chevron had to deal with at El Segundo. The same day that the Sierra Club lawsuit was settled in 1988, the *Los Angeles Times* reported that the largest oil leak in the country had been discovered there. A twelve-foot-thick, 250-million-gallon lake of oil had accumulated under the vast refinery. The plume also reached under part of the neighboring community of Manhattan Beach, where gasoline vapors had begun to seep into people's homes. Chevron initiated a twenty-year clean-up program in which it continues literally to drill for the spilled oil under its plant, with the cost of recovery estimated at more than $100 a barrel. Furthermore, the company estimates that it will only be able to clean up two-thirds of the spill.[68]

Nor were the company's problems limited to Los Angeles. A growing public consciousness in the late 1980s and the enforcement of regulations were causing problems for Chevron across the country. There were pipeline spills and neighborhood evacuations in Texas. There were major violations and spills at an offshore platform near Santa Barbara, California. There were a series of explosions, more than seventy fires, widespread violation of worker safety laws and accusations of "environmental racism" in Richmond, California. And there were air pollution violations in Philadelphia, to name but a few.[69] All of this combined to damage the company's image and its bottom line.

Meanwhile, Chevron's exploration, drilling and mining activities came under attack—primarily by indigenous peoples. Its efforts to drill in the Arctic National Wildlife Refuge (ANWR) were rebuffed by protests from the indigenous Gwich'in peoples, the environmental lobby and resistance in Congress. The uranium mine it shared with DuPont in Panna Maria, Texas, was found to be leaking and polluting groundwater, while its Mount Taylor, New Mexico, uranium mine, the deepest of its kind in the world, situated on a sacred Navajo mountain, was found to have contaminated community wells nearby.[70] In Montana's Rocky Mountains, in an area of national forest adjacent to Glacier National Park—one of the last remaining pristine habitats of the grizzly bear and home of the Blackfoot Indians—Chevron's exploratory wells and drilling plans came under fire from both the Blackfoot and environmentalists concerned about the endangered grizzly.[71]

Chevron was not the only oil corporation running into environmental obstacles at nearly every turn. Activists and the laws they deployed as weapons in their war to clean up the United States were a threat to the entire industry. This was most clearly reflected in the howls heard from the global giants as compliance costs took hefty bites out of their profits. The Unocal Corporation, for example, complained that the U.S. petroleum industry was spending as much as $50 billion a year on environmental controls between 1989 and 1993—more than double the 1989 profits of the top 400 oil and gas corporations.[72] The public's demand that corporations produce oil without destroying the environment was building toward crisis proportions for the oil corporations. Even Chevron's employees, 85 percent of whom consider themselves "environmentalists" and 37 percent of whom rank themselves as "strong environmentalists," contributed to this green surge.[73] The distress culminated in 1989 with the *Exxon Valdez* spill.

"Thank God it was Exxon and not Chevron," said company executive William Mulligan, reflecting the relief of the rest of the oil industry that the world's most publicly scrutinized and economically costly environmental disaster hadn't happened to them.[74] Indeed, any one of the global giants could have run aground with such a spill, foundered in the national media spotlight and then been submerged in a costly series of legal battles. (In one suit alone, Exxon was found liable for more than $5 billion in damages.[75]) The *Exxon Valdez* became a graphic symbol of the impacts and arrogance of the oil corporations and a rallying point for environmentalists. The spill also turned out to be a pivotal moment in which the corporate response to environmentalism shifted from one of resistance and confrontation to a strategy that emphasized co-optation. Ironically, rather than Exxon it was Chevron, perhaps more than any other oil corporation, that was leading the way.

Greening the Pipeline?

From ancient rainforests of Papua New Guinea to halls of power in Washington, D.C., the people of Chevron like to give a geographical explanation for the vanguard role they say they've played in dealing with environmental issues. Listen again to Mr. Mulligan: "With our corporate headquarters in San Francisco, with our company having its roots in California, we were on the cutting edge, we were the point on the learning curve, we were in the hot bed of environmentalism as a corporation; so I think we've had to adapt to the movement earlier than our East Coast predecessors." With California environmentalists regularly protesting in front of their corporate headquarters, Chevron realized, perhaps somewhat earlier than its cohorts, that the multibillion-dollar "burden" posed by environmental issues and the environmental movement was not going away. "As a result," observes Mulligan, "people have had to reconsider their earlier views and make a transition to essentially a new view of what the private sector role is in that New World Order, so to speak."[76]

Chevron moved quickly. In 1989 it set a new strategy and then wrote a corporate environmental policy, reorganized its already existing environment-related activities and integrated them more centrally into the corporate hierarchy. It took a series of steps, detailed below, that measurably diminished some of its most serious environmental impacts. It also designated the vice-chairman of its board and a vice-president to determine the environmental policy of the corporation. And it created new positions and rewrote job descriptions so that it could claim that 400 of its staff worked on "environmental issues." It promoted reforestation and other ecologically oriented projects for employee participation in an apparent effort to boost company morale. The corporation also stepped up its donations to environmental groups, launched an environmental advertising campaign and became intimately involved in a number of high-level governmental and non-governmental environmental advisory councils. By 1991 the company had published one of the industry's first "environmental reports"—printed on recycled paper. With a crystal-clear satellite image of the Middle East emblazoned on its cover, the report paints a generally positive picture of Chevron's relationship with environmental issues.[77] In the introduction, Chevron chairman and CEO Ken Derr declares, "Chevron has worked hard for many years to earn its reputation as one of the petroleum industry's most responsible companies. We're proud of that reputation, and we plan to build on it."[78]

Tall, broad-shouldered and silver-haired, Ken Derr has played a central role in Chevron's transformation. He has advised U.S. policy makers on how to accommodate their environmental mandates to corporate America's wants and needs, serving as the only oil industry representative on both the Bush Administration's President's Commission on Environmental Quality and the Clinton Administration's President's Council for Sustainable Development. Derr was also one of four oil industry representatives on the Business Council for Sustainable Development at the United Nations Earth Summit.

There is no doubt that Chevron's initiatives and those of the oil industry in general have cleaned up their act in the U.S. and other industrialized nations. Indeed, Chevron and many of its employees deserve credit for the hard work they've done to mitigate a series of environmental problems endemic to the oil industry. But it is essential to understand that they've usually done so when at least one of three key, often interrelated factors is present. First, Chevron and most other oil companies are compelled to clean up when the government moves to enforce environmental laws. Second, they will embark on environmental initiatives when their endeavors can save money or generate profits for the company. And third, they can be pushed to make changes in environmentally destructive behavior in response to prolonged public criticism and protest. It is important to understand these dynamics in order to grasp how change in corporate behavior has come about.

Regulation and government enforcement have played a key role in curbing industry's most flagrant abuses and in pushing corporations toward cleaner production. In 1994, for instance, Chevron spent almost $1.5 billion on environmental programs—nearly equivalent to the profits the company declared that same year. It holds another $1.2 billion in reserve for "environmental remediation" of Superfund and other sites it has polluted and still $1.5 billion more in reserve for costs primarily related to the ecological restoration of oil, gas and coal sites it abandons around the world.[79] This is not so different from other oil corporations; overall, according to the American Petroleum Institute, the U.S. oil industry spent nearly $8 billion on the environment in 1990 and projected that this cost would increase by another $15 billion to $23 billion a year by the turn of the century.[80]

The industry in general and Chevron in particular tout such expenditures as evidence of their green commitment. Yet such boastfulness tends toward exaggeration. According to Greg Karras, an analyst with Communities for a Better Environment, "the oil industry consistently overestimates its environmental costs by an average of tenfold."[81] What's more, most of the industry's environmental money is spent complying with legislation passed in response to major campaigns mounted by environmental groups—laws that Chevron and the oil industry usually opposed the passage of and later attempted to undermine. Indeed, Chevron spent a significant amount of its environmental capital expenditures in the early 1990s on altering facilities to produce cleaner-burning fuels (reformulated gasoline) in order to bring Richmond, El Segundo and other refineries into compliance with federal and state air quality regulations.[82]

Chevron, along with most oil and chemical companies, has also responded to pressures by implementing environmental programs when it has made clear-cut economic sense to do so. Whereas in the past, corporations such as Chevron didn't pay much attention to environmental issues, whether they were potentially profitable or not, these have become what Mulligan calls "no-brainers," initiatives that one would have to be stupid not to undertake. Thus, for instance, the company's Save Money and Reduce Toxics (SMART) program was a no-brainer initiated in 1986 in an attempt to comply with RCRA regulations. Through SMART, Chevron reduced the land disposal of hazardous waste by 70 percent in less than ten years, developing in the process a number of source reduction and recycling programs, thus cutting the company's costs.[83] It has also built cogeneration facilities at many refineries, reducing the amount of energy it takes to operate them, therefore saving money and reducing emissions at the same time. Overall, Chevron improved its energy efficiency by 6 percent between 1991 and 1993, saving the equivalent amount of energy that it would take to power half a million U.S. homes for an entire year.[84]

Direct pressure from environmental and community groups has also forced the company into action time and again. Three examples illustrate the point. In Richmond, after a long battle with Communities for a Better Environment, Chevron agreed to cut its refinery's chemical discharges into San Francisco Bay, and did so by 90 percent in only six years.[85] Similarly, in 1993 at El Segundo, ongoing pressure from Heal the Bay, the Natural Resources Defense Council, the American Oceans Campaign, and the Surfrider Foundation forced Chevron to go beyond legal requirements and extend its effluent pipelines from the surf zone out 3,500 feet into Santa Monica Bay. Chevron's decision came only after stubborn resistance on its part, which included financing a "risk assessment" study that demonstrated that "exposure to potentially carcinogenic substances" in its discharge water "does not have an adverse impact on human health."[86] However, waterborne protests by surfers who continued to complain of eye, sinus and skin infections were sullying the company's image. And the threat of legal action was looming. Finally, Chevron shifted its stance when it realized that it could use an old, decommissioned pipeline to reroute the pollution farther out to sea, cutting costs from the $10 million estimate to build a new pipeline to $2 million. With this less economically painful alternative in hand, Chevron flew its environmental flag, declaring that "our decision to voluntarily move forward with this project exemplifies our intent to remain an environmental leader."[87] Thus, roughly seventy years after it had begun dumping, Chevron extended the last major source of industrial pollution in swimming and surfing areas of Santa Monica Bay out to sea.[88]

Meanwhile, at almost the same time in Austin, Texas, a community of working-class Latino and African-American residents was locked in a pitched battle against six oil companies, including Chevron, Exxon,

Texaco and Mobil. The citizens wanted to close down a group of storage cisterns known as a "tank farm" that the corporations operated jointly in the middle of their neighborhood. The tank farm was so much a part of this neighborhood of poor people of color that children literally played in the shadow of the cisterns. Pipelines ran under tattered tract homes at such a shallow depth that, according to local resident Mary Hernandez, "people can feel their houses shake when the gas is pumped through the pipes."[89]

While regulators and the companies had been aware for many years that the tank farm had leaked significant amounts of gasoline and jet fuel into the groundwater, no one had told the community.[90] Citizens who were living right next to the tanks, and who were already suffering nosebleeds, rashes and respiratory problems from airborne toxics, only found out about the underground contamination in 1992 after they forcefully raised the issue. "It was a total disregard for the rights of the people," asserts Susana Almanza, an organizer with People Organized in Defense of the Earth and her Resources (PODER, Spanish for "power"). "For so long these commissions that were set up to regulate were taking care of the corporations," she charges. When they discovered the magnitude of the problem, which was also affecting children at three elementary schools and one high school within a mile of the tanks, the citizens became angry, and then they mobilized through PODER.[91] It was what Travis County Attorney Ken Oden called "a study in grassroots democracy" in which "the citizens were way out ahead of the government."[92] PODER, the East Austin Strategy Team (EAST) and their allies held community hearings, conducted health surveys and organized protests. They denounced a pattern of environmental racism in Austin and across the United States, pointing out that hazardous facilities were located disproportionately in poor communities of color that had little or no political clout.[93]

The oil corporations resisted every step of the way. First, they denied the problem. "I don't think we're doing anything that is endangering anyone's health," said Chevron's Neal Miller in a March 1992 statement typical of each of the tank farm corporations. They worked behind the scenes to portray community activists as extremists.[94] Throughout the entire process, says Almanza, Chevron, the supposed environmental leader, was "the worst" of all the oil companies, taking out advertisements in Latino and African-American newspapers in an attempt to debunk government health studies while the other companies remained quiet. "Chevron," she remarks, was "very outspoken, very nasty."[95]

Finally, in late 1992 and early 1993, with pressure from PODER continuing and with County Attorney Oden conducting a criminal and civil investigation, the six oil companies agreed, one by one, to close down their tank farm operations and move to an unpopulated zone, while cleaning up the community they had contaminated. Almanza and her allies, who many thought were crazy for taking on the oil giants in the first place, declared it "a victory for the people."[96]

These three factors—enforcement of environmental law, economic incentives and public pressure—have driven the major oil corporations to mitigate and reduce the destructive nature of many of their activities. But when the prize is big profits from exploiting new reserves of crude in ecologically fragile zones that government has declared off-limits, Chevron has been known to utilize its newfound corporate environmentalism as an offensive weapon. As William Mulligan spins it, the oil industry's new environmental consciousness and policies, along with the cleaner nature of new oil-drilling technology, will make it safe to produce in ecologically sensitive areas such as ANWR, offshore Florida and offshore California. Today, "we have different companies with better programs, greater awareness," he announces. "Whatever you're going to do is going to be done better than it was ever done before, or at least minimize the potential for any kind of risk to the environment. ...We would like to believe," he says, "that we could safely explore in all areas."[97]

Chevron's manipulation of the environmental issue was clear to local citizens and city officials in Santa Barbara, California, who fought the company tooth and nail in the late 1980s and early 1990s. Fearing a *Valdez*-like spill in the Santa Barbara Channel—a biologically rich fishing zone and recreational area—activists, local fishermen and government officials wanted to prevent Chevron from sending tankers from its offshore Point Arguello field through the channel while en route to Los Angeles and the El Segundo refinery.[98] In the battle that ensued, Chevron used not only its political clout, but also its environmental charm, to get its way. As Linda Krop, an attorney with the Santa Barbara–based Environmental Defense Center, observes, Chevron came across as "young environmental types" who "promised the world." But when it came down to it, "they completely reneged on all their promises," violating conditions of permits they were granted, misstating the levels of toxic hydrogen sulfide in the oil and single-mindedly pursuing their objective of sending tankers through the channel.[99] Ultimately, Chevron won the battle.[100]

Indeed, Chevron has used a number of "environmental" initiatives to further its objectives. It has attempted to stymie international regulation through its presence on the BCSD at the Earth Summit. Its chemical subsidiary helped launch the Chemical Manufacturers Association's Responsible Care program, an initiative designed to resuscitate the industry's credibility in the face of widespread pollution and accidents. And it may have succeeded in deflecting or softening criticism from the environmental movement by making donations to a number of environmental organizations, such as the World Wildlife Fund, the Nature Conservancy and the Audubon Society.[101]

Yet beyond these techniques, what most belies the company's—and for that matter much of corporate America's—purportedly green intentions is the anti-environmental offensive that Chevron and many of its counterparts launched in tandem with the 104th Congress in 1995. Chevron helped lay the groundwork for this offensive for a number of years by making numerous donations to front organizations, or so-called Wise Use groups, which have helped forge an anti-environmental ideology and build an organized constituency in favor of extensive deregulation in the United States. For instance, Chevron has funded Citizens for the Environment, an organization that has no membership base and that advocates strict deregulation of corporations as the solution to environmental problems. Chevron has also donated money to the right-wing Mountain States Legal Foundation, founded by former Interior Secretary James Watt; to the National Wetlands Coalition, which lobbies to remove obstacles to the development of wetland areas; and to Oregonians for Food and Shelter, a pro-pesticide lobby. Other groups that have benefited from Chevron's generosity include the Global Climate Coalition, the pro-mining, anti-environmental People for the West and the Pacific Legal Foundation, which has filed court challenges to clean water, hazardous waste and wetlands protection laws.[102]

Chevron also played an integral role in supporting academic research to develop the concept of risk assessment, pledging $1 million for studies in 1987 and funding a major public television program on the subject in 1991.[103] Risk assessment was subsequently adopted by the Clinton Administration as a central principle in environmental decision making and then pushed by the Republican-dominated 104th Congress as *the* overriding criterion for implementation of environment, health and safety laws. By applying a risk-benefit analysis to such decision making, risk assessment places economic considerations above often intangible human health and ecological factors, thus undermining government's ability to regulate corporate activities in the public interest.

By preparing the political, ideological and policy ground for an anti-environmental counterattack, Chevron and its colleagues were ready to take the field when the Republican majority swept into the 104th Congress. As Chevron's William Mulligan told the *San Francisco Chronicle*, "The industrial sector spent years on defense, then the ball was punted; now we're on offense." [104] Chevron's aggressive strategy included participating in Project Relief and the National Endangered Species Act Reform Coalition. Both are corporate groups that authored much of the Republican deregulatory agenda and actually wrote legislation that was introduced by congressmen. [105] Thus while Chevron continues to argue that its environmental expenditures are bottom-line proof of its green credentials, it has been a leader in the charge to undermine the very laws that compelled it to clean up some of its act in the first place.

While much of the deregulatory offensive has now been pushed back, Chevron and its corporate brethren continue to claim that current controls are overly burdensome and that their self-regulating environmental approach can do the job. Yet the company's U.S. record during the early 1990s (a time in which its new environmental policies were already in force) suggests otherwise. Indeed, the primacy of the company's bottom line over environment and human health became quite clear in 1996, when it refused to move an oil pipeline that the city of San Francisco said could, in the event of an earthquake, severely contaminate 2.5 million people's drinking water in the Bay Area. [106]

San Francisco had cause for concern. For while Chevron has made strides in some areas, a series of spills, fires, accidents and an ongoing flow of hazardous waste continue to plague its operations. [107] Between 1989 and 1993, for example, the number of environmental citations regulators dished out to Chevron's U.S. operations increased by 44 percent. [108] These penalties, which the company blames on the increasing number and complexity of regulations, are indicative of the ongoing, severe impact of Chevron's drilling, transportation, refining and distribution.

Such problems continue to be pervasive throughout the oil industry, whose refineries, pipelines, oil wells, supertankers and storage tanks continue to spew oil. This pollution contaminates streams, rivers and beaches, killing wildlife and threatening the drinking-water supplies, health and property values of communities across the country. All told, the U.S. petroleum industry continues to leak, spill and waste a total of

280 million barrels of oil every year—equivalent to 1,000 *Exxon Valdez* spills annually.[109] Such a large and ongoing problem clearly demands tighter regulation and enforcement. It also demonstrates the urgent need to develop strong energy conservation measures as well as ecologically sound alternatives to oil.

The Global Gambit

One oil industry response to environmental controls at home has been to move operations abroad. This gambit is part of the accelerating process of economic globalization that makes foreign investment increasingly attractive for the petroleum transnationals. Globalization has pried open previously forbidden foreign oil reserves, fostering a situation in which huge new "fat" fields can be exploited at relatively low cost. At the same time, newly opened markets and/or fast-growing demand in places such as China and Southeast Asia open up huge new horizons for refining and sales, prompting the majors to put further emphasis on the global market.[110]

While all of the big oil corporations have been multinational entities since the beginning of the twentieth century, 1989 was the first year that the U.S. oil industry began spending more on exploration and production abroad than it did at home. And while as recently as 1990 Chevron still spent more than half of its exploration and production monies in the United States, by 1996 it was spending a full 61 percent of this capital abroad.[111] As a company annual report explains, "Attractive opportunities overseas combined with limited business opportunities in the U.S. due to stringent regulatory barriers, drilling bans and a dwindling number of high-potential exploration opportunities have resulted in a shift in investment emphasis."[112] Thus Chevron, along with most of the rest of the oil industry, is following the path of least resistance, moving its search for oil to Asia, Africa, Latin America and the former Soviet Union, where large untapped resources are more profitably extracted, markets are booming, environmental regulation is looser and labor is cheaper.

While emerging exploration opportunities and expanding markets are the primary forces driving the globalization of the oil industry, environment is also a factor. It can be argued that by producing growing proportions of oil outside the industrialized North, the oil industry is shifting a portion of the environmental burden of the North's oil consumption to the South and East. What's more, Chevron has blamed environmental factors for playing a central role in its sale of two major

U.S. refineries that accounted for about 25 percent of its domestic capacity. The sale of its Port Arthur, Texas, and Philadelphia refineries saved the company an estimated $2 billion over five years, most of which would have been spent complying with environmental regulations. The money from the sales was reportedly shifted overseas to finance ventures such as building a pipeline to pump oil from Kazakhstan.[113]

Corporations such as Chevron are clear that they will not be investing in new refineries in the United States. For one, the market for refined products is already saturated. What's more, community opposition to the toxic hazards of the petrochemical industry is omnipresent. Building a new refinery in the United States is a "tough, tough sell because it's one of those kinds of smokestack industries," says Chevron's William Mulligan. "It's almost akin to a nuclear power plant," he comments. "There aren't too many places that are willing to grant that kind of permission and be willing to have one in their backyard."[114] Indeed, the only new refineries Chevron is building these days are in rapidly industrializing areas such as Thailand and China, two of the fastest-growing fuel markets in the Asia-Pacific region.[115] Environmental controls in these countries are weaker than in the industrialized North, while local communities are often uninformed of the potential hazards.

The impacts of this industrial migration are significant. The flight of the petroleum industry combined with the failure of the U.S. government to pursue a strong alternative energy development path is fostering an ever greater U.S. dependence on imported oil.[116] The global oil corporations are also leaving behind a beleaguered, unemployed workforce along with a decaying, increasingly leaky and accident-prone U.S. infrastructure in order to build pipelines, refineries and oil wells on the global petroleum frontier.[117]

Like much of the rest of corporate America, the oil corporations have successfully participated in lobbying the U.S. government to take the lead in pushing for "free trade and investment" as the centerpieces of an increasingly liberalized and globalized new world economic order. With freshly opened, burgeoning new markets available, U.S. corporations are now attempting to use the global economy as a wedge to dismantle U.S. environmental standards in the name of jobs and economic competitiveness. William Mulligan elaborates:

> As economic globalization has occurred, what it's doing is counterbalancing the environmental movement. Where things were being done early on primarily for environmental reasons, now people are begin-

ning to say "time out," we don't have unlimited resources just to spend on every kind of identified environmental problem. . . . So there's a sense of balance and priority that's creeping into it driven by the desire to be competitive globally. Let's face it. We could have the highest standards in the world. We could try to project leadership in this area of the environment, but by the end of the day you may be going out of business simply because there are other places in the world that may not hold themselves to the same high standards . . . as a result, you're going to have to compete with them.[118]

As discussed in Chapter One, this kind of approach sets up a race to the bottom of the regulatory barrel. On the global playing field, corporations are not only pitting communities or local or regional governments against one another as they traditionally have, but they are playing entire nations against one another. Globalization weakens the hands of organized labor and environmentally concerned constituencies, while undermining the sovereign control of national governments across the map. Meanwhile, the visible hand of the highly mobile, tremendously powerful transnational corporations becomes stronger. The common good takes a back seat to the interest of the corporate bottom line. In this scenario, according to companies such as Chevron, self-regulation and so-called free market environmentalism should take care of the environmental problem, replacing the unwieldy governmental controls that have been imposed upon them. Unfortunately, with the "counterbalancing" effect of globalization, the rules of the so-called free market tilt the playing field toward more oil development while undermining governments' ability to reign in the global oil corporations and promote alternative energy and transportation policies.

A clear example of this dynamic can be found in the energy provisions of the North American Free Trade Agreement (NAFTA). NAFTA allows governments to subsidize oil and gas development while leaving regulations that might provide subsidies for energy efficiency and conservation initiatives unprotected—open to be sanctioned by the agreement's secretive dispute-resolution panels as "barriers to free trade." Thus the "counterbalancing" influence of globalization cited by Mulligan heavily favors the interests of the oil majors over the imperative for more ecologically sustainable and economically efficient resource use in the United States. The agreement further exposes the ecologically sensitive northern Canadian and coastal Mexican regions to unbridled fossil fuel development.[119]

The oil industry's global gambit cuts like a two-edged sword. While it creates an international market that serves to undermine environmental controls and initiatives (such as energy conservation and demand-side management) in countries such as the United States, it also increasingly brings to other nations the problems that the populations of the industrialized North have been suffering for decades. These problems are made worse by the lack of accountability that the oil transnationals operate under in much of the global economy. Indeed, in many parts of the world oil is spilling and leaking and burning up in ways that are virtually unimaginable in the United States.

In the mid-1990s, for example, increased exploitation of the Russian Arctic's oil fields by a number of transnational oil companies, including Conoco, Gulf Canada, British Gas and others, escalated the amount of petroleum pouring through the already faulty pipelines of the former Soviet Union. This virtually uncontrolled flow contributed to massive, ecologically devastating spills in the Komi and other regions in 1994. According to Greenpeace, the Western oil corporations cut deals with the Russian government whereby they reap profits based on how much oil they pump rather than how much arrives at the other end. Even when twenty-three holes developed in the pipelines and Komi authorities called on them to halt, the transnationals refused to stop pumping their oil.[120]

Many of the considerations that have forced the oil majors to clean up their acts at home—factors such as governments with the capacity, power and, when pressed by the public, the political will to force a corporation to stop its abusive behavior—are absent in many foreign investment-dependent nations. Factors such as vocal environmental movements with some democratic access to and influence over governmental decision making are also absent or severely limited in countries such as Indonesia, Burma or Nigeria, where dictators reign. Moreover, just getting by on a daily basis is often the top priority for the many millions of poor affected by the oil industry.

Chevron's environmental record abroad is a cloudy one. While it has shifted an increasing amount of its resources to the global oil game, Chevron has conveniently focused its corporate environmentalist spotlight on domestic operations. Little information is available, either from the company or from external sources. Its environmental report states that Chevron carries out environmental audits of its international operations, yet it is not at all clear what these audits have revealed. Company officials such as William Mulligan insist that when abroad Chevron follows "industry standards." Yet Chevron does not present any international information about air emissions, hazardous waste or oil spills in its environmental report. In fact, the company claims that "because each country has different oil spill reporting requirements, Chevron does not collect oil spill data in non-U.S. waters."[121] Caltex is not even mentioned in Chevron's environmental report, despite the fact that it appears prominently in its annual report's discussion of operations, in its submissions to the U.S. Securities and Exchange Commission and as a profitable line item on the company's balance sheet.

What is clear is that of the nearly $1.5 billion that Chevron says it spent on the environment in 1994, less than $200 million was accounted for outside the United States.[122] Caltex reported spending an additional $365 million on environmentally related capital and operating expenditures.[123] (Since Chevron owns half of Caltex, its share can be calculated as $182.5 million). This brings the total Chevron spent outside the United States to less than $383 million—or about 22 percent of all its environmental spending. It is safe to say that much of this money is probably spent in areas such as the North Sea and Japan, where regulations are stiff, while Chevron's huge operations in Nigeria and Indonesia probably receive proportionately less funding. Moreover, Chevron's international environmental spending is quite low when compared to the fact that more than half its profits come from its international operations.[124] Chevron's environmental expenses are lower abroad, while its international operations garner more profit than at home. This seems to confirm what is already obvious—the company is following lower standards internationally than it does at home. Of course, this also suggests that its environmental impact is disproportionately high outside the United States.

In fact, while Chevron appears to be far from the worst oil corporation in terms of its international environmental record (such a distinction might be reserved for Texaco or Shell), some anecdotal evidence points toward what may be a pattern of serious problems throughout Chevron's global empire. Chevron brags, for instance, that between 1989 and 1993 oil spills in U.S. waters decreased by 97 percent.[125] But in 1990, a year in which Chevron reports spilling 252,000 gallons of oil in the entire United States, just one Caltex spill in the Philippines added up to nearly twice that total. The Caltex-contracted tanker *My Fernando,* which was delivering a load of oil to the company's Philippine refinery, sank off Bataan, spilling more than 460,000 gallons of oil, spelling disaster for more than 6,000 fishing families living in five towns nearby, and taking a serious toll on the already beleaguered marine life in the area. Furthermore, the Caltex refinery in Bataan—the largest in the Philippines—reportedly suffers smaller spills into the bay on a regular basis, causing continuous problems for these fisherfolk.[126]

In Sumatra, Indonesia, Caltex's massive operations within a 32,000-square-kilometer government-granted concession have come under fire from local Riau communities as well as from national and international environmental groups. Trees are reportedly dying, fish populations are declining and rivers are polluted. Scientists from Greenpeace who tested river water near six Caltex "gathering stations" in 1993 charged that the company has allowed "large-scale releases" of contaminants into the freshwater systems that "have led to irreparable environmental damage" and "severe long term hazards to human health."[127] Caltex has also reportedly leased rainforest land claimed as traditional territory by the indigenous Sakai to an Indonesian company that is clear-cutting it and planting palm oil plantations.[128]

In Nigeria, Chevron operates in the Niger Delta, an ecosystem once described as one of the most fragile in the world. It has now been labeled the most endangered delta on the planet.[129] Environmental problems in Nigeria include a plethora of spills that have destroyed agricultural and fishing grounds, toxic drilling wastes dumped in unlined pits, natural gas flared right next to villages, acid rain and the virtual decimation of numerous subsistence economies.[130] While Royal Dutch Shell, the leading oil producer in Nigeria (responsible for half of all oil pumped in the country) has come under heavy international fire for the social and environmental disaster it has created in the territory of the Ogoni people there, little is known about Chevron's Nigerian operations, which make up roughly 20 percent of its international oil and gas production.[131] The company boasts that it has helped form one of the first "oil spill cooperatives" in the country and claims that only a small portion of its operations are in Ogoni territory.[132]

Yet Chevron's presence in Ogoniland was sufficient for Ken Saro-Wiwa—late Nigerian author, president of the Movement for the Survival of the Ogoni People (MOSOP) and winner of various environmental awards—to identify it, together with Shell, as the cause of serious social and ecological disruption. Saro-Wiwa, who was executed by the Nigerian government on trumped-up murder charges in 1995, used strong words to describe the impacts of the oil transnationals on his people:

> The result . . . has been the total destruction of Ogoni life, human, social, cultural and economic. . . . What Shell and Chevron have done to Ogoni people, land, streams, creeks and the atmosphere amounts to genocide. The soul of the Ogoni people is dying and I am witness to the fact.
>
> I hear the plaintive cry of the Ogoni plains mourning the birds that no longer sing at dawn; I hear the dirge for trees whose branches wither in the blaze of gas flares, whose roots lie in infertile graves. The brimming streams gurgle no more; their harvest floats on waters poisoned by oil spillages.
>
> Where are the antelopes, the squirrels, the sacred tortoises, the snails, the lions and tigers which roamed this land? Where are the crabs, the periwinkles, mudskippers, cockles, shrimps and all which found sanctuary in mudbanks under the protective roots of mangrove trees?
>
> I hear in my heart the howls of death in the polluted air of my beloved home-land; I sing a dirge for my children, my compatriots and their progeny.[133]

The brutal Nigerian military dictatorship, bloated and corrupted by $10 billion a year in oil revenues, silenced Saro-Wiwa.[134] While Shell denies it, some accounts finger the oil giant as complicit in his execution.[135] Saro-Wiwa and MOSOP were certainly threatening the flow of oil revenues in Nigeria. Indeed, MOSOP's protests were inspiring action against Shell and Chevron not only in Ogoniland, but across the country, paralyzing operations in dozens of locations, including Opuama, where a convoy of villagers in canoes took over a Chevron drilling platform, demanding compensation for pollution.[136]

The severity of the government's crackdown in Ogoniland following Saro-Wiwa's hanging sent the signal that such threats to corporate and government interests would not be tolerated. Or as Naemeka Achebe, general manager for Shell Nigeria, put it in early 1995, as he defended the Nigerian regime, "For a commercial company trying to make investments, you need a stable environment. . . . Dictatorships can give you that. Right now in Nigeria there is acceptance, peace and continuity."[137] Conversely, while the government provides a stable investment climate, Shell's, Chevron's and other oil corporations' ongoing presence in the country has continued to help prop up Nigeria's brutal military regime.

Nigeria and Indonesia are but two examples of the destructive social and ecological impacts of oil drilling in tropical areas. Similar problems have occurred elsewhere in Africa, Asia and Latin America. Perhaps most notorious is the case of Chevron's Caltex partner, Texaco, which spilled an estimated 16.8 million gallons of oil (50 percent more than the *Exxon Valdez*) into the fragile rivers, creeks and lagoons of Ecuador's Oriente region of the Amazon forest over a seventeen-year period. Texaco, other transnational corporations and Ecuador's national oil company have also spewed more than 4 million gallons of untreated toxic drilling waste into the rainforest every day for years. With their traditional lifestyles and ecosystems disrupted, the indigenous people in Ecuador's oil zones suffer malnutrition rates that reportedly surpass 70 percent, while cancer, birth defects and other health problems linked to petroleum have soared.[138]

Such abuse tarnishes the environmental image that the global oil corporations are projecting at home. As Ecuadoran indigenous leader Valerio Grefa observes, "These corporations say they are green, but this isn't true. If they can't even be green in the United States, then they certainly won't be green in countries like Ecuador, Bolivia and Peru, where they can basically do whatever they want."[139] The corporate response, across the board, whether it be Ecuador, Nigeria or Burma, is that they have followed the laws of the land. As Michael Trevino, public affairs manager for Texaco Latin America/West Africa, explains, his company's operations "have always been conducted in strict accordance with the laws of the countries in which we were operating and the environmental practices of the time."[140]

Changing times, however, have made mere compliance with weak environmental laws insufficient. Local uprisings, often of indigenous people against abusive transnational corporations, are taking place the world over. The Ogoni in Nigeria and a coalition of indigenous groups that rose up against the oil companies in Ecuador are two examples. This, combined with growing international concern for both indigenous peoples' rights and rainforest conservation, have posed significant barriers to transnational corporations trying to extract oil from beneath the rainforests' fragile soils. In response, some companies have invented more sophisticated strategies that seek to mitigate the social and ecological impacts of their activities in order to most efficiently extract resources.[141] Chevron's operations in Papua New Guinea exemplify this tropical manifestation of corporate-driven "sustainable development."

Disneyland in the Rainforest

The setting is stunning. High mountains drop off into steep ravines cut by cascading waterfalls. A jewel of a lake sits nestled among rolling, rainforested hills. An abundance of rivers wind through steamy jungle flatlands until they reach the sea. From the air, one can see an occasional village or agricultural plot dotting this green carpet, rich in life. Until recently, with the exception of the occasional missionary, the myriad tribal groups that live in the vicinity of Lake Kutubu and in the Kikori Basin had very little contact with the world beyond theirs. Most have only known slash-and-burn agriculture, hunting and gathering. Things changed, however, when Chevron established the Kutubu Joint Venture in the late 1980s. Managing the project for a group of investors that includes Mitsubishi, British Petroleum, the giant Australian concern Broken Hill Properties and the Papua New Guinea (PNG) government, Chevron created a high-tech outpost for the global economy in the midst of this idyllic natural setting populated by tribal people.

Walking into the Chevron compound from the surrounding area is like taking a leap through time. In a matter of minutes one hurtles from the Foe and Fasu people's jungle villages of thatched rattan walls and grass ceilings to a Disneyland-like reality. Inside the barbed-wire fences and beyond the security guards is a world furnished with satellite dishes, state-of-the-art computers, gourmet catering, a hospital, smiling clean-cut Americans and a fleet of hundreds of shiny-white four-wheel-drive vehicles. More than ninety miles of newly carved roads snake throughout what feels like a rainforest theme park, while an airstrip intersects its center. Twenty-one wells quietly suck oil from the ground, a mini-refinery processes fuel for the compound's automobiles and airplanes and a pipeline sends 140,000 barrels of crude a day 165 miles through the jungle, under the rivers and into the ocean, where it arrives at a loading terminal platform. From there, supertankers take it to Australia, China, South Korea, Japan, Hawaii and sometimes as far as El Segundo and Richmond for refining. Chevron set up this outpost of modernity in roughly one year. To do so, it employed military-style operations in which, at their peak, three Hercules C-130 transport planes made five runs a day, importing everything from storage tanks and televisions to toilet paper.[142]

A technology workshop in the compound is there to build or repair almost anything imaginable. Indeed, for the ceremonies that officially opened the pipeline in late 1992, Chevron built a twenty-foot-high model of a smoking volcano and imported a fifty-foot-tall inflatable cockatoo for a gala performance of the myth of Lake Kutubu. Fireworks exploded in the air as a parasailor descended from the sky and a narrator's voice boomed over loudspeakers. The narrator told the ancient story of Lake Kutubu's birth for the government officials and corporate executives sitting in the newly built grandstands, as well as the local villagers representing various tribal groups in the area (some of whom donned face paint, headdresses and spears to perform traditional dances for the dignitaries).[143] This larger-than-life Disneyfication of local mythology—billed by Chevron as a "mystical blending of legend and modern life"—was part of an ongoing, comprehensive and systematic effort by the company not only to impress its investors and PNG national leaders, but also to win the hearts and minds of the native population.

With local government in the Kutubu area virtually nonexistent, Chevron, the stateless corporation, functions almost as a state unto itself—acting as a global company cum development agency. By 1994 it had spent more than $3 million (money that goes a long way in rural PNG) on development projects run by a community affairs division staffed by more than fifty professionals. In contrast to the behavior of many other oil development projects around the world, this group carries out work on public health, community development, small business development, land tenure, agricultural extension and more. It has put water tanks in every village, built schools and medical outposts, run sewing and cooking workshops, set up portable sawmills, taught hygiene and built latrines. "We've taken on the government's extension program for them and we're interfacing with them," says Papua New Guinean Gai Pobe, Chevron's government relations and community affairs coordinator at Kutubu.[144]

Just as most so-called aid to the Third World is motivated by a government's own self-interest (or to support investment by its corporations), Chevron's sophisticated development assistance in Kutubu is geared to get oil out of the ground as smoothly as possible. This is not to say that there aren't well-meaning, highly skilled and knowledgeable people working for Chevron. There are. But the bottom line is that if the communities are happy, "we're gonna be able to do what we want to do," explains the man in charge, community affairs manager and Chevron veteran Jim Price. The company will go so far as to fly helicopters out to remote villages to bring spare parts for a portable sawmill in an area where it is prospecting for oil. It's "the best insurance we have around us of not having a Bougainville," Price maintains, referring to the guerrilla war being waged against a multinational mining corporation by disgruntled locals elsewhere in PNG.[145] Chevron's Gai Pobe puts it more bluntly. "We're keeping the people with the spears and arrows out," he asserts.[146] In sum, while the extension workers on the ground may be dedicated to their cause, the essence of Chevron's development assistance is to implement a preemptive rural pacification program designed to avoid costly strife that would interrupt the flow of oil and stain the company's image.

Chevron's efforts to engineer a stable business environment also have an environmental component. Given the tremendous biological diversity of the Kutubu and Kikori areas and their nearly pristine state when the oil project began, Chevron correctly anticipated that its efforts would draw international environmental attention. Integrating environmental issues into its ground-floor planning, the company, to its credit, undertook a series of initiatives to minimize its destructive impacts, thus distinguishing the Kutubu joint venture from the socio-ecological debacles in places such as Nigeria and Ecuador. The company laid much of its pipeline on the Kikori River in an attempt to minimize the risk of sabotage and spills. The pipeline itself carries cathode protectors that send an electrical current through it in order to detect corrosion. A computerized warning system and the segmentation of the pipeline allow for a relatively quick shutdown in case of a spill. At its wells, Chevron is reinjecting drilling waste and much natural gas, although it continues to flare some. It has also instituted a hazardous waste management program.[147]

Finally, Chevron gave the World Wildlife Fund (WWF) $3 million over three years to develop a community-based management plan to protect the rainforests in the project area. But some critics see this move as environmental pacification—buying convenient green cover in case of an accident. "Chevron's gotten WWF in there as an insurance policy," says British environmental researcher George Marshall. "If there's an oil spill, they'll just roll out the panda."[148] Chevron officials don't disagree, explaining that the WWF was brought in to provide a buffer against both environmental destruction and "against international environmental criticism."[149]

While Chevron's collaboration with the WWF has succeeded to some degree in keeping international criticism at bay, it appears that the WWF is in over its head in terms of halting environmental destruction related to the petroleum venture. According to wildlife experts, ongoing air traffic and other vehicular activity at and around the Chevron camp has scared away most game and bird life in the vicinity of the lake, ruining local hunting and diminishing the area's biodiversity.[150] And, in an internal report, one of the WWF's foremost experts on tropical forests makes dire predictions for the future of the Lake Kutubu area. "Uncontrolled and devastating logging, unfortunately, is the probable future for the accessible forests along all the new roads in the Lake Kutubu region," writes respected scientist Gary Hartshorn.[151]

What's more, Chevron's move in 1995 to begin exploiting new oil strikes in the nearby Gobe region has cast the company's social and environmental commitments into doubt. The cultural terrain of Gobe (it is home to more than twenty-eight clan groups who are laying claim to royalties from the oil) is far more complex than that of Kutubu and may well prove to be overwhelming for the company's community affairs division. Chevron is also building roads close to Gobe's biologically sensitive terrain, which is considered by the WWF to be a priority conservation area. Moreover, landowner companies set up by Chevron are upgrading a road that runs from the southern highlands near Kutubu down through the lowland rainforests of Kikori and out to the sea—something the company had promised the WWF and others would not happen.[152] At Kopi, Chevron planned to join forces with a small Houston-based corporation to help it build an oil refinery for national consumption—a project bound to have significant impacts on the communities and ecosystems nearby.[153] Chevron's road network may well allow Malaysian transnationals, who received government timber concessions for Kikori in 1995, to edge ever closer to the pipeline, threatening not only pristine rainforest ecosystems, but also the oil's safe flow to the Chevron sea terminal.[154] The WWF, which was supposed to work with Chevron to provide economic alternatives for communities tempted to sell their rights to these pristine rainforests, has only slightly slowed the destruction's pace.[155] The future may well bring additional environmental problems to Chevron's PNG operations. With shifting riverbeds in a seismically active area, the part of Chevron's pipeline that runs under the river is extremely vulnerable. In fact, a shift in the Kikori River in May 1993 left more than a half-mile of pipe unsupported for some time, exposing it to breakage. Increased shipping traffic on the river from growing logging operations also threatens the pipeline in shallow areas.[156]

Chevron's preemptive rural pacification program may run into other troubles as well. As Greenpeace's Lafcadio Cortesi, who works closely with community groups in PNG, comments, Chevron's operations threaten to "foster dependence, disrupt village life, displace customary institutions and ultimately take control of the direction in which development goes out of Papua New Guinean hands and put it into the hands of corporations with very different interests and world view."[157] The introduction of a cash economy has been known to wreak havoc on indigenous societies, marginalizing non-cash-earning subsistence and communal activities and leading to malnutrition, deterioration of health and a spiral of dependency.[158] In the case of Kutubu, the company's public health coordinator, Dr. Nadeem Anwar, observes that while "Chevron brought in the virtues, it brought in the vices too." According to Anwar, alcoholism and domestic violence have both increased as a result of the project.[159] The failure of some businesses set up by Chevron in an effort to foster self-sufficiency suggests that transferring Western development models to tribal groups may not, in the end, be overly successful either. In sum, Chevron's development agency is running up against the classic pitfalls that plague most such programs; by attempting to mold the local people in its own Western image, it may be undermining their cultural integrity, and with it their tools for survival.[160]

In the end, the extent of the social and environmental disruption that Chevron's operations will cause in Papua New Guinea depends, more than anything, on whether or not additional fields are discovered and developed. Either way, it's a lose-lose proposition for the people of PNG. If the country's oil industry expands beyond the Kutubu and Gobi fields, then Chevron's project may wind up serving as a Trojan horse that will open up PNG to large-scale oil development. The more oil that flows, the greater the loss of cultural and biological diversity, and the greater the chances that Kutubu and its surroundings will follow in the unfortunate footsteps of Bougainville, Nigeria or Ecuador. On the other hand, if no more oil fields are found and exploited, Chevron and its partners may well abandon PNG in the first decade of the twenty-first century. When they go, they will leave a quite Westernized, but impoverished and dependent, group of indigenous peoples behind. Until that day comes, Chevron will continue to dominate the Kutubu region.

Indicative of Chevron's profound influence are the local people who have switched from traditional tribal designs in yellow, black or white face paint and have been seen adorning their faces with the company's red, white and blue standard. Indeed, the people of Kutubu have become members of a global tribe, stakeholders of a great transnational nation; they are People of Chevron.

Heat Wave

While the effects of oil discussed throughout this chapter are all serious, Chevron's and the petroleum industry's largest environmental impact— the one that most threatens their bottom line and the green image they've developed—is global warming. In fact, the corporate response to the broad scientific agreement that serious measures must be taken now to avoid potentially catastrophic climate change later belies one of the fundamental arguments of corporate environmentalism: that ecological sustainability and corporate profitability can run hand in hand. Severe reduction in the use of fossil fuels, key to averting global climate change, will not be profitable to Chevron or its oil industry cohorts. And these corporations know it. But if the planet is to escape the threat of global warming, changes must run counter to many corporations' financial interests, or these interests must fundamentally change.

The primary source of greenhouse gases in the world is energy use and production, which contributes an estimated 57 percent of the gases responsible for global warming. CFCs, as well as other gases such as methane and nitrous oxide (some of which result from fossil fuel production and use), also contribute to global warming. But the burning of oil, gas and coal, which provides about 85 percent of the world's total energy, is the number-one culprit.[161] The industrialized North, which represents 25 percent of the world's population, ignites more than 70 percent of these fuels, while the other 75 percent of the world who live in the South consume less than 30 percent.[162] Globalization is changing this scenario, however. Increased consumption of oil, gas and coal is providing the underpinnings for rapid economic growth in parts of Asia and Latin America. According to Sir Peter Holmes, chairman of Royal Dutch Shell, the Third World's oil consumption increased by two-and-a-half times in a recent twenty-year period and could well double again by the year 2010.[163] The Institute of Southeast Asian Studies estimates that by 2025 the Asia-Pacific region will release more carbon dioxide into the atmosphere than any other region of the world. And by the year 2050 China's carbon dioxide emissions alone are expected to exceed the entire output of the OECD, a group of the most industrialized nations in the world.[164] Yet today, and cumulatively speaking, it is still the European Union, Japan and, most of all, the United States that are primarily responsible for greenhouse gases, in both absolute and per capita terms.[165] At the same time, increasingly stateless global corporations are bridging this North-South gap; their Earth-spanning operations are responsible for more than 50 percent of all greenhouse gas emissions, regardless of national boundaries.[166] This fact has put companies such as Chevron in the hot seat.

The oil industry's response to the looming greenhouse crisis consists of a series of defenses. Its first line of defense is to deny and question the science. Using a scant number of dissenting climatologists, it has pounced on the slightest uncertainty both as to whether global warming may occur and how severe it may be—despite the broad scientific consensus. But as Chevron's CEO Ken Derr has observed, flat-out negation of the problem invites unflattering comparisons to the tobacco industry's response to cancer studies. Rather, as a second line of defense, Chevron and other oil corporations call for more studies—for a full airing of the science. In this spirit, Derr has gone so far as to cite studies that suggest that greenhouse-induced climatic alterations will be mild and maybe even beneficial.[167] This tactic of delaying and questioning, while calling for conclusive proof before action is taken, is reminiscent of the stand that corporations such as DuPont, Hoechst and ICI took with regard to CFCs and ozone depletion. Even though it was a near scientific certainty that continuing CFC production would lead to ozone depletion and all its social and ecological consequences, these corporations called for more studies and more proof, delaying the phase-out of these highly destructive chemicals for fifteen years, until the first ozone hole had actually appeared.[168]

The third line of defense involves circular logic. The oil industry regularly asserts that there are no credible, viable alternatives to fossil fuels currently available. Therefore, government policy should not favor alternatives over oil. Rather, technological fixes such as "low emission" fossil-fuel-burning vehicles are the most desirable options. This, of course, only delays the development of alternatives that might replace oil, such as new generations of technologies for solar, wind and hydrogen power.

"The effort to tilt the playing field away from oil and toward alternatives," declares Derr, has "the potential to do great harm not only to the petroleum industry but to the interdependent global economy as well." This is the industry's fourth line of defense—the argument that meeting the challenge of climate change is not only unviable economically, but may bring on economic catastrophe. As Derr alleges, "the cost of a forceful mandate to curtail the burning of fossil fuels is almost beyond calculation."[169] It is true that if oil production were to cease tomorrow, the world economy would collapse. But if fossil fuels continue to be produced and burned at current rates, or those rates continue to increase at their current pace, the economic impacts of climate change will also be catastrophic. There is no doubt that major cutbacks in fossil fuel use and the phasing in of alternative energy need to occur in an orderly fashion so as not to spur tremendous economic upheavals. This is certainly possible, if the political will exists.[170] The catch here, of course, is that the political will of governments is tied up in the tentacles of the very corporations resisting this change, which brings us to the fifth line of defense.

The fossil fuel industry uses the above arguments to lobby consistently against all national and international legislation aimed at addressing climate change. For instance, in the international arena, the fossil fuel lobby has been unrelenting in its efforts to undermine the intergovernmental effort to address the greenhouse crisis through the Climate Convention. But even Chevron recognizes that it is only a matter of time before the oil industry becomes obsolete. As William Mulligan remarks, "We are a mature industry. We've been around for a hundred years. And just like everything, there's a beginning, there's growth, there's maturity and there's ultimately death. And we recognize those kinds of curves . . . and we're looking to ensure our financial future . . . as an entity. And we have to begin to think about transitions too."[171] Unfortunately, Chevron, along with the rest of the oil majors, is working steadily to see that death (or "transition") occurs far into the future. As part of a trend common in the oil industry, Chevron has sold off much of its noncore business and is focusing almost exclusively on petroleum. Meanwhile Ken Derr has announced that new technologies will double the current fifty-year supply of proved reserves of petroleum. This hundred-year period, which, in Derr's words, is "far beyond any meaningful planning horizon," will give the world "ample time for an orderly transition to an era of genuine alternatives."[172] A twenty-first century based on petroleum, however, may well mean that we all surf the oil pipeline right into a stormy and turbulent greenhouse world.

Wipe-out

As we have seen throughout this chapter, Chevron's greener hue, be it in Kutubu or California, does not change the fundamental reality that oil is a dirty business with a vast array of environmental and social impacts. Nor does it alter the collision course that the petroleum industry is on. Building an artificial reef for surfers, as Chevron is now doing to pacify its waterborne critics in El Segundo, will do nothing to stem the rising tides that global warming will bring. Hundreds of millions of coastal dwellers from Manhattan Beach to Bangladesh may well be inundated, suffering tremendous economic, ecological and social destruction as a result of climate change.

The coming years will surely see natural gas touted by petroleum corporations as the transition fuel that moves the world away from oil and toward a solution to the planet's climate woes. Yet natural gas emits only 30 percent less carbon dioxide when it is burned than oil does. It also often leaks significant amounts of the potent global warming gas methane when it is produced and transported.[173] It is not the answer. Nor is coal. Fossil fuel use must be severely curtailed now, even though the fossil fuel corporations oppose this step. One of the best mechanisms for achieving this could be the Climate Convention. Such an international agreement—which mandates reductions in carbon dioxide emissions and keeps the oil transnationals in check—must be enforced by ongoing political pressure from local communities, environmental groups and national governments alike. The problem is that the Climate Convention continues to be stymied by a powerful corporate lobby and foot dragging by those nations up to their necks in oil. Consequently, oil production and consumption are expanding unhindered, in tandem with economic globalization.

As this occurs, the degree of responsibility that countries of the South bear for climate change will no doubt increase. The nations of the South must face up to this reality and take responsibility for it. But so must international institutions such as the World Bank, along with the governments and corporations of the industrialized North, for these are the actors who bear the lion's share of the blame for pushing the South onto a fossil-fuel-dependent energy path. To redress this situation, the South must be given the economic incentive and technological opportunity (and it must develop the political will) to leapfrog over the mistakes made by the North, rather than basing its future on an ecologically bankrupt model of energy development.

At the same time, the most fundamental change must happen in the oil majors' home countries. For it is in the industrialized North that energy consumption is still overwhelmingly the highest and has been so throughout the hydrocarbon age. The question again is whether or not people can organize to generate the political will to stand up to the oil giants and build alternative economic models based on environmentally sound, equitably distributed energy production. The future leaves us very little choice. For unless there is a fundamental transformation away from fossil fuels, the petroleum companies that have generated oil's wave of power and prosperity and ridden it throughout the last century will send the Earth spinning into a terrible wipe-out—one that could leave us gasping for breath.

Chapter Four

Island of Dreams

Mitsubishi and Japan's *Keiretsu*

The experience of Japan . . . should be a lesson for the rest of the developing world. . . . Japan's economic growth was based on massive aggression in all areas of life.
                                                        Jun Ui, *Industrial Pollution in Japan*

You cannot tell the story of the economic development of Japan without telling the story of the Mitsubishi companies.
                                                        Mitsubishi Public Affairs Committee

For decades Shin Kiba (which translates as "New Wood Place") has served as one of two Tokyo ports of arrival for timber transport ships returning from faraway lands. Over time, transnationals such as Mitsubishi, Sumitomo and Itochu have brought to Japan a diverse sampling of logs from around the world. When one country's forests are depleted, a new source is developed and its resources transported to this global clearinghouse of wood. Indeed, the logs passing through Shin Kiba have come from the formerly vast but today fast-disappearing forests of the Philippines, Malaysia, Indonesia, Burma, Papua New Guinea, North America, Chile, Siberia and the Solomon Islands, to name a few. More than 3,000 ships loaded with logs, plywood, wood chips for paper, and even disposable chopsticks arrive in Japanese ports every year, making the country and its 125 million inhabitants the largest importer of wood products—both tropical and temperate—in the world.[1]

When a boat full of logs arrives in Shin Kiba, union dock workers roll the timber into the bay, tie it into rafts and float it across a channel to vast ponds—giant saltwater warehouses filled with the remnants of some of the world's most ancient forests. The logs move through the holding ponds at a fairly rapid rate, as they are scooped up by giant blue cranes and mechanically rolled along into plywood factories. There they are peeled into thin sheets and glued into precisely measured boards, mostly destined for short-term deployment as *konpane*—plywood molding for concrete in the domestic construction industry.[2] Once used, the *konpane* is thrown away or incinerated.[3]

Just to the north of Shin Kiba is an ironic spectacle. Protruding from a spit of reclaimed land known as the Island of Dreams sits a botanical garden enclosed in glass—the Yumenoshima Tropical Plant Dome. Every week, thousands of Tokyo residents visit this artificial rainforest to stroll on its concrete paths, past orchids, tree ferns, rosewoods, king palms and waterfalls. In the "forest" there is a model village hut made of palm fronds. There are exhibits as well as a video that describe "the effect that tropical and subtropical plants have on our lifestyles." The soothing sounds of birds and animals are piped in. Just outside the greenhouse sits a giant fifteen-foot-high, ten-foot-wide stump of a tree that once towered 150 feet, donated by the state government of Sabah, Malaysia, a territory that has already exported a large portion of its forests to Japan.

Of course, in this sanitized tropical fantasyland, which a promotional brochure calls a "real green, dreamy island," there is no mention of the fact that the world's forests and the peoples who live in them are quickly disappearing, and that the "lifestyles" of Japan, North America and Western Europe are behind this destruction. There is only a hollow, ringing slogan: "Rediscovering the Relationship Between Humanity and Plants."[4] What's more, this rainforest mirage is powered by trash; the Island of Dreams, which is built on top of an old garbage dump, is also the location of two of Tokyo's sixteen "waste to energy" incinerators. These plants burn the waste generated by Tokyo's 12 million inhabitants, as well as the construction industry's discarded *konpane* plywood.[5] As byproducts, they produce toxic smoke and ash.

This is Dream Island. It is a microcosm of Japan, one of the greatest destroyers of forests in the world, yet a country that projects an image of environmental sensitivity with the likes of artificial plant domes that mimic nature. Like Corporate America, which has appropriated and reshaped the American Dream, and like their European counterparts, who are molding the European "Community" into a corporate union, the transnationals that make up "Japan Inc." have transformed virtually their entire country into an "island of dreams"—a nuclear-powered, neon-lit, plastic-wrapped society that mass produces and mass markets an ecologically unsustainable lifestyle.

Corporate Clans

More than any other entities, the country's corporate clans, the *keiretsu*, have created and perpetuated the dream island culture that pervades contemporary Japan. Six giant *keiretsu* dominate much of Japan's economic activity and thereby have a significant impact on environmental issues domestically and around the world. A uniquely Japanese form of corporate organization, a *keiretsu* is a group, or "family," of affiliated transnationals with broad power and reach. Operating globally, integrated both vertically and horizontally, and organized around their own trading companies and banks, each major *keiretsu* is capable of controlling nearly every step of the economic chain in a variety of industrial, resource and service sectors. It can research and develop a technology, plan its production, finance and insure the project, extract resources from virtually anywhere in the world, transport them back to Japan or elsewhere, process them, produce an item, package it, promote it and then distribute and sell it globally. While Japanese corporate and government leaders deny or play down the existence or relevance of the *keiretsu*, their presence and vitality have been well documented by Japanese and Western scholars alike.[6]

Coordinating many *keiretsu* activities are the *sogo shosha*, or trading companies. In terms of revenue, the trading companies of the top four *keiretsu*—Mitsubishi, Mitsui, Itochu and Sumitomo—are the largest corporations in the world, with sales for each topping $160 billion in 1994. The nearest Western rival is General Motors ($154 billion), while Exxon, one of the largest oil companies in the world, grossed "only" $100 billion in the same year.[7] Meanwhile, in terms of assets, the top eight banks in the world are all Japanese *keiretsu* members. These banks outflank their Western counterparts by a large margin; the U.S. financial giant Citicorp, for example, ranks only thirtieth globally.[8] In addition to the trading companies and banks, which are considered to be the flagships of each group, every major horizontally organized *keiretsu* is made up of a core group of about thirty corporations specializing in areas such as electronics, heavy industry, mining, timber, pulp and paper, petroleum, chemicals, autos, steel and insurance. These core companies are bound together economically through a series of trading arrangements, cross-ownership structures, financing relationships and steering committees that meet "informally."[9]

Despite the fact that there are nearly a hundred large corporate groups in Japan and thousands of small ones, and although their clout has diminished somewhat in recent years, the Big Six—Mitsubishi, Mitsui, Dai Ichi Kangyo, Sumitomo, Sanwa and Fuyo—clearly dominate the nation's economy. More than half of the top 100 Japanese corporations are core members of one or another of the Big Six *keiretsu*. Only a very few, such as the maverick corporation Sony, can be said to be truly independent. And while small firms of less than a thousand employees make up more than half of all sales and assets in the Japanese economy, many derive income as subcontractors for the *keiretsu*. Furthermore, the group of 182 core corporations most tightly linked to the Big Six control 25 percent of the economy's assets, giving them a significant degree of power over the country's economic affairs.[10] The tight relationship between the corporations and government in Japan—an association that leads many analysts to point to the country as a model of state-sponsored capitalism—also gives the Big Six a major say in the policies of their government. Given the exceptional level of concentrated political and economic power they hold, as well as their global reach, it is easy to surmise that these mammoth corporate clans have a significant environmental impact on their home country and, more broadly, on the Earth's ecosystems.

The best known, most prestigious and largest *keiretsu* is the Mitsubishi Group of companies. Yoichi Kuroda, coordinator of the Japan Tropical Forest Action Network, describes the Mitsubishi Group as a "mini-Japan."[11] There are more than 160 corporations, employing more than half a million people, that make up the Mitsubishi Group. In turn, these entities hold shares in roughly 1,400 separate Japanese companies, while another 700 or so "related firms" are dependent on the Mitsubishi Group.[12]

Indeed, the core Mitsubishi companies are ranked as global leaders in most key economic sectors and are involved in an array of activities that range from making chopsticks to building rocketships. In 1995 the Mitsubishi Corporation, the group's general trading company, or *sogo shosha*, was ranked by *Fortune* magazine as the largest corporation on the planet, with revenues topping $175 billion.[13] Mitsubishi Bank is the largest commercial banking company in the world, with assets of nearly $820 billion.[14] Mitsubishi Group member Meiji Mutual is the sixth-largest mutual life insurance company on Earth, with assets of more than $90 billion. Mitsubishi Motors and Mitsubishi Chemical have reached the ranks of the world's top-ten vehicle producers and top-ten chemical companies, respectively. Mitsubishi Electric is one of the top-

ten electronics companies and one of the fifty largest industrial companies in the world, with annual sales approaching $33 billion, making it
30 percent larger than American high-tech powerhouse Motorola.
Mitsubishi Heavy Industries is the largest industrial and farm equipment manufacturer on the planet. Other core group members include
Mitsubishi Materials (the world's twelfth-largest metals company), Kirin
Brewery (the fourth-largest beverage company), Mitsubishi Oil (the
twenty-eighth-largest petroleum refiner) and Asahi Glass (third in building materials).[15] The combined revenues of the twelve Mitsubishi companies listed in *Fortune* magazine's "Global 500" are comparable to the
combined gross domestic product of Mexico and Central America, or
the Netherlands and New Zealand—take your pick.[16] Such prominence
on the global economic map prompted Professor Hiroshi Okumura, an
expert on Japanese corporations at Kyoto's Ryukoku University, to quip
that the world is undergoing a process of "Mitsubishi-fication."[17]

While the Mitsubishi Group's global reach is certainly extensive, it is
even more dominant at home. The revenues of the same eleven companies mentioned above make up roughly 11 percent of Japan's entire
GDP.[18] The *sogo shosha,* Mitsubishi Corporation, is Japan's number-one
fossil fuel trader, importing oil from countries such as Vietnam and
Papua New Guinea and handling 50 percent of Japan's liquefied natural gas imports, which come primarily from Australia, Brunei, Malaysia
and Venezuela.[19] Mitsubishi Materials is the country's number-one non-
ferrous metal producer, importing platinum, copper and other raw
materials from Mitsubishi-financed ventures as far away as Chile and
South Africa.[20] Mitsubishi Heavy Industries is Japan's number-one gas,
oil, coal-fired and nuclear power plant maker, ship and rocket builder,
and heavy machinery producer. Mitsubishi Heavy, which builds Patriot
missiles, is also Japan's number-one defense contractor—no small market, considering that Japan's "nonoffensive" military's budget is the
world's third largest.[21] Mitsubishi Chemical is Japan's largest integrated
chemical corporation.[22] Asahi Glass was Japan's top producer of ozone-
depleting CFCs and leads the field in producing their replacements—
HFCs and HCFCs. Mitsubishi Estates is Tokyo's top landowner, controlling, among other assets, a good portion of the capital's high-value
downtown real estate, an area known as Mitsubishi Village. It is estimated that Mitsubishi food companies specializing in the production,
transport and distribution of canned products, grain, beef and fish
directly or indirectly feed about 25 percent of the entire Japanese popu-

lation.[23] Much of Japan washes this food down with alcohol produced by the *keiretsu* member Kirin, Japan's largest brewer.[24]

However, the Mitsubishi Group does not derive its power and profits merely from the individual companies that make up its clan. It and the other Big Six *keiretsu* enjoy the added strength that comes from the synergy created through joint projects carried out among member companies. The flagship corporations—the banks and *sogo shosha*—use their reciprocal trade and financing relationships with other *keiretsu* members as the primary vehicles to arrive at a highly sophisticated level of collaboration.[25] Reciprocal trade networks function more or less as follows: The *sogo shosha* Mitsubishi Corporation might pay the Mitsubishi shipping company Nippon Yusen (insured by Group member Tokio Marine) to ship copper to Japan that was mined by a Mitsubishi project in Chile with equipment built by and bought from Mitsubishi Heavy in Japan. In Japan, Mitsubishi Materials will buy and then smelt the copper in a factory that was financed by Mitsubishi Bank. Once processed, the copper may be sold to Mitsubishi Heavy Industries, which will use it to build air conditioners. It may then sell these to Mitsubishi Motors' auto factories in Japan and the United States. In addition to the air conditioners, Mitsubishi Motors' U.S. operation gets windshields from Mitsubishi Group member Asahi Glass, starters and cruise controls from Mitsubishi Electric, engines and transmissions from Mitsubishi Motors in Tokyo and steel from Mitsubishi International, Mitsubishi Corporation's wholly owned subsidiary.[26]

Given the size and reach of its diverse activities, and due to the fact that it is more heavily focused in polluting industrial sectors than other *keiretsu*, the Mitsubishi Group may well be the single most environmentally destructive corporate force on Earth. As we shall see, various members of the Mitsubishi Group have come under attack on numerous occasions for the environmental problems they have created. Yet it would require a global undertaking of major proportions to document comprehensively the combined impacts of the *keiretsu*. In the timber industry, for example, while non-Japanese companies or subcontractors may actually cut the trees, the big *sogo shosha* catalyze and promote deforestation through activities such as financing logging, organizing the imports, furnishing credit for processors in places such as Shin Kiba and providing a distribution network in Japan.[27] As Dr. Hidefumi Imura, a former official with Japan's Environment Agency, describes the impacts of these trading houses, "their effects are [often] indirect, but the implications are serious. The impacts are greater than those of mere factories."[28]

This chapter briefly documents the historical evolution of the Mitsubishi Group as an emblematic Japanese *keiretsu*. In doing so, it attempts to provide insight not only into the magnitude of the Group's environmental impacts in a number of areas, but also into the interplay of environmental issues with the various stages of Japan Inc.'s economic development and the emergence of the Island of Dreams.

From Samurai to Cold Warriors

In the late nineteenth century, during the Meiji Restoration, the young Yataro Iwasaki, son of a samurai family serving the Tosa feudal clan, began an independent shipping business. His steamships bore flags marked with three triangular water chestnuts that would later be transformed into the three-diamond logo of the Mitsubishi Group.

According to the *keiretsu*'s official history, the company got its first big break in 1874, when a competing shipping company refused a government request to transport munitions to Taiwan: "Mitsubishi grabbed the brass ring, shipped the munitions, and paved its way for even greater future success." A year later the company received thirty ships from the government as a reward for its patriotism. This was the beginning of a long, collaborative relationship between the Japanese government and Mitsubishi, characterized, as the official history explains, by Mitsubishi operating under the "protection of the government to help Japan compete with foreign nations."[29]

In the early twentieth century, the Iwasaki clan expanded into coal mining and shipbuilding. By the end of World War I the family-run Mitsubishi *zaibatsu* (holding companies that were predecessors of the *keiretsu*) controlled more than seventy subsidiaries, branches and affiliates, including oil, petrochemical, electric and aircraft companies. Mitsubishi and the two other big *zaibatsu*—Mitsui and Sumitomo—continued to accumulate wealth and power. By the 1930s these three groups dominated more than half of all production in most sectors of Japanese industry.[30] By the outbreak of World War II about a dozen *zaibatsu* controlled 80 percent of Japan's industry, commerce and finance.[31] Mitsubishi's Zero fighter was considered both the embodiment of the advanced *zaibatsu* technological capabilities and a symbol of Japan's military prowess.

Widely seen as partially responsible for Japan's aggressive expansionism and antidemocratic tendencies, the *zaibatsu* were disbanded after the war and splintered into thousands of smaller companies by the U.S. Occupation Command. Mitsubishi's trading company was, according to the official history, "miserably fragmented" into 139 separate trading corporations. To keep the *zaibatsu* from reemerging, the U.S. military government, led by General MacArthur, sold their stock off to the public, barred *zaibatsu* family members from assuming positions of power in the remnants of their old empires and prohibited the use of their corporate names. MacArthur also instituted an antimonopoly law modeled on U.S. antitrust legislation and promoted "democratization" measures that included the legalization of trade unions and land reform policies.[32]

These reforms, however, were short-lived, as the advent of the Cold War caused U.S. policy makers to view Japan in a new light. Fearing that the country could potentially ally itself with the Soviet Union or an emergent communist China, and needing an industrial and military staging ground for the Korean War, the United States did an about-face and suddenly converted occupied Japan into a bastion of anticommunist containment in Northeast Asia.[33] Such a policy shift, which included neutralizing the antimonopoly law, sat well with U.S. corporations such as General Electric and Standard Oil, which upon seeing their lucrative prewar ties with the *zaibatsu* undermined by MacArthur's efforts had complained that the democratic reforms were "anti-American," "socialistic" and likely to lead to the "communization of Japan."[34]

Consequently, the reconstruction of Japan shifted from an effort to defuse the corporate power of the former *zaibatsu* to one of placing them at the center of a strategic alliance that brought Japan into the fold of the U.S. Cold War. This alliance was achieved through the political mechanism of a security agreement (formalized in a treaty in 1960), through CIA support for the ruling Liberal Democratic Party and through the economic mechanism of joint ventures between Japanese and U.S. transnational corporations.[35] As analysts Joel Kotkin and Yoriko Kishimoto write, "In many respects the creation of the much feared 'Japan Inc.' was in large part a function of American foreign policy."[36]

Under these Cold War conditions, the fragmented components of the former *zaibatsu* coalesced like mercury. For example, repeated mergers among the 139 splintered trading companies that had formed Mitsubishi's prewar *sogo shosha* yielded four big corporations. By 1954 these four had come together into what is today the Mitsubishi Corporation. Other Mitsubishi companies were allotted small shares in the new *sogo shosha*—shares that when combined into one bloc amounted to a controlling interest. In this way, the practice of cross-shareholding began. It remains one of the economic forces that bind the *keiretsu*.[37]

Today the modern *keiretsu* is a decentralized yet cohesive, flexible yet nearly impenetrable corporate entity. In the *keiretsu*, power rests not in the hands of one family or one executive and board, but rather under the collective control of the corporate group's member companies. In some ways the *keiretsu* have become stronger than their *zaibatsu* predecessors. As Japanese business management specialist and professor Maruyama Yoshinari writes, when "seen in terms of Japan's rapid postwar economic growth and the global reach of *keiretsu* operations, there can be no question that the economic dominance of the Big Six is greater [today] than before the war."[38] The *keiretsu* have also mastered the technology introduced to them by U.S. corporations. "In many cases we are now more competitive than they are," boasts Kentaro Aikawa, former president of Mitsubishi Heavy Industries.[39]

The root causes of Japan's domestic environmental crisis, as well as of its significant impacts abroad, can be found embedded in the structural foundations of its post–World War II economy. Indeed, much of the promise that MacArthur's reforms held out to small- and medium-scale businesses, farmers, fisherfolk and workers—change that was inherently, if not consciously, more ecologically sustainable—was buried under the avalanche of procorporate Cold War policies. Japan experienced rapid growth not through the flowering of grassroots economic initiatives (although the initial reforms did create the space for new companies such as Sony to emerge), but rather through *keiretsu* collaboration with U.S. corporations in the development of the country's nuclear, petrochemical and other heavy industries, as well as in resource extraction from abroad.[40] This U.S.-Japanese alliance would ultimately evolve into an accommodation between the two powers whereby the ongoing U.S. military presence in the Asia-Pacific served as a canopy for the rapid integration of the region around the Japanese economy. Reciprocally, Japan grew and developed within the confines of the U.S. geopolitical strategy and economic framework.[41]

A prime example of this collaborative relationship can be found in the evolution of the Japanese nuclear industry—one of the most serious and contentious environmental issues in Japan today. Japan currently has the fourth-largest nuclear power program in the world. Its forty-seven functioning reactors, which provide more than 25 percent of the country's electricity, are frequently focal points of protests by communities throughout the country.[42] Roughly half of these plants were built by Hitachi and Toshiba (members of the Mitsui and Sumitomo *keiretsu* respectively) in collaboration with the American corporation General Electric. Another twenty were built in a joint venture between Westinghouse and the Mitsubishi Atomic Power Industry (MAPI). Such collaborative arrangements began in the early 1950s, helping the *keiretsu* to reemerge as the dominant economic force in Japan and as integral players in the new U.S.-Japanese alliance.[43] In fact, according to Dr. Jinzaburo Takagi of the Tokyo-based Citizens' Nuclear Information Center, the Mitsubishi Group used MAPI, a joint project of more than forty Mitsubishi companies, as a vehicle for its reunification.[44] For their part, by providing nuclear technology and know-how to the *keiretsu*, Westinghouse and General Electric helped tie the U.S.-Japanese strategic alliance together with the politically and economically powerful (and highly profitable) nuclear thread. In doing so, they also created Japanese nuclear corporations in their own image.

Given the genesis of the industry, it is not surprising that the troublesome issues surrounding Japanese nuclear power today—including the risk of catastrophic accidents, the insoluble problem of waste disposal, the question of plutonium reprocessing and the industry's attempts to export nuclear power—are similar to those debated in the United States. For example, many of the plants built through the U.S.-Japanese alliance have become increasingly dangerous with age. An accident at the Mitsubishi/Westinghouse-built Mihama II light water reactor in 1991, in which fifty tons of primary coolant leaked into the secondary circuits, heightened what were already ongoing protests throughout Japan by local communities living beside nuclear plants. The near-catastrophe stirred a national debate on the deteriorating safety of Japan's eight oldest reactors, five of which were built by Mitsubishi/Westinghouse. The accident also strengthened the resolve of communities opposed to the Japanese government's plans to build thirty more light water reactors in various parts of the country by the year 2010.[45] As in the United States, popular opposition has virtually halted plans to build new reactors, forcing Japanese corporations to seek to export their technology, especially to the fast-growing economies in places such as China and Indonesia.[46]

The growth of Japan's forest products industry, which today makes up the fourth-largest import sector in the island nation, parallels that of its nuclear industry.[47] At the end of World War II the forest acreage available to Japan was cut almost in half when it lost a number of colonies—nations or regions it had subjugated in part to gain access to natural resources such as timber. In fact, before and during the war, Japan depleted most of its own, as well as Korea's and Taiwan's, commercially viable forests.[48] Rebuilding in the early postwar era and pressured by U.S. military demands for construction materials during the Korean War, the country found itself continuing to harvest trees at three times its own rate of forest growth. Recognizing the unsustainability of the situation, the U.S. military government recommended that Japan implement forest conservation measures so as not to completely deplete its resources during reconstruction.[49] The United States did not want Japan to build up economic ties with the Soviet Union, whose vast Siberian timber resources were close by.[50] Consequently, the United States offered new sources of wood. The U.S. timber corporation Weyerhaeuser quickly stepped into a collaborative trading relationship with the Mitsubishi Corporation; basically, Mitsubishi served as Weyerhaeuser's agent, importing raw logs and sawn timber to feed wood-starved Japan. Other Japanese trading companies developed similar relationships with various U.S. multinationals.[51] In 1957 the U.S. government also offered a group of Japanese corporations direct access to Alaska's Tongass National Forest, the largest surviving temperate rainforest on earth, leading to the formation of the Alaska Pulp Company (APC).[52]

The APC was designed to involve all the leaders in the recovering Japanese timber industry. It included among its ranks the trading companies Mitsui, C. Itoh (now Itochu), Marubeni and Mitsubishi.[53] The U.S. Forest Service gave the APC a fifty-year contract to cut up to 5 billion board feet of timber at a subsidized rate in return for a $66 million investment in a pulp mill and saw mill. The APC deal was the first major Japanese commercial venture in the United States after the war.[54] Ultimately it proved important for three key environmental reasons. First, together with the raw logs shipped from companies such as Weyerhaeuser in the U.S. Pacific Northwest, it established a flow of resources from the United States to Japan. As Japan became an increasingly powerful export-oriented economic force, this resource flow grew in importance, helping to ease the U.S. trade imbalance created by Japan's export of items such as automobiles and electronics. This dynamic continues today, contributing to the ongoing unsustainable harvesting of U.S. forests.[55] Currently, wood products are the sixth-ranking U.S. export to Japan.[56]

Second, the APC deal provided the initial impetus for a global Japanese timber industry that grew exponentially in the following decades. In the Philippines, for example, Japanese transnationals, including the Mitsubishi Corporation, surpassed U.S. companies that in prewar days had made the then U.S. colony Southeast Asia's number-one timber exporter. By the 1960s Japan had supplanted the United States as the archipelago's top log export market. Over the next thirty years Japanese corporations accounted for as much as 70 percent of Philippine forests logged. By the early 1990s the country's supply was almost completely exhausted.[57] Indeed, Philippine exports to Japan peaked in the early 1970s and then slowly receded as Japanese timber transnationals moved progressively into Indonesia, Malaysia and Papua New Guinea in their search for raw logs.[58]

Third, the legacy of air pollution, water pollution, deforestation and antitrust violations that the APC venture left behind also fits the global pattern of behavior by the Mitsubishi Group and its *keiretsu* cousins. The APC pulp mill, whose emissions were a regular source of contention in the community of Sitka where it was located, racked up hundreds of thousands of dollars in U.S. government fines for air and water quality violations.[59] Located on the shores of picturesque Silver Bay in southeast Alaska, the pulp mill poisoned this resource-rich source of local livelihood with sludge and dioxin-contaminated waste, prompting the U.S. Environmental Protection Agency (EPA) to list it among the top-ten polluters in the American West.[60] In 1983 the APC, along with the U.S. timber company Louisiana-Pacific, was found to be in violation of antitrust laws for conspiracy to create monopoly control of the southeast Alaska logging industry and the Tongass National Forest by fixing prices, restraining trade and in the process wiping out more than one hundred small, local logging and milling operations.[61] The APC was also found by a federal judge to have carried out "transfer-pricing," whereby it fixed timber prices at extremely low levels in order to avoid U.S. taxes and transferred the profit to Japan.[62]

In 1990 the APC was ordered to stop dumping waste into Silver Bay, a rich source of up to 800,000 pounds of salmon a year.[63] In 1993 the company shut down its pulp mill and fired 400 workers after the U.S. Forest Service, under pressure from environmental groups such as the Southeast Alaska Conservation Council and the Sierra Club, finally removed the massive subsidies to the company for cutting old-growth forest, giving respite to 3 million acres of the Tongass National Forest.[64] In 1995, despite protests from Republican congressmen, the EPA moved to list Silver Bay as a Superfund site, forcing the APC to pay for studies to determine dioxin levels in the local fishery and making the company potentially liable for damages.[65]

Economic Miracles and Ecological Debacles

Another area of economic activity that was a postwar focal point around which Japan's *keiretsu* reamalgamated was the petrochemical industry. A central component in the original industrialization of the country, it was the key contributor to the rapid economic growth of the 1950s and 1960s dubbed the "Japanese economic miracle." With the proliferation of petrochemical technology during the 1920s and 1930s, a number of *zaibatsu*-run oil refineries and chemical factories had already emerged before the Second World War. But American bombs destroyed 85 percent of the country's total refining and storage capacity. This devastation, combined with the Cold War's procorporate orientation, provided an entree to the large U.S. and European oil corporations. Multinationals such as Shell and Caltex moved in to work with MacArthur's government and build (or rebuild) alliances with Japanese companies. The occupying American government used its powers to broker these reunions, allowing Japanese companies to remain intact (rather than being dismantled) if they cut deals with foreign oil companies. In return for access to a Japanese market poised to boom, the oil majors provided the new technology, capital and cheap crude that fueled rapid industrialization in Japan.[66] Oil consumption increased more than fifty-fold between 1950 and 1970, while per capita income grew ten-fold. This spurred the widespread growth of consumerism that, for instance, saw the number of households with refrigerators rise from 5 percent to nearly 95 percent.[67]

Bottom-line-oriented high-speed industrialization also resulted in environmental scourges such as Minamata disease (mercury poisoning), *itai-itai* disease (cadmium poisoning) and Yokkaichi asthma (sulfur dioxide pollution). Called "some of the most intense environmental destruction the world has ever seen," the social and ecological impacts of the contamination that caused these industrial diseases were so serious that a new word, *kogai* (meaning "destruction of the public domain"), was coined to describe the devastation.[68] Corporate *kogai*, which spread far beyond these three notorious cases, also catalyzed the emergence, in the 1960s and early 1970s, of the country's militant environmental movement, which, in turn, fundamentally changed the way Japanese companies do business. "We had a very rude awakening," says Takuya Negami, senior executive officer at Kobe Steel, one of the top-twenty industrial corporations in Japan. "One morning we found that we were almost criminals."[69]

Gray-haired, bespectacled, dressed in blue jeans and black tennis shoes, Yoshiro Sawai stands on a small spit of land in the port city of Yokkaichi, near Nagoya. He points to a labyrinthine behemoth of pipes and tubes, storage tanks and towering stacks. The giant petrochemical complex dwarfs the traditional Japanese houses in a neighboring fishing village—the mighty, contorted face of modernity towering over the squat yet stalwart remnants of tradition. "Back in the 1960s you could see the smoke, feel the vibration, smell the smell. People became active," recounts Sawai, who, as a trade union member and a victim of Yokkaichi asthma, helped lead the fight against six polluting Yokkaichi factories, three of them Mitsubishi companies.[70]

Yokkaichi was once a fishing and trading port. Its sparkling beaches stretched up and down Ise Bay, its waters teemed with mackerel, octopus and other sea life, while the surrounding land, filled with rice paddies and fields of bright yellow wildflowers, was rich and fertile. In 1955 government and corporate planners decided to turn an old navy refinery into the site of the largest of Japan's three new petrochemical facilities. By 1959 the complex, its night lights glistening, was operating twenty-four hours a day, and Yokkaichi residents rejoiced at their "million-dollar view." But the people living in and around Yokkaichi, who considered it an honor that their region would play such an important role in rebuilding Japan, did not suspect the horrors that awaited them.[71]

The main factory at the Yokkaichi complex, and also the most polluting, is the Showa oil refinery. Owned jointly by Mitsubishi Chemical* and Royal Dutch Shell, Showa takes crude oil pumped in by supertankers coming from places such as the Middle East, Indonesia and Papua New Guinea. It refines the crude into heavy oil for the power plant that provides electricity for Yokkaichi city and energy for the fac-

---

* Mitsubishi Chemical was formed in 1994 by the merger of Mitsubishi Petrochemical and Mitsubishi Kasei; for purposes of simplicity, these companies are referred to as Mitsubishi Chemical.

tories in the complex. Other refined products include gasoline, kerosene and naphtha—a key petrochemical feedstock. Plants in the Yokkaichi complex run by Mitsubishi Chemical (in joint ventures with Monsanto and BASF) use the naphtha to produce a vast array of industrial chemicals, the building blocks of modern industrial society.[72]

Like their counterparts throughout Japan in the 1950s and 1960s, Mitsubishi Chemical and other companies at the Yokkaichi complex subordinated everything to the drive for big profits and economic "development." Inevitably, those residents who had been marveling at their "million-dollar view" began to pay a heavy price. Sulfur and nitrogen oxides poisoned the air, ultimately leading to the now notorious Yokkaichi asthma. Hazardous waste wound up in open pits. Elementary school playgrounds stood in the shadows of oil storage tanks. Outfall pipes spewed effluent containing cadmium, mercury and arsenic into the bay. Oil spilled from tankers and pipelines, devastating coastal inlets, bays and beaches. Factories were rocked by explosions. Acid rain wilted flowers and corroded fishing boat propellers. Fish caught in the area smelled and tasted foul.[73] By 1960 the local government determined that 70 percent of all fish within five miles of Yokkaichi were inedible. Markets around Japan began rejecting Yokkaichi fish, and thousands of people lost their livelihood. While the local government provided some compensation, "what we really wanted," said one disgruntled fisherman, "was for the companies to stop polluting and give us back our clean sea."[74]

Not only did the Mitsubishi companies and their partners keep on polluting, they denied all responsibility for the pollution and throughout the 1960s pushed forward with plans to build more factories and expand their operations in Yokkaichi. Even as the severity of Yokkaichi asthma worsened and increasing numbers of people suffered the agony of acute respiratory distress—even as more than a thousand people stopped breathing altogether, dying from overexposure to the sulfur dioxide emissions from the Showa refinery and other Yokkaichi factories—the companies did precious little.

As the pollution increased in the mid-1960s, people in Yokkaichi and in similar places throughout Japan overcame their traditional reticence to protest publicly and began to take direct action. Fisherfolk plugged outfall pipes while residents took to the streets demanding blue skies and clean seas. These protests evoked mostly cynical reactions from the companies and their allies in government. Mitsubishi Chemical provided oxygen tanks to the hospital treating the asthma victims.[75] Companies in the complex planted trees and raised the height of their smokestacks in order to disperse the pollution. While bolstering public relations efforts, raising the stacks served only to expand the area affected by excess sulfur dioxide from 26 to 67 percent of the city.[76] Meanwhile, in league with the corporations, the mayor of Yokkaichi fed irate residents the Japanese version of a line delivered by apologists for pollution the world over: "The air pollution is nothing to worry about," he said. "You smell miso when you pass by a miso shop. You smell an industrial complex when you have one in your neighborhood."[77]

By the late sixties, frustrated victims began to pursue a series of legal strategies, filing four major pollution lawsuits. These legal actions were taken by people suffering from Yokkaichi asthma and by the victims of *itai-itai* disease (literally, "ouch-ouch" disease, because of the painful side effects of cadmium exposure), while two separate cases were brought by Minamata disease (named for the place where massive mercury poisonings first appeared in Japan) victims from different prefectures. With antipollution protests mounting throughout the country, these lawsuits had strong public backing from labor unions, doctors, teachers, academics, students, housewives, fisherfolk, farmers, artists, journalists, film producers, actors and some sectors of the news media.[78] This broad-based mass movement was, for a while, able to break the powerful corporate-state linkage and helped ensure the successful outcome of the lawsuits.

While the Minamata poisonings received more international public attention, Yokkaichi was perhaps the most significant of the big four pollution cases. For while the Minamata poisonings were caused by Chisso Chemical—an independent company whose technological and economic prowess began to decline in the 1960s—Yokkaichi embodied the *keiretsu*-conjured "economic miracle" and therefore the future of Japan.

When the Yokkaichi, Minamata and *itai-itai* victims won their lawsuits, and companies such as Mitsubishi Chemical and Chisso were found guilty of destroying the environment and people's lives, Japan's corporations and government were shocked into action. Their response was to address the worst abuses with legal, technological, financial and geographical remedies. The government legislated a body of environmental law that included strict corporate liability for environmental damage. It also created a national environment agency to enforce it.

Corporations responded to these regulatory regimes by developing end-of-the-pipe environmental technologies.[79] Indeed, Mitsubishi Heavy Industries became the global leader in producing air pollution control devices; by the early 1990s it was generating more than $3 billion in annual revenues from the business.[80] The courts also awarded some victims monetary compensation for their suffering although thousands were excluded from the legal settlements. In Yokkaichi, the citizens further won the right to inspect the industrial facilities. Moreover, Yokkaichi activists succeeded in halting Mitsubishi Chemical's plans to build a massive, 300,000-ton-per-year ethylene facility as an addition to the complex.

"They are trying to bury the past," exclaims veteran activist Yoshiro Sawai, as he earnestly explains to a visitor how the mayor of Yokkaichi, who previously worked for a Mitsubishi company, recently canceled plans to build a display about the antipollution struggle in the new city museum. "They say there's no problem now. They say they've overcome the problem."[81] Indeed, as the brochure for the Showa refinery asserts today, Mitsubishi Chemical and its partners "are trying to preserve the clean refinery, with the high quality fuel for the blue sky, with the complete effluent water treatment for the sea, and with the green trees for nature."[82] Sure enough, while there is still a whiff of oil in the air, the skies over Yokkaichi along with the water of the neighboring seas are bright blue, punctuated only by fluffy white plumes floating out from the megacomplex of refineries, power plants and chemical factories. A tree or two is also visible. Legal strictures and the Mitsubishi Group's "environmental" technology have succeeded in virtually eliminating the sulfur dioxide problem and minimizing the heavy metal effluent they were found liable for dumping into the sea.[83]

Yet while Yokkaichi asthma is fading into the forgotten past, the environmental crisis still lurks just below the green surface of the Island of Dreams. Although corporate communicators and government bureaucrats tell the Japanese public and foreign visitors that actions taken in the 1970s have resolved most environmental problems, their posture is deceptive. As scholar Jun Ui explains, the government and corporations created "an illusion whereby the people are led to believe that all the problems of the environment have been solved. . . . Government information highlights only the successes but fails to indicate the failures or the situations in which industrial power was allowed to ride roughshod over environmental considerations."[84] The issue of the poisonous, asthma-causing, potentially carcinogenic, yet much less perceptible nitrogen oxide (NOx) is a case in point. The court did not rule on nitrogen oxide in the Yokkaichi case; thus the government and corporations have not been compelled to address the problem. It is also very expensive to install the technology necessary to lower NOx levels. Thus while 90 percent of NOx reduction is technologically possible, very few factories in Yokkaichi and throughout Japan installed NOx reduction equipment after the protests and lawsuits of the 1960s.[85] More recently, the government, under corporate pressure, has watered down the already weak NOx laws that are on the books. Not surprisingly, ongoing industrial growth along with a nearly seventeen-fold increase in the number of motor vehicles in Japan between 1960 and 1990 have caused NOx air pollution to grow; as a result, while asthma has diminished from its alarmingly high levels in Yokkaichi, a success touted by the corporations and government, cases are on the rise nationally.[86]

The Yokkaichi complex is also still producing tons of hazardous waste—part of a larger dilemma throughout the country that is both masked and aggravated by the official posture. Japanese corporations officially produce just a fraction of the hazardous waste that their counterparts in the United States do, allowing them to project themselves as less polluting. Yet Japan's numbers are kept artificially low by the government's narrow definition of hazardous waste, which excludes entire categories of toxics that are listed in many other countries. This also allows what many define as hazardous waste to be disposed of in a less stringent manner. Indeed, well under 1 percent of all industrial waste in Japan is defined as hazardous.[87] Overall industrial waste production continues to rise throughout the country; by 1990 it had reached 390 million tons, or more than three tons per person, a rate that rivals that of the United States.[88]

The Export of Kogai: Globalizing the *Keiretsu*

Coinciding with the antipollution movement's victories in the early 1970s was Japan's accelerated economic expansion into East Asia. The combination of growing regulatory pressure at home and widening investment horizons in the region made it a fairly logical proposition to quell domestic dissent and avoid the high costs of pollution control by siting some dirty industrial facilities elsewhere. Countries such as the

Philippines, South Korea, Taiwan, Thailand, Malaysia and Indonesia became targets for the export of *kogai*.

While sulfur dioxide pollution rapidly declined in Yokkaichi and elsewhere in Japan in the 1970s, South Korea experienced concomitant increases. Growing Japanese and U.S. investment in petrochemical and industrial complexes, the failure of these corporations to bring with them the pollution control devices required at home and local government repression of environmentalists combined to spur an 11 percent annual growth rate in pollution-intensive industries. By 1978 South Korea, which accepted U.S. and Japanese dirty industries with open arms, achieved the status of world-class polluter when a United Nations study singled out Seoul's air as having "the highest sulfur-dioxide content of the world's major cities."[89] Similar problems were occurring in the rest of the region, where cheap labor, lax environmental standards and undemocratic governments made for attractive investment opportunities. In 1974 Asahi Glass, a Mitsubishi Group company, was found by activists to be dumping mercury into Thailand's Chao Phraya River.[90] Around the same time, Kawasaki Steel, a member of the Dai Ichi Kangyo Group, located the most polluting portion of its metal works on the island of Mindanao in the Philippines. This was done, according to Japanese activists, to "dodge the strong anti-pollution sentiments and pressure from anti-pollution groups" in Chiba city, near Tokyo. In the process, the Marcos dictatorship evicted more than 2,000 villagers from their lands, so as to make room for the factory.[91] In Indonesia, Semarang Diamond Chemical, owned jointly by Showa Chemical, Mitsubishi Corporation and Indonesian investors, began operations near the city of Semarang in central Java in 1977. Soon after, neighboring villages' well water was poisoned, their rice plants withered and their fish died.[92] At the same time that this pollution export was occurring, Japanese natural resource extraction—including mining, forestry, oil and coal—from the Asia-Pacific region and elsewhere was growing exponentially.

By the mid-1980s Japan had emerged as the major economic power in East Asia and much of the Pacific, supplanting U.S. dominance and sending yet another surge of hazardous industry into the region. The September 1985 Plaza Accords on currency realignment, agreed to by the ministers of the world's five most powerful economies, aimed to shift some of the weight of global economic power from its nearly singular post–World War II resting place on the shoulders of the United States. In essence, the Plaza Accords meant that the ever more vigorous economies of Japan and Germany were to take on more central roles.[93] The agreement nearly doubled the value of the yen against the dollar, thus increasing the price of Japanese manufactured goods. Conversely, the Plaza Accords radically increased the yen's buying power, opening the floodgates for a torrent of Japanese capital to rush into the Asia-Pacific area, making it the second-largest target of Japanese corporate investment after the United States.[94] By the end of 1992, cumulative Japanese investment in Asia (mostly Southeast Asia) was triple what it was in 1985 and almost twice the size of cumulative U.S. investment there.[95]

Japan has become the core economy in an informal, yet de facto, Asia-Pacific trading bloc—the fastest-growing economic region on Earth in the last two decades of the twentieth century. Japan is the number-one exporter to the region. It is also the second-largest importer of goods from the region, after the United States. All in all, it is the region's top trading partner and its largest aid donor—aid that is often used strategically and efficiently to support Japanese corporate expansion (See Chapter Five). Most importantly, while high-speed industrialization has made economic "tigers" out of many East Asian countries, such as Taiwan and South Korea, Japan has maintained control of much of the economic capital and technology—machinery and high-tech components—that underlie these new "miracle economies." As a U.S. government study notes, much of the high-speed, export-oriented economic growth in East Asia is now "financed and controlled by Japanese multinationals." The study suggests that "a casual survey of low end Japanese consumer electronics goods and cameras in the market today will show that while the name may be Sony, Canon or Sharp, the country of origin is likely to be Malaysia, Thailand or China."[96] Additionally, while new transnational corporations such as Taiwan's premier chemical company Formosa Plastics, the Thai agribusiness conglomerate Chareon Pokphand, the Malaysian logging transnational Rimbunan Hijau and the South Korean *chaebol* (similar to the *keiretsu*) such as Daewoo, Samsung and Hyundai have entered the ranks of the world's top corporations, they are not as independent as they may seem. They may compete with Japanese corporations for a piece of the action in the lucrative U.S. market, but at the same time they are highly dependent on Japanese technology and finance. Hyundai, for example, makes its bestselling Excel subcompact car with an engine designed by Mitsubishi Motors and a transmission both designed and manufactured by Mitsubishi Motors. Mitsubishi also owns 15 percent of Hyundai Motors.[97] As the U.S. government study concludes, "for all intends [sic] and purposes, some countries' industrial policies appear practically to be made in Tokyo."

In their more candid moments, Japanese corporate executives and government officials don't argue with such assertions. Listen to Hisahiko Okazaki, Japanese ambassador to Thailand in the early 1990s, who, writing in the Tokyo magazine *This Is*, declares that while the dramatic increase in direct investment from Japan "is already a grand spectacle . . . it has only just begun." Asserting that Japan can afford to triple its overseas investment without destabilizing its domestic base, Okazaki explains that growing Japanese ventures in the region are designed to incorporate the Asia-Pacific nations into "*an overseas keiretsu system* with captive imports and captive exports" [emphasis added]. By building this regional platform, he remarks, "the Japanese economy will expand globally." Japan is clearly building such a platform today in an effort to optimize the competitiveness of its corporations in the age of globalization. While in his analysis Ambassador Okazaki ignores the export of pollution-intensive industries discussed above, he describes three subsequent waves of Japanese corporate investment in East Asia. The first wave, writes Okazaki, was the movement of a number of automobile and consumer electronics operations offshore. This has been followed by a second wave of smaller Japanese subcontractors that supply parts to these industries. The third wave, which Ambassador Okazaki anticipated in 1992 and now appears to be under way, is based on "the relocation of heavy chemical manufacturers."[98]

The Mitsubishi Group's recent activities in the Asia-Pacific region confirm the ambassador's predictions of this third wave. In the early 1990s Mitsubishi Chemical completed work on a major petrochemical complex in South Korea as well as a polyvinylchloride complex in Indonesia.[99] Mitsubishi Corporation is aggressively expanding the Group's chemical business into China, building a 300,000-ton-per-year ethylene plant in Guandong Province and leading a Big Six joint venture to develop and manage a major $4 billion petrochemical facility in Liaoning Province.[100] The Group is extending its chemical empire to India, where it plans to build a polypropylene polymer facility with the German company BASF, and is also investing in pesticide production.[101] Japan's other major *keiretsu* appear to be following similar patterns. By developing this "overseas *keiretsu* system" these corporations are not just exporting dirty industry, but as described in Chapter Five, they are also playing their part in the dynamics of globalization, seeking cheap labor, lax environmental controls and new markets.

Japan's central role in creating Asia's "miracle economies" has also been a key factor in generating the region's environmental crisis. What until very recently were primarily traditional agricultural societies have been rapidly transformed into economies based on mass industrial extraction, production, consumption and disposal of resources. The telescoping, into a few short decades, of industrial development processes that evolved over much longer periods of time in industrialized countries such as the United States has had traumatizing effects on the environment and people of the region.[102] Farmers and villagers are pushed off their land or poisoned by pesticides. The seas are either contaminated by agribusiness run-off and toxic development or overfished by industrial fishing, or both. The air in most large urban areas is grossly polluted, and more often than not drinking water is contaminated by toxic chemicals.[103] The rapid escalation of the environmental crisis in the region has also given birth to an increasingly vital environmental movement demanding clean air, land, water and food. This region-wide protest has cast the economic "success" of East Asia's industrialization in a different light.[104]

It was in this context of growing environmental problems and protest that the case of Asian Rare Earth emerged as one of a number of incidents that illuminated the ecological and social impacts of rapid economic growth in the region. This case, in which a Mitsubishi company played a central role, began as part of the initial round of Japan's hazardous exports in the 1970s. Over time it evolved in tandem with East Asia's economic boom, emerging in the public spotlight in the early 1990s at a moment when the managers of the Island of Dreams were moving to consolidate and escalate their investment, influence and control in Southeast Asia. The exposure it received sent pulses of shock and embarrassment back up through the hierarchies of corporate Japan.

Meenakshi Raman stands no taller than five feet. Often dressed in a khaki shirt and jeans, this vivacious young Malaysian woman of Indian descent does not look like the type to make *keiretsu* executives tremble in their blue suits or the Malaysian government turn its powerful security apparatus on red alert. But anyone who has been in a legal tangle with Ms. Raman knows that she is not to be taken lightly. It was Raman and her colleagues at the Consumers Association of Penang who worked with local villagers in the small town of Bukit Merah to take Mitsubishi Kasei (now Mitsubishi Chemical) and its Malaysian joint venture partner in the Asian Rare Earth (ARE) company to court for poisoning them with radioactive waste. Compounds such as rare earth chloride and rare earth carbonate are extracted and refined from a byproduct of tin mining known as monozite mineral. These compounds are used in Japan, elsewhere in East Asia and in the United States in the manufacture of computers, medical and communications lasers, magnets for motors and color televisions. One of the byproducts of rare earth production is thorium hydroxide, a low-level radioactive material that is discarded as waste. Asian Rare Earth produced 250 tons of this waste annually, and the company was accused of indiscriminately dumping it behind the factory in old broken barrels and plastic bags, prompting the residents of Bukit Merah to sue the company for negligence.[105]

Rare earth compounds used to be produced in Japan, until the process was determined by authorities to be environmentally hazardous. In 1969 the Japanese government established regulations that raised the cost of waste disposal to the point where Japan's rare earth industry began to relocate production. In 1973 Mitsubishi Kasei decided to set up a factory in Malaysia, a country rich in tin and therefore monozite.[106] The ARE company, owned 35 percent by Mitsubishi Kasei, finally began operations in 1982. Its factory, located within half a mile of more than 1,000 Chinese-Malaysian villagers, became the focal point of conflict.

Despite Mitsubishi Kasei's and ARE's vehement denials of any wrongdoing, various medical experts and scientists who testified in court found that it was extremely likely that the people of Bukit Merah were suffering from radiation poisoning. A former employee told the courtroom that the company put no stipulations on how he was to dispose of the radioactive thorium hydroxide waste, which he subsequently dumped in various uncontrolled sites. Not surprisingly, sometime after this incident, a Japanese professor recorded unusually high levels of radiation on the outskirts of the plant. During the trial, three cases of childhood leukemia surfaced within a six-month period, a rate that was forty-two times higher than the national average. A disproportionate number of children were found to be suffering from lead poisoning (lead is also a byproduct of rare earth processing and a potential indicator of radiation exposure). Some newborn children suffered neurological problems, and others developed brain tumors. The rate of miscarriages, prenatal deaths and neonatal deaths in the plant's vicinity amounted to more than five times the national average.[107]

In 1992, after seven years of litigation—with all of the evidence in, the testimony of some of ARE's witnesses discredited and thousands of villagers from the Bukit Merah area demonstrating outside the High Court for ARE's closure—Judge Peh Swee Chin ruled in favor of the villagers and against Mitsubishi Kasei and its joint venture partner, ordering the plant shut. The ruling resounded throughout Malaysia, the rest of Southeast Asia and Japan. Facing calls by Japanese Diet members for laws to regulate Japanese corporate activities abroad, confronted with severe criticism from some government agencies and blasted by the Japanese media for betraying "the spirit of the times," Mitsubishi Kasei was intransigent.[108] The company's senior executive, Masao Sato, told the director general of Japan's Environment Agency that the ruling was the result of overly strict pollution control standards in Malaysia.[109] In turn, Mitsubishi's attitude caused concern in the Malaysian government that the country would no longer be seen by global corporations as having a "favorable" investment climate. As many people expected, in early 1994 the much more political Malaysian Supreme Court overturned the High Court's ruling on appeal, citing a lack of evidence. With this legal victory in hand, Mitsubishi Kasei closed the ARE factory and began importing most of its rare earth from an intermediary in China.

Despite the fact that Mitsubishi Kasei and the Malaysian government kept any legal precedent that would hinder future investment from being established, the villagers still achieved their objective. Moreover, as Meenakshi Raman comments, the case had a powerful effect on communities throughout Malaysia by "exposing the double standards of transnational corporations like Mitsubishi, while serving as an example of how people, if they are organized, can make a difference."[110] In Japan, the ARE case stirred a debate about the role and responsibilities of Japanese corporations operating abroad. The calls for regulation of Japanese transnationals' overseas activities—regulations that could potentially conflict with international trade agreements such as GATT—did not get very far in the Diet. But the Mitsubishi Group and Japan's other *keiretsu* realized that if they did not address the environmental impacts of their companies' foreign investments, they were setting themselves up to be buried by an avalanche of national and international criticism. As Nobuo Kojima, a Japanese lawyer who assisted Ms. Raman and her colleagues in the lawsuit, comments, "Before this case

Japanese corporations never considered the environmental effect outside Japan. Now environment is on their checklist for foreign investment."[111]

In response to the ARE case, in an attempt to avoid legislation that
would control their activity, in recognition of the growing global climate of environmental concern and anticipating future environmental
problems related to Japanese foreign investment, the Japanese Federation of Economic Organizations, Keidanren—a more powerful
Japanese version of the Chamber of Commerce—created a voluntary environmental code of conduct called the Global Environmental Charter.
Established in 1991, these guidelines, says Mr. Kojima, "are quite good
on paper, but reality is something else." As Keidanren itself admits, a
large percentage of Japanese companies have not followed through on
the Charter with their overseas subsidiaries and affiliates.[112] But "when
a problem happens," remarks Kojima, "every company hides behind the
guidelines. So we are quite suspicious about how they execute the
guidelines in reality."[113]

For its part, Mitsubishi Kasei, stung by the ARE case, put the environment on its checklist in its own sort of way. According to Kenzo
Tamura, manager for Mitsubishi Kasei's public relations department, the
next time the corporation locates an environmentally sensitive project
abroad, it will take care in choosing a less activist village.[114] A problem
that the Mitsubishi Group and other *keiretsu* face, however, is that there
will definitely be more activist villages in Malaysia and elsewhere as a
result of ARE and similar cases. Certainly, ARE and tragedies like the
Bhopal disaster have prompted transnational corporations to proceed
with more caution and fewer double standards when investing in the
Third World. Yet the transnationals are clearly moving forward with
gusto, pouring billions of dollars into the expansion or relocation of
dirty industries like chemical manufacturing. When it becomes necessary, they step behind the green veil of environmental charters, mani-
festos and public relations departments designed to improve the corporate image. They also regularly remove themselves from direct responsibility by subcontracting the dirty work. Thus their most destructive
activities become less and less visible, as is the case with Mitsubishi
Kasei's (now Mitsubishi Chemical) new source of rare earth. Located in
China, where government repression guarantees less activist villages,
the rare earth processing is contracted out to a Chinese company and
exported through a small trading company.[115] The project might be
financed by a Mitsubishi company, the technology licensed by

Mitsubishi Chemical, and the product used by Mitsubishi Electric to build computers and televisions, but the *keiretsu*'s visible responsibility is now many steps removed. Dream Island's polluters have once again maneuvered to become invisible.

Timber Transnationals and Forest Blockades

Corporate Japan has demonstrated its ability to hide behind surrogate companies and cloak itself in green camouflage. This is the case not only when it comes to domestic environmental issues or the relocation of hazardous industry to the Third World, but also with regard to Japan's massive natural resource procurement and processing activities. It is especially true in terms of the Big Six *keiretsu*'s socially and environmentally destructive logging operations, which have come under scathing attack from environmentalists around the globe. The Mitsubishi Group once again plays a central role in this drama.

As one of its myriad economic activities, the Mitsubishi Corporation functions as a global wood products transnational, operating in both tropical and temperate regions of the world. Through investments, joint ventures and contract arrangements, its logging and milling operations are devastating some of the richest forests of the planet. In Sarawak, Malaysia, for instance, Mitsubishi joint ventures and subsidiaries harvested rainforest logs and milled plywood for more than two decades, terminating operations in 1995. The Mitsubishi Corporation is a major purchaser and marketer of plywood from Indonesia in tandem with Barito Pacific, a local corporation that took over Mitsubishi's 550 square miles of timber concessions when the government there banned raw log exports.[116] The Mitsubishi joint venture Eidai do Brasil is one of the largest milling operations in the Brazilian Amazon; the company subcontracts to log suppliers who, in their search for quality raw material, have penetrated some of the deepest, most pristine reaches of the Amazon Basin.[117] Despite resistance from local communities fighting for their resource rights, the Mitsubishi Corporation's Bolivian joint venture, Suto Limitada, is cutting tropical forests in the Bolivian Amazon, including endangered mahogany. In Chile, the Mitsubishi Corporation owns a wood-chip mill, Astillas Exportaciones (Astex), which purchases its raw material from local suppliers, spurring the destruction of native forests (wood chips are used for pulp and paper production). Forestal Tierra Chilena, a company owned jointly by Mitsubishi Corporation and Mitsubishi Paper Mills, is converting native forests in territories traditionally occupied by indigenous Mapuche communities into ecologically destructive monocrop eucalyptus plantations.[118]

The Mitsubishi Corporation's forest operations are just as widespread in the world's northern boreal forests. The *sogo shosha* is not only a major importer of tropical timber into the United States, but is also one of the largest wood exporters from the U.S. Pacific Northwest.[119] Purchasing from Weyerhaeuser, as it has done historically, Mitsubishi exports enough U.S. Douglas fir and hemlock logs to Japan to fill 140 football fields six feet high every year. The corporation's exports of American-milled wood chips could fill another 174 fields.[120] The Mitsubishi Corporation imports logs and sawn wood from Siberia and the Russian Far East—tapping that region's vast temperate forests inhabited by various indigenous peoples, as well as the endangered Siberian tiger.[121] In Alberta, Canada, the Mitsubishi Corporation is the majority owner of the largest chlorine bleach pulp and paper mill in the world, called Al-Pac. Built with Canadian government subsidies, it supplies paper to Europe, Asia and North America. And in British Columbia, the Mitsubishi Corporation built the largest disposable chopstick factory in the world.[122]

Other *sogo shosha* such as Sumitomo, Itochu (Dai Ichi Kangyo Group), Marubeni (Fuyo Group), Nichimen (Sanwa Group), Nissho Iwai (Sanwa and Dai Ichi Kangyo) and Mitsui carry out logging, milling pulp and paper, purchasing, transport and wood marketing operations more or less equivalent to Mitsubishi's in size and scope. Yet according to the San Francisco–based Rainforest Action Network (RAN), which has mobilized an ongoing boycott against Mitsubishi in the United States—the *keiretsu*'s most important foreign market—"the Mitsubishi Group is the worst destroyer of rainforests [both tropical and temperate] in the world."

Both RAN and the World Rainforest Movement, an international network of activist organizations, have singled out the Mitsubishi *keiretsu* for this ignominious distinction for five key reasons. First, in addition to Mitsubishi's *sogo shosha*, a wide range of Group members play active roles in forest destruction. Mitsubishi Heavy builds mill equipment. Mitsubishi Bank provides financing. Mitsubishi Motors makes logging trucks. As a partner in Chevron's operations, Mitsubishi Oil explores for petroleum in the pristine forests of Papua New Guinea. And in Burma, the Mitsubishi Corporation is both helping to build a natural gas pipeline through the country's pristine tropical forests, while also purchasing teak taken from the country's rainforests.[123] Despite ongoing protests by local communities, Mitsubishi Materials is developing copper mining operations in the biologically diverse and extremely threatened forests of Ecuador's Choco region. Nippon Yusen is a major timber shipper. Tokio Marine provides insurance. While other *keiretsu* may have similar arrangements, RAN insists that "we have identified no other corporate family with as broad an involvement in forest exploitation activities."[124]

Second, Mitsubishi has a record of forest destruction that dates back more than fifty years. This cumulative damage is a significant factor in Mitsubishi's ranking. Third, RAN notes that the Mitsubishi Corporation's forest-related activities bring with them a long record of price fixing, antitrust violations, transfer-pricing and other alleged violations of the law, making it "one of the worst" forest products groups "in terms of legal transgressions." Fourth, the Mitsubishi Corporation's extensive and sophisticated public relations campaign has not only obfuscated many of the issues, but, as RAN observes, has become "a model which other logging companies have quickly emulated to mask their destruction." And fifth, when the Mitsubishi Group's and its subsidiaries' global imports and exports of tropical and temperate timber are added up, RAN believes that it may in fact be the largest wood products group in the world. All of this combines to make it possibly the largest single destroyer of forests on the planet.[125] Such a distinction may be hard to prove, as more accurate calculations have been made extremely difficult by Japanese industry associations, which have increasingly restricted information. The Mitsubishi Group has also become adept at hiding its role in forest destruction. The case of Southeast Asia is a prime example.

As the Mitsubishi Corporation and other *sogo shosha* became targets of international criticism in the 1980s, many began fading into the woodwork, making themselves less visible while allowing lower-profile, less vulnerable Southeast Asian corporations to act essentially as subcontractors to Japan's demands. The Japanese *sogo shosha* do the buying, but they are doing less and less of the cutting. Instead, Malaysian, Thai, Indonesian and South Korean timber corporations are chopping up as much of the region's remaining forests as they can get their hands on and shipping the wood overseas, primarily to the Japanese market. This change also fits into the general pattern of economic development in the Asian region, where processing and manufacturing is shifting from high-wage Japan to lower-wage countries. Indonesian and Malaysian corporations, for example, are grabbing ever larger market shares in the plywood industry, consuming some of this wood domestically as their economies continue to grow, while exporting significant amounts to the U.S., European, Chinese, Taiwanese, South Korean and Japanese markets.[126] The situation in Papua New Guinea, the central battlefield in Southeast Asia's timber wars in the 1990s, is indicative of the shift in Japanese strategy and the emergence of new Asian "tiger" transnational corporations, many of whose regional activities function in the interests of the *keiretsu*.

Nearly 80 percent of Papua New Guinea (PNG) is covered by the fourth-largest remaining stand of tropical rainforests on the planet; only in the Amazon, Congo and Indonesia can larger tracts be found.[127] Papua New Guinea is a rugged paradise, a place where many of the hundreds of linguistically diverse cultures had never encountered the wheel until they saw tires rolling along under the wings of a bush plane. The horizon is punctuated by active volcanoes whose smoke pirouettes into the heavens and whose occasional eruptions spew lava over towns and villages. The palm-fringed coasts are ringed by coral reefs that teem with life under the refracted rays of a blazing sun. But as the global economy runs head on into remnants of the Stone Age, some of these last great tropical forests and the people in them are being mowed down.

This is a relatively recent phenomenon. In the 1970s various Japanese timber companies, such as Nissho Iwai and Honshu Paper, set up subsidiaries on the coastal fringes of PNG's timber reserves, a vast resource base the size of California, commercially valued at $70 billion.[128] The Mitsubishi Corporation came in a little later, beginning operations in 1984 by creating a "national" company named United Timber, which it directly financed and from which it exclusively purchased high-quality logs. United undermeasured, undergraded and underpriced its log exports, allowing the Mitsubishi Corporation to pay lower taxes and to secretly transfer profits out of PNG and into a Hong Kong tax haven. United Timber was found by the Barnett Commission, an official PNG government inquiry, to be guilty of transfer-pricing $1.5 million out of the country in less than two years, exclusively for the benefit of Mitsubishi.[129]

Taken alone, this may seem like a trivial amount of money for a global giant such as Mitsubishi. But it was not an isolated incident for the company, nor for Papua New Guinea. Mitsubishi has employed similar practices in other parts of the world, as discussed earlier in the case of the Alaska Pulp Company. And, according to the Barnett Commission, in the two-year period between 1986 and 1987, PNG lost more than $31 million in foreign exchange earnings and taxes, or about 15 percent of the industry's total earnings, to transfer-pricing carried out primarily by Japanese corporations. Barnett writes that these transnationals were "roaming the countryside with the self-assurance of robber barons, bribing politicians and leaders, creating social disharmony and ignoring laws in order to gain access to, rip out, and export . . . valuable timber." [130]

Since then, the forest crisis has intensified in PNG. The abuses that the Barnett Commission exposed have become even more widespread and entrenched than before. [131] What has changed is that this broad expansion of deforestation has not been led on the ground by the Japanese, but rather by a single Malaysian logging corporation, Rimbunan Hijau Sdn. Bhd. (in English, "Green Forest"). It is estimated that Rimbunan Hijau controls an astounding 60 to 80 percent of timber exports from PNG. [132] However, Japanese trading companies, including Mitsubishi, still import significant quantities of logs from the country.

Rimbunan Hijau and most of the new transnational Malaysian logging corporations got their start in the ancient rainforests of Sabah and Sarawak in Malaysian Borneo. Japanese corporations supplied both the credit and the market that enabled these ethnic Chinese-owned and -run companies to emerge as powerful players in the Southeast Asian logging industry. [133] They made fortunes cutting Malaysian Borneo's sparsely populated tropical forests and selling the logs to companies such as the Mitsubishi Corporation for export to Japan, South Korea and Taiwan, leaving the area's indigenous Iban, Kayan, Penan and other peoples very little, if anything, to show in terms of economic gain. In fact, the logging operations in Sarawak in the 1970s and 1980s wrenched many indigenous peoples from subsistence-oriented lifestyles into a market economy, upsetting patterns of customary land rights, disrupting traditional social structures and destroying their resource base—leaving behind a legacy of pollution, soil erosion, siltation, poverty and hunger. [134]

Sarawak and Sabah's dwindling forests, growing legal and direct-action protests by indigenous peoples against the destruction of their traditional lands and way of life, shifting economic dynamics in the region and increasing international criticism all prompted change in the early 1990s. Japanese corporations increasingly removed themselves from direct logging, while the Malaysian corporations, having converted many of Sarawak's forests into liquid assets, sought to reinvest some of those financial resources in a national plywood industry, oil palm plantations and new logging operations overseas.[135] With bans on log exports from the devastated rainforests of Indonesia (1985) and Thailand (1989), and a total ban on any logging in the few remaining virgin forests of the Philippines (1992), these corporations have expanded their operations to the Solomon Islands, Papua New Guinea and even South America.[136]

As a result, the amount of wood exported from PNG quadrupled between 1980 and 1992 and continued to increase dramatically as other tropical timber supplies in the region dwindled. Between 1992 and 1993, for example, exports increased by more than one-third, jumping from 6.6 million cubic feet to nearly 9 million cubic feet (roughly 3 million trees a year).[137] And while the Japanese *sogo shosha* are not directly involved in the bulk of the country's multimillion-dollar logging operations, they continue to procure the majority of PNG's timber resources. Thus they wash their hands of the destruction their demand wreaks and that corporations like Rimbunan Hijau carry out, including changing the course of rivers, destroying community gardens, polluting traditional water supplies and ripping up coral reefs so that log ships bound for places such as Shin Kiba can pull into isolated areas.

And while the trees of PNG's vast rainforests are sent off to Japanese and Korean sawmills and plywood factories, the development the corporations promise local villagers is most often an illusion.[138] Similar to the situation in Sarawak, very little benefit is accruing to the local people, who are often divided and conquered by the logging corporations— conned into selling off the land and forests that have sustained them for generations.[139] Consequently, Papua New Guinea spirals into deeper poverty and ecological instability, the Malaysian corporations and some corrupt PNG government officials get rich and the Japanese corporations get their logs without getting their hands dirty.

Green Dreams

After coming under fire for its activities in Malaysia, PNG and elsewhere in the world, the Mitsubishi Corporation moved to address its international critics, promoting itself as a global environmental leader. The first step it took was in 1989, when it created a Committee for Global Environmental Problems. Then in 1990 it established an Environmental Affairs Department to carry out its policies.[140] This department has become the principal voice for the *sogo shosha* on forest and other eco-

logical issues. As mentioned in Chapter One, it immediately responded
to its critics by placing the blame for deforestation on the poor. It also
began to deny involvement in destructive projects, claiming that its logging policy was "based on sustainable forest management."[141]

Stating that "we are working with the sincere intention of sustaining
the rainforests, not only for the good of the environment, but for the
future of our fellow human beings in Asia and around the world," the
Environmental Affairs Department launched a series of proactive initiatives.[142] It started research into alternatives to the plywood *konpane*
molding used in the construction industry. It sponsored experimental
reforestation projects in Malaysia and Brazil designed to rehabilitate
devastated tropical rainforest ecosystems by planting native species—a
potential model, Mitsubishi suggested, that if successful could be applied throughout the world.[143] Leading up to the 1992 Earth Summit,
the Mitsubishi Corporation's chairman, Shinroku Morihashi, joined the
Business Council for Sustainable Development, declaring that "we believe a business cannot continue to exist without the trust and respect
of society for its environmental performance." The Mitsubishi Corporation has also participated in Keidanren's new Nature Conservation
Fund, which collaborates with Conservation International, the Nature
Conservancy and other environmental organizations to support projects around the world.[144] It has created an environmental foundation in
the United States headed by the director of its public relations department there, and it prints its business cards with green ink on tree-free
paper.[145]

While many of these initiatives succeeded in drawing a green veil
over the face of the Mitsubishi Corporation's environmental destruction, they had little effect on its fundamental approach to the forest
products industry, and a number were found to be lacking. For instance,
the Environmental Affairs Department's $3 million pilot program to
restore rainforests was so costly—$40,000 per hectare over the first three
years—that it could not hope to replicate this effort on a scale relevant
to the problem. Moreover, overall forest destruction in places like
Sarawak, spurred by demand from corporations such as Mitsubishi, pro-
ceeds at such a pace that restoration projects cannot keep up. Indeed,
when pressured, the leader of the project himself, Yokohama University
professor Akira Miyawaki, acknowledged that the best way to preserve a
rainforest ecosystem is to stop cutting it down.[146]

The reforestation project has, however, helped Mitsubishi's public
relations effort to green its image.[147] For instance, it played a prominent

role in a comic book funded by the Mitsubishi Corporation, produced by the Japanese Ministry of Education and distributed to every high school library in Japan. In the comic, entitled *For Gaia*, a Mitsubishi employee is shocked by "Japan-bashing" allegations in the U.S. press that his company is destroying the rainforest. Mitsubishi then sends him to Southeast Asia to discover the truth. There he finds the poor destroying the forest and Mitsubishi replanting it.[148] Fortunately in this case, environmentalists protesting the comic book's distribution caused such a scandal that the Ministry of Education was forced to recall it.[149]

Despite this setback, the company's environmental affairs department continued its activities, touting its tree planting, blaming the poor and denying Mitsubishi's complicity in the world deforestation problem. They did so, much to the dismay of some inside the Mitsubishi Group. As one senior manager from a Mitsubishi core company laments, "The Mitsubishi Corporation's environmental protection section is only for public relations. They don't think seriously about environment. Essentially they want to earn money. That's Mitsubishi Corporation's attitude. . . . This is a very sad issue for me." The official also cites similar "conservative" approaches to the environment in other leading group companies such as Mitsubishi Heavy Industries and Mitsubishi Electric.[150]

Campaigners from the Rainforest Action Network and the Japan Tropical Forest Action Network (JATAN) have come to similar conclusions. After nearly five years of organizing a U.S. boycott of all Mitsubishi products—from Kirin beer to Nikon cameras to Mitsubishi televisions—of carrying out civil disobedience at Mitsubishi Motor shows, and of taking other high-profile actions, RAN got the Mitsubishi Corporation to the table. By calling for citizens to boycott all Mitsubishi products, these organizations have aimed to change not only the *keiretsu*'s practices, but to trigger a transformation of the entire Japanese and, indeed, the world forest products industry.[151] Once in negotiations, however, the company was intransigent. "Their response to us every step of the way," says RAN's former Mitsubishi Campaign coordinator Michael Marx, was "only PR. There's been no movement."[152] JATAN coordinator Yoichi Kuroda concurs, assessing the Mitsubishi Corporation's response to the campaign as "damage control."[153]

However, some opportunities to move this corporate giant have arisen. As Marx observes, "Occasionally Mitsubishi discovers an opportunity to make money and transform its operations at the same time." And RAN has molded its strategy into three prongs to take advantage of this crack in the *keiretsu*'s seemingly impenetrable structure. While keeping up the boycott, it has first proposed to the Mitsubishi Corporation that it can improve its image by turning truly green, halting all new logging in old-growth forests and developing alternative products such as nonchlorine-bleached paper produced with agricultural byproducts rather than wood products. Second, it has shown the *sogo shosha* how such a shift could be profitable for it in the short term. And third, it has argued that such changes are inevitable in the future and that the Group's long-term profitability and competitiveness will be enhanced by an early transformation. "They may be buying it," says Marx, putting an optimistic spin on the situation. "But they will never acknowledge that changes they may make were caused by this campaign." [154]

Given Mitsubishi's and other *sogo shosha*'s abilities to coordinate activities within their groups, they have tremendous potential both to mitigate a broad spectrum of environmentally destructive behavior and, in the longer term, to lead far-reaching technological and economic transformations that could make large contributions toward global environmental sustainability. In spite of the environmental affairs department's public relations orientation, the Mitsubishi Group has begun to awaken to the ecological implications of its economic actions, realizing that it has more than just a green image problem. It has been forced to see that its wide-ranging activities have enormous environmental impacts— effects whose repercussions are not at all good for business, let alone the health of the planet. Perhaps it may just be possible for Mitsubishi to respond to the RAN campaign and other sources of pressure by transforming itself into a leader in promoting sustainable forest products.

What's more, in response to the growing market for environmental goods and services, various Mitsubishi companies are conducting in-depth research on developing "environmental" products, including remote sensing devices to track environmental trends, plastic *konpane*, recycled paper and solar-energy-based water purification systems. In China, a Mitsubishi company participated in a deep-well drilling project as a part of a national program to increase drinking water supply and quality. And Mitsubishi Corporation has brought desulfurization technology to Eastern Europe.[155] Between twenty and thirty of Mitsubishi's core companies meet once or twice a month to share information on environmental trends and business development, creating the potential for significant advances in the broad array of fields in which Mitsubishi is involved.

However, Mitsubishi's potential to direct its prowess along the path of sustainability is tainted by the green spin it attempts to give its traditional activities. For instance, some of the efforts that the Group labels environmentalist, such as developing advanced nuclear technology, are not socially and environmentally sound ventures. Indeed, much of the "environmental business" that the Mitsubishi Group says it is carrying out to promote "sustainable development" is what many consider to be part of the problem. These projects include hazardous and solid waste incinerators, "low emission" chlorine bleach pulp mills, monocrop eucalyptus plantations, natural gas operations and a solar-driven salt mine, which provides a key input to chlorine production at the expense of the last pristine breeding ground for the California gray whale in Baja California, Mexico. Most of these activities are facing local, national and international resistance. What's more, some of the environmental trends that Mitsubishi tracks (perhaps with cruder technology than remote sensing devices) turn out to be the strategies, tactics and activities of those opposing their projects. In 1993, for example, when the nuclear fuel reprocessing issue was heating up in Japan, the government and major utilities contracted with the Mitsubishi Corporation to use its vast global network to conduct a study of Greenpeace's antinuclear activities.[156]

If the Mitsubishi Group is to transform itself into an agent that promotes sustainability, it must forge deeper change than simply labeling some of its most destructive activities "green." Such change would entail phasing out entire areas of economic activity that are at the root of Mitsubishi's and the Big Six's power and history. Such transformation is highly unlikely without very organized, powerful, ongoing international pressure that is orders of magnitude stronger than the initiatives of Japan's antipollution movement of the 1960s. An important first step in this direction is for ordinary Japanese citizens to break out of the artificial bubble that encases the Island of Dreams. By doing so, they can confront the unsustainable nature of their country's resource consumption and lifestyle, addressing the role that they as individuals play, but also seeking to exert more democratic control over seemingly omnipotent entities such as Mitsubishi and the rest of Japan Inc.

Chapter Five

Toxic Empire

The World Bank, Free Trade and the Migration of Hazardous Industry

Sustainable development recognizes that poverty is the ultimate polluter and hunger has no environmental conscience.

Frank Popoff, Chairman, Dow Chemical Corporation

Inequity . . . allows the powerful and rich to usurp a disproportionate and unsustainable share of natural resources, while forcing the weak and poor to overstrain whatever little resources are left with them. It allows the powerful to defile and pollute the water, air and soil, while forcing the weak to bear the consequences of such defilement.

Ashish Kothari, Indian Environmentalist

As transnational corporate investment accelerates in the "emerging markets" of the Third World, so does the environmental crisis. Indeed, it can be said that economic globalization is facilitating the Southward expansion of polluting production and consumption patterns that until recent decades had been largely limited to the countries of the industrialized North. Some of the rhetoric behind this surge, which in 1995 had reached nearly $100 billion a year—increasing the Third World's share of all direct foreign investment to nearly 40 percent—claims that it will promote "sustainable development" to alleviate poverty.[1] The reality is something different.

This chapter attempts to uncover the true nature of this toxic empire of chemical facilities, oil refineries, auto factories, tree plantations, pulp mills, power plants and a myriad of other ventures that continue to spread across the globe in the name of development. It examines four of the empire's most important facets. It looks first at the role that the World Bank, International Monetary Fund and other multilateral and bilateral development institutions play in promoting and creating the conditions for transnational corporate investment in the Third World. Second, the chapter examines the relationship between transnational corporations and free trade agreements. Third, it documents the movement of hazardous industry from the Northern industrialized nations to the countries of the South, examining the double standards involved in this migration and three general paths that such toxic globalization takes. And fourth, it looks at the corporate world's response to the environmental crisis its investment is generating.

The Corporate Development Banks

Every year the World Bank and its regional counterparts, such as the Asian Development Bank, the Inter-American Development Bank, the African Development Bank and the European Bank for Reconstruction and Development, collectively known as multilateral development banks (MDBs), lend $45 billion to the so-called developing world. This money in turn leverages support by bilateral aid agencies, private finance and other sources for projects and programs whose total cost is estimated at well over $130 billion.[2]

The ostensible goal of this "development finance" is to alleviate poverty in the Third World by stimulating economic growth. Yet in many respects these loans, which have integrated vast human populations and expanses of natural resources into the world economy, deliver far greater benefit to the governing elite of stratified Southern societies, to transnational corporate contractors and investors and to the globalization agenda of the donor governments of the industrialized North than they do to the impoverished billions whom they are supposed to serve. It is well documented that a broad array of MDB-financed projects and economic policy proscriptions have contributed to a deepening spiral of social and ecological poverty throughout the South.[3] Such destruction has prompted international campaigns aimed at reforming or halting individual projects, as well as reforming or closing down the MDBs themselves.

Bruce Rich, prominent World Bank critic and senior attorney at the United States–based Environmental Defense Fund, cogently describes the conditions that have generated these protest campaigns:

Massive internationally financed development schemes were unleashing ecological destruction and social upheaval in areas larger than
many American states or European countries. Huge forests had been
destroyed, gigantic river basins filled with dams, and vast agricultural
expanses consolidated into larger holdings for export production at
tremendous ecological cost. What was occurring was not a reasonable,
measured process to increase economic welfare, but the destruction of
natural and social systems whose endurance are the prerequisite, and
the goal, of any sane project for longer term human development.[4]

Much has been said about the losers in this MDB-engineered development; and much has been said about the World Bank's hubris, about its
technocratic arrogance, its economistic condescension, its lack of
accountability, its draconian secrecy and its elitist approach to development; but very few observers have identified who the winners are in this
global game of monopoly.

When the United States and its allies created the World Bank at the
Bretton Woods Conference in 1944, they expected that one of its primary functions would be to guarantee private investment in distant and
politically volatile lands where it appeared too risky for corporations to
go it alone.[5] Since that time the Bank's policies have deliberately and
consistently advanced corporate expansion to nearly every corner of the
so-called underdeveloped world. And they continue to do so, even
though such investment often clearly runs contrary to the World Bank's
official mandate of poverty alleviation. As analyst Cheryl Payer wrote in
1982, in an observation that is even more relevant today, "to the extent
that greater advantage for foreign investment is incompatible with the
alleviation of poverty and the satisfaction of human needs (a possibility that is never entertained in the Bank's ideology), poverty . . . is likely to *increase* as a result of the Bank's intervention."[6]

The policies of MDBs have consistently served corporate interests in
five key ways. The first and most obvious way that the transnationals
benefit from MDB and bilateral aid is through contracts. In what is
essentially a quid-pro-quo relationship, large corporations based in the
countries that provide the MDBs with capital receive lucrative contracts
for MDB-financed projects. Similarly, governments in Western Europe,
North America and Japan often provide bilateral development assistance with either the assumption or the stipulation that it be spent on
products made in the donor country or on contracts with corporations

from that country. It is this profitable relationship, not meeting the needs of the poor, that is the *raison d'être* of development finance. Indeed, government officials in the Northern industrialized countries regularly justify the MDBs' existence with evidence that these institutions are an economic boon, rather than a burden, to their economies. Listen to Lloyd Bentsen, former secretary of the Treasury in the Clinton Administration testifying to the U.S. Senate in 1993: "Last year, the U.S. contributed $1.6 billion to the multilateral development banks. The banks, in turn, awarded U.S. companies procurement contracts amounting to more than $2.2 billion. The difference is 39 percent. That's a 39 percent bonus." The bulk of these contracts went to hundreds of giant transnationals who make up a virtual "Who's Who" of corporate America. Bentsen further claimed that those 1992 contracts created 42,000 U.S. jobs and concluded that "the economic and financial benefits we receive from the banks have been much greater than our contributions to them."[7]

Overall, net disbursements by the World Bank (i.e., the balance of gross disbursements minus repayments to the Bank for previous credits) totaled just over $7 billion in 1993. But the borrowing countries paid out nearly an equivalent amount of money in contracts—$6.8 billion, to corporations from the twenty-four rich OECD nations—leaving only marginal positive cash flows going into the coffers of recipient countries. The International Development Association, an arm of the World Bank designed to lend money to the poorest of the poor countries, doled out more money to British corporations for contracts in 1993 than it committed in future loans to Bangladesh, one of the most impoverished nations on Earth. Similarly, Switzerland, home to only 6 million people and some of the world's largest transnationals, got more money than Mali or the Philippines.[8] Most of Japan's *sogo shosha* are also major contractors for the Bank, Mitsubishi being the largest. Moreover, the *sogo shosha* often play the role of coordinator for megaproject consortia of global corporations from the Triad.[9]

Many of these projects have adverse social and ecological impacts. In the case of the Kedung Ombo Dam project in central Java, Indonesia, for instance, the World Bank teamed up with the Export-Import Bank of Japan to build a dam for irrigation, flood control and power generation. The dam, which was built by Japanese companies Nichimen and Hazama Gumi Construction, displaced nearly 30,000 rice farmers.[10] Japanese corporations also secure a multitude of contracts from the Asian Development Bank (ADB). For instance, after a bitter battle in Masinloc,

Zamables, the Philippines, the ADB, together with the Import-Export Bank of Japan and the Philippine central government, succeeded in evicting local residents in order to build two coal-fired power plants. The contract for the second plant, which threatens the ecological integrity of coral reefs and mango groves and whose design does not even meet Philippine government air quality standards, let alone those in Japan, has been granted to a member of the Mitsubishi Group.[11]

The second way in which multilateral and bilateral aid has benefited corporate interests is by building infrastructure such as roads, electrical grids, dams and power plants, which often serve to lay the groundwork for further transnational investment. Unfortunately, the creation of such infrastructure has also repeatedly led to social and environmental debacles. Japan, which is the single largest bilateral aid donor in the world, directs roughly one-third of its Overseas Development Assistance (ODA) to infrastructure. This ODA, which has prompted many cases of human rights violations and environmental destruction, serves the interests of Japanese corporate expansion and accelerated resource extraction. For instance, 99 percent of the power generated by the Asahan Dam in Indonesia, built by Japanese ODA, disappears into an aluminum refinery owned by a Japanese-Indonesian joint venture. In the same fashion, a road built with Japanese aid in Sarawak, Malaysia, opened up ancient forests, home to various indigenous peoples, to Japanese and Malaysian timber corporations.[12]

Similarly, in Central America in the 1950s, the U.S. bilateral aid agency USAID and the World Bank provided loans to build roads that allowed local hacienda owners to expand export-driven cotton production on the region's Pacific coast. Transnational chemical companies benefited immensely from this "development" with 40 percent of all U.S. pesticide exports going to Central America from the mid-1960s through the 1970s, mostly for use on cotton.[13] Meanwhile, peasants pushed off their land by this process were herded along USAID- and MDB-built roads into the region's eastern rainforests, where they were encouraged to clear vast jungle areas. Once denuded, these lands were also swept into the export economy as MDB-promoted cattle ranching produced beef for fast food and pet food transnationals such as Burger King and Ralston Purina. Between 1970 and 1980 alone, this dynamic destroyed 15 percent of Central America's rainforests, one of the richest reserves of biological diversity in the world.[14]

World Bank infrastructure lending in the transportation sector has also supported corporate expansion, promoting the growth of the auto industry in the Third World rather than more accessible and ecologically sound rail transport. While in the 1950s the Bank's lending for railways was twice that for highways, this situation reversed itself in the 1960s, when road building became the largest element of this loan sector.[15] By 1993, 74 percent of the Bank's $3.2 billion in transportation loans went to road and highway construction.[16] As Cheryl Payer writes, "This emphasis on road building, in the Third World as in the developed countries, amounts to a substantial subsidy to the motor transport industry."[17] Indeed, the Bank's transport policies directly support the automotive transnationals, which, as is discussed later in this chapter, are rapidly expanding their Third World markets, thus exacerbating the already significant contribution that road vehicles make to local air pollution and global climate change.

Lending for energy infrastructure has similarly catered to corporate interests while virtually ignoring environmental consequences and failing to promote alternatives. Throughout Asia, for example, the MDBs and bilateral aid agencies are building coal-fired power plants and promoting the development of other ecologically destructive energy schemes designed to fuel rapid economic growth and foreign investment in the region. China, the largest power market in the world, is, with the help of the MDBs and bilateral aid, adding on a staggering 12,000 megawatts of power every year—an amount equivalent to two-thirds of the output of southern California's electrical grid. Much of this power, which is generated by coal, oil, gas and nuclear energy, provides the infrastructure for rapid industrialization in China and helps make the country the world's leading non-OECD recipient of foreign direct investment.[18] Meanwhile, MDB support for alternative energy development such as solar and wind power is virtually nonexistent. This situation is replicated on a global scale with the World Bank spending 40 percent of all its energy loans on oil and gas development, 15 percent on coal and most of the rest on electrical transmission and fossil-fuel-powered generators. Less than 3 percent of all Bank energy lending goes to renewable energy and energy efficiency projects.[19]

The third way in which the World Bank and other MDBs support corporate interests is through their newfound environmentalism. As they have come under increasing fire for their socially and environmentally destructive behavior, these institutions have moved to address their critics. Parallel to the corporate response to environmentalism, the MDBs have taken a series of steps to absorb the ecological question into their agenda. Thus, for instance, in the mid-1980s, the World Bank, in conjunction with the UN Food and Agriculture Organization and the World Resources Institute—a Washington, D.C., think tank—created the Tropical Forest Action Plan (TFAP). Assailed by a number of critics in the North and South as a "fraud" that used a few conservation and watershed management programs essentially to promote the expansion of an export-oriented timber industry, the TFAP soon lost credibility. But its spirit and intent lived on within the World Bank.[20]

By the onset of the 1990s the Bank had initiated a "forest management and protection" project in the West African country of Guinea; the effort turned out to be an initiative to deforest two-thirds of the remaining pristine rainforest in the country. And a 1990 World Bank forestry conservation project in the Ivory Coast put a half-million-hectare rainforest under the management of the same corporations that had pillaged the country's timber resources during two previous decades. This logging project, which was approved in 1990 under the Bank's supposedly "environmental" forestry policy, also set the stage for the potential displacement of more than 200,000 people who depended on the forest.[21] Such programs, fashionably dressed in green, promote business as usual. As the United States–based Environmental Defense Fund's Korinna Horta comments, many of the World Bank's so-called environmental policies continue to involve "taking control away from local resource users and handing it over to those with power in the global economy. . . . Forests are given to the corporations for 'protection' while people are expelled."[22]

A similar dynamic has taken place with the advent of the Global Environment Facility (GEF), a multibillion-dollar joint project of the World Bank, the UN Development Programme and the UN Environment Programme. Created during the lead-up to the Earth Summit and essentially controlled by the Bank, the GEF's mandate is to provide concessionary financing or grants to promote such goals as biodiversity conservation, the protection of international waters, limiting ozone depletion and reducing releases of global warming gases. Yet many of its projects appear to be furthering more traditional World Bank goals.[23] Such was the case with a "model" GEF natural resources management project in the Congo, which was designed to integrate isolated rainforests into the global economy by opening them up to corporate logging under the pretense of protecting them.[24]

In addition to providing green cover for ongoing exploitation, GEF concessionary financing has also served to sweeten the financial pot for recipient governments and corporate contractors to the World Bank.[25] In 1993, for instance, the Nigerian government attempted to garner $25 million in GEF money to supplement an $82 million World Bank loan for a joint project with the Chevron Corporation.[26] Ironically, the GEF money comes from a fund earmarked for projects aimed at preventing climate change, a phenomenon that Chevron, claiming the absence of scientific proof, officially argues should be further studied rather than acted upon. Such a position, however, didn't prevent the oil giant from working with the Nigerian government to seek GEF grants to subsidize its $1 billion venture designed to capture escaping natural gas from its oil fields in Nigeria and market it throughout West Africa.[27] The GEF money might have further greened the company's image, while making the project even more profitable. But Chevron encountered obstacles along the way. These came in the form of resistance from a lone soul in the U.S. government who contested the loan in official comments, questioning whether the GEF "should be engaged in an activity which essentially provides a subsidy to a multinational oil company."[28]

The fourth way in which MDB policies serve corporate interests is through so-called policy-based lending, or structural adjustment. From the 1980s onward, the piecemeal, project-based relationship between the MDBs and Third World governments became secondary as the World Bank/IMF attained a position from which it could dictate macro-economic policies and effectively wrest sovereign control of entire economic sectors from Southern governments. In the throes of a deep debt crisis and in the face of monumental geopolitical shifts along the east-west axis, Southern states dropped much of what had ostensibly been nationalist development strategies and ideologies. Instead, left with little other choice, they began to follow World Bank and IMF structural adjustment policies with a newfound, near religious zeal. By 1996 about one-quarter of all World Bank lending was in the form of structural adjustment programs.[29]

These lending policies effectively deconstructed much of the Third World nation-state. They did so by conditioning loans designed to resolve balance of payments crises on the privatization of national industries, the removal of barriers to foreign investment in key sectors, the "reform" of financial systems, the gutting and privatization of social and environmental services and the redirection of economies toward an increasingly export orientation. Together, all of these components of adjustment effectively pried open previously protected markets to escalating foreign investment while pitting Third World nations even more fiercely against one another in a competition to be chosen by transnational corporations as integral components in their global plans.[30] These changes are largely responsible for the escalating corporate investment that many "developing" nations have experienced in the first half of the 1990s.[31]

In this way, the World Bank and the IMF opened up huge new horizons for the transnationals. At the same time, structural adjustment increased poverty and inequality, while heightening environmental degradation by intensifying the exploitation and export of natural resources.[32] Transnational corporations also assumed responsibility for a number of environmental problems as they bought up what had been state-owned power plants, chemical factories, mines and forests. Moreover, the World Bank's adjustment policies exacerbated the South's environmental crisis in no small part, as Philippine scholar Walden Bello writes, through an "ideological bias . . . against any disincentives that might stand in the way of the operation of market forces. . . . This translated into opposition on the part of the economic authorities to effective environmental regulation by the state."[33]

The fifth and newest way in which the MDBs serve corporate interests is by either directly lending to or investing in transnational corporate projects and providing risk insurance for their endeavors in the Third World. By cutting back key sectors of the nation-states that the World Bank and its sister institutions are chartered to lend to, the MDBs have, in a sense, been working themselves out of a job. Undaunted, however, they are remaking themselves as investors and bankers for the transnationals. This shift has also allowed the MDBs to sidestep some of the environmental and social controls that more than a decade of activists' campaigns had forced upon them. Michelle Chan, an analyst with Friends of the Earth, explains:

> Just as public pressure is having an impact on the accountability of the MDBs, they are changing their role from direct lenders to catalysts for private enterprise and private money flows. In the past few years the World Bank has been channeling a mounting proportion of its lending portfolio into the International Finance Corporation (IFC), which provides money for private-sector development rather than government sponsored initiatives.[34]

Founded in 1956 as part of the World Bank Group, the IFC was a little-known entity until the mid-1980s. Since then it has increased its total financing by more than 360 percent in a ten-year period. By 1995 the IFC was making nearly $3 billion in loans and equity investments for 213 corporate projects in sixty-seven countries.[35] The IFC's support for and participation in these investments leveraged another $15 billion in financing for these corporate ventures.[36] The World Bank has also created a new entity, the Multilateral Investment Guarantee Agency (MIGA), to provide risk insurance for corporate investment in Southern nations. And, with the new slogan "catalyst for private capital flows," the Bank itself has jumped into the private investment business. Overall, the World Bank Group (International Development Agency, IFC, MIGA and the World Bank itself) takes credit for supporting "about $25 billion of private-sector finance a year, or 10 percent of all investment by private enterprise in developing countries."[37]

Meanwhile, the Inter-American Development Bank (IDB) is following a similar path, establishing a new private sector department and a corporation that lends to and invests in businesses operating in Latin America and the Caribbean. The IDB works in tandem with corporations and groups of investors such as one led by former World Bank official Moeen Qurshi and former U.S. Treasury Secretary Lloyd Bentsen. With initial captialization of $300 million provided by the American International Group—a global insurance company—and the General Electric Capital Corporation, Bentsen's group is sinking money into power plants, telecommunications and transportation systems primarily in the region's six richest countries. Bentsen, who is also a former governor of the IDB, hopes his fund will realize profits of 25 percent a year. As the *New York Times* writes, "in the Washington tradition of revolving doors, former officials of these banks are taking advantage of these new business opportunities."[38]

While the MDBs and their investment partners may be making big profits investing in big projects, their chartered mission of eradicating poverty is usually neglected by the "free" market. As Swiss MDB critic Peter Bosshard puts it, "policy changes and finance are geared towards big, often foreign companies, while the informal sector and small enterprises which create most employment are left to fend for themselves." What's more, note Bosshard and others, "the private sector lending guidelines of the World Bank Group so far have not supported a strengthened role of civil society, but rather undercut the normal accountability standards of the World Bank."[39] A quick glance at IFC lending also shows that many of the investments and loans it makes are in the most environmentally hazardous economic activities, such as power plants, mining, chemical, petrochemical and oil refining, timber, pulp and paper, food and agribusiness, and the automotive industry.[40] This is particularly troublesome considering that the IFC is not constrained by the minimal environmental and public participation safeguards that organizations such as the Sierra Club, the International Rivers Network, Friends of the Earth and others have fought hard to impose on the World Bank.

Promoting private investment in the Third World is not necessarily a bad thing. But when it comes at the cost of social equity and ecological sustainability it is a questionable endeavor at best. The World Bank Group and its regional cousins would best serve their mandate of eradicating poverty and promoting sustainable development by subsidizing, guaranteeing, financing and investing in ventures that foster organic agriculture, solar and wind power, public transportation, chlorine-free, tree-free paper made from agricultural byproducts and the like. If these global economic institutions are not able to promote such transformations, even after much touted "reforms," it may be high time for governments to close them down and replace them with institutions that will do the job.

Toxic Trade

The changes set in motion by structural adjustment in the 1980s—changes that were both macro-economic and profoundly political in nature—have been institutionalized and deepened by the trade and investment agreements that were established or strengthened in the first half of the 1990s. The Uruguay Round of GATT and the creation of the new World Trade Organization (WTO), the North American Free Trade Agreement (NAFTA), the plans to expand NAFTA throughout much of Latin America, the South American Common Market (MERCOSUR) and the European Union all serve as international frameworks that aim to guarantee that the sweeping shifts initiated by structural adjustment will last. Under these "free" trade regimes, the governments of the world formally abdicate their sovereign control over numerous facets of international trade and investment as they become more deeply integrated into the corporate-led global economy. The proposed Multilateral Agreement on Investment (MAI) aims to deepen these changes by granting the transnationals even more rights in the international arena. As discussed in Chapter One, this has created a situation where national governments are increasingly being forced to comply with a set of global rules and regulations arrived at and enforced not by the democratic discourse of their citizens, communities and elected officials, but rather by these unaccountable global economic institutions.

Crucial for the purposes of this discussion is the fact that the transnationals have played a central role in shaping and promoting the free trade agenda. For instance, the International Chamber of Commerce (ICC), the single largest international association of corporations, provided coordinated leadership for lobbying efforts on behalf of the Uruguay Round of GATT. The case of NAFTA is similar and even more explicit. During the two-year NAFTA debate in the United States, large U.S. corporations formed a myriad of pro-NAFTA organizations, sent wave after wave of lobbyists to do battle on Capitol Hill and carried out a major public relations campaign in favor of the embattled agreement. One analysis prepared by the Washington, D.C.-based Institute for Policy Studies found that USA*NAFTA, the leading pro-NAFTA organization in the United States, composed of about 2,300 U.S. corporations and corporate lobby groups, was dominated by polluting industries. The study discovered that of the thirty-five corporate "state captains" in charge of pro-NAFTA lobbying efforts, nearly one-third ranked among the top-thirty U.S. toxic polluters, including DuPont, Kodak, General Motors and Monsanto. Also, the majority of these companies had been eliminating U.S. jobs and shifting work to Mexico, where most were planning to expand.[41] What's more, a study by the Ralph Nader organization Public Citizen found that official U.S. government "Trade Advisory Committees" mandated by Congress to be "fairly balanced in terms of points of view" were overwhelmingly stacked with corporate executives. The study concluded that the Trade Advisory Committees, which "wield strong influence over trade issues that could endanger the environment or consumer health and safety," include a disproportionately large number of corporations that have followed "a pattern of lawlessness and disregard" for these very issues.[42]

Since global corporations dominate international trade and investment, it is in their interest and within their reach to shape the rules to their liking. By doing so the transnationals can more freely extract and process ever greater quantities of natural resources while expanding their sales to the far corners of the Earth. This is precisely why they have aggressively pushed the free trade agenda. The global and regional economic rules and regulations set by the new trade agreements provide frameworks for corporations to create integrated "regional core networks" that emanate from a transnational's home country. According to the United Nations, individual countries are increasingly becoming cogs in these regional wheels, part of multicountry production and service networks that operate in the context of the European Union or NAFTA. (As we have seen, in the case of East Asia, Japanese corporations have created such networks without formal trade agreements.) Thus the nation-state is fading into the background, giving "rise to an international production system, organized and managed by transnational corporations."[43]

In essence, these trade regimes serve as international regulatory structures for this globalization, or as Martin Khor, director of the Third World Network, has written, global trade agreements are designed to function as "world economic policemen to enforce new rules that maximize the unimpeded operations of transnational corporations."[44]

In the case of India, the changes that free trade is bringing are dramatic and jolting for the country's diverse cultures. As in many parts of the world now, the words "liberalization," "privatization" and "globalization" roll off people's tongues as part of everyday conversation. Men clad in fluorescent turbans and chewing betelnut and women dressed in colorful traditional saris gather around the neighborhood television set to watch Asia's satellite network, Star TV, where bikini-clad blondes gyrate on a Los Angeles beach to an exotic MTV beat. In between music videos, advertisements tout the fruits of globalization and the ethic of consumerism. The Indian middle class—a consumer market that conservative estimates place at 100 million people (only one-ninth of India's population, but still larger than the populations of Germany, Switzerland and the Netherlands combined)—is being inundated with the commodities of the American Dream.[45]

The new investments that are pouring into the country, comments the New Delhi–based Public Interest Research Group, "are enticed on terms which can only be described as 'predatory.'"[46] Coke and Pepsi, once exiled by a nationalist Indian state, are back and taking over nearly every bottling plant in the country, wiping out national industry. McDonald's is entering the market with plans to erect thirty-one sets of "golden arches" around the country and buying up land for breeding the lambs necessary to cater to Hindu lamburger munchers. Cargill and ICI see India as one of the world's great future exporters of sunflower oil.[47] Consequently, India's food security is increasingly compromised as more and more of the countryside is blooming in sunflowers, the seeds for which are controlled by a few transnationals. More than ever, pesticides are a booming business in India. The players include Dow, DuPont, ICI, Ciba-Geigy, Atochem and Mitsubishi. The potential these transnationals see in India is huge. As a DuPont official told the *Economic Times* of India, "In Japan, the average use of pesticides per hectare is 10 kilograms, in India it is 450 grams [less than one-half of one kilogram]. Considering that India is an agricultural economy, the industry has ample scope to grow."[48] Mitsubishi and numerous other corporations are also plying the country's coasts with their industrial fishing fleets, displacing fishworkers, depleting resources and threatening the local way of life of millions of coastal fisherfolk. Their catch of prawns, cuttlefish, tuna and shark mostly ends up on the tables of U.S. and Japanese consumers.[49]

India has relaxed its controls on foreign investment in order to accede to GATT/WTO and attract a growing flow of capital. In the process, a number of environmental laws are being rolled back as growing foreign investment rolls in.[50] This trend is similar to the moves against U.S. environmental controls that occurred in the early 1980s and again in the mid-1990s. The Indian experience is also comparable to that of a number of countries around the world that are experiencing the environmental impacts of structural adjustment. This includes a number of components. The exploitation and export of natural resources has accelerated. Prohibitions against siting industrial facilities in ecologically sensitive zones have been eliminated, while conservation zones are being "denotified" (stripped of their status) so that cement plants, bauxite mines, prawn aquaculture and luxury hotels can be built. Similarly, forestry regulations appear to have been loosened for the pulp and paper industry, fisheries controls undermined by transnational and national corporations and mining laws watered down for the mining corporations.[51]

India's broad economic opening has not gone without resistance. In fact, the country's popular movements—organized labor, peasants, fisherfolk, nongovernmental organizations and women's groups—have been in the forefront of the international response to structural adjustment, GATT/WTO and growing corporate penetration of their lives. While some of this response has fed the fires of right-wing Hindu fundamentalist nationalism, a great deal of it has harkened back to the experience of Mahatma Gandhi and India's struggle for independence and self-sufficiency, while also looking forward to building new, more democratic forms of governance (see Chapter Seven).

Protest has taken many forms. In the city of Bangalore, for instance, angry farmers raided Cargill's offices, making a bonfire of its documents in 1993. "We're ransacking the ransackers," says Professor M. D. Nanjundaswamy, the small, bearded and bespectacled leader of the Indian farmers' seed movement (KRRS). Nanjundaswamy charges that the government's liberalization policies and growing corporate investment are leading to "a perennial colonization" and the "increasing impoverishment of farmers," who make up 75 percent of India's population.[52] Perceiving GATT as implementing intellectual property rights and patenting regimes to transfer control of genetic seed stocks, and therefore their agricultural future, from the local community to transnationals such as Cargill, nearly half a million KRRS members took to the streets to protest against the GATT in 1993.[53]

The opening of the fisheries sector to transnational companies has also evoked nationwide protests, work stoppages and strikes by the thirteen unions comprising India's National Fishworkers Forum (NFF). These protests, which began in 1994, have been aimed at ending all foreign participation in the country's fisheries industries. "We are going up against the World Bank, the IMF, the GATT," observes Tom Kochery, chairperson of the militant NFF, which believes these international institutions are promoting the demise of a traditional way of life. "It's better to get killed than to live in the face of such demonic market forces," he quietly comments.[54]

By 1995 India's antitransnational, antiglobalization movement was gaining strength. A prolonged and broad-based campaign charging price gouging, the absence of competitive bidding and corruption forced joint venture partners Enron, General Electric and Bechtel to at least temporarily abandon plans to build the country's largest power plant near Bombay; the retreat of the Enron-led project meant not only the tabling of a $2.8 billion investment venture, but was also a symbolic blow that shook other corporations' confidence in India's investment climate.[55]

With the power sector in partial retreat and a series of actions being taken against Coke, Pepsi and Kentucky Fried Chicken, India's popular movements were flexing their muscles, making a statement for all the world to hear. Sometimes the movement was marked by xenophobic nationalism (the Enron campaign was joined by the militant Hindu Fundamentalist BJP party, which rode it to power in Maharashtra state, only to then turn around and cut a deal with Enron and reinstate the project). Indeed, these organizing efforts signaled the possibility that antiglobalization forces can drift toward fascism. Paradoxically, and more optimistically, they also revealed to the world that it is possible for grassroots movements promoting cultural, economic and ecological sustainability to emerge and challenge the manifest destiny of corporate globalization.

The Migration of Hazardous Industry

Despite growing protest movements in India and elsewhere, the structures of the global economy, engineered by the World Bank and cemented by free trade agreements, have combined with stronger environmental regulations in the Northern industrialized countries to accelerate the migration of polluting industries to the Third World. Indeed, the form and function of corporate globalization make it eminently reasonable for the toxic empire to expand in this way.

Such logic was clearly stated in 1992 by Lawrence Summers, who at the time was the World Bank's chief economist. In what became an infamous memo leaked to environmental organizations in Washington, D.C., Summers wrote to a Bank colleague, "just between you and me, shouldn't the World Bank be encouraging *more* migration of the dirty industries to the LDCs [least developed countries]?" Arguing that many Third World countries hold various comparative advantages, such as cleaner air and less costly human life (as measured by lost wages when a worker's health is impaired), Summers added, "I think the economic logic behind dumping a load of toxic waste in the lowest wage country is impeccable and we should face up to that."[56]

While Summers, who went on to become a high-ranking official in the Clinton Administration, attempted to explain away his comments as ironic humor, his memo served to put the world economy's ongoing dynamics into stark relief. Indeed, such double standards exist not only in the theoretical realm of Summers's musing memo, but also take many forms in the real world. It is well documented, for instance, that double standards were partially responsible for the 1984 Bhopal gas disaster, in which a Union Carbide pesticide factory spewed more than forty tons of lethal methyl isocyanate (MIC) gas into the slums of Bhopal, India, killing, according to government figures, more than 6,600 people and injuring well over 70,000—many permanently. (Death and injury claims actually filed by citizens exceed 16,000 and 600,000, respectively.)[57] Safeguards to prevent runaway chemical reactions in Carbide's Bhopal pesticide plant were well below standard practices employed by the company in the United States. Much of this had to do with the parent company's cost cutting in operation and maintenance of the factory. It also had to do with the fact that because regulation and enforcement standards in India were (and continue to be) far below those in the United States, the corporation felt no compulsion to maintain higher standards that could have prevented the tragedy.[58]

Despite the ringing warning given by the Bhopal disaster, double standards continue to flourish. A United Nations survey of the Asia-Pacific region found that transnational corporations regularly "adopted lower environmental standards in their operations in developing countries than those in developed countries, thus exposing workers and communities in developing countries to dangers that would not be accepted in developed countries." The report attributed the ongoing prevalence of double standards to corporations' "greater concern over maximizing profitability . . . rather than ensuring maximum safety of their operations."[59]

Many corporations and industry associations will argue that there is nothing wrong with their standards being lower in the Third World than they are at home, so long as they are following their host country's laws. This, as we have seen, is the response that many oil corporations make to critics of their operations around the world. Giving their reasoning a further twist, corporate spokespeople often suggest to their detractors that they wouldn't want to trample Third World sovereignty and imperiously impose Northern values and Northern laws on Southern countries. Yet, as has been discussed, the dynamics of the world economy are such that most Third World countries are in competition with one another to attract foreign investment. Governments are hesitant to tighten or enforce their regulations for fear of creating an unfavorable climate that discourages transnationals from investing or precipitates the flight of corporations already in their countries.[60] Many global corporations appear to be fully aware of these situations and regularly take advantage of them to keep their costs down—threatening to move or actually uprooting operations in the cases where governments impose regulations—effectively imposing their interests on Southern countries' legislative and regulatory processes.

Even when transnational corporations follow higher standards than those their host governments require (something that their superior technological, financial and management resources often make possible), these standards are frequently still *lower* than what the corporations must follow at home. In this way corporations can take advantage of the differential between often abysmal conditions in many Eastern European and Southern countries and increasingly high standards in the industrialized North, and export hazardous or obsolete technologies in the name of sustainable development.

Even the corporations that do implement equivalent standards in their operations abroad are often replicating the problems they cause at home. (Indeed, some of these are problems that point to the fundamental unsustainability of certain industrial activities.) For instance, the United Nations found that electronics firms operating in the Philippines maintained similar standards there as they did in places such as California's Silicon Valley.[61] Yet corporate activity in the Silicon Valley, home to more federal Superfund sites than any other region of its size in the United States, leaves much more to be desired in terms of environmental quality and human health.[62]

What's more, such equivalent standards may cause greater impacts in places ill equipped to handle them. In the South pollution is compounded by widespread poverty, including a lack of adequate housing, public health services, transportation and communications infrastructure, and water supply.[63] In the case of the ongoing sale of leaded gasoline in the South, for example, conditions of underdevelopment exacerbate the impacts. As Nigerian physician Dr. Jerome Nriagu has observed, "Because of the narrow streets and overcrowding in urban areas, because of the prevalence of contaminated dusts both indoor and outdoors, because of poor nutrition and health, poor hygienic conditions and the preponderance of pregnant women and children, the populations of developing countries are much more susceptible to the hazards of environmental lead contamination."[64] Similarly, in Bhopal, the pattern of urban poverty typified by the crowded slums of rural migrants that sprang up next to the Union Carbide plant was, as author Larry Everest writes, "central in turning the gas leak in Bhopal from a 'typical' industrial accident into a disaster of immense proportions."[65]

The situation is analogous in rural areas. When people live on the edge of fields being sprayed by pesticides, or when workers are illiterate and unable to understand written instructions and warnings, the hazards of pesticide use increase.[66] Industrialization can also have greater effects on communities that are highly dependent on local resources for sustenance than on communities that are part of a more complex economy. DuPont, for example, fought for nearly ten years to relocate a nylon plant from Richmond, Virginia, to the Indian state of Goa. Local critics, who eventually defeated the project, pointed out that the factory would have had a far greater impact on the small "lifeline" rivers used to supply drinking and irrigation water in Goa than it did on the James River in an industrial zone in Richmond, where DuPont was in compliance with the U.S. Clean Water Act.[67]

The case of agricultural biotechnology adds yet another dimension to this predicament. The growing competition among transnationals such as Cargill, Monsanto, Hoechst-Roussel and others to develop and globally market transgenic crops (plants that have been genetically engineered to retain traits from other organisms) threatens the survival of centers of crop diversity, most of which are located in the Third World. These geographic areas, where a great many of the planet's staple crops originate, contain a diverse wealth of varieties. The global proliferation of transgenic crops, approved as safe in countries such as the United States, threatens to contaminate these centers and reduce the diversity of strains of various food crops, thus undermining the genetic basis of the world's future food supply. As the Union of Concerned Scientists reports, "An assessment of risk in the United States cannot take into account all the environmental variables confronted by a crop used in different countries in different parts of the world. . . . Unfortunately . . . countries where most centers of diversity are found are among those least likely to have the resources needed to protect against the risks of the technology."[68] Thus, a technology deemed safe in the North may be devastating not only to specific areas in the South, but to the global storehouses of genetic knowledge located there.

Beyond all of these issues is the question of the speed with which industrialization is taking place. So many Southern societies are witnessing such rapid industrial development that processes that took many decades to develop in the industrialized North are being compressed into a few short years of high-speed industrialization. This concentrated evolution of industrial development prompted the United Nations to observe that the environmental crises experienced in the South "are sometimes worse than those experienced by developed countries when they were at the same stage of development."[69] However quixotic it may seem, there is a strong argument to be made that in many cases standards should be higher and regulations stricter in the Third World than they are in the United States, Japan or Western Europe.

When it migrates from the North to the South, or from the West to the East, hazardous industry typically follows one of three distinct but interrelated paths. The first path is that of the "pollution haven." This thoroughfare is filled with transnational corporations that relocate their operations, export their products or send off their hazardous waste primarily to avoid environmental regulations in the North. The second path is traversed by those corporations going for a "package deal" by which they relocate their operations in order to obtain a bundle of benefits such as cheap (often nonunion) labor, tax breaks, government subsidies or support and lax environmental controls. The third, and by far the most popular, path is followed by the "Marlboro Men," those global corporations that are expanding rather than relocating, riding off into the frontier to carry the manifest destiny of economic globalization to the rest of the world.

Pollution Havens

In the 1980s, barge after barge of toxic waste was exported to the Third World as fines mounted and landfills overflowed in the North.[70] In the latter part of the decade, environmental campaigning and Southern government opposition gave birth to the Basel Convention, which has subsequently prohibited many forms of international waste trade.[71] Despite this ban, products such as pesticides and other chemicals banned or severely restricted by the United States, Western Europe and Japan because of their acute toxicity, environmental persistence or carcinogenic qualities are still regularly sent to the Third World. Every year, for example, U.S. corporations export 100 million to 150 million pounds of pesticides that are banned or unregistered in the United States. This amounts to one-quarter of the U.S. pesticide export market.[72]

As public concern rises and controls on pesticide production tighten in the North, corporations are also shifting production to the South. The Swiss company Sandoz, for example, was responsible for the worst river spill in history in 1986 in which thirty tons of the extremely hazardous organophosphates disulfoton and parathion spilled into the Rhine, killing fish, wildlife and plants for hundreds of miles. Sandoz responded by "cleaning up" its operations and moving 60 percent of its organophosphate production to Resende, Brazil. After another ton of disulfoton almost spilled into the Rhine in 1989, Sandoz moved the rest of its production of this hazardous chemical to Brazil and India.[73]

Today pesticide production and use is deeply integrated in the agricultural systems and economies of the Third World, creating growing environmental problems and mounting human tragedy.[74] In the 1980s the World Health Organization made the admittedly conservative estimate that every year unintentional pesticide poisoning killed 19,000 people, while another million suffered the acute and severe ill effects of poisoning. An extremely disproportionate number of these deaths and poisonings occurred in the Third World.[75] Other estimates that look more broadly at the combined number of acute and less severe Third World occupational pesticide poisonings have pegged the number at 25 million cases annually.[76]

Corporations from various other industries also seek shelter from environmental controls in pollution havens. Asbestos provides a classic example. In North America and Western Europe asbestos was completely banned or highly restricted when concerns about health hazards and liability took hold. As a result, the 1980s saw asbestos companies build up their marketing efforts in Asia, Africa and Latin America. Asbestos continues to be exported to or produced in the Third World by transnational corporations, especially those from Canada, who lead the industry. Today transnationals produce asbestos cement that is still regularly used as building material in nearly every Latin American country. Asbestos is also manufactured by global corporations under unsafe conditions in Tunisia, the Middle East, the Philippines, Nigeria, Malaysia, Sri Lanka, South Korea and South Africa.[77]

The mining industry is also seeking pollution havens. As the Control Risks Group, a corporate investment advisory service, reports, "Tighter environmental regulation at home has helped prompt the expansion abroad of North American and European mining companies."[78] And as discussed in Chapter Four, Japanese corporations sought pollution havens abroad in response to the environmental movement in their home country.

The production of leaded gasoline provides still another example. Beginning in 1975, the United States, Japan, Canada and Australia virtually eliminated the use of leaded gasoline, and the rest of the industrialized world reduced lead use as well. Yet, taking advantage of a pollution haven, DuPont continued to produce leaded gasoline in Mexico and market it throughout Latin America until 1992; the United States–based Ethyl Corporation produced it in Canada and marketed it throughout the world until 1993; and as of 1997, Associated Octel, a subsidiary of Great Lakes Chemical Corporation, continued to produce the profitable yet deadly product for the world market.[79] As a result, children in Third World cities such as Bangkok and Mexico City have among the world's highest levels of lead in their blood.[80]

The export of hazardous products and industries to pollution havens continues with the advent of new technologies. For instance, the Sandoz corporation sold biotechnology products such as bovine growth hormone in Central and Eastern Europe during a time that the European Community had placed a moratorium on marketing the product because its risks had not been fully investigated.[81] The trend also continues to play itself out as environmental movements emerge in the newly industrializing countries. For example, after running into stiff opposition from Taiwanese environmentalists, who averaged one antipollution demonstration a day in the late 1980s, Taiwan's Formosa Plastics sought to relocate a $7 billion petrochemical plant in the pollution haven of China's Fujian Province.[82] And, as discussed in Chapter Four, Mitsubishi relocated its rare earth plant a second time, from Malaysia to China, in response to heated protest.

Finally, the existence of pollution havens in the South gives corporations leverage in their efforts to bargain down standards in the North. In 1995, for example, timber transnational Boise Cascade closed mills in Oregon and Idaho and moved operations to Guerrero, Mexico. There it found a haven of lax environmental regulations, a repressive political climate and new investment opportunities fostered by NAFTA. The company then used the threat of relocating more of its operations to Mexico as part of an attempt to weaken U.S. environmental standards. "How many more mills will be closed depends on what Congress does," Boise Cascade spokesperson Doug Bartels told the *Idaho Statesman*. "The number of timber sales will determine our decision to move south."[83]

The Package Deal

For many corporations relocating from the North to the South, or from the West to the East, lax environmental controls are often just one, sometimes minor component of a larger package of incentives that entice them to seek out the comparative advantages of relocation. Corporations going the route of the "package deal" can be found in a growing number of countries geared toward high-speed, export-oriented industrialization. Nations such as Taiwan, South Korea and Malaysia welcome transnationals that seek cheap labor and anti-union policies. Government repression of unions in these countries also creates conditions in which workers have very little political space to organize against hazards in the workplace and lax health and safety standards.

Along with these "advantages," corporations have often found weak or nonexistent environmental regulation of their toxic emissions to be a cost-saving bonus. Such "favorable investment climates" have also led to the hollowing out of industry in the Northern industrialized countries, helping to undermine union power and environmental control at home. The industrialization along the U.S.-Mexican border is a prime example of this phenomenon.

More than 3,400 factories known as *maquiladoras* are located on the Mexican side of the stretch of border that winds through the North American desert from the Pacific Ocean to the Gulf of Mexico. Many of them belong to major U.S. transnationals, such as DuPont, General Motors and Motorola, who have packed up some of their operations in the United States and moved South. Indeed, more than half of the largest 100 U.S. corporations have *maquiladora* operations.[84] They have crossed the Rio Grande seeking some of the lowest wages in the world (in 1994 people working in the *maquiladoras* earned $3.75 a day, less than their counterparts in Taiwan or South Korea). Located in and around hot, dusty border towns such as Juarez, Matamoros and Tijuana, producing electronics, automobiles and other consumer goods amidst striking poverty, the *maquiladoras* are second only to oil and petroleum products in capturing foreign exchange for Mexico. These sweatshops, which primarily employ and exploit young women who have migrated from other parts of Mexico seeking a livelihood, are the model of economic growth upon which much of NAFTA was based.

Indeed, the *maquiladoras* have allowed U.S. transnationals to cast aside their worries about environmental compliance and rejoice in the "freedom" of free trade. One survey conducted in the border town of Mexicali by the Colegio de la Frontera Norte revealed that more than one-quarter of the *maquiladoras* there considered stiff environmental regulations in the United States and weaker ones in Mexico to be either the main factor or a factor of importance in their decision to leave the United States.[85] A case in point is the General Telephone and Electronics (GTE) Corporation. In the mid-1980s more than 200 workers from GTE's Albuquerque, New Mexico, plant, many of them suffering from several forms of cancer they claimed were brought on by exposure to workplace solvents, sued the company. During the resolution of the lawsuit, GTE moved the most hazardous section of the plant just across the border to Juarez, Mexico.[86]

The *maquiladoras* have generated what has become a notorious series of environmental problems dubbed by one environmental group as "a

2,000-mile-long Love Canal." Researchers and journalists have time and again chronicled hazardous industrial wastes flowing into ravines, sewers and rivers. For example, the New River, which flows from Mexico's Baja California into the Imperial Valley in the United States, is laden with more than a hundred toxic chemicals. U.S. health officials advise people not to go near this body of water, which is considered one of the most polluted rivers in the world. Overall, in a spot check done by U.S. toxics researchers, 75 percent of *maquiladora* industries were found to be dumping toxic waste directly into public waterways.[87] At more than one-third of the industrial sites that one group of scientists visited, they found clear and flagrant violations of U.S. and Mexican standards that went "far beyond what we would expect at similar facilities in the U.S." They also observed canals "flowing close to people's homes" where children played, livestock drank and people fished in water that "contained high levels of volatilizing toxic wastes that will expose the residents to high risks of cancer, birth defects and other diseases." In the city of Matamoros, these hardened investigators found "some of the most repugnant conditions that the researchers have ever seen."[88] While the debate that swirled around NAFTA generated initiatives to clean up the *maquiladora* zone, the social and environmental situation along the border has deteriorated since the agreement was implemented.[89]

In China a similar, perhaps even more serious situation is evolving. *Maquiladora*-type zones have sprung up in Guandong and Fujian Provinces, attracting billions of dollars of investment, making these areas the fastest-growing free trade zones in the world. While the environmental problems in these "special economic zones" have not been as well documented as those of the *maquiladora* region, a similar dynamic of migratory corporations exploiting low wages and lax environmental controls is clearly at work. New Toyotas, Nissans and Mitsubishis push through waves of bicyclists, heralding a new day for this Asian giant as the South's number-one recipient of foreign investment. Tractors and giant shovels tear up the red earth to build more factories, while petrochemical smokestacks breathe fire into the air, like poisonous dragons lording over peasant farmers who stoop to water, weed and rake rows of vegetables in the fast-disappearing fields. Both national and transnational corporations based in Hong Kong and Taiwan have relocated numerous production facilities to China, taking advantage of average wages that are roughly one-tenth what they are in the now prosperous Asian Tiger nations (which were low-wage zones only two decades ago).[90]

The Marlboro Men

Today, the process of economic globalization is the single most power-ful force in driving the migration of hazardous industry to the Third World. Many transnational corporations are no longer seeking pollu-tion havens or carving out enclaves in zones of cheap labor and lax environmental regulation so as to export back to their home markets. Rather, through the dynamics of globalization, scores of corporations are setting up shop both to export back to their home markets, as well as to sell their products—be they Marlboro cigarettes, Solvay polyvinyl chloride (PVC) piping, Kellogg's cornflakes, Caltex gasoline, Ford Motor cars, Mitsubishi nuclear power plants or Jack Nicklaus golf courses—to the capital-hungry governments and burgeoning consumer classes in previously out-of-bounds places such as India, Russia, China, Mexico and Brazil.

Of course, transnational corporations have long had a presence in many of these countries. Union Carbide, for instance, first set up shop in India in the early 1960s under an "import substitution" program sim-ilar to those that existed in many other nations. But the deepening globalization of the world economy has provided an opportunity for the transnationals to expand into this new territory en masse. Con-sequently, as discussed in Chapter One, foreign direct investment and the growth of polluting industries in the largest countries of the South and East has skyrocketed.

Sometimes the globalization of an industry coincides with a process of saturation, stagnation and decline, partially brought about by envi-ronmental and health pressures in the industrialized North. This is cer-tainly the case with the tobacco industry, whose addictive product cre-ates bodily environmental pollution that can lead to cancer, heart dis-ease and death. As the severe health effects of tobacco have become increasingly clear and cigarette smoking is ever more restricted in the North, the industry's home market has stagnated and begun to shrink. While fighting for survival against declining sales at home, the Marl-boro Man and his cohorts have moved on from the great American cig-arette frontiers. They are now expanding primarily in Asia, but also in Africa, Latin America and Eastern Europe. U.S. cigarette exports to Asia, for example, more than doubled between 1986 and 1989, and this growth shows no signs of abating.[91]

The strategy employed by many other industries parallels that of the tobacco corporations. The chlorine industry, for example, is stagnating in the North and migrating to the South. As described in Chapter One, chlorine production, itself a hazardous process, results in organochlo-rine byproducts, many of which (such as dioxin) are tremendously per-sistent, bioaccumulative substances that are some of the most toxic and problematic hazardous wastes in the world. As scientific understanding of chlorine grows, so does political organizing to phase it out, replace it and ban it in the North. The industry is confronting increasing pressure to phase out chlorine in paper production and the use of building mate-rials such as polyvinyl chloride, as well as to eliminate the discharge of organochlorine waste. Additionally, chlorine-producing corporations such as Dow, Solvay and ICI face a mature and somewhat stagnant mar-ket in the North, where they have been selling their products for decades. The expansive opportunities of deregulated globalization beck-on it to the South. Thus the chlorine corporations are building produc-tion facilities in Brazil, Mexico, Saudi Arabia, Egypt, Thailand, India, Taiwan and China—to name a few. In India alone there are twenty-six separate proposals to build chlorine-related factories for domestic con-sumption and export.[92]

The nuclear power industry is following a similar pattern. The combi-nation of economic stagnation and tough, hard-won environmental controls are limiting the industry's potential for expansion throughout the industrialized North. Therefore, nuclear giants such as Mitsubishi, Toshiba, Hyundai, Westinghouse, General Electric, Asea Brown Boveri and Framatome are competing to sell nuclear power plants to the rapidly industrializing countries. As an official from the Mitsubishi Corpora-tion's nuclear fuel department explains, "If Japan's nuclear industry is to survive the next century, we have to develop foreign markets."[93] Opportunities abound in Asia, where the market for the years 1995–2005 was estimated to be $100 billion. China alone has plans to build more than thirty reactors.[94]

A similar expansion scenario is emerging in the case of the automo-bile industry. While car ownership continues to grow at a slow pace in the United States (2 percent) and Western Europe (4 percent), it is booming in places such as South Korea and Thailand, which in the early 1990s witnessed annual growth rates of 25 and 40 percent respectively.[95] In China, which has experienced roughly 20 percent growth rates in auto production in recent decades, the U.S. Big Three automakers, along with Toyota, Mitsubishi and Daimler-Benz, are rushing into joint ven-tures with state-owned companies to capture a share of a growing mar-ket whose annual production is expected to double from 1.5 million cars in 1994 to 3 million by the turn of the century.[96] Similarly, the number of cars in Mexico City grew an astounding 60 percent between 1990 and 1993.[97]

These burgeoning markets are bringing augmented profits to the ten global automotive corporations that produce 70 percent of the world's cars.[98] They are also encouraging further expansion by the global oil corporations. What's more, governments that might otherwise focus on serving a broader segment of their countries' populations by improving public transportation are compelled to follow the automobile route by the dynamics of the world economy. In China, the *New York Times* observes that the government has "seized on the auto industry as one of four heavy industries whose growth can help sustain the country's rapid economic expansion over the next two decades. . . . Just as the automobile captured the American dream at the expense of mass transit, China's leaders are eager for the giant internal consumer market to move to the next stage of materialism."[99] This development path is encouraged by institutions such as the World Bank, which, as discussed earlier, effectively subsidizes the proliferation of the auto industry.

Such expansion is contributing to escalating local environmental problems in already smog-choked, gridlocked urban centers such as Beijing, Mexico City, Santiago, Bangkok, Warsaw and Moscow. The spread of the automobile is also exacerbating the threat of climate change, with motor vehicles responsible for 20 percent of world carbon dioxide emissions in the early 1990s.[100] Overall, the globalization of the car culture is proliferating an environmental problem that spells potential disaster for the world's environment and the health of the people living in it. As the Malaysia-based Third World Network writes, "If the Third World tries to match Western levels of dependence on the car and other forms of personalized transport, our planet is doomed."[101]

The Lessons of Bhopal

Identifying the three paths that hazardous industry takes when it migrates from North to South provides a framework for understanding how corporations globalize their polluting activities. But the events in the decade following the 1984 Union Carbide gas disaster in Bhopal, India, provide a number of insights as to the nature of this toxic empire. Bhopal continues to be a warning at once ignored and heeded. Signs of this warning include the disaster's impoverished victims, who have waged an unrequited struggle for justice. They have been ill served by the Indian government, which failed to pursue their case aggressively in court, opting instead to settle with Carbide. A central reason for this is that Bhopal occurred precisely at the moment the fundamental shift from Third World nationalism to neoliberal globalization got under way. It happened just as the government of India was beginning to undergo structural adjustment, liberalizing its economy and opening up to increasing levels of foreign investment. Bhopal and its aftermath were a warning that this path was fraught with human, environmental and economic peril consisting of more hazardous investment and the loss of economic independence. But the leadership of the Indian government, which was quickly buying into the globalization scenario, did not want the political fallout from Bhopal to undermine its efforts to create a stable and desirable investment climate for transnational corporations. In this sense, while Bhopal might have helped change the course of history, it was instead largely ignored. The consequences could be dire. As leading Bhopal activist Abdul Jabbar Khan predicts, "GATT will bring more Bhopals. The Indian government has not listened."[102]

As for the U.S. government, it didn't want to see the precedent of one of its corporations being held accountable at home, in a U.S. court of law, for its activities abroad. Coinciding with this was the fact that litigation was bounced from U.S. to Indian courts, where it ended in an unfair settlement. Thus Carbide, the party responsible for the deaths of thousands of men, women and children, was able to settle out of court for $470 million—a modest sum when compared, for instance, to the $5 billion awarded to plaintiffs litigating after the *Exxon Valdez* spill (in which no human being died). By striking this deal, Carbide also kept any damaging international legal precedent of corporate liability from emerging.[103]

Despite these injustices, Bhopal has served as a wake-up call to corporations, governments and citizen groups alike. It was to the Third World what Hooker Chemical's Love Canal was to the United States, what Hoffman-LaRoche's Sveso explosion in Italy was to Europe, what Minamata, Yokkaichi and *itai itai* illnesses were to Japan. It signaled that disasters can occur at any time. It also demonstrated that seemingly local problems of industrial hazards and toxic contamination are often tied to global dynamics. Until recently, little was done in India or other Third World countries to control, regulate or manage pollution and industrial hazards. Yet Bhopal signaled that the heady rush of rapid industrialization had begun to give way to reveal some inevitable toxic side effects. Bhopal was a dramatic, but not unique, manifestation of a growing toxic empire in the South.

The corporate world looked up and took notice. Indeed, while surviving the trauma, the Union Carbide Corporation was permanently scarred by the Bhopal incident. In 1982 the company was a self-described "global powerhouse"—an important manufacturer of agricultural chemicals, the top U.S. producer of industrial gases, the world leader in polyolefins and the producer and marketer of such top brand names as Eveready batteries and Prestone antifreeze. A decade after the disaster, Carbide had been reduced to less than one-sixth its former size.[104] This cutback came about as a result of Carbide's strategy to restructure and divest itself of assets. By doing so, the company avoided a hostile takeover attempt and gave its stockholders and top executives bountiful compensation (in contrast to the relatively small settlement the Bhopal victims received). The strategy, in the words of Ward Morehouse of the New York–based International Council on Public Affairs, also "placed a significant proportion of Carbide's assets beyond the [legal] reach of the victims . . . and effectively immunized the company against a consumer boycott."[105]

The incident is also deeply engraved in the psyches of lawyers, public relations officers, managers and chief executives across the corporate planet. And it has translated into some behavioral changes, prompting many corporations operating in India and elsewhere to conduct safety audits of subsidiaries, reevaluate manufacturing processes, institute new production processes and upgrade or replace old equipment. All of this is designed to reduce the risk of a massive, sudden toxic release. "A company would be very foolhardy to let this sort of thing [Bhopal] happen," contends Pratip Chatterjee, the man in charge of ICI India's corporate planning a decade after the disaster. "I mean, look at Union Carbide. They've had to dish out so much money."[106]

The behavior of ICI since 1985 provides an example of the corporate world's response to Bhopal. The British chemical giant, whose Indian subsidiary manufactures pesticides such as paraquat as well as other chemical products, increased the attention it paid to health, safety and environment issues in Bhopal's aftermath. Chatterjee explains that whereas before Bhopal top management viewed the one person in charge of environment and safety as "wasting people's time," today that role is seen as "a vital function." Since Bhopal, Chatterjee explains, ICI India has instituted mandatory reporting on safety, health and the environment in its manufacturing design and operations. And in the early 1990s, for example, 30 to 40 percent of ICI India's capital expenditures were for environment-related projects, a lot of which were "done to make up for being complacent" in the past. The company's new safety and environmental consciousness is also a useful tool for managing public opinion. As Chatterjee candidly observes, ICI is "getting mileage out of" its post-Bhopal policies "in terms of overall image." Yet despite the substantive changes and the corporation's new green look, Chatterjee admits that ICI India does not adhere to standards as strict as its parent company in the United Kingdom—standards that are them-selves faulty.[107]

The U.S. chemical giant DuPont learned its lessons from Bhopal in a different sort of way. As noted earlier in this chapter, beginning a year after Bhopal, the company attempted for a decade to export a nylon plant that produced the material for synthetic, heat-resistant tires for airplanes and automobiles, from Richmond, Virginia, to the state of Goa, India. In the face of ongoing, militant opposition from Goan resi-dents and community activists (who finally defeated the proposal), the leading private producer of toxic waste in the United States sought to sell itself as a leader in pollution control. It also tried to build its image by placing regular environmental advertisements in India's national newspapers. Furthermore, DuPont downplayed the potential danger of its factory; at a public forum, a company representative flown in for the event told residents that "making nylon 6,6 is like baking a cake—here is the flour and there are the eggs."[108] The insulted and angered resi-dents didn't buy the half-baked analogy, nor did DuPont itself. Apparently haunted by the specter of Bhopal, DuPont, in its early nego-tiations with the Indian government, had sought and won a remarkable clause in its investment agreement that absolved it from all liability in case of an accident.[109]

Globalizing the Environment Industry

Pollution in many rapidly industrializing nations has become increas-ingly difficult to ignore. Bhopal was only the most graphic manifesta-tion of this reality. Today, according to a survey by the Control Risks Group, which advises transnationals on the saftey of investing in "emerging markets," corporations perceive environmental activism as the fastest-growing threat to their investments in the South and the East.[110] Similarly, governments see their citizens' activism in the face of growing environmental problems as a threat to their security. Thus, seeking to maintain social stability and consequently a warm invest-ment climate, a number of Southern governments are beginning to emulate their Northern counterparts by applying the "solutions" to corporate contamination provided by the environment industry (see Chapter Two). Of course, globalizing end-of-the-pipe pollution control technologies has presented another lucrative business opportunity for the Northern transnationals. For while the Third World and Eastern Europe make up less than 10 percent of the global environment industry's revenues, these countries still comprised a $22 billion market in 1993. This market was projected to grow to be worth $35 billion by 1998.[111]

The governments of the United States, Japan and the European Union are working assiduously to give their corporations an edge in the stiff competition for burgeoning new "environmental markets" in the South and East. For instance, with the interests of United States–based corporations in mind, the U.S. Agency for International Development and the EPA are building relations with and providing training programs for policy makers and bureaucrats from various countries who are developing their nations' regulatory bodies.[112] The Japanese government is carrying out similar programs under the auspices of the International Center for Environmental Technology Transfer (ICETT), an arm of the Ministry of Trade and Industry based near the city of Yokkaichi. This center trains Third World engineers, researchers, entrepreneurs and planners "so that Japan's environmental technology may be transferred smoothly and effectively to foreign nations."[113]

Transnational corporations are also exporting an approach to regulation that serves their investment strategies. In a clear conflict of interest, for example, WMX Technologies has helped write the laws that will govern its own operations in Mexico. Carlos Margain, then president of the WMX subsidiary ChemWaste Mexico, boasted in 1992 that "ChemWaste has already helped the government write 50 reference terms which outline parameters for environmental regulation."[114] Meanwhile, another WMX subsidiary, Rust International, takes credit for helping the Mexican environmental agency write its air pollution regulations, characterizing this intervention as "playing an important role in Mexico's much-publicized environmental movement."[115] Still another subsidiary, Waste Management International, has played a similar role in Indonesia.[116]

Much of the "environmental" technology exported to Asia, Africa, Latin America and Eastern Europe is being financed by the MDBs and bilateral agencies. Mexico, for example, is spending some $2.5 billion to address air pollution problems in its capital, almost half of which will come from foreign governments and MDBs.[117] What's more, in September 1993 the Mexican government signed a $3 billion joint loan agreement with the World Bank for environmental clean-up, including solid and hazardous waste management as well as water and sanitation systems.[118] The North American Development Bank, created during the NAFTA debate, is also financing U.S. corporate hazardous waste management projects on the border.[119]

Of course, helping provide services such as potable drinking water is an important role that the environment industry and its proponents can play in the Third World. Yet in far too many cases the industry, led by WMX and other global corporations, is pushing inherently limited, often obsolete, sometimes hazardous end-of-the-pipe systems on industrializing nations. Indeed, under a green guise, hazardous technologies are masquerading as solutions as they follow familiar paths, migrating from North to South and from West to East.

Incineration is a case in point. With a saturated market and after more than a decade of popular protest against this technology's social and ecological impacts, the hazardous waste incineration business has stagnated in the industrialized North. Meanwhile, exports to the Third World and Eastern Europe are on the rise.[120] For instance, just after the Clinton Administration announced a moratorium on new incinerators in 1993, U.S. consultants were pushing the technology in Malaysia at what the Third World Network's Sobhana William describes as "rock bottom prices."[121] Taiwan is building more than twenty waste-to-energy incinerators.[122] And in Argentina, despite a dearth of public information, Greenpeace documented more than eighteen incinerator proposals in 1995.[123]

To make matters worse, the environment industry's technological fixes and regulatory models are regularly introduced into political contexts where there is a lack of the limited right-to-know laws and other democratic rights that have been won by worker and environmental movements in many industrialized countries over the last twenty years. In such situations, the effectiveness of technology and regulations tends to be undermined or neutralized by the absence of political pressure from below. In the Philippines, for example, the Mitsui and Marubeni corporations set up a copper refinery on the island of Leyte in the 1970s. While the Marcos dictatorship did not press these transnationals to install air pollution control devices (required in Japan), they *were* ordered to install water pollution controls. But according to Japanese environmental lawyer Nobuo Kojima, because the companies were interested in maximizing their profits, and since there was no legal enforcement, the corporations rarely activated their environmental technologies. As Kojima comments, "They had beautiful antipollution devices. But without a social system to enforce their use, those luxurious machines won't function." Ultimately, says Kojima, political pressure from affected communities must force strong standards to be created and enforced. "Where people protest, the standards will be higher. However, where local people are oppressed by a central government, the pollution will be higher. . . . We don't just need technology," he says, "but a social and political system to stop pollution."[124]

The Toxic Dilemma

Environment and safety issues are undeniably increasingly high on corporate agendas in the age of globalization. However, the role they play in the board rooms, law offices and spin control centers of these global giants is a questionable one. It is true that many corporations are trying to be more careful so as to avoid future Bhopal-like accidents. And increasing numbers are attempting to manage the waste they create. At the same time, observes Satinath Sarangi, an activist who has worked for more than a decade with the victims in Bhopal, corporations have become "more cunning in how they handle things."[125]

Ed Woolard, chairman and former CEO of DuPont, once dubbed himself the corporation's "chief environment officer" in an effort to raise the company's green profile. "In a sustainable world economy, we can expect a new paradigm," he says. "We will have to let local needs determine the products we offer, instead of taking existing products and trying to fit them to local needs. The needs themselves will be defined . . . in the context of ecological impact and resource availability as well."[126] Yet corporations have almost never acted this way unless they are forced to. They didn't when they bought out public transport systems in the United States in order to promote automobile sales. They don't when they're promoting the car culture, cigarette culture and chlorine culture throughout the Third World. Union Carbide didn't in Bhopal. DuPont certainly didn't act in such a fashion in Goa, India, spending a decade fighting to build a nylon factory that virtually no one in the area wanted.

The controversy surrounding DuPont's nylon project was precisely about corporate development impinging on a local economy. It was about a choice between a global corporation producing heat-resistant airplane tires as part of a regional production system in the global economy and the preservation and evolution of a traditional way of life. It was about red-tile-roofed villages surrounded by fruit trees, rice fields, tilting coco palms and patches of tropical forest versus a chemical factory equipped with incinerators that release dioxin into the air but are still called "environmental" technology. It was about whether or not the streams that flow through this community would be poisoned or not; whether local people's needs or a global corporation's bottom line would be met.

Development as it is currently promoted by the MDBs, international trade agreements, industrialized governments, transnational corporations and the elites of Southern countries is premised on the extension of the toxic empire to the far corners of the Earth. As discussed, the ideology that promotes economic growth at all costs views such expansion as the key to "sustainable development." Yet in reality such toxic globalization is militating against making development sustainable and equitable, while allowing global corporations and national elites to further enrich themselves.

Northern countries need to reduce their consumption of resources and their production of waste. But it is not a solution for people of the North to allow corporations held in check at home to export their dirty production processes to the South, while still enjoying the commodities and economic benefits that this production yields. Southern countries need to develop and grow, but if they follow the seductive path laid out for them by the transnational corporations, MDBs and other engineers of development, they will face ever greater ecological destruction. Moreover, existing global environmental problems such as climate change will no doubt be exacerbated. Unfortunately, the way out of this trap is not simple, nor is it clear.

Many Third World governments find themselves in a toxic dilemma. National and transnational corporations are already producing considerable pollution within their borders. These are tangible problems that affect rivers, sewers and oceans—problems that they must do something about. Certainly, it is essential to clean up pollution disasters created by the *maquiladoras* on the Mexico–United States border or the hazardous excesses of industrialization in places such as Brazil, Poland, South Korea and Taiwan. Yet by applying the same flawed solutions to the problems—solutions, such as incineration, that are discredited and on the decline in the North—the entrance of the transnational environment industry into the Third World and Eastern Europe serves, in many cases, to cast a façade of environmental management over an environmentally destructive development model, limiting other options for more ecologically sustainable and socially equitable development.

Thus the dilemma: the environment industry's approach to environmental protection has become a fundamental component of a model of toxic globalization—a malignant form of economic growth promoted by the forces driving the world economy. Yet such "environmental" technology is often the only "solution" available to the growing toxic crises in the countries of the South, and it is arguably better in many cases than dumping a load of toxic waste directly into a river. By following the path that the environment industry provides, however, and adopting the flawed end-of-the-pipe regulatory approach so often taken by the North, the South is missing an opportunity to develop in a healthier, more ecologically sound and more democratic fashion than have the rich, industrialized nations.

In seeking solutions, the spirit of the ongoing struggle for justice by the victims of Bhopal may cast a guiding light. Ultimately, the lessons of Bhopal can be found in the winding back alleys of Nigam Nagar Colony, the slums near the old Union Carbide factory. Sitting quietly in a modest house is Sabra Bi. The mat on the floor serves as a bed. The kitchen has a small camping stove, with a couple of blackened pots and pans hanging above it. Ms. Bi is a member of the Bhopal Women's Gas Disaster Victims Association, whose slogan is "We are the women of Bhopal. We are not flowers. We are flames!" She survived the invisible flames of tragedy in 1984. More than a decade later she and her group are still fighting not only for better health care to treat the ongoing problems caused by Union Carbide, but also to hold the corporation accountable for the disaster—to extradite the former CEO of Union Carbide, Warren Anderson, to India and try him for criminal negligence. They are working to prevent other Bhopals from happening elsewhere. As Ms. Bi explains, "If they are punished, then other companies will be careful and it will be known that we, the people of Bhopal, hit back." [127]

Chapter Six

The Emerald City

Advertising, Public Relations and the Production of Desire

Pay no attention to the man behind the curtain.　　The Wizard of Oz

A tiny blue butterfly flutters across the television screens of millions of viewers. A narrator's voice explains Chevron's program to save this endangered species and rhetorically asks his audience, "Do people really do that so a tenth of a gram of beauty can survive?" The narrator then drives home the theme of the advertising campaign with the slogan "People Do." Unmentioned and hidden from view is the fact that the sand-dune-dwelling El Segundo blue butterfly makes its home within a barbed-wire-fenced compound atop the United States' largest underground oil spill. Viewers are not aware that the butterfly flaps and flutters within the confines of one of the largest sources of pollution in the Los Angeles Basin—Chevron's El Segundo refinery.

The "People Do" campaign consists of more than twenty advertisements that tout similar projects in similar places across Chevron's empire. The television and magazine spots create the impression that Chevron, one of the world's major polluters, is a caring, green, butterfly-, fox- and bear-loving group of people. These advertisements are but a ripple in the powerful current of corporate environmental advertising that has flooded the airwaves and print media. This cascade of propaganda is designed to recast the negative image that many transnationals have been tagged with. It aims to convince the public that those they heretofore saw as eco-villains are actually environmentalists. It strives to placate concerned employees and shareholders. And it is geared to sell product.

This practice of environmental whitewash, commonly known as corporate "greenwash," was best defined by the environmental group Greenpeace as a situation "where transnational corporations are preserving and expanding their markets by posing as friends of the environment and leaders in the struggle to eradicate poverty."[1] This chapter takes a close look at advertising and public relations (PR), the industry largely responsible for developing and implementing the communications strategies that facilitate this illusion for the transnationals.

Environmentalist-businessman Paul Hawken writes that, in general, despite some significant advances over the last few decades, "environmental ad campaigns represent the limit and extent to which corporations are presently willing to accept ecological truths."[2] Indeed, the transnationals have gone to great lengths to conjure up a mirage of sustainability rather than transform their reality. In an effort to appropriate the symbols, language and message of environmentalism while continuing to promote ever expanding consumerist societies, they have created a world of image and myth—a global Emerald City in which all things radiate a feel-good verdant hue and people shop happily as they sing their favorite corporate jingles.

Building the Emerald City

Modern public relations emerged in the first decades of the twentieth century, invented by men such as Ivy Lee and Edward Bernays. These PR pioneers were hired by big corporations, including John D. Rockefeller's Standard Oil, to stave off government regulatory efforts and to turn around what was then a strong anticorporate public sentiment.[3] The role that the descendants of Lee and Bernays have played in shaping and distorting environmental issues can be traced back to the 1962 release of Rachel Carson's *Silent Spring*, the book credited with catalyzing the modern environmental movement.[4] In response to *Silent Spring*, the Chemical Manufacturers Association (CMA, called the Association of Manufacturing Chemists at the time) recruited a young man named E. Bruce Harrison, whose job was to develop a coordinated response among the major U.S. chemical corporations to *Silent Spring*'s stinging and prophetic account of the ecological impacts of pesticides such as DDT. In his capacity as one of the world's first anti-environmental "flacks"—his title at CMA was "manager of environmental information"—Harrison sowed the seeds of the corporate PR response to modern environmentalism.[5] Working with public relations representatives from DuPont, Dow, Monsanto, Shell and W. R. Grace, Harrison developed a strategy to combat Carson and the fallout from her book. This effort was described by public interest newsletter *PR Watch* as "the PR equivalent of a prolonged carpet bombing campaign." During that period, Harrison and his cohorts devised tactics that have since been honed as key weapons in the industry's "crisis communications" arsenal.[6]

David Brower, who was executive director of the Sierra Club at the time, recalls Harrison's effort, noting that "the vigor of the chemical industry's defense mechanisms, mixed with the vitriol of apologists, was something to watch." According to Brower, the "consuming fury" with which the chemical companies fought Carson's book even engulfed the Sierra Club's board of directors for a time, as they wavered before finally adopting a sound policy with regard to pesticides.[7] Despite their ultimate failure to convince the Sierra Club, Harrison and the chemical corporations did succeed in casting considerable public doubt on Carson's critique. Since *Silent Spring*, Harrison has remained in the forefront of the PR industry. Today the E. Bruce Harrison Company's clients include more than eighty Fortune 500 companies, as well as associations such as the Global Climate Coalition.[8]

Harrison's trailblazing efforts to rebut *Silent Spring* and rehabilitate the chemical industry's image were followed by what former Madison Avenue advertising executive Jerry Mander recalls as a "burst" of corporate environmental advertising.[9] As the contemporary environmental movement built momentum in the mid- to late-1960s, undermining public trust in many a corporation, newly greened corporate images flooded the airwaves, newspapers and magazines. This initial wave of greenwash was labeled by Mander and others at the time as "eco-pornography."[10]

It seemed that everyone was jumping on the bandwagon. It was a time when the antinuclear movement was coming into its own. In response, notes Mander, the nuclear power division of Westinghouse ran four-color advertisements "everywhere, extolling the anti-polluting virtues of atomic power" as "reliable, low-cost . . . neat, clean, safe." (The latter-day versions of these ads now promote nuclear power as the answer to global warming.) Meanwhile, in the year 1969 alone, public utilities spent more than $300 million on advertising—more than eight times what they spent on the antipollution research they were touting in their ads. Overall, Mander estimated that oil, chemical and automobile corporations, along with industrial associations and utilities, were spending nearly $1 billion a year on "ecopornography" and in the process were "destroying the word 'ecology' and perhaps all understanding of the concept."[11] This incipient greenwash continued at a steady level through the first Earth Day in 1970 and into the Reagan years.

As the 1980s produced the Bhopal, Chernobyl and *Exxon Valdez* disasters, the environmental movement gained in strength. In response, greenwash advertisements became even more numerous and more sophisticated, peaking in 1990 on the twentieth anniversary of Earth Day. It was during that year of eco-hoopla that "corporate environmentalism" came into its own in the United States. The transnationals came to recognize that increasing numbers of consumers wanted to buy green products. In fact, in the early 1990s, one poll found that 77 percent of Americans said that a corporation's environmental reputation affected what they bought.[12] In another U.S. poll, 84 percent of the people regarded corporate environmental crimes as more serious than insider trading or price fixing.[13]

In response to this phenomenon, the corporate world went to great lengths to market itself and its products as the greenest of the green. One-fourth of all new household products that came onto the market in the United States around the time of "Earth Day 20" advertised themselves as "recyclable, "biodegradable," "ozone friendly" or "compostable."[14] Simultaneously, some of the world's greatest polluters spent millions putting on a shiny new coat of green paint—both literally and figuratively. The oil company ARCO, for example, concealed its Los Angeles facility behind a façade of palm trees and artificial waterfalls in what one commentator labeled an "industrial version of cosmetic dentistry."[15] DuPont worked with Madison Avenue giant BBDO to produce an ad full of seals clapping, whales and dolphins jumping and flamingos flying, all set to Beethoven's "Ode to Joy," to project its newfound green image. And Dow Chemical, the world's largest producer of environmentally hazardous chlorine, used the image of planet Earth to tout its "ongoing commitment" to the environment, which it claims can be traced back to the founding of the company.[16]

Similarly, across the Pacific, nuclear giant Hitachi was billing itself in advertisements as "a citizen of the Earth." The brewery Suntory, a member of the Sanwa *keiretsu*, produced a new beer called "The Earth." The company's advertising tag line, "Suntory: Thinking About the Earth," was emblazoned on cans of beer.[17] And a Mitsubishi Corporation joint venture clear-cut vast swaths of hundred-year-old aspen forests in Canada, producing 6 million to 8 million pairs of disposable chopsticks a day and exporting them to Japan, where they were sold as "chopsticks that protect nature."[18]

In Europe, greenwash was no less prevalent. The Swiss chemical corporation Sandoz, in an effort to rehabilitate its image after the 1986 Basel spill, ran advertisements depicting a forest, a tranquil pond and a clean river running through the scene. To a certain degree, the advertisement was accurate; by 1990 Sandoz had relocated its hazardous chemical production from Switzerland to Brazil and India.[19] Meanwhile, the British Corporation ICI, which for years was the world's number-two producer of ozone-depleting CFCs until it was forced to phase them out, advertised its shift to HFCs and HCFCs—global-warming gases and ozone depleters respectively—as ushering in "a new generation of ozone friendly fluorocarbons."[20]

This toxic greenwash also spilled into the Third World. In Malaysia, ICI produced a blatantly deceptive full-color newspaper advertisement whose headline trumpeted "Paraquat and Nature Working in Perfect Harmony."[21] The ad, which described paraquat as "environmentally friendly," contained a series of outrageous assertions about the highly toxic herbicide that has poisoned tens of thousands of workers in Malaysia alone, is banned in five countries and is listed as one of the "dirty dozen" by the Pesticide Action Network.[22] In New Delhi, DuPont ran a weekly environmental advertisement in *The Times of India* in which it portrayed itself as an ecological champion.[23] The Brazilian transnational Aracruz Cellulosa advertised to a global audience that its monocrop plantations, which make it the world's leading producer of chlorine-bleached eucalyptus pulp, are a "partnership with Nature" and promoted itself as a model for sustainable development.[24] In Argentina, Exxon publicized its financial support for a wetlands project with the tag line "There's a tiger that cares for the deer."[25] And in Russia, Chevron aired its "People Do" advertisements in an effort to overcome public opposition to its oil drilling plans.[26]

As economic globalization spreads, the world appears to be drowning in greenwash. This state of affairs was epitomized at the 1992 UN Earth Summit in Rio when the Summit's secretary-general, Maurice Strong, created an Eco-Fund to finance the event. The Eco-Fund franchised rights to the Earth Summit logo to the likes of ARCO, ICI and Mitsubishi group member Asahi Glass.[27]

It was in 1985 that Chevron launched its "People Do" advertisements. Still going strong more than ten years later, the "People Do" series is a textbook case of successful greenwashing. It began when Chevron asked itself whether or not it would pay to tailor an advertising campaign to a "hostile audience" of "societally conscious" people concerned about such issues as offshore oil drilling.[28]

Produced at a cost of $5 million to $10 million a year, the campaign consists of an expanding series of advertisements, each of which features a different Chevron "People Do" project. In addition to the butterfly "preserve" at the El Segundo refinery, the ads have publicized artificial reefs made of old gas-station storage tanks the company sank off the coast of Florida, its efforts to protect grizzly bears near one of its drilling sites in Montana, and artificial kit fox dens in the Central Valley of California. Other advertisements publicize company projects in Australia and Canada.[29]

"People Do" has been criticized on a number of levels. For instance, Chevron is spending much more on promoting its image through these projects than it does on the projects themselves. Producing one thirty-second advertisement may cost $200,000, while the El Segundo butterfly program costs the company only $5,000 a year. This estimate does not include the millions Chevron spends buying magazine space and TV air time.[30] Moreover, critics charge that the ads are misleading. A number of the "People Do" projects, such as programs to protect grizzlies in Montana, waterfowl in Mississippi, eagles in Wyoming and kit foxes in California, are programs that are mandatory under the law. Yet the advertisements either fail to mention or downplay this fact.[31] Herbert Chao Gunther, director of the Public Media Center in San Francisco, comments that "the ads are a selective presentation of the facts with a lack of context. Chevron implies that maybe we don't need a regulatory framework because the oil companies are taking care of it."[32]

Indeed, it appears that one major factor motivating Chevron's "People Do" campaign is the transnational's deregulatory agenda. An investigation of "People Do" by a local San Francisco television station discovered that although Chevron sells gasoline across much of the country, the corporation has only aired its ads in the top three oil-producing states of the continental United States—California, Texas and Louisiana—locations where it drills for and refines most of its oil and, consequently, where it is most heavily regulated. Confronted with this evidence, Chevron spokespeople insist that "People Do" is not a "political advocacy program" (if it were found to be so, their advertising might no longer be tax deductible). But the only other place in the United States where Chevron airs its "People Do" advertisements is in

Washington, D.C., hardly a nationally significant gasoline market.[33]

Despite public skepticism and criticism by environmentalists, the "People Do" strategy seems to have worked. Polls conducted by Chevron in California two years after the campaign began show that it had become the oil corporation people trusted most to protect the environment. The greenwash also paid off at the gas pump. Among those who saw the commercials, Chevron sales increased by 10 percent, while among a target audience of the potentially antagonistic, socially concerned types, sales jumped by 22 percent. Thus Chevron's man in charge of public affairs research could conclude that "it does pay to advertise to hostile audiences."[34]

Over the years, various initiatives have emerged to promote a greater degree of truth and accountability in advertising. In the 1960s and 1970s U.S. public interest organizations unsuccessfully pushed for the implementation of a "fairness doctrine" that would have allowed responsible opposing points of view free air time to rebut corporate claims.[35] On a more positive note, tobacco advertising is now prohibited on television in most industrialized democracies, while alcohol ads and ads aimed at selling unhealthy items such as junk food to children are under fire.[36] Moreover, one of the major points that organizers of the international Nestlé boycott won in 1981 was the implementation of a World Health Organization code of conduct. The code calls on governments to prohibit advertising and promotion of infant formula that is hazardous in Third World settings where it is frequently mixed with contaminated water.[37]

A number of initiatives have also emerged to stem the tide of greenwash. The U.S. Federal Trade Commission has issued a series of green guidelines aimed at halting deceptive greenwash ads.[38] And in 1990 a task force of eleven state attorneys general issued a report that called for environmental claims to be "as specific as possible, not general, vague, incomplete or overly broad."[39] In France and the Netherlands environmentalists have introduced a twelve-point advertising code to their national legislatures. Independent green-labeling regimes have also emerged in a number of countries. The best of these efforts attempt to create independent criteria to evaluate the environmental effects of a product throughout its life cycle.

Another strategy employed by activists and government officials working to rein in the promotion of hazardous products has been to fight fire with fire. In California, for example, a voter-initiated tobacco tax has financed a powerful billboard advertising campaign carrying the message "Smoking Kills" to counter the tobacco industry's ads. And nonprofit organizations such as the San Francisco– based Public Media Center have carried out a plethora of national and international advertising initiatives in support of campaigns against environmentally and socially destructive corporations. Despite being outspent by their transnational opponents, these efforts have proved to be a highly effective component of broader organizing strategies for social and environmental justice.

Despite these initiatives, however, as media ownership becomes increasingly concentrated in the hands of a few giant corporations, and as economic globalization promotes ever expanding media reach into the growing consumer markets of the South and East, greenwash and the ecologically unsound consumption patterns that accompany it continue to flow.

Global Images and the Production of Desire

The profound influence that corporations wield over the words and images fed to the general public seriously affects how we live our lives, how we see the world and how we understand the nature of the environmental crisis along with the changes needed to correct it. Direct corporate control of the media has become increasingly concentrated since the Second World War. In 1945 more than 80 percent of U.S. media outlets were considered independent of large corporations. By 1982 just fifty corporations controlled more than half of all major U.S. media, including newspapers, magazines, radio, television, books and film. By 1993 this number had shrunk to fewer than twenty.[40] By 1995 the trend had intensified as U.S. telecommunications, computer and media corporations merged and acquired one another at a breakneck pace.

Despite protests of objectivity by media leaders, this centralization of ownership results in severely skewed reporting that undermines democratic discourse and the role it should play in promoting ecological sustainability. For instance, when producing a piece in the 1980s on boycotts, an NBC reporter failed to pursue the story of the largest boycott of the day—the one that the group INFACT was running against General Electric (GE) for making nuclear weapons. It is no coincidence that GE owns NBC. Such a conflict of interest allowed one of the United States' largest conglomerates to pass unscrutinized by the people who get their news from NBC. And when the network ran a documentary praising nuclear power (without mentioning that its parent company is a major nuclear power plant builder), or when the network's news division ran a series of segments about a new device to detect breast cancer (without mentioning that the device is manufactured by GE), the supposedly "objective" media came very close to resembling a glorified corporate public relations and marketing operation.[41]

The terms of debate and freedom of the press itself are also severely limited by the pervasiveness of economically motivated self-censorship. Television networks and news magazines regularly refuse to run stories on the social or environmental impacts of a particular product, corporation or industry. The reason? According to the Washington, D.C.–based Center for the Study of Commercialism, such coverage would jeopardize their portion of the more than $3 billion that corporations spend every year on advertising in U.S. media markets alone—money that some corporations are not bashful about threatening to withhold.[42]

Corporate control of the media is even more pronounced in Japan. Dentsu, the largest advertising company in the world, which works for almost every major Japanese transnational, handles about one-quarter of the $34 billion spent on advertising in Japan every year. This is a tremendous percentage when one considers that Young and Rubicam, Dentsu's U.S. counterpart, handles less than 4 percent of the U.S. market. Japan's commercial TV stations are highly dependent on Dentsu, whose mighty weight in advertising gives it a significant degree of influence over the content of what gets put out over the airwaves and in publications. Dentsu's control is bolstered by its ownership stake in a number of TV channels, newspapers and news agencies such as the Kyodo News Service and Jiji Press. Finally, Dentsu controls the Video Research Company, the national rating agency (nominally independent in most countries) that determines whether or not a TV show will be successful.[43]

Dentsu's activities have included the censorship of messages on environmental and consumer issues that might damage its clients' prestige. Dentsu has successfully supressed stories on arsenic-laced milk and the deaths caused by a Japanese pharmaceutical company's cold medicine. Furthermore, an executive for the advertising and communications giant once bragged that when the *Yomiuri* newspaper invited consumer advocate Ralph Nader to visit Japan, Dentsu successfully broke up a planned two-page special report and compelled the paper to tone down its fragmented coverage. It simultaneously pressured the *Mainichi* newspaper to run a "moderate" story on the consumer movement, downplaying Nader's perspective.[44] And Dentsu, along with its sister agencies Hakuhodo and Tokyu, have also been responsible for the propagation of a good deal of the greenwash advertising to be found throughout Japan.

Already so prevalent in the United States and Japan, corporate control of the media is increasing in the European Union as well. In the 1980s governments privatized public broadcasting monopolies in Belgium, France, Italy, Germany, Norway, Portugal, Spain and Switzerland. This opened Western Europe to a deluge of advertising on a scale comparable to that in the United States. Today the European Union boasts a common television market of more than 330 million consumers, many of them ecologically conscious, who spend $4 trillion in disposable income—a fat target for advertisers.[45]

Corporate control of the media is increasing in the South and East as well, aided by the proliferation of World Bank/IMF structural adjustment policies and free trade regimes.[46] In Latin America, privatization and free trade agreements have not only spurred global corporations to buy up local businesses and implement regional production and distribution systems, but have also prompted networks such as NBC, CNN and Mexico's Televisa to expand and create regional programming. Consequently, advertising agencies are moving toward producing single spots for single products that are aired from Tijuana to Tierra del Fuego. As one analyst notes, the time is not far off when "consumers throughout the Americas will start the day with the same cereal, juice, cheese and other processed foods. . . . When the brands will be the same, the containers identical, the advertising campaign one."[47] In Asia, the *Wall Street Journal* reports that Rupert Murdoch's highly successful Star TV, which beams MTV and the BBC news, along with Chinese and Hindi language programming across the region, was initially created as "the ideal advertising format for Asia's increasingly affluent consumers."[48]

This growing reach of transnational corporate media and advertisers, and with it the globalization of the Western ideology of consumerism, lends continuity to a process that began hundreds of years ago. As Anthony Simoes, who works with the Goa Foundation on India's southwest coast, observes, "Satellite television softens up the population for the multinationals just the way Christianity softened up the population for colonialism." The only difference, he notes, is that Christianity had some moral underpinnings.[49]

The globalization of images and products is facilitated by the globalization of technology that has led a growing number of people to buy televisions. Between 1980 and 1990, a decade in which the real average income in Latin America dropped by 40 percent, the number of televisions per capita in the region *increased* by 40 percent.[50] Similarly, during roughly the same period the number of televisions in India jumped from 3 million to 14 million. About half the world's population now has access to commercial television broadcasts.[51]

By promoting the same products, lifestyles, role models and values across the planet, television advances the global sprawl of a homogeneous culture of consumption—what Vandana Shiva has referred to as a "monoculture of the mind"—that is ravaging and replacing the vast diversity of more than 6,000 cultures around the world. This ethic of boundless consumption underpins the accelerating depletion and despoilation of the world's natural resources. In the South and East, people are abandoning traditional, often sustainable ways of life in favor of consuming resources extracted, manufactured and marketed by transnational corporations. And while the Northern industrialized countries do next to nothing to reduce their profligate consumption of resources, the globalization of American consumption patterns lures more and more people into participating in an utterly unsustainable lifestyle that is already destroying the planet's life-support systems. In this way the destruction of the world's cultural diversity is intertwined with the destruction of the world's biological diversity—and with it the ecological equilibrium of the Earth.

Many corporate leaders deny that the transnationals and the media they control are responsible for rising consumption patterns in the North or South. Kobe Steel executive Takyua Negami, for example, like so many of his counterparts throughout the corporate world, insists that "the corporation's activities are a shadow of the people's desire. If the people don't want to spend more, then there are no sales. So it's not really the corporation which is leading the people. It's the people's desire which gives the corporation its room for growth."[52]

On one hand, Negami's contention rings true. Individual consumers must take responsibility for their role in the environmental and social impoverishment of the planet. On the other hand, he unfairly places the blame for many of the world's social and ecological crises on individual rather than global dynamics, thus absolving the transnationals of their substantial share of the blame. Indeed, there is a compelling argument to be made that corporations *produce* the desire to consume their products—that artificial needs are created and demand stimulated by advertising and media strategies that beam MTV or "Lifestyles of the

Rich and Famous" to the far corners of the Earth. As the Malaysian Consumers' Association of Penang (CAP) opines, "By endowing an aura of glamour and superiority on modern and foreign (or 'foreign-style') products, advertising has dramatically subverted the indigenous cultures and products of Third World peoples." CAP reports that radio and magazine ads have been so effective in Malaysia that they have persuaded the families of fishermen to shun their local catch and buy canned sardines.[53]

Indian scholar Rajni Kothari argues that "if people were asked to choose between drinking water and television or air to breathe and cars, most would opt for water and air." While this is effectively "the choice before the world," Kothari continues, "it is never allowed to be presented as such."[54] Rather, as author John Berger observes, advertising creates its own narrow terms of debate:

> Within publicity, choices are offered between this cream and that cream, that car and this car, but publicity as a system only makes a single proposal. It proposes to each of us that we transform ourselves, or our lives, by buying something more. . . . publicity turns consumption into a substitute for democracy. The choice of what one eats (or wears or drives) takes the place of significant political choice. Publicity helps to mask and compensate for all that is undemocratic within society. And it also masks what is happening in the rest of the world.[55]

The Wizards of PR

In their exposé of the public relations industry entitled *Toxic Sludge Is Good for You*, John Stauber and Sheldon Rampton point out that "'publicity' was once the work of carnival hawkers and penny-ante hustlers smoking cheap cigars and wearing cheap suits."[56] The Wizard of Oz fits this description. "The man behind the curtain" in the famous movie— the great and all-powerful Oz—turned out to be nothing more than a washed-up carnival stunt man who had puffed himself up into a grand illusion. By contrast, "today's PR professionals," Stauber and Rampton write, "are recruited from the ranks of former journalists, retired politicians and eager-beaver college graduates anxious to rise in the corporate world. They hobnob internationally with corporate CEOs, senators and U.S. presidents. They use sophisticated psychology, opinion polling and complex computer databases so refined that they can pinpoint the prevailing 'psychographics' of individual city neighborhoods."[57]

These are the wizards of PR. The services they provide for the Emerald City have grown in prominence in the decades since E. Bruce Harrison launched the assault on Rachel Carson and *Silent Spring*. In the last thirty years or so, the transnationals have increasingly integrated PR into the ground floor of their strategic planning. Take, for instance, the case of the *Exxon Valdez*, in which PR played a central role before, during and after the crisis.

In the late 1970s the Exxon corporation implemented a PR strategy that helped set the stage for the disaster. At the time, Exxon and its oil industry partners were seeking to create optimal conditions for extracting oil from Alaska's North Slope, running a pipeline across the state's wilderness tundra terrain and tankering it out of Valdez Harbor, through Prince William Sound and down to the continental United States. Exxon worked vigorously to counteract its critics in Alaska. It went out of its way to oppose and delay what it called "unnecessarily strict regulations on tankers" transiting the Valdez Narrows.[58] The company was especially concerned about Alaska's proposals to raise taxes on oil tankers transiting the sound that didn't comply with the state's regulations. At the same time, Exxon worked with the rest of the oil industry to combat proposed requirements for double-hulled tankers in the western United States.[59]

To counter a series of proposals considered "detrimental to the oil industry," Exxon created a "grassroots" campaign to lobby Alaska's state legislature. In an "action plan" for the 1977 legislative session, the oil giant outlined its strategy, which contains many of the key components that the PR industry continues to use today:

> Selected information . . . will be sent with personalized letters to opinion leaders around the State. These contacts will be asked to write or telephone their legislators to communicate their views. A "grass roots" contact list of Alaska business leaders, labor leaders, educators, native leaders, media owners and industry contractors and suppliers will be developed. Personal visits will be necessary to develop many of these contacts. Public relations and advertising programs also will be conducted to gain public support for fair taxation policies toward the oil industry. Included in the advertising program will be newspaper, radio and television ads. The public relations program will include media briefings, tours, radio and TV interviews, a speakers' bureau and preparation and distribution of printed materials. In addition, a letter-writing campaign will be organized among Exxon employees in the Anchorage office.[60]

As William Greider thoroughly documents in his book *Who Will Tell the People?* such PR blitzes often have the effect of subverting the democratic process by overwhelming critics' voices and muscling the corporate agenda through the legislative arena.[61] Indeed, in the case of Alaska, big oil won the battle with opponents of tankering in the Valdez Narrows. Disaster struck a decade later.

With the *Exxon Valdez* spewing oil from its hold in the spring of 1989, public relations activity intensified. Exxon hired several PR firms to help it try to control the media spin on the story. The PR factor in the wake of the *Valdez* spill was so prominent (if ineffective) that Lloyd's of London, together with more than 100 other insurance companies, sued Exxon. In addition to insisting that the spill resulted from "willful, wanton, reckless and/or intentional misconduct," the insurance companies charged that Exxon's efforts to voluntarily "clean up" the oil spill immediately after the *Valdez* disaster were a public relations gimmick undertaken "solely for the purpose of preserving its corporate image." The companies insisted that they would not pay Exxon's cosmetic clean-up expenses since "there is no coverage for losses incurred as a result of public relations incidents."[62]

In the ensuing years, the spin continued. In 1993 the corporation launched what the *Wall Street Journal* described as "a full-scale campaign within the scientific community to try to dispel the widespread belief that Alaska's Prince William Sound suffered long-term environmental damage from the 1989 spill." The "scientific" evidence that Exxon presented was in marked contrast to studies performed by many independent scientists.[63] The company has also disseminated its version of the truth to school children across the United States (discussed later in this chapter). And in 1996 a federal judge accused Exxon of acting like "Jekyll and Hyde" by "behaving laudably in public and deplorably in private." The judge, H. Russel Holland, was referring to a secret agreement between Exxon and seven seafood processing companies that sued for losses from the *Valdez* spill. Under the terms of the agreement, which the judge labeled an "astonishing ruse," the seafood companies received $70 million from Exxon in 1991. While Exxon's chairman, Lee Raymond, claimed publicly and to the court that it doled out the $70 million as a gesture of good will with no strings attached, this turned out not to be true. The seafood companies had agreed to kick back any punitive damages they might win. When a jury awarded plaintiffs $5 billion, the seafood companies claimed $750 million of it, which, unbeknownst to the public or the court, they were obligated to return to

Exxon. When this scheme came to light, it was disallowed by U.S. District Court Judge Holland.[64]

Although Exxon's efforts have failed to deflect most of the negative publicity and legal liabilities for the Alaska spill (in many cases the company has perpetuated its negative image), the few corporations that dominate the public relations industry are playing an increasingly pivotal role in environmental politics around the world. Stauber and Rampton write that "PR experts—at Burson-Marsteller, Ketchum, Shandwick, Bruce Harrison and other firms—are waging and winning a war against environmentalists on behalf of corporate clients in the chemical, energy, food, automobile, forestry and mining industries."[65] Public relations corporations, many of which are subsidiaries of the world's largest advertising agencies, manage what they call "integrated communications" strategies. These schemes regularly combine the use of slick greenwash ads and the placement of "real" news stories in the media with services ranging from "green" marketing plans to espionage and "crisis management" to the orchestration of fake grassroots (or "astroturf") campaigns to high-brow lobbying.

Yet very few people have ever heard of, let alone seen, these wizards. Opaquely omnipresent, they stand behind the curtain stealthily churning out the special effects that prop up the Emerald City. Even if one looks closely, it is difficult to get beyond the smoke and mirrors. The public relations industry is made up almost exclusively of relatively small corporations that don't sell stock to the public and therefore are required to provide very little information to the general population about their activities. Moreover, as Kevin McCauley, a senior editor at *O'Dwyer's PR Services Report*, a monthly news magazine on the industry, relates, "nobody really knows how big the PR industry is because no one knows exactly what it entails."[66]

Nevertheless, some figures on the industry are available. For instance, the world's top fifty advertising organizations, which include most of the parent companies of the largest PR firms, grossed more than $18 billion in 1991, with more than 70 percent of that income concentrated in the top-ten corporations.[67] Meanwhile, conservative estimates place annual revenues for the United States–based PR industry at $10 billion. Of those sales, so-called environmental PR accounts for roughly 10 percent of the total.[68] If internal corporate expenditures are included, this amount would be much higher.[69] What's more, despite its relatively small revenues (compared to other corporate sectors), the PR industry packs considerable clout. The estimated 150,000 PR flacks who work to "place," "handle" and "massage" stories in the United States, for example, actually outnumber the country's 130,000 journalists.[70]

To better understand the reach and influence of the PR industry, it is worth taking a closer look at the most powerful of the wizards, Burson-Marsteller, and its parent company, Young and Rubicam, which has more than 300 offices in sixty-four countries. The Young and Rubicam Group is a global leader in every communications field. Its annual profits top $1 billion. Through its various subsidiaries Young and Rubicam carries out advertising, public relations, direct marketing, "identity consulting and design," as well as specialty work in areas such as "health care communications." It wholly owns the Bravo Group, which specializes in Hispanic communications in the United States, and has a joint venture with Japan's Dentsu that spans fourteen countries, giving it reach into Japan and the burgeoning markets of Asia while also bringing in Japanese clients seeking representation in the United States and elsewhere. Additionally, Young and Rubicam operates in Europe, Africa, Latin America and the Middle East.[71]

Young and Rubicam's Burson-Marsteller (BM) subsidiary is the top public relations firm in the world, with annual profits of nearly $200 million. In turn, BM owns a number of subsidiaries, including two high-powered Washington, D.C., lobbying firms and one in Brussels, the capital of the European Union. "Our global reach," claims BM, "our experience and our people make Burson-Marsteller a part of more corporate and marketing communication decisions than any other firm in the world." Indeed, the list of more than a hundred clients who benefit from BM's services contains the names of many of the world's largest transnationals, including Asea Brown Boveri, Chevron, Ciba-Geigy, Dow Chemical, DuPont, Ford Motor, Genentech, General Electric, ICI, Kerr-McGee, Rhone-Poulenc Rorer, Sandoz, Scott Paper and Shell.[72] Burson-Marsteller also handled the image of the Business Council for Sustainable Development (BCSD) at the Earth Summit.[73]

In addition to serving corporate clients, BM works for governments. It promoted Nicolae Ceausescu's repressive Romania as a good place to do business and also worked for the Argentine military dictatorship in the 1970s to improve its image at a time when the generals were under international fire for "disappearing" an estimated 35,000 people.[74] It did PR for the South Korean government, which was concerned about its reputation as an oppressive regime during the 1988 Seoul Olympics.[75]

And in Washington, D.C., during the NAFTA negotiations, BM served as the Mexican government's top lobbyist, leading the twenty-four lobbying, PR and law firms Mexico had hired.[76]

Burson-Marsteller and its industry colleagues are always there for the transnationals when disaster strikes. They provide "PR SWAT teams" that specialize in "crisis communications"—the jargon for putting the best corporate spin on a chemical factory explosion, an oil tanker running aground or environmentalists holding a sit-in at company headquarters. The PR industry also provides ongoing "issue management" services. As a brochure from Burson-Marsteller explains:

> Often corporations face long term issue challenges which arise from activist concerns (e.g., South Africa, infant formula) or controversies regarding product hazards. . . . Burson-Marsteller issue specialists have years of experience helping clients to manage such issues. They have gained insight into the key activist groups (religious, consumer, ethnic, environmental) and the tactics and strategies of those who tend to generate and sustain issues. Our counselors around the world have helped clients counteract activist-generated health concerns about food additives, safety concerns about medical devices, ethical concerns about advertising, liability controversies on product hazards and political issues such as South Africa.[77]

In addition, the PR industry provides "grassroots communications services." These include infiltrating activist organizations and putting together front groups to support their clients' interests. As an example, in British Columbia (B.C.), Canada, known as the "Brazil of the North" for its serious deforestation problem, BM designed a "grassroots" coalition, the B.C. Forest Alliance. The group brazenly insists that it is a nonpartisan citizens' group that wants "a B.C. solution to B.C.'s problems." Yet the B.C. Forest Alliance, in addition to being supported by the Canadian timber transnational MacMillan Bloedel, is also funded by many decidedly nonlocal timber corporations operating in western Canada, including the United States' Weyerhaeuser and Japan's Mitsubishi (Crestbrook Industries). At one point, the Alliance hired a Burson-Marsteller employee as its executive director.[78]

In 1997 BM organized a similar astroturf campaign called the Foundation for Clean Air Progress. It was part of a broad, multi-front corporate blitz against EPA administrator Carol Browner's efforts to tighten standards for soot and smog.[79]

Corporate Codes and Classroom Clout

One manifestation of the PR response to environmentalism is the proliferation of corporate and industry-wide environmental guidelines and principles. A primary function that these voluntary codes of conduct serve is to evade public demands for strong government regulation and control of industrial activity. For instance, the International Standards Organization (ISO)—a private-public organization dominated by large transnational corporations—is serving as a global forum to create standards for environmental management, performance and eco-labeling. While the ISO standards may help implement strong uniform standards in places where they might otherwise not exist, its work is problematic for a number of reasons, including the following. First, the management standards lack any mechanisms for public accountability or oversight. Second, the organization is moving toward adopting an eco-labeling system that provides only information on how a product is made, rather than a judgment about whether it is ecologically sound or not. Third, as the ISO rules become recognized international standards, WTO may well use them to strike down other, stricter environmental controls as trade barriers. And fourth, it is serving as a diversion from the creation of internationally binding standards.[80]

Another prominent corporate code is the Chemical Manufacturers Association's Responsible Care program. Responsible Care emerged in the wake of the Bhopal disaster. In the words of E. Bruce Harrison, it "was born out of a negative public image of the chemical industry" and intended "to reassure worried publics—especially neighbors of chemical plants—that nearby facilities are being operated safely, and that the company that owns the facilities cares about their employees and the community."[81]

Playing a strong leadership role in Responsible Care, while also producing advertisements trumpeting its commitment to the environment, is Union Carbide. Yet in 1994, ten years after Bhopal and the founding of Responsible Care, Carbide, the tenth-largest chemical company in the United States, had more than three times the number of reported spills than its next-worst competitor and had the second-worst health and safety record of any company in the industry.[82] Carbide also found itself under continual fire for failing to work with employees and community groups to resolve these problems.[83] Once this record is examined, it becomes clear that Responsible Care has been aimed more at resuscitating Carbide's and the industry's image than at working toward a safe and clean environment.[84]

E. Bruce Harrison points out that Responsible Care has served as a very important PR tool for the chemical industry. He observes that the program "provides a credible rationale for maintaining . . . independence from the codes of conduct, such as the Valdez Principles, developed by organizations outside the business community." [85] Thus when stockholders of several chemical companies raised the Valdez (or CERES) Principles—proposed by the Coalition for Environmentally Responsible Economies, a grouping of activist organizations and institutional investors from churches and pension funds—they were hit with a corporate PR blitz. As Harrison explains,

> envirocomm [his term for green PR] was kicked into higher gear. Companies communicated heavily about environmental commitment, with and without reference to the proposed code, and made sure the subject was covered before, during and after the annual meeting season. . . . How did companies say no to CERES? When asked by the news media if they would sign the CERES Principles, companies answered generally in the same way: *No, we are not signing. We have our own set of principles regarding environmental protection and stewardship. Here is what it says. . . .* " [86]

Ultimately, CERES bent to corporate pressure in the early 1990s and, in Harrison's words, amended its principles to make them "more acceptable to the businesses they once attacked." Since that time, corporations such as General Motors and Sun Oil have bolstered their images by signing on to CERES.[87]

While corporations, industry groups and PR firms are fending off movements for greater public control and accountability, they are also infiltrating educational systems in an effort to preempt the emergence of a new generation of critical environmental activists. Such initiatives, which date back to the 1970s in the United States, have picked up steam in the 1990s, while also spreading to other countries. The greatest culprit in this endeavor is Exxon, which is rewriting the history of the *Valdez* oil spill for an audience of the nation's impressionable youth. While an Alaska jury was awarding 10,000 fisherfolk, 4,000 Native Alaskans and another 20,000 plaintiffs more than $5 billion in damages from Exxon, the company was distributing, free of charge, its version of the truth to 10,000 elementary school teachers, for viewing by kids who were too young to remember the devastating oil spill in Prince William Sound. While the jury determined that the spill had destroyed much of the plaintiffs' livelihood, damaging fishing and native hunting grounds, the Exxon video—which is filled with shots of stoic scientists cleaning cute, furry marine mammals—told a new generation of potential environmentalists and soon-to-be consumers that the spill did not decimate wildlife in Prince William Sound. Adding to this facelift is the high-tech, interactive Exxon "Energy Cube," a boxed set of activities and lesson plans distributed gratis, on a national level. The Cube's curriculum encourages students to make "real-world energy choices." Yet there is no discussion in the Cube of the ecological impacts of fossil fuels, and the only way to win one Monopoly-like game is to choose an oil-driven energy path.[88]

Exxon is only one participant in the corporate invasion of public schools. As the *Philadelphia Inquirer* puts it, "The next time your child's class turns to its lesson plan on the environment, it is likely that the materials the teacher passes out will have been supplied by Procter & Gamble . . . Or Browning Ferris Industries . . . Or Exxon, Chevron or Mobil."[89] For instance, the Procter & Gamble program, "Decision Earth," which was distributed to 75,000 schools, touts clear-cut deforestation as ecologically beneficial because it helps "create new habitat for wildlife." The American Coal Foundation provides a curriculum that makes no mention of acid rain or global warming, but rather helps students "identify the reasons coal is a good fuel choice." And the American Nuclear Society supplies teachers with a "Science/Social Studies Fair Kit" that provides step-by-step instructions for building a model nuclear reactor. The Society writes off the problem of nuclear waste, telling students that "anything we produce results in some 'leftovers' . . . whether we're making electricity from coal or nuclear, or making scrambled eggs!"[90]

Direct advertising has also infiltrated the classroom. A project called Channel One, developed by Whittle Communications and now owned by Kohlberg, Kravis, Roberts, generates nearly $100 million a year in advertising revenues by providing junior and senior high schools with free television sets. In exchange, the schools show twelve minutes of programming a day, including two minutes of commercials. Seen by more than 8 million students in 40 percent of U.S. secondary schools, Channel One is an ideal venue for product placement, guaranteeing advertisers access to "the largest teen audience in television history."[91]

The transnationals' ability to carve out this niche from the U.S. educational system can be attributed, in large part, to the ongoing government divestment from public education—a component of the neoliberal agenda. As education funds have been cut and many schools—particularly in poor districts in large urban areas—nearly bankrupted, most teachers are increasingly starved for material. Often, they are all too happy to accept slick, corporate-produced curricula. Nevertheless, a grassroots rebellion against Channel One is brewing. Students involved with the feisty national youth group "Unplug" have staged walkouts and filed lawsuits around the country, forcing Channel One to be thrown out of school in some communities. Meanwhile, the National Education Association (NEA) launched a campaign in 1994 to divest teachers' and other school employees' pension funds from corporate advertisers on Channel One. Says NEA's president, Keith Geiger, "we're proving that Americans want community-based, not corporate-imposed, education for their children."[92]

False Harmony and Anti-Environmental Backlash

One of the strategies developed by the PR industry has been its attempt to position its corporate clients to divide and conquer the U.S. environmental movement. It has done so with a two-track strategy. First, it moved to promote "partnerships" between large polluting corporations and the most establishment-oriented environmental organizations; this had the effect of co-opting, or influencing to a degree, some of the mainstream groups while simultaneously driving a wedge between these organizations and the more progressive elements of the environmental movement. At the same time, it pursued a second track aimed at fomenting an anti-environmental backlash.

Declaring that the era of confrontational politics is finished, PR firms geared up in the early 1990s to promote cooperation and "harmony" among adversaries in the environmental debate. "The Cold War is over between environmental activists and companies," declared *O'Dwyer's PR Services Report* in 1994. "Each side now is willing to work with the other on projects designed to improve the environment." Such collaboration, *O'Dwyer's* observed, helps improve a corporation's reputation among environmentally aware consumers while it increases the cash flow for environmental organizations.[93]

A number of mainstream environmental leaders, such as the World Resources Institute's president, Jonathan Lash, use similar imagery. Lash insists that in order to achieve "sustainable development" there is "no choice but to take a collaborative approach." He compares the growing harmony among mainstream environmental groups, corporations and government with the end of the Cold War and the "velvet revolutions" of Eastern Europe, as well as with the African National Congress's ascent to power in South Africa. Lash suggests that just as change was achieved "without violence" in these situations, the U.S. government, corporations and the mainstream environmental groups are working together to stave off the threat of "a much more confrontational approach" to addressing the environmental question.[94]

While Lash proposes close cooperation among corporations, environmental organizations and government, some critics see this approach as a deception and a sell-out. Many grassroots organizers insist that violence is already being done and that corporations are the perpetrators. Lois Gibbs, director of the Citizens Clearinghouse for Hazardous Waste, whose activism emerged from her experience as a housewife battling Hooker Chemical's Love Canal debacle, asks, "How do you negotiate with someone who's killing your kids?"[95]

Indeed, Lash's agenda, and that of most corporations and many mainstream environmental groups, is not to seek revolutionary transformations such as those that occurred in Eastern Europe or South Africa, but rather to give the status quo a greener hue. A similar tactic has been used to stifle U.S. social movements since the 1960s. As anthropologist Laura Nader writes, "In an effort to quell the rights movements (civil rights, women's rights, consumer rights, environmental rights) and to cool out the Vietnam War protesters, harmony became a virtue extolled over complaining or disputing or conflict."[96]

By serving as a matchmaker between environmentalists and corporations, the public relations industry has played an important role in promoting such false harmony. Firms such as Hill and Knowlton have urged corporations to develop collaborative projects, make donations, advertise in green magazines and secure seats on environmental groups' boards of directors. By doing so, they argue, corporations can muffle or quell future criticism by these groups.[97] This indeed has become a key tactic for many transnationals. Craig Smith, president of Corporate Citizen, a business think tank, observes that corporations "in industries that pollute or extract natural resources . . . forge alliances with nonprofit adversaries in the hope of circumventing regulations."[98]

Such partnerships are seen as part of a strategy to divide and conquer the environmental movement. According to Ronald A. Duchin, senior vice-president at the PR firm Mongoven, Biscoe & Duchin, the gambit is to isolate more progressive elements of the environmental movement by co-opting the mainstream. "If your industry can successfully bring about these relationships," he says, "the credibility of the radicals will be lost."[99]

Examples of corporate America intertwining itself with mainstream U.S. environmental organizations are abundant. The World Resources Institute (WRI), for example, has more than thirty "corporate support-ers," many of whom are major polluters. It also has a number of corpo-rate leaders sitting on its board of directors, but claims it does not "have the expertise" to judge the environmental impacts of transnationals that give it money. At the same time, Nina Kogan, WRI's director of cor-porate relations, justifies its acceptance of money from Chevron, Citibank, DuPont and WMX among others because they're "the com-panies most actively trying to develop solutions."[100] Similarly, the National Audubon Society, which says it is "very discriminatory" about who it accepts money from, lists WMX, Cargill, Chevron, Dow, DuPont, Ford, Motorola, Scott Paper and a number of other environmentally destructive entities among the more than sixty major corporate donors that provide it with well over $1 million a year.[101]

Corporate donations make up only about 2 percent of Audubon's income—an average proportion for a mainstream environmental group. But there are also other strains of potential corporate influence. For instance, numerous individuals connected to a variety of polluting cor-porations have sat on Audubon's board of directors.[102] Other U.S. orga-nizations receiving significant corporate support include Conservation International (CI), the World Wildlife Fund (WWF) and the National Wildlife Federation (NWF), which has created a Corporate Conservation Council in which members pay $10,000 each to participate.[103] The Nature Conservancy, which buys large parcels of land for preservation, receives at least $10 million annually in corporate donations.[104] Overall, according to Losing Ground, award-winning journalist Mark Dowie's study of the U.S. environmental movement, corporate donations to environmental groups have averaged $20 million a year since the Exxon Valdez spill.[105]

This relationship coincides with support among many green groups for the corporate ideology that claims free and open markets will lead to ecological sustainability paired with economic growth. Nowhere was this consonance clearer than when many of the corporate-funded envi-ronmental groups threw their support behind NAFTA. These organiza-tions joined ranks with almost all of the large United States–based transnationals to support the Clinton Administration's push for NAFTA's passage. To their credit, Audubon, NWF, WWF, CI, the Natural Resources Defense Council and the Environmental Defense Fund (the latter two do not take significant corporate money) pushed for environmental safeguards to be included in the agreement. But while these organizations might have seen supporting NAFTA as a pragmatic tactic intended to make the agreement environmentally friendly, the relatively minor concessions that Clinton offered served more as a wedge to divide the environmental movement than as a way to "green" the agreement. Indeed, the environmental movement split between the pro-NAFTA free-marketeers and opponents of the agreement such as the Sierra Club, Greenpeace, Friends of the Earth, Public Citizen, the Southwest Network for Economic and Environmental Justice and others.

This division of one of the strongest U.S. constituencies that was critical of the agreement helped NAFTA slide through Congress. By forsaking confrontational tactics in favor of a false harmony approach, the mainstream organizations abandoned the stratagems that gave them so many victories in the past. In the end, the pro-NAFTA environmentalists ended up with an ineffective, narrowly scoped, toothless environmental commission. In this way, false harmony further strengthened the corporate hand while institutionalizing environmentally and socially destructive trade, investment and resource consumption.[106]

"I think you'll be surprised at the business community," says Dow Chemical Company's vice-president and corporate director, Dave Buzzelli, with a disarmingly friendly smile. "If you want to sit down and talk about the forest products industry becoming a sustainable industry and have a discussion with them about thirty years from now, you'll be amazed about the kind of discussions you can have. If you talk about it happening next year, you won't be amazed at the kind of resistance you'll get." [107] Of course, missing from Buzzelli's invitation to dialogue is the fact that at current rates much of the remaining unprotected old-growth and ancient forests in the continental United States and much of the rest of the world will be gone in thirty years.

In recent times corporations have been highly successful at drawing environmental groups into dialogue. Some of these interactions have been productive, but many have created "solutions" that come at the expense of affected local communities and grassroots organizations on whose "behalf" some large environmental groups enter into negotiations. The most famous of the "partnership" agreements, and the one that PR specialists such as Dale Didion and E. Bruce Harrison consider to be a landmark, is the deal struck between the Environmental Defense Fund (EDF) and the McDonald's Corporation. A joint task force composed of representatives of the two organizations put together a plan to eliminate McDonald's use of styrofoam containers in the United States. As *O'Dwyer's PR Services Report* comments, "The plan paid off for both sides. Not only did McDonald's achieve EDF's goal of cutting the amount of waste, it also improved its corporate image."[108] The accord was widely hailed as promoting nearly unprecedented collaboration between corporate America and environmental groups.

However, what seems like a win-win situation has a dark side. The so-called landmark agreement also set another kind of precedent: by bringing EDF into the fold, McDonald's was able to sidestep highly organized and more militant grassroots efforts against its wasteful practices. By the time EDF had moved onto the scene, the Citizens Clearinghouse for Hazardous Waste (CCHW) had already been waging a three-year national grassroots campaign to force McDonald's to clean up its act. McDonald's refused to meet with community leaders working with CCHW, but rather enlisted EDF in a partnership that marginalized CCHW. While it was CCHW's national grassroots action that forced McDonald's to seek out a mainstream group, EDF formed a task force with McDonald's without inviting CCHW to join. By doing so, EDF appropriated the issue, cut a deal with McDonald's and received widespread credit for cooperating with corporate America.[109] As CCHW's director, Lois Gibbs, contends, "One thing McDonald's did not want consumers to know was that their local actions nationwide could significantly change corporate practices. So the PR was that EDF convinced them."[110]

Such partnerships can also create situations in which Northern environmental groups work against the wishes and interests of their "colleagues" in the South. The collaboration between the Natural Resources Defense Council (NRDC) and Conoco, DuPont's oil subsidiary, provides a harsh lesson in this respect. Conoco's plans to drill for oil on the land of the Huaorani people in the Ecuadorian Amazon drew spirited opposition from the Huaorani, Ecuadorian environmental and human rights organizations and a number of U.S. environmental groups. Seeking to neutralize this resistance, Conoco approached NRDC and entered into closed-door negotiations with them. Meeting in New York City, they agreed that Conoco would set up a $10 million foundation in Ecuador in exchange for NRDC dropping its opposition to the drilling. The problem was that no one had consulted the Huaorani. Consequently, NRDC ran into trouble when the confidential minutes of its meeting with Conoco were leaked to environmental groups, evoking outrage from Ecuadorian and less conciliatory U.S. environmentalists, who accused the group of "environmental imperialism." The backlash killed the deal, prompting Conoco to pull out of Ecuador and invest its resources in Siberia.[111]

In 1992 an anonymous corporate source was quoted in the *Corporate Philanthropy Report*, remarking that "many companies are using their donations to buy time with environmentalists until their environmental reform effort pays off."[112] That time came in 1995. Indeed, by the time the Republican-controlled 104th Congress had swept into power and begun its deregulatory barrage, much of the groundwork for "environmental reform" had been laid.

As the transnationals lulled some environmental organizations into complacency, and as segments of the environmental movement drifted away from the grassroots and toward the boardrooms and corridors of government power, corporate America pursued the second route in its two-track stratagem: building the foundations for an unprecedented onslaught on environmental regulation. They did so partly by helping to bankroll a series of anti-environmental think tanks and "grassroots" organizations with names such as the Center for the Defense of Free Enterprise, the National Wetlands Coalition and the Evergreen Foundation, known collectively as the "Wise Use Movement."[113]

While to some degree the Wise Use groups do represent disaffected small business owners, landholders and other ordinary citizens in the United States, many receive significant corporate support. What's more, their calls to open up public lands, wilderness areas and national parks to mineral, energy and oil exploration fit snugly into the corporate deregulatory agenda.[114] And although their memberships and budgets are quite small, the influence of these organizations, along with a number of corporate front groups, has been vastly inflated through the machinations of the PR industry, which helped generate the very effective impression in the media and in the halls of Congress of a bottom-up rebellion against environmentalism.

As John Stauber and Sheldon Rampton write in *Toxic Sludge Is Good for You*, the PR industry has gained much ground for its corporate clients, "turning the definition of 'grassroots politics' upside down by using rapidly evolving high-tech data and communications systems to custom design 'grassroots citizen movements.'" Known inside the industry and out as "astroturf," these PR initiatives can, for a fee, instantly manufacture a public constituency to support or oppose a legislative proposal in which a corporation or group of companies has a specific interest. The slickest of these efforts are artfully designed by Burson-Marsteller, Ketchum Communications and others to appear to members of Congress as real grassroots initiatives.[115]

While rolling this artificial turf into Congressional chambers, lobbyists representing environmentally destructive transnationals were also able to play a more crucial role than ever inside the offices of the Republican leadership. There they worked hand in hand with these officials, under the rubric of the Contract with America, in a bald-faced attempt to dismantle the government's ability to regulate and control corporations' negative impacts on the environment.[116]

By 1995 the two-track corporate strategy of co-optation and backlash began to falter. Some of the contradictions arose at the President's Council on Sustainable Development (PCSD), a blue-ribbon environmental commission established by the Clinton Administration. The PCSD, which was co-chaired by WRI's Lash and Dow's Buzzelli, was comprised of the leadership of seven big environmental groups, nine corporate chief executives and various Cabinet secretaries of the Clinton Administration. It was mandated to come up with a blueprint for "sustainable development" in the United States.[117]

Many of the corporations represented on the PCSD were self-styled environmentalists. All of them also made donations to PCSD member groups such as Audubon, WRI, NWF and the Nature Conservancy.[118] Yet while the PCSD members sat around the negotiating table, eight of the nine corporations were also helping to bankroll the anti-environmental backlash.

For instance, PCSD members Enron and Chevron supported the National Wetlands Coalition, a driving force behind the rollback of wetlands protection. The Global Climate Coalition, an industry lobbying group working to fend off regulations aimed at curbing global warming, is funded in part by PCSD leaders Dow and Chevron. The Center for the Defense of Free Enterprise, the Wise Use Movement's premier think tank, receives money from presidential commission member Georgia-Pacific. Project Relief, the corporate coalition that helped define the Contract with America's deregulatory agenda, was underwritten by numerous corporations, including Chevron, as well as the Chemical Manufacturers Association, in which Dow is an active member. The Clean Water Task Force, which worked assiduously to cripple the Clean Water Act, was comprised of PCSD members General Motors, Georgia-Pacific, the American Petroleum Institute (of which Chevron is an active member) and the CMA, among others. The list goes on.[119]

When confronted with the reality that the corporations they had been "partnering" with over recent years were attempting to overturn much of the work they had accomplished since the first Earth Day, the leadership of the mainstream environmental groups began to have second thoughts. "It will be a great tragedy for me, if . . . collaboration . . . is brought to an end because of the effort to undermine the environmental laws of the country," said the Natural Resources Defense Council's long-time president, John Adams. "But it could well be that we will see much less collaboration over the next five years, as a result of what is taking place today."[120]

Ultimately, as environmentalists mobilized public opinion against the Contract with America, the PCSD served as a vehicle to help contain the effort to undermine environmental laws. The corporate members of the PCSD were forced to agree publicly that existing laws were not to be dismantled, but rather were a point of departure for a new regulatory framework.[121] Yet despite this more promising turn of events, corporate America and its public relations counselors continued to move vigorously, both in an effort to regain lost ground and to capture new terrain.

Characteristic of these ongoing endeavors was Exxon's brash attempt to recover damages it claims to have suffered from the *Exxon Valdez* debacle. In 1995 the corporation filed suit in the U.S. Court of Claims to obtain compensation from the government for income lost since its ship the *Valdez* (now renamed the *Mediterranean*) has been prohibited from operating between Alaska and San Francisco.[122] Meanwhile, in an even more symbolic turn of events, environmentalists struggled to hold the line against the National Park Service becoming the ultimate icon of corporate greenwashing. In the last days of the 104th Congress, the Clinton Administration supported a Republican initiative to sell corporate sponsorships for the country's national parks. "Even companies with a record of environmental violations can become an official sponsor, thus buying a green image they do not deserve," charged the Natural Resources Defense Council. "Are we really ready for the Pepsi Old Faithful or the Kodak Grand Canyon?" asked the NRDC as it urged citizens to pressure the president and Congress to stop the bill.[123]

While the corporate parks bill died a quiet (if perhaps temporary) death with the end of the 104th Congress, 1997 began with the 105th Congress promising to carry on essentially the same anti-environmental, deregulatory agenda, albeit in a less audacious, subtler fashion.[124] This left the terms of much of the national environmental debate restricted to questions about how certain environmental statutes such as the Clean Air Act, the Superfund and the Endangered Species Act might be enforced or rewritten—a far cry from the measures needed to reverse the environmental crisis and bring corporations under greater democratic control.

Chapter Seven

Grassroots Globalization

Reclaiming the Blue Planet

We are not a market; first and foremost we are a people.
La Falda Declaration, from the Second Meeting
of Chemical and Paper Industry Workers
of the South American Common Market (MERCOSUR)

Every local community equipped with rights and obligations constitutes a new global order for environmental care.
Vandana Shiva, Indian Environmentalist

As dawn bathes Mexico City's central plaza, or Zócalo, in a hazy light, hundreds of *campesinos* and indigenous people from the faraway state of Tabasco arise. They roll up their makeshift bedding, assemble in rows of three and begin a procession toward Los Pinos, the residence of President Ernesto Zedillo. They have come from more than 600 miles away, marching for forty days and finally camping in the Zócalo to protest electoral fraud and to demand, in their words, "democracy, liberty and social justice."

As they pass by the National Stock Exchange—one of the country's primary links with the global economy—the peasants suddenly switch targets. They stop and then rush the doors, blocking all entrances just one half-hour before the day's transactions are to begin. The Exchange is forced to shut down for nearly two hours. News and police helicopters hover overhead and riot squads equipped with tear gas assemble. The newspaper *La Jornada* reports from the scene, describing the clash of two very different Mexican realities:

> The businessmen yuppies, with their Hermes Italian silk ties, Armani suits . . . Florsheim shoes . . . Burberry's shirts, and Ralph Lauren after-

shaves . . . are exasperated by the demonstration. Meanwhile, the
Chontal Indians and peasants remain seated, sandals off, *itacates* at one
side. Their dark bodies give off the smell of various days' sweat. Their
stern faces observe the executives and brokers who may have never
before been so close to people from the Mexican countryside—or perhaps only know them from TV.[1]

With police surrounding them, and the director of the Exchange
pleading with the protesters to allow one hundred people into the
building "to begin transactions," one of the group's spokespeople, left-
ist opposition leader Andrés Manuel Lopez Obrador, explains why they
are there. The Stock Exchange, he says, "is the clearest example of the
practices that have sunk Mexico and its people." Asserting that the liberalization of the Mexican economy has caused *campesinos* to lose their
land, workers to lose their jobs and those employed to have their buying power drop to levels of sixty years ago, Lopez continues: "In the last
twelve years of hunger and sacrifice, in which the workers and peasants
have been forced to survive in inhumane conditions, we have seen the
corporate profits on the Exchange grow."[2]

As tensions mount and the police prepare to move in, the protesters
clear out, avoiding a violent confrontation. But they have made their
point, not only to President Zedillo, but also to corporations and
investors from around the world who hold a stake in Mexico.

The Mexico City protest, which took place in June 1995, is one of a
growing number of grassroots mobilizations around the world against
the impacts of globalization. As the centers of political and economic
power shift from the nation-state toward an international economic
system increasingly dominated by transnational corporations, shifting
also are the strategies, tactics and targets of movements working for
social and environmental justice. The presidential palace, center of
power in the universe of Mexico's one-party state, is less and less relevant. Increasingly pertinent—and vulnerable—is the National Stock
Exchange, which, since it was opened to international investors, has
become a symbol of Mexico's growing subordination to the prerogatives
of the corporate-driven world economy.

The specter of disenfranchised peasants blockading, even briefly,
Mexico's access to international capital and international capital's access
to Mexico, provides us with a glimpse of the future. It presents the
prospect of a world in which those seeking social justice and ecological

sanity on the national and even local levels take their demands into the global arena. The old 1960s slogan "Think globally, act locally" is no longer sufficient as a guiding maxim. Rather, taking a cue from the peasants of Tabasco, civil society—popular movements, non-governmental organizations, labor unions, academics, doctors, lawyers, artists and others around the world—must confront the essential paradox and challenge of the twenty-first century by developing ways of *thinking and acting both locally and globally at the same time*. For without a host of fresh, innovative and coordinated international approaches firmly anchored in a diversity of local realities, the world's social and environmental movements will be rendered increasingly ineffective before the transnational power and mobility of the global corporations in the age of globalization.

Such collaborative initiatives are emerging in a scattershot fashion across the globe. Communities and organizations are increasingly working together across national boundaries to combat corporate abuses. Groups throughout the world are campaigning jointly around a diversity of issues ranging from Mitsubishi's deforestation to Union Carbide's ongoing denial of accountability for the Bhopal gas disaster. Indigenous peoples from Nigeria to British Columbia are increasingly working together to save the natural and cultural integrity of their resources from corporate and governmental intervention. Some organizations, such as the Pesticide Action Network, have secretariats in every continent dedicated to collaborative efforts to phase out some of the world's deadliest agricultural chemicals. Other organizations, such as Greenpeace and Friends of the Earth, have offices in dozens of countries working on coordinated campaigns aimed at curbing corporate-led destruction of the global environment. Similar international efforts are also emerging from the South. The recently created Ecuador-based group Oil Watch works with activists throughout the Third World to combat the abuses of transnational oil corporations in the tropics. And the Malaysia-based Third World Network, whose representatives operate in various countries in Asia, Africa and Latin America, has helped lead the critique of GATT and the World Trade Organization as new structures for global corporate governance.

The kinetic activity in all of these areas begins to provide a picture of a somewhat dispersed but burgeoning process of grassroots globalization. Communities the world over are breaking their isolation and entering into direct contact and collaboration with one another. As a document entitled *From Global Pillage to Global Village*—the product of a post-NAFTA meeting of more than seventy United States–based grass-roots organizations—optimistically declares:

> The unregulated internationalization of capital is now being followed by the internationalization of peoples' movements and organizations. Building peoples' international organizations and solidarity will be our revolution from within: a civil society without borders. This internationalism or "globalization from below" will be the foundation for a participatory and sustainable global village.[3]

Unfortunately, the current level of organization and approach of most of those working to build grassroots globalization still comes up well short. Corporate globalization continues apace, and civil society has so far been unable to significantly slow or change, let alone reverse, its destructive course. Even many of the examples of successful international collaboration cited in this book have been thwarted by the mobility that transnationals enjoy in the world economy. For instance, when Mitsubishi responded to international pressure by shutting its rare earth processing plant in Malaysia, it immediately subcontracted that work to two companies in China (see Chapter Four). Despite sporadic triumphs at the local, national and even international levels, the Corporate Planet continues to appropriate the Blue Planet for its profit-driven motives.

As advocates of social and environmental justice attempt to navigate the uncharted territory of corporate globalization, this chapter aims to provide a compass and some rough sketches of a map that may help point in the right direction. It is an attempt to contribute to the discussion of how the existing diversity of efforts to exert democratic control over corporations might develop a strength and power to work successfully in a consistent, strategic and systematic fashion to build a powerful form of grassroots globalization that can challenge structures of corporate rule.

Campaigning for Reform

Throughout the world, community groups, indigenous peoples, popular movements and non-governmental organizations continue to apply pressure on corporations to both clean up their act and transform their activities into ones that are ecologically and socially sound. As discussed in previous chapters, many such campaigns have forced companies to change their behavior. Corporations operating in various communities around the world have halted or significantly reduced their pollution of local water, land and air resources in response to campaigns against such abuses. Consumer boycotts, or sometimes the mere threat of them, have forced corporations to change their destructive behavior in a specific realm. Some campaigns have succeeded in convincing transnationals, on a local—and sometimes on a national or company-wide—basis to provide their workers not only with better wages, but also with improved health and safety conditions inside factories. Others have successfully employed public pressure and legal action to force companies to withdraw a hazardous product from the market, or have forced projects to be canceled and entire operations to be closed down or moved. And, finally, still other campaigns waged against corporations or against problems caused by one or more industrial sectors have resulted in the promulgation of national and international laws that have forced transnationals to change how they do business.

Of course, all of these efforts have elicited a sophisticated series of corporate responses ranging from sincere efforts to promote sustainability, to the export of pollution problems, to multifaceted attempts to co-opt the environmental issue itself. Yet despite all the resistance they continue to encounter, and despite the formidable structural impediments to thoroughgoing change, environmental and social movements have forced significant shifts in some corporate behavior and are continuing to do so, making the world a better, cleaner place to live than it might otherwise be.

Paradoxically, fighting corporate-caused problems chemical by chemical, forest by forest, shoreline by shoreline or even national law by national law may ultimately be a losing battle. Yet this approach can form the basis for the broader, deeper, more structural changes necessary to truly safeguard the world's environment and people from corporate abuse. This opportunity exists precisely because the fate of an old-growth forest or the ongoing production of organochlorine compounds is increasingly linked to the dynamics of the world economy. People's local concerns are inexorably parlayed into the global arena as local, single issues are drawn deep into transnational webs, requiring the escalation of international solidarity and collaboration.

One way the challenge of grassroots globalization is being met is through the worldwide proliferation of communications technology, which is bringing social and environmental movements from around the world ever closer together. The power of global communications became apparent in 1989 as the Chinese pro-democracy movement took over Tianamen Square in Beijing. Fax communications poured out of China, providing up-to-the-minute information to the news media and organizations working in solidarity with the pro-democracy movement.

The use of global communication networks for social change has expanded in the 1990s with the diffusion of the Internet. Nearly instantaneous communication between organizations and communities working on similar issues around the world has increased. The worldwide Association for Progressive Communications (APC) has built dozens of national and regional computer networks that are utilized by environmental, women's, labor, social justice and peace organizations across the planet. As Roberto Bissio, who directs the Uruguay-based Third World Institute, writes, the Internet not only provides decentralized, effective, low-cost communications among non-governmental organizations, but also "the informal, inter-active nature of this technology makes it possible to include grassroots communities right up to the international level in dynamic dialogue and collaboration on different strategic issues." Indeed, the APC-affiliated group known as NGO-Net, which Mr. Bissio helped found, is successfully linking grassroots communities and activists across the Third World, giving them numerous opportunities, including the chance to lobby intergovernmental organizations such as the United Nations on intergovernmental accords such as the Biodiversity Treaty.[4]

The Internet can also serve as a tool for those campaigning on specific issues. For instance, the Rainforest Action Network spurred thousands of individuals visiting its page on the World Wide Web to send computer-generated faxes to the Mitsubishi Corporation. The messages, urging the global giant to curb its deforestation, complemented a number of other tactics RAN employed to force Mitsubishi to sit down at the negotiating table. Meanwhile, an Internet project called Corporate Watch provides easily accessible, in-depth information to people around the world who are campaigning against the abuses of transnational corporations.[5]

Of course, international corporate campaigns were not born with the Internet. The Nestlé boycott in the 1970s mobilized activists, health care professionals and government officials in dozens of countries in both the North and South to put pressure on Nestlé to stop marketing a powdered substitute for mother's milk that was leading to higher infant mortality in the Third World. While limited in its success, it is hailed as a model for transnational organizing and the effort to build grassroots globalization.[6]

Similarly, the campaign to force divestment from South Africa during the era of apartheid proved that concerted ongoing international pressure on a group of corporations could help change the structure of an entire nation in a positive way. The divestment campaign successfully used United Nations resolutions, popular boycotts, public pressure, grassroots organizing, direct action and other tactics in countries all around the world to pressure a number of transnational corporations and large institutional investors (such as universities) with stakes in those corporations to quit doing business in South Africa. Divestment contributed to the enormous international political and economic pressure that put an end to apartheid.

One of the lessons of the anti-apartheid campaign is that it often takes pitting one powerful entity (corporate investors) against their erstwhile allies (the apartheid government) to leverage change. This message is now being heeded by those seeking to reverse global-warming trends who find themselves up against the oil industry. In order to confront these most powerful corporations, some environmental groups are turning to a most unlikely ally—the insurance industry. Large insurance corporations such as Swiss Re and Lloyd's of London are becoming alarmed by the potential impacts of climate change. They face possible financial ruin from the increasing frequency and severity of storms, drought and the like that global warming will bring. For this reason, the global insurance and reinsurance industry has become a wedge that can potentially dislodge the global oil corporations' grip on the status quo.[7] The presence of insurance industry lobbyists at the Berlin Climate Summit in 1995, for example, marked these corporations' formal entrance into the global-warming debate. It immediately strengthened the hand of environmental groups, thereby creating a corporate counterbalance to the so-called carbon club of lobbyists from the oil, coal, auto and chemical industries.[8]

New tactics are also emerging that involve the strategic use of technological innovation combined with mobilization of consumer constituencies to push and cajole entire industrial sectors to adopt more environmentally sound products and production methods. The various campaigns against bleaching paper with chlorine, for example, now point to technology that can produce excellent quality paper products by bleaching with oxygen- or hydrogen peroxide–based processes as substitutes for chlorine. The existence of this new technology and the growing demand for it, combined with political pressure brought about by grassroots organizers, have led a number of governments to legislate the phase-out and eventual ban of chlorine-based paper production. This has forced a growing number of paper corporations to invest in chlorine-free technology. The entire German paper industry, for instance, is totally chlorine free, and the rest of Europe is moving quickly in that direction.[9]

Perhaps the most successful and creative example of the strategic use of technological innovation as a catalyst for change is Greenpeace's effort to transform the refrigeration industry. Its effort has focused on moving away from the harmful CFC substitutes (HFCs and HCFCs) promoted by the world's major chemical companies and toward new technologies based on relatively benign butane- and propane-driven refrigeration technology. During the 1980s and early 1990s Greenpeace unsuccessfully attempted to pressure major German and English refrigeration corporations to create a new technology that didn't use ozone-depleting chemicals. Both the companies and their governments repeatedly told Greenpeace and others that developing such technology was ill considered and unsafe. Convinced by 1992 that the chemical industry's desire to retain the refrigeration market for CFC substitutes was intractable, the environmental group teamed up with independent researchers whose innovative work to produce ozone-friendly fridges had been rejected by the refrigerator corporations. Together they quickly developed the prototype for an alternative refrigeration system and then found a state-owned refrigerator company in the former East Germany to mass-produce the Greenfreeze model. This was especially fortuitous since the factory was about to be eliminated and its workers thrown out of work as a result of German unification. Instead, it began a new life as a privatized corporation named FORON, producing the Greenfreeze refrigerator for a guaranteed market of Greenpeace Germany members who had pre-ordered fridges. The ready-made market allowed the Greenfreeze project to take off.

The more than 30,000 advance orders that rolled in from Greenpeace members for Greenfreeze also shocked the refrigerator transnationals into action. Before the first Greenfreeze had rolled off the assembly line, German corporations such as Bosch-Siemens, Liebherr and Miele—all of whom had previously rejected the more environmentally sound alternative—realized that they would have to produce ozone-friendly refrigeration in order to stay competitive in the German market. They quickly came up with prototypes and, once they decided to move, transformed their production lines to turn out their own version of Greenfreeze within a matter of weeks. Soon the Swedish giant Electrolux joined in. Greenpeace had succeeded in breaking the tight link between the chemical and refrigeration corporations not only in Germany but—with the exception of the United Kingdom—throughout Europe. By 1994 these corporations (including FORON) were producing 8 million Greenfreezes a year in Europe, accounting for more than 50 percent of the region's entire production and 15 percent of the world market. This, in turn, piqued the interest of Japanese corporations. As Yoichi Fujimoto, head of Japan's Electrical Manufacturers Association, commented on the Greenfreeze phenomenon, "It's no laughing matter now that Siemens and the other big makers have taken it on. It poses a threat." [10]

But that is not the end of the story. Greenpeace then began to disseminate the technology—which it intentionally did not patent—around the world, offering it to small companies in Australia, Argentina, Colombia, Pakistan, Kenya and Ghana, as well as to state corporations in India and China, free of charge, thus providing these entities with an alternative to their dependence on the large chemical companies. The campaign has also involved the European governments, whose aid agencies are now promoting European corporations' versions of Greenfreeze in India and China. And it has even begun to have some limited success in pressuring the Montreal Protocol Fund (which, as discussed in Chapter Two, is controlled by the World Bank and advised by the large chemical corporations) to finance small national refrigeration companies to develop Greenfreeze projects in the Third World. [11]

In a world where transnationals increasingly control knowledge, information and technology, thereby determining what gets produced and how it gets made, Greenpeace was able to break through those barriers by developing and disseminating an alternative technological model. They used cheap, readily available technology and inputs—technology that the transnationals claimed either didn't exist, wasn't safe or wasn't economically viable—and they forced the transformation of an entire industry in Europe, thus opening the door to worldwide change. As a Greenpeace publication describes its own campaign:

> The story of Greenfreeze shows how it is possible for an environment group to take a new form of direct action, one which harnesses the expertise of technologists to the political and market power of consumers to force change where conventional campaigning is not enough. . . . The precedent set by Greenfreeze offers the hope that environmental groups will be able to unlock the scientific, technical and human potential for environmental solutions which are currently

ignored or suppressed in order to allow profit from pollution to continue. . . . The Greenfreeeze story shows that change is possible, and
that even powerful industrial strangleholds can be broken.[12]

Despite their international approach, neither Greenfreeze nor any of
the other campaigns mentioned above can, by themselves, go beyond
a piecemeal, case-by-case approach in their efforts to change how corporations operate. They can only force the transnationals to be fleet-
ingly accountable to local communities, national governments and
international institutions. These campaigns are valuable for a number
of reasons, however. First and foremost, they are generating specific
solutions to specific problems: leading Nestlé to implement more ethi-
cal marketing practices, compelling Mitsubishi to halt its dumping of
radioactive waste in a Malaysian village, empowering local activists to
lobby the United Nations and phasing out the refrigeration industry's
use of ozone-depleting chemicals. When taken together, such individual victories add up to broader change.

These campaigns are also empowering to the activists, consumers
and government officials who get involved in them. They demonstrate
that there are creative and effective ways to create change, promote justice, build democracy and save the environment. Moreover, the mere
existence of an active, vibrant movement carrying out a series of campaigns challenging corporations keeps the political, economic and public relations pressure on the transnationals to continue innovating and
developing new, cleaner technologies and products.

Finally, these campaigns hold a great potential to serve as building
blocks toward a more fundamental change—the transformation of political power to an order that will make corporations truly accountable
to the public good. The divestment campaign against apartheid is an excellent example of such a building block.[13]

Yet engaged as they are at local, national and international levels, all
of these campaigns have the common problem of having to wage their
battles on a playing field that is most often (and increasingly) tilted in
favor of entrenched corporate interests. This is often due to a corporation "buying" a handful of local elected officials or national congressmen, or the political clout a transnational acquires when it invests in a
community or a country. It is attributable to national and international systems of accounting and subsidies that determine that it makes
more "economic sense" to pursue the more destructive of two options.

It is also dictated by the international regulatory framework established by GATT/WTO and other free trade accords that leaves less and less room for alternatives. And the tilt toward corporate interests is exacerbated by the fact that the transnationals control the bulk of money invested in research and investment in new technologies—money that is rarely invested in the interests of sustainability.

Some activists are beginning to address this disequilibrium in a way that goes beyond international collaboration on single-issue campaigns. They are doing so by attempting to build grassroots globalization in a way that redefines and restructures the playing field—moving to tilt it toward sustainability, justice and democracy. In order to achieve this, movements throughout the world are challenging the mainstream dogma that equates "free market" capitalism with democracy, and are instead advocating political change that reins in corporate power and subordinates it to participatory democratic mechanisms at the local, national and international levels.

Piercing the Penumbra

Ralph Nader, long-time consumer advocate and critic of the transnationals, has remarked that the creation of free trade pacts such as NAFTA and GATT could be the "greatest blunder in the history of the modern global corporation." Until the Uruguay Round of GATT was created to provide a framework for corporate globalization, the transnationals operated in what Nader describes as a more or less "private penumbra." But "now that the global corporate strategic plan is out in print," he reasons, "it gives us an opportunity." [14]

In the newly emerging structures of the world economy—NAFTA, GATT and the World Trade Organization (WTO)—citizens have found "handles" with which to respond to the process of corporate globalization. By organizing in reaction to the negotiation of these global and regional accords, social movements around the world are identifying and targeting not just single issues, but rather the structures that underpin an emerging system of governance increasingly by and for corporations. Labor, environmental and consumer groups are also forging close working relationships, building common agendas and implementing joint strategies across their specific issue interests and across national borders. One of the best examples of this is the evolution of nongovernmental alliances that grew out of the NAFTA negotiations.

As the debate concerning NAFTA began to heat up in 1991, these alliances were nearly nonexistent. But despite the lack of experience that many of the advocacy organizations from Canada, the United States and Mexico had in terms of working internationally or "cross-sectorally," the collaboration grew out of necessity. These joint efforts arrived at some significant achievements. True, those who aimed to defeat NAFTA were unsuccessful in doing so, and those who fought for side agreements on environment and labor issues ended up with weak and largely toothless accords. Yet in spite of these setbacks, in a few short years activists did succeed in forcing a broad public debate on "free trade" and the corporate interests it serves—whereas before there had been none—and placing environmental and labor issues at the center of it. As historian Jeremy Brecher writes, in the United States, "the near defeat of NAFTA reveals pervasive popular doubt about the wisdom of an unregulated international market. The struggle against NAFTA represented the first major effort by Americans who have been hurt by global economic integration to do something about it."[15]

The relationships forged among environmental, labor, consumer, farmer and religious organizations during the intitial NAFTA negotiations have deepened. Many have lasted beyond the specific NAFTA debate, evolving into collaborative efforts to address the social and environmental ramifications of the corporate-driven integration of the economies of the United States, Canada and Mexico and to propose alternative development paths. By the time negotiations to integrate Chile into NAFTA began in 1995, more than 175 environmental organizations, labor unions, human rights groups, indigenous peoples' organizations and religious institutions from the four countries sent a joint letter to their presidents expressing deep concern for "the growing gap throughout the Americas between the wealthy beneficiaries of deregulated integration and the growing numbers of poor people whose jobs are being displaced or eliminated and whose wages, rights and environments are being eroded." The organizations called for "economic integration in the hemisphere that places the rights of workers, indigenous peoples, farmers, consumers and women, as well as the protection of the environment at the center of the integration agenda."[16]

The breadth and depth of organizations participating in the debate on the integration and globalization of the world's economies continues to grow as the environmental and labor movements use NAFTA expansion, MERCOSUR, the WTO and the MAI as organizing vehicles to ride across national and single-issue boundaries, building the process of grassroots globalization.

The emergence of the Zapatistas in Mexico represents another type of response to the process of economic integration that NAFTA consolidated. The Zapatistas first appeared in the public eye on January 1, 1994—the day NAFTA went into effect—when they launched a guerrilla offensive in the southern Mexico state of Chiapas. Their presence; their critique of Mexican society, politics and economics; and their demands provoked what may be called the first real crisis of the age of globalization. Their dramatic uprising shook the image of prosperity and development projected by the corporate and governmental proponents of liberalization, privatization and free trade regimes everywhere. The crisis also pointed to both old and new ways of responding to the social, political, economic and, implicitly, ecological impacts of globalization.

During NAFTA negotiations in the early 1990s, Mexico was held forth as a shining example of the transformation of a once ardently nationalist Third World state to a model of economic neoliberalism. Sustained rates of economic growth, the opening up of protected markets, the selling off of state-owned industries, escalating transnational corporate investment and a booming stock exchange were all hailed as indicators of Mexico's vigor and potential as an "emerging market" in the world economy.

The Zapatista National Liberation Army (EZLN) emerged from Chiapas's Lacandon rainforest to remind Mexico that despite the McDonald's and Wal-Marts sprouting up in its major cities, and despite the more than $40 billion in foreign investment that flowed into the country over the five years leading up to NAFTA's implementation, a huge proportion of its people were mired in poverty as deeply, if not more so, than ever before.[17] As Subcomandante Marcos, the best known of the Zapatistas, described it, "Thousands of Indians, armed with truth and fire, with shame and dignity, shook the country from the sweet dream of modernity."[18]

Significantly, as the first guerrilla movement to emerge in Latin America after the Cold War, the Zapatistas moved beyond the polarized terrain of superpower rivalry and its accompanying political and ideological burdens. They did not aim to seize state power, but rather they called for the democratization of the Mexican state and an end to marginalization and misery for the vast number of poor, not only in Chiapas, but throughout the country. These demands posed a problem not only for the monolithic Mexican government and its more than seventy-five years of one-party rule, but by demanding democracy and social justice, the Zapatistas also threatened to destabilize the investment climate in Mexico and in emerging markets around the world, thus posing a direct menace to the agenda of corporate globalization.

Indeed, a small group of mostly indigenous people living in an isolated rainforest zone of southern Mexico projected their reality, the plight of Mexico's poor, and by implication, that of three-fifths of the world's population who are marginal to the world economy, to the center of the international stage. By doing so, the Zapatistas highlighted some of the greatest contradictions of globalization: not only are the majority of the world's peoples peripheral to or victims of the corporate world order, but their aspirations for basic rights—ranging from democratic participation to housing and food to clean air and water—are anathema to it.

Wall Street confirmed this analysis in its own sort of way. As Dalal Baer, an adviser to Bear, Sterns & Company put it, Mexico faced a dilemma: on the one hand, it was under pressure to open up its political system (augmented by the Zapatista insurgency); on the other hand, she observed, "Financial markets might not respond positively to increased democracy because it leads to increased uncertainty."[19] In Mexico the interests of the forces of economic globalization and the interests of democracy did not intersect. Rather, they had become starkly opposed to each other.

One U.S. corporate response to the Zapatistas came from Chase Manhattan Bank, which has billions of dollars invested in Mexico. In a memo leaked to the public and widely distributed on the Internet, a senior Chase analyst wrote that "While Chiapas, in our opinion, does not pose a fundamental threat to Mexican political stability, it is *perceived* [emphasis added] to be so by many in the investment community. The government will need to eliminate the Zapatistas to demonstrate their effective control of the national territory and of security policy."[20] Thus the mere *perception* of instability became a threat to investor confidence and therefore to real economic stability both in Mexico and, by means of a 1990s-style global financial domino effect, in the world economy.[21] To resolve this public relations crisis, the memo called for military intervention. Not surprisingly then, right after Mexico received a $50 billion loan designed by the U.S. government to bail it out of its financial tailspin and thus stabilize a jumpy world economy (the loan was guaranteed by Mexico's petroleum revenues), the Mexican military moved into Chiapas's rainforests in an unsuccessful effort to root out the Zapatista insurgency.

The New Anticolonialism

While the process of economic globalization has propagated a new form of colonialism, or what Indian journalist Chakravarthi Rhagavan has referred to as "recolonization," one of the ways social movements the world over have responded to this dynamic is by harkening back to anticolonial movements of the past. Such is the case in Mexico, where the Zapatista insurgents not only built on five centuries of indigenous resistance to colonialism, but also took up the banner of Emiliano Zapata, a hero of the Mexican Revolution. By doing so, they positioned themselves as guardians of a deeply ingrained tradition of revolution that is counterposed to foreign domination and in favor of local self-government and land reform.[22]

The situation in India is similar. There, burgeoning peoples' movements against globalization and the growing control of the country's economy by transnational corporations and international lending institutions are reaching back to the relatively recent history of the country's movement for independence against British colonialism. And while resistance to globalization in India is still by no means as broad or powerful as was the anticolonial movement led by Mahatma Gandhi and Jawaharlal Nehru, it is clear, says leading opposition figure George Fernandes, that "for the first time [since 1948] there is a genuine feeling that our independence is at stake."[23]

In response to the waning economic and political sovereignty of the Indian state, organizers are drawing on the country's rich history of nonviolent protest for political independence and local self-sufficiency. "This is the land of *Satyagraha*.* This country produced Mahatma Gandhi and nonviolently threw out the colonizers. And we are very confident of throwing out all of the powers that are trying to colonize India now," asserts M. D. Nanjundaswamy, who led a movement of hundreds of thousands of farmers against the Cargill corporation's agricultural forays into central India (see Chapter Five).[24]

In some cases the transnationals seem to be obliging their Indian critics by following the well-worn paths of history. Cargill, for example,

---

* Literally translated as "truth" (or "soul") "force," *Satyagraha* was the essence of Gandhi's philosophy and strategy of nonviolent civil disobedience. In his words, *Satyagraha* aimed at the "vindication of truth, not by infliction of suffering on the opponent, but on one's self." Quoted in Lewis Fischer, *Gandhi: His Life and Message for the World* (New York: New American Library, 1954).

which in a few short years has become one of the largest traders of agricultural commodities in India, moved in 1992 to initiate a massive salt-mining enterprise in the Kutch region of the state of Gujarat—home of Mahatma Gandhi. This struck a powerful chord for many, as salt was one of the issues upon which India's independence movement was forged. Gandhi himself led the famous salt *Satyagraha* civil disobedience march in 1930 and the ensuing campaign aimed at making India self-sufficient in salt, a basic commodity it was forced to import under British rule.[25]

So when the New Delhi government gave Cargill its blessing to move in and begin producing salt for Japan and the East Asian market (salt is a key input for, among other things, chlorine production), it touched a raw nerve. Labeling Cargill the "New East India Company," activists launched a "second salt *Satyagraha*" in 1993. In addition to pursuing a legal strategy to protect small-scale salt producers in the region from the U.S. transnational, tens of thousands of people, including members of parliament, students and youth, trade union leaders, representatives of other popular movements, non-governmental organizations and local salt manufacturers, participated in a series of protests, including a march that followed the reverse route of Gandhi's famous *Satyagraha*. With the protest building toward a planned blockade of the port of Kutch and Gandhi's simple, powerful words "We will make salt" echoing across the land, Cargill pulled out.[26]

From the corporate perspective, Cargill was wise to quit the fight when it did. The salt issue, carrying with it as deep an historical and symbolic resonance as the Boston Tea Party does for the United States, or perhaps as the nationalization of oil does for Mexico, could have catalyzed a significant backlash not only against Cargill, but against the opening of the Indian economy in general. Yet while Cargill bailed out before the *Satyagraha* built into a national movement, it was an important moment. As the New Delhi–based Public Interest Research Group observes, this victory marked "the beginning of the larger struggle against the new economic policies of the government which strike at the very roots of a self-reliant and socially oriented economy."[27]

Since that time, one of the most vibrant movements in the world against the negative impacts of globalization has emerged in India. Millions of farmers, fisherfolk, union workers, urban dwellers and others have engaged in various forms of protest against the growing transnational corporate penetration of the Indian economy. And to a large degree they base their organizing on their country's recent struggle against colonialism, including the principles of *Satyagraha, swadeshi* (economic independence) and *charkha* (self-sufficiency).* As the *Sunday Times of India* reports, "Their philosophy . . . must seem like heresy to the champions of globalisation." Yet for these organizations, which serve as a voice for the hundreds of millions of people who subsist on the country's natural resources, "*swadeshi* is an imperative, much more so today than 50 years ago. For in this period a process called 'development' has deprived more and more people of direct control over their immediate environment and means of livelihood."[28]

Some activists in the United States are also evoking their heritage of anticolonialism in an effort to build greater democratic control over corporations. Looking back to the War of Independence against England and the creation of the United States of America, they have uncovered a hidden history of citizens' and local governments' efforts to maintain sovereign control over corporations. In the late 1700s, after overthrowing British rule and severing the political and economic links between the former colonies and corporations such as the East India and Hudson's Bay Companies, which had been chartered by the English Crown, citizens moved to create mechanisms that would allow new U.S. corporations to exist, but under strict control at the state level. As Richard Grossman and Frank Adams write in their widely circulated pamphlet *Taking Care of Business: Citizenship and the Charter of Incorporation*:

> Having thrown off English rule, the revolutionaries did not give governors, judges or generals the authority to charter corporations. Citizens made certain that legislators issued charters, one at a time and for a limited number of years. They kept a tight hold on corporations by spelling out rules each business had to follow, by holding business owners liable for harms or injuries, and by revoking charters. . . .
> Citizens shared the belief that granting charters was their exclusive right. . . . The power of large shareholders was limited by scaled voting, so that large and small investors had equal voting rights. Interlocking directorates were outlawed. Shareholders had the right to remove directors at will. . . . The penalty for abuse or misuse of the charter was not a

---

* *Swadeshi* was also a term popularized by Gandhi. *Charkha* is the spinning wheel that Gandhi used as a symbol of the *swadeshi* campaign to create homespun cotton cloth in order to free India from its dependence on the cotton mill trade with Great Britain.

fine or slap on the corporate wrist, but revocation of the charter and
dissolution of the corporation. Citizens believed it was society's inalien-
able right to abolish an evil.[29]

Grossman and Adams go on to document how, as U.S. corporations
grew in power and reach through the 1800s, they were able to undermine many of the accountability mechanisms created by the states. By
the early twentieth century, ongoing corporate lobbying and gambits
that played states off against one another had convinced most legislatures to diminish citizen authority over corporate structure, governance, production and labor, to extend the length of charters and to
grant corporations limited liability. Meanwhile the courts reinterpreted
the U.S. Constitution, granting corporations equal status with individual citizens, including protection under the Bill of Rights and the Four-
teenth Amendment. The courts also granted corporations a variety of
rights and privileges that went beyond what citizens were entitled to
under the law.[30]

Despite the distortion of the chartering process from a mechanism
designed to foster corporate accountability to democratic institutions to
one that has given U.S. transnationals increasingly free reign, original
chartering laws remain on the books in various states. A renewed understanding of the power inherent in these laws has given rise to a number
of budding efforts to revoke corporate charters. "We are challenging
who has authority here—the corporations or the people," asserts
Grossman.[31]

While not yet forcing corporations into courts of law, the concept of
challenge is spreading. In Washington State, a local chapter of the grassroots environmental group Earth First! issued a mock certificate of dissolution that declared the Weyerhaeuser corporation "guilty of gross
felony criminal conduct," including having "irreparably degraded the
environment of the Northwest [United States], Canada, Asia and other
areas." The "certificate" called for the revocation of Weyerhaeuser's
charter, the abolishment of the company and the seizure of its assets.[32]
Without legal standing, Earth First!'s call for dissolution is nevertheless
based on existing legal doctrine.

More importantly, the group's action reflects other efforts brewing
across the United States to recall the political and legal heritage of the
American Revolution in order to build a contemporary response to corporate power. This response, in the words of activist Peter Kellman, aims

first "to create a debate . . . which questions the authority and legitimacy of corporations to rule our society." Ultimately, say Kellman and a growing number of activists throughout the nation, the goal is to replace "corporate, anti-democratic institutions that consolidate power in the hands of a few, with democratic institutions that disperse power and wealth in the hands of the many."[33]

These are lofty, distant goals, yet many of those working on environmental, labor, consumer, health and other issues in the United States are coming to realize that the question of democracy versus corporate governance underpins their issues. Thus they are increasingly drawn to the common cause of seeking alternatives to corporate globalization. What's more, as corporate power grows, increasing numbers of citizens are becoming indignant. A 1996 poll conducted for the Washington, D.C.–based Preamble Center for Public Policy found that seven in ten people favor stronger government actions to curb corporate irresponsibility. "Ire at large corporations crosses race, class and political lines," write the Center's pollsters. "It's so intense that, for the majority of citizens, it now rivals or exceeds anger at government. Most significant and most surprising, anger at corporate America has begun to translate into broad public support for government action to make corporations act more responsibly—and has the potential to change the nation's political landscape."[34]

Not all those who want to change the U.S. landscape intend to carve progressive political contours into it. Right-wing ideologues and movements have also reacted to corporate globalization with a new brand of nationalism that carries with it fascist and often racist tendencies. In the wake of the 1995 Oklahoma City bombings, for example, newscasts carried video clips of right-wing militia members decrying NAFTA and GATT as affronts to U.S. sovereignty. And in his campaign for the 1996 Republican presidential nomination, right-wing zealot Patrick Buchanan elicited popular support by denouncing the tyranny of giant corporations. In the anticorporate groundswell that briefly followed, even fellow Republican Bob Dole, a favorite son of corporate America, was compelled to criticize the excessive power of the transnationals. In fact, Buchanan's xenophobic populism drew far more attention to the issue in a few short months than progressive activists and politicians had been able to muster over a number of years. While resonating with the public's discontent, such criticism is packaged as part and parcel of a hate-filled political agenda that is not only antigovernment and anti-corporate, but also anti-immigrant, anti-Semitic, and deeply racist.

Similar trends are emerging in other parts of the world. In France, for instance, one of the most prominent leaders in the fight against GATT was neofascist politician Jean-Marie LePen. In Russia ultranationalists such as Vladimir Zhirinovsky exploit public unease with the presence of foreign corporations to build their right-wing agenda. And in India the Hindu fundamentalist BJP party has taken advantage of the movement against economic globalization and transnational investment to, in the words of its general secretary, K. N. Govindacharya, "bring the focus back to emotional nationalism, which is our political ground."[35] By building temporary alliances with left-wing political parties and popular movements, and by appropriating the Gandhian concept of *swadeshi*, the BJP is using popular sentiment against globalization as a vehicle in its efforts to seize political power.[36] By building a new religious-based right-wing anticorporate nationalism, the BJP threatens to undermine efforts to achieve social justice, ecological sustainability and peaceful coexistence between Hindus and Muslims in India.

These disparate yet strikingly similar responses point to the potential that exists within right-wing forces to appropriate pervasive public discontent with corporate globalization, forging it into a platform that is at best conservative-nationalist and at worst neofascist. The political solutions these forces offer will inevitably be at odds with the central principles of ecological sustainability, social equity and democratic participation that form the basis for almost every progressive movement against the destructive forces of corporate globalization. As historians Jeremy Brecher and Tim Costello write, "An exclusive focus on national interests distorts people's understandings of what is really going on in the global economy." What's more, they point out, nationalist answers to globalization that rely on absolutist interpretations of national sovereignty undermine "efforts to address such global problems as environmental destruction, nuclear proliferation, overpopulation and human rights." Brecher and Costello further argue that the direction the response to globalization takes could easily turn toward either progressive and humane solutions or ugly right-wing answers. Whether the movements that are emerging to combat globalization "protect narrow special interests, lash out in chauvinistic rage at political scapegoats, or take a more constructive direction," they write, "will be crucial to the future of politics worldwide."[37]

Reclaiming the Blue Planet

As the world moves into the twenty-first century, corporate globalization has become the dominant economic—and to some degree political—paradigm. In response, various social movements are emerging to challenge its reign, presenting both danger and opportunity. The danger is that the xenophobic nationalist reaction will arise as the foremost voice of opposition. The opportunity is that the nascent forces of grassroots globalization, which are weaving an emerging web of activism and building networks across the Earth, have a chance to step forth with alternatives to both the Corporate Planet and its neofacist detractors.

Reclaiming the Blue Planet from the clutches of corporate globalization will not be a simple task. It must be achieved by creating and implementing mechanisms for democratic control over corporations and economies. Such democratization involves redefining both the concept of corporate accountability and the concept of "the corporation" itself. Corporate accountability is presently understood by many people as a corporation's nonbinding response to the demands of those affected by its activities. It is variously defined as a transnational's responsibility to its investors, the responsiveness of a corporation to the demands of its workers or of a local community in which it is operating, or as a company's voluntary reporting of environmental information. Indeed, corporate accountability is increasingly confused with corporate self-regulation.

True corporate accountability, however, is something much broader and more profound than the above definitions. It means that a company can be held strictly accountable to the laws and democratic processes of communities, governments and the global framework in which it operates. At the heart of such democratic governance should lie the concept that corporations do not have any inherent right to exist, but rather are granted that right by "the people" and therefore must answer to the public. Thus the people, through a process of democratic political representation, should have the right to define "the corporation"— what it is, and what it can and cannot do. If a company knowingly sells defective products or consistently violates the law, the public should be able to petition the government to revoke its charter and dismantle it by liquidating its assets.

With corporations under more democratic control, their power can be curbed. Monopolies can be broken up. Economies could become focused more on sustainability. Such a climate could foster a decentralized, ecologically oriented market economy based on the development of alternative clean technologies, organic agriculture, worker-controlled enterprises, small businesses, municipal corporations, alternative trade associations, banks that are truly dedicated to the eradication of poverty, community empowerment and greater equity between North and South, and more.

Building such a vision—one that would dismantle global capitalism as we know it—may seem to be a Quixotic quest, a tilting at skyscrapers of sorts. Yet many interim steps can be taken at the local, national and international levels to build democratic control over corporations while fostering alternative economic development. Following are some of the broad outlines of what such a transformation might entail.

Local Democratization

Creating mechanisms that empower communities at the local level with rights, obligations and information is essential for achieving democratic governance of corporations. As Vandana Shiva argues in her insightful essay "The Greening of Global Reach," while transnational corporations are parochial entities emanating from a very local area and projecting themselves globally, the converse is also true. Local communities, when taken as a group, are truly global, or "planetary," entities. Although often isolated from one another, they share many characteristics, such as a spiritual and tangible connection with the Earth and her resources. This connection provides the foundation of a nearly universal ethic of sustainability that spans just about every culture on Earth, and which runs counter to the growth and profit-accumulation ethic of corporate capitalists. Thus, suggests Shiva, equipping local communities with the right to timely, accurate and comprehensible information about corporate and governmental development projects, and with the right to reject such projects—in other words, democratizing decision-making processes at the local level—constitutes what she calls "a new global order for environmental care."[38]

Such empowerment could go a long way toward breaking up corporate control and decentralizing power, placing communities in command of their resources, ecosystems, economies, politics, cultures and destinies. It could also alleviate many current social and environmental disasters and prevent many in the future.

How local democratization can feed into broader, larger-scale national and international political processes without being co-opted or corrupted is a difficult question. This forms part of the paradox and challenge of thinking and acting both locally and globally.

National Democratization

The pervasive corporate role in government, which permeates most nations, must be addressed in order to forge democratic control over corporations. Such a change implies reinventing the nation-state in a fashion that transforms it from an elitist, unaccountable, overly bureaucratic, often corruption-ridden entity to a new model of governance that is an expression of grassroots democracy.

It must be recognized, however, that the tide is moving swiftly in the opposite direction, spawning only eddies of resistance. As Indian scholar Rajni Kothari lucidly points out, the "right" has co-opted the "left's" critique of the nation-state and used it to promote its free market agenda:

> While there is no doubt that too much dependence on the State had
> produced a structure of power and authority, at once insufficient and
> oppressive, as was indeed continuously pointed out by the left-cum-
> liberal critique of the State . . . today that very critique is being hijacked
> for a wholly opposite and right wing purpose by the proponents of
> globalization. . . . It has . . . become the basis for reinforcing privatiza-
> tion and debunking not just the public sector but the State as such, not
> just the bureaucratic excesses but democratic politics itself, not just cor-
> ruption in public life but the public arena as a whole.[39]

Thus criticisms of the overcentralizing, antidemocratic nature of the state, of too much "big government," are being used by corporate interests and right-wing ideologues to attempt to dismantle as much of it as possible. Nevertheless, argues Kothari, the nation-state must not be discarded, rather the tide must turn and the state must be reinvented as an instrument of democracy and popular participation that promotes the interests of the poor, of labor and of the environment in this age of globalization.[40] Or as Jorge Castaneda, one of Mexico's most prominent dissidents, puts it, the state "must be radically overhauled, without necessarily shrinking."[41]

Of course, this is nothing less than an agenda for revolutionary change. The transformation of the nation-state requires that powerful, broad-based movements arise and break the tight, interwoven link between corporations and government. If achieved, such a change

could create the political space for democratically accountable legisla-
tors (instead of representatives beholden to corporate contributions) to
shift government subsidies away from the pockets of large corporations
in the petroleum, nuclear and timber industries, for example, and
toward support for the development of alternative, ecologically sound
technologies and industries, as well as education, health and social programs for the poor. It could facilitate the introduction of environmental accounting and government support for other mechanisms, such as
green taxes, that promote sustainability. Such changes could alter regulatory structures so that the big transnationals would lose many of the
unfair advantages they currently enjoy, thus permitting small business
to thrive. In a country like the United States, it could provide for the
possibility of stringent national charters for corporations, rather than
the current state-based system that has allowed half of the top 500 U.S.
corporations to seek haven in Delaware, where regulations are the weakest.[42] It could open the door for a Constitutional amendment that
would deprive corporations of their Supreme Court–granted legal status
as individual persons. And it could give government the mandate to
ban particularly harmful production processes, products or entire industries—such as the nuclear or chlorine sectors—while implementing programs that would provide transitional support along with meaningful
education and retraining for workers.[43] It could also effectively regulate
the onslaught of corporate advertising and reverse the concentration of
mass media ownership, allowing for a greater democratization of information.

Greater democracy at the national level in the Northern industrialized countries could have a number of global repercussions as well. For
instance, communities in countries such as Costa Rica, Colombia,
Ecuador and India that have attempted to sue U.S. corporations such as
Dow Chemical, Shell and Texaco for destroying their lives and resources
would have a much better chance of gaining standing in U.S. courts of
law—something that has, until now, been quite difficult to achieve.
Parliaments, diets, and congresses less influenced by transnational corporations would be much more likely to extend national product bans
on deadly pesticides, hazardous pharmaceuticals and products such as
asbestos to the export of such lethal merchandise as well. These legislatures could also mandate that the corporations they charter follow the
highest standards throughout their international operations. Conversely, if countries in the South and East exerted more democratic con-

trol over corporations, they would be more readily able to apply social and environmental criteria to screen and control foreign investors.[44]

Global Democratization

Finally, true accountability means that international institutions such as the United Nations must be imbued with greater transparency and democracy themselves, while taking more significant steps to govern the behavior of transnational corporations on a worldwide level. In this age of globalization many regulations, standards and market mechanisms must be global as well. For too long the transnationals have gotten away with playing governments against one another in a gambit to undermine workers' power and environmental laws. A system of global governance needs to be designed to control transnational corporations while raising labor and environmental standards across the board. Such a role could be undertaken by the UN and financed by a modest tax on international financial transactions, as originally proposed by Nobel economist James Tobin. The income generated by such a tax would at once lessen the UN's dependency on the world's richest governments and provide it with more resources than all international agencies currently have at their disposal.[45]

While advocating such a shift may be swimming against the tide, it is not pure fantasy. The Canadian and French governments have recently considered a Tobin-style tax. What's more, there are already a number of international regulatory systems and accountability mechanisms in place that, while they may be inadequate in many respects, provide a point of departure. Most fall under the direct aegis of the United Nations. Although the UN today is a less pivotal player on the world stage than it once was, it must be reformed, revived and reinvigorated. While the WTO and the multilateral development banks are dominated by the most economically powerful nations in the world, the United Nations is based on a one-country–one-vote principle. Thus, apart from the Security Council, where the most militarily powerful nations dominate, there is a semblance of democracy. Universal declarations on human rights, indigenous peoples, international labor codes and environmental conventions negotiated under UN auspices are all examples of positive forms of globalization that hold significant potential as international legal mechanisms that could well regulate corporate behavior globally.

As a United Nations study points out, "Despite large gaps and great disparities between the regions, there is now a significant body of rules of international environmental law at the regional and global levels. Those rules, in one way or another, affect every geographic and political region and state, and influence, directly or indirectly, virtually every type of industrial activity, including TNCs [transnational corporations]."[46] This body of law could be further strengthened, elaborated upon and refined to address directly the unique, often stateless nature of global corporations. As we move into the greenhouse age, for example, it is possible and foreseeable that protocols will be attached to the Climate Convention that specifically regulate and control the activities of the corporate sectors most responsible for climate change. Protocols similar to the Biodiversity Treaty could be created to force greater accountability from fisheries, forestry and biotechnology transnationals.[47] The United Nations is also working on an intergovernmental treaty to phase out and ban persistent organic chemicals such as chlorine. While facing a tough, uphill battle, this accord, if implemented, would force fundamental transformations for chemical transnationals such as Dow, Solvay, and Mitsubishi Group member Asahi Glass.[48]

The potential that such agreements hold, however, is seriously diluted not only by corporate lobbying against them, but also by the dynamics of corporate globalization. The increasing power that is concentrated in institutions that define themselves as primarily economic in orientation, such as GATT, WTO and the World Bank, serves to weaken the more socially, environmentally and politically oriented United Nations. This has profound political ramifications that must be addressed. Indeed, mechanisms for global corporate accountability that don't subordinate this de facto system of corporate governance to more democratic institutions oriented to the prerogatives of ecological sustainability and social justice will ultimately fail.

The only way that these ideas about reclaiming the Blue Planet will be transformed into reality is through pressure applied by the forces of grassroots globalization—pressure that includes ongoing campaigns, boycotts, strikes and direct action to effect change. Part of this effort will entail refashioning specific strategies aimed at saving a forest or banning a chemical so that they include a focus on corporate globalization. As Canadian activist Tony Clarke explains, "Conventional modes of action—lobbying governments, consumer boycotts, shareholder campaigns, and litigation measures—need to be re-evaluated and reworked for the central task of dismantling corporate rule."[49]

Another component will be to invent new ways of thinking, seeing and organizing. Candido Grzybowski, executive director of the Brazilian Institute for Social and Economic Analysis, puts it this way:

> We must use a different approach to think about globalization, taking alternative globalizations into consideration. For this, the conventional hegemonic way of thinking dictated by neoliberalism and by "free market" consensus is not very helpful. It is necessary that we, as citizens of the planet Earth committed to democracy, build our own agenda, our own way of viewing issues and tasks, our own priorities. We can't ignore other approaches and their proposals, but let's not limit ourselves to them. Let's face up to them![50]

The road of grassroots globalization will be an arduous one. Yet in many respects this journey continues along a path well traveled and chronicled by those seeking justice throughout history. This route has taken many different political, cultural, technological and moral turns over the centuries, but the quest continues unabated. The curve that we are rounding now, at the close of the twentieth century, finds the stark, monolithic flatlands of corporate globalization stretched out before us, extending to the foreseeable horizon of history.

Yet it is becoming clear that the terrain is more varied and less alien than it may first appear. The path toward sustainability and democracy has not disappeared. It can be found by reading the compass of the world's valiant history of struggles for social justice. New road maps, new vehicles and new tools for organizing within the topography of globalization will also be required. It may take a generation or more to forge a passage that can point the way for the world's diversity of cultures to reclaim the Blue Planet. But it can be done. And when that day arrives, we will round another bend to find that our journey in search of justice carries on.

Notes

Introduction

1. Richard L. Grossman and Frank T. Adams, *Taking Care of Business: Citizenship and the Charter of Incorporation* (Cambridge, MA: Charter Ink., January 1993), pp. 6–10.
2. UNCTAD, *World Investment Report 1995: Transnational Corporations and Competitiveness* (New York: United Nations Conference on Trade and Development, Division on Transnational Corporations and Investment, 1995), pp. xix–xx.
3. Cited in Rhys Jenkins, *Transnational Corporations and Uneven Development: The Internationalization of Capital and the Third World* (London and New York: Methuen, 1987), pp. 1–2.
4. While unwieldy for the purposes of this book, Barnet and Cavanagh define seven groups of nations: (1) the wealthy, industrialized OECD countries, (2) the newly industrializing countries, (3) countries aspiring to industrialize, (4) the former communist countries of Eastern Europe, (5) most of the OPEC countries, (6) forty poor countries located mostly in Latin America and Africa and (7) the forty-seven "poorest of the poor" nations, almost all located in Africa. Richard J. Barnet and John Cavanagh, *Global Dreams: Imperial Corporations and the New World Order* (New York: Simon & Schuster, 1994), pp. 281–87.
5. Greenpeace, *Beyond UNCED* (Amsterdam: Greenpeace International, June 1992), p. 4.
6. UNRISD/79/C.14 (Geneva: United Nations Research Institute on Social Development, May 1979), cited in Ibid., p. 4.

Chapter One: The Corporate Planet

1. See Wolfgang Sachs, "The Blue Planet: An Ambiguous Modern Icon," *The Ecologist*, vol. 24, no. 5 (Sept.–Oct. 1994), pp. 170–75.
2. These webs are cogently described throughout Richard J. Barnet and John Cavanagh, *Global Dreams: Imperial Corporations and the New World Order* (New York: Simon & Schuster, 1994).
3. Henrique Rattner, "Globalizaçao: Em Direçao a 'Um Mundo Só'?" (Paper pre-

sented at the Seminar on Globalization and Sustainable Development, Rio de Janeiro, 31 August 1995).

4. Despite all its flaws, the UN has helped globalize and legitimize certain values through the Universal Declaration of Human Rights, the International Labor Organization's conventions supporting workers' rights, various agreements and declarations advocating indigenous peoples' rights and a series of treaties and conventions aimed at establishing internationally agreed upon environmental rights.

5. See Rajni Kothari, *Growing Amnesia: An Essay on Poverty and the Human Consciousness* (New Delhi: Viking-Penguin, 1993), pp. 87–89.

6. See Richard L. Grossman and Frank T. Adams, *Taking Care of Business: Citizenship and the Charter of Incorporation* (Cambridge MA: Charter Ink., January 1993).

7. "Global 500: The World's Largest Corporations," *Fortune*, 7 August 1995, p. F-1, reports Ford and GM's combined 1994 revenues at $283.4 billion. The World Bank, *World Development Report 1995* (Oxford: Oxford University Press, 1995), p. 167, puts sub-Saharan Africa's GDP at $269.4 billion.

8. "Global 500," p. F-1, figures place the combined big six *sogo shosha* revenues at $928.7 billion, while the World Bank, *World Development Report 1995*, pp. 166–67, tables show South America's total GDP (minus the Guyanas) adding up to $938.3 billion.

9. This figure does not include banking and financial institutions. Sara Anderson and John Cavanaugh, *The Rise of Global Corporate Power* (Washington, D.C.: Institute for Policy Studies, September 25, 1996), p. 1.

10. See Phillip I. Blumberg, *The Megacorporation in American Society: The Scope of Corporate Power* (Englewood Cliffs, NJ: Prentice-Hall, 1975), pp. 16–63.

11. UNCTAD, *World Investment Report 1995: Transnational Corporations and Competitiveness* (New York: United Nations Conference on Trade and Development, Division on Transnational Corporations and Investment, 1995), pp. xix–xx.

12. Harris Gleckman and Riva Krut, *The Social Benefits of Regulating Transnational Corporations* (Portland, ME: Benchmark Environmental Consulting, 1995), p. 2.

13. UNCTAD, *World Investment Report 1995*, pp. 3–4. Global sales generated by corporations' foreign affiliates "were worth $5.2 trillion in 1992, exceeding worldwide exports of goods and (non-factor) services worth $4.9 trillion in that year."

14. Paul Hawken, *The Ecology of Commerce: A Declaration of Sustainability* (New York: Harper Business, 1993), p. 92.

15. UNTCMD, *World Investment Report 1992: Transnational Corporations as Engines of Growth* (New York: United Nations, Transnational Corporations and Management Division, Department of Economic and Social Development, 1992), p. 99.

16. UNCTAD, *Trends in Foreign Direct Investment, Report by the UNCTAD Secretariat,* E/C.10/1994/2 (Geneva: United Nations Economic and Social Council, Commission on Transnational Corporations, 2–10 May 1994), p. 16.

17. "Multinationals: Back in Fashion," *The Economist,* 27 March 1993, p. 6.

18. Barnet and Cavanagh, *Global Dreams,* p. 21.

19. Vandana Shiva, "The Greening of Global Reach," *Third World Resurgence,* no. 14–15 (Oct.–Nov. 1991), p. 58.

20. See, for example, Eduardo Galeano, *Open Veins in Latin America: Five Centuries of the Pillage of a Continent* (New York: Monthly Review Press, 1973), pp. 21–70.

21. Page Smith, *A New Age Now Begins: A People's History of the American Revolution,* vol. 1 (New York: McGraw Hill, 1976), pp. 373–75.

22. Grossman and Adams, *Taking Care of Business,* pp. 6–21.

23. "Introduction to the Fortune 500 Largest U.S. Corporations," *Fortune,* 15 May 1995, p. 227.

24. William Greider, *Who Will Tell the People? The Betrayal of American Democracy* (New York: Simon & Schuster, 1993).

25. The Clinton Administration is no different in this respect. See Nadav Savio, "The Business of Government: Clinton's Corporate Cabinet," *Multinational Monitor,* April 1993, pp. 24–26.

26. Friends of the Earth, *The Green Scissors Report: Cutting Wasteful and Environmentally Harmful Spending and Subsidies* (Washington, DC: Friends of the Earth and the National Taxpayers Union, January 1995); Friends of the Earth, *Dirty Little Secrets: Polluters Save While People Pay—Exposing 15 of the Tax Code's Most Unfair Tax Breaks* (Washington, DC: Friends of the Earth, April 1995).

27. See Walter LaFeber, *Inevitable Revolutions: The United States in Central America* (New York: Norton, 1984), pp. 34–58, 111–26; Richard J. Barnet and Ronald E. Muller, *Global Reach: The Power of the Multinational Corporations* (New York: Simon & Schuster, 1974), pp. 81–83.

28. David E. Sanger, "Salesman in Chief: Clinton Puts a Foot in the Opening Door of the Global Market," *New York Times,* 24 November 1993.

29. David E. Sanger, "How Washington Inc. Makes a Sale," *New York Times,* 19 February 1995; David E. Sanger and Tim Weiner, "Emerging Role for the CIA: Economic Spy," *New York Times,* 15 October 1995.

30. Tom Hilliard, *Trade Advisory Committees: Privileged Access for Polluters* (Washington, DC: Public Citizen, 1991).

31. Keith Schneider, "Gore Says Clinton Will Seek to Block Waste Incinerator," *New York Times,* 7 December 1992; ———, "Ohio Incinerator Cleared Over Objection by Gore," *New York Times,* 18 March 1993; "Environmental Preview," "Gore on a Von Roll," "Green Light for Von Roll," "Greenpeace Calls a Judge," *Wall Street Journal,* editorial pages, 30 December 1992, 8, 12, 19 January 1993; L. J. Davis, "Where Are You, Al?" *Mother Jones,* November–December 1993, pp. 44–49.

32. Mark Dowie, *Losing Ground: American Environmentalism at the Close of the Twentieth Century* (Cambridge: MIT Press, 1995), pp. 182–85.

33. Robert D. Hershey, Jr., "A Hard Look at Corporate 'Welfare'," *New York Times*, 7 March 1995.

34. Sumiya Toshio, "The Structure and Operation of Monopoly Capital in Japan," in Tessa Morris-Suzuki and Takuro Seiyama, eds., *Japanese Capitalism Since 1945* (New York: M. E. Sharpe, 1989), pp. 121–22.

35. Takuya Negami, interview with author, Tokyo, 25 January 1994.

36. UNTCMD, *World Investment Report 1992*, pp. 34–39.

37. Ibid.

38. Nicholas Hildyard, "Maastricht: The Protectionism of Free Trade," *The Ecologist*, vol. 23, no. 2 (Mar.–Apr. 1993), pp. 45–51.

39. Barnet and Cavanagh, *Global Dreams*, pp. 385–402.

40. David C. Korten, *When Corporations Rule the World* (San Francisco: Kumarian Press/Berrett-Koehler, 1995), p. 203.

41. Ibid., p. 208.

42. Hildyard, "Maastricht," p. 47.

43. Barnet and Cavanagh, *Global Dreams*, pp. 53, 259–358.

44. UNTCMD, *World Investment Report 1992*, p. 100.

45. UNTCMD, *World Investment Report 1992*, p. 233.

46. Hawken, *Ecology of Commerce*, p. 3.

47. Kenneth T. Derr, "Oil and Its Critics: The Facts and the Future" (Remarks delivered to the Cambridge Energy Research Associates Executive Conference, Houston, 8 February 1994).

48. For instance, see S. Fred Singer, "Climate Claims Wither Under Luminous Lights of Science," *Washington Times*, 29 November 1994; Sallie Baliunas, "Frozen Fantasies of Flaky Science," *Washington Times*, 2 February 1996; Robert C. Balling, Jr., "Keep Cool About Global Warming," *Wall Street Journal*, 16 October 1995. For a critique see Tom Athanasiou, *Divided Planet: The Ecology of Rich and Poor* (Boston: Little, Brown, 1996), pp. 256–61; Union of Concerned Scientists, "Who Majors in Junk Science?" *UCS Backgrounder* (n.p., n.d.).

49. U.S. Reps. John Doolittle and Tom DeLay, for example, have claimed that "there has not been a sufficient showing of scientific evidence to justify" a rapid phase-out of ozone-destroying chlorofluorocarbons. William K. Stevens, "GOP Seeks to Delay Ban on Chemical Harming Ozone," *New York Times*, 21 September 1995; see also Janet S. Wager, "Double Exposure," *Nucleus* (Union of Concerned Scientists), vol. 17, no. 4 (Winter 1995–96).

50. Gregg Easterbrook, *A Moment on the Earth: The Coming Age of Environmental Optimism* (New York: Viking-Penguin, 1995). For a rebuttal of Easterbrook see *Moment of Truth: Correcting the Scientific Errors in Gregg Easterbrook's "A Moment on the Earth"* (New York: Environmental Defense Fund, 1995).

51. World Meteorological Organization, *Scientific Assessment of Ozone Depletion:*

1994, Global Ozone Research and Monitoring Project Report No. 37 (Geneva: World Meteorological Organization, 1995); ———, *Scientific Assessment of Ozone Depletion: 1991*, Global Ozone Research and Monitoring Project Report No. 25 (Geneva: 1991); Johanthan P. D. Abbott and Mario J. Molina, "Status of Stratospheric Ozone Depletion," *Annual Reviews of Energy and Environment*, vol. 18 (1993), pp. 1–29.

52. Jack Doyle, *Hold the Applause! A Case Study of Corporate Environmentalism as Practiced at DuPont* (Washington, DC: Friends of the Earth, 1991), pp. 37–57.

53. See Jessica Mathews, "In Denial About Global Warming," *Washington Post*, 29 January 1996; Ross Gelbspan, "The Heat Is On: The Warming of the World's Climate Sparks a Blaze of Denial," *Harper's*, December 1995, pp. 31–37.

54. Gelbspan, "The Heat Is On," pp. 31–37; William K. Stevens, "Scientists Confront Renewed Backlash on Global Warming," cited in Athanasiou, *Divided Planet*, pp. 258–59.

55. Intergovernmental Panel on Climate Change, *Climate Change: The IPCC Scientific Assessment* (Cambridge: Cambridge University Press, 1990); John T. Houghton et al., *Climate Change 1992: The Supplementary Report to the IPCC Scientific Assessment* (Cambridge: Cambridge University Press, 1992); Bert Bolin et al., *Climate Change 1995: The IPCC Second Assessment Report* (Cambridge: Cambridge University Press, 1996); William K. Stevens, "Scientists Say Earth's Warming Could Set Off Wide Disruptions," *New York Times*, 18 September 1995.

56. For instance, fossil fuel (oil, gas and coal) industry production, about half of which is controlled by big transnational corporations, is responsible for 8 percent of all carbon dioxide emissions and a great deal of the methane released into the atmosphere—both potent contributors to global warming. The automotive industry, almost completely composed of large corporations many of which have historically resisted efforts to promote public transportation and fuel-efficient vehicles, contributes to about 20 percent of projected global warming. Corporations that build fossil-fuel-burning energy plants, metallurgical industries and chemical corporations also make major contributions to climate change. Arjun Makhijani, *Climate Change and Transnational Corporations*, Environment Series No. 2 (New York: United Nations Centre on Transnational Corporations, 1992), pp. 1–9, 35–100.

57. Al Gore, *Earth in the Balance: Ecology and the Human Spirit* (New York: Houghton Mifflin, 1992), p. 148.

58. Ibid., p. 148.

59. *National Biennial RCRA Hazardous Waste Report, 1987*, EPA-530-SW-091-061.

60. Hazardous waste production actually dropped to 197.5 million tons in 1989 and then jumped to 305 million tons in 1991. By 1993 it had dropped

down to 235 million tons—still higher than 1987 (*National Biennial RCRA Hazardous Waste Report 1989, 1991*). The 1993 figures come from RCRA statistics available in 1995. If waste that is exempted for a variety of administrative and political reasons is taken into account, annual U.S. toxic waste production reaches the two-ton-per-person figure. Ninety-nine percent of all this hazardous waste comes from only 2 percent of the estimated 650,000 commercial and industrial sources in the country (Gore, *Earth in the Balance*, pp. 146–48).

61. Cited in Gary Cohen and John O'Connor, eds., *Fighting Toxics* (Washington, DC: Island Press, 1990), p. 16.

62. Devra Lee Davis et al., "Decreasing Cardiovascular Disease and Increasing Cancer Among Whites in the United States from 1973 Through 1987," *Journal of the American Medical Association*, vol. 271, no. 6 (February 9, 1994), cited in *Rachel's Hazardous Waste News* (Environmental Research Foundation), no. 385 (14 April 1994).

63. U.S. Environmental Protection Agency, "Health Assessment for 2,3,7,8-TCDD and Related Compounds," public review draft, EPA/600/EP-92/001 (Washington, DC: U.S. Environmental Protection Agency, 1994); Michael J. DeVito et al., "Comparisons of Estimated Human Body Burdens of Dioxinlike Chemicals and TCDD Body Burdens in Experimentally Exposed Animals," *Environmental Health Perspectives*, vol. 103, no. 9 (September 1995). For well-documented but more popular presentations see Theo Colborn, Dianne Dumanoski and John Peterson Myers, *Our Stolen Future* (New York: Dutton, 1996); Lois Marie Gibbs, *Dying from Dioxin* (Boston: South End Press, 1995).

64. In Europe, for instance, the Barcelona Convention, comprised of twenty-one Mediterranean nations, agreed to eliminate discharges of persistent, bioaccumulative substances, particularly organochlorines. The Paris Commission, comprised of thirteen nations on the Northeast Atlantic, along with the European Union, agreed to eliminate similar discharges, as did the North Sea Conference. And in North America the International Joint Commission on the Great Lakes called for the "banning or sunsetting" of "the manufacture, distribution, storage, use and disposal" of persistent, toxic and bioaccumulative chemicals. See Michelle Allsopp, Pat Costner and Paul Johnston, *Body of Evidence: The Effects of Chlorine on Human Health* (London: Greenpeace International, 1995), pp. 72–74.

65. Daryl Kimball, Lenny Siegel and Peter Tyler, *Covering the Map: A Survey of Military Pollution Sites in the United States* (Washington, DC: Physicians for Social Responsibility and Military Toxics Project, 1993).

66. In the aluminum industry, for example, six transnationals control 63 percent of mining, 66 percent of refining and 54 percent of smelting capacity. Makhijani, *Climate Change*, p. 77.

67. Intel produces roughly 5,000 wafers a week in one plant in New Mexico. SWOP, *Intel Inside New Mexico* (Albuquerque: Southwest Organizing Project, 1994), pp. 34–35.

68. Tekla S. Perry, "Cleaning Up," *IEEE Spectrum* (International Association of Electric and Electronic Engineers), February 1993.

69. United Nations figures cited in Kenny Bruno, *The Greenpeace Book on Greenwash* (Washington, DC: Greenpeace International, 1992), p. 9.

70. World Health Organization, *Public Health Impact of Pesticides Used in Agriculture* (Geneva: World Health Organization, 1990), p. 85; J. Jeyaratnam, "Acute Pesticide Poisoning: A Major Global Health Problem," *World Health Statistic Quarterly*, vol. 43 (1990), pp. 139–43.

71. Henk Hobbelink, *Biotechnology and the Future of World Agriculture*, Span. ed. (London: Zed Books, Ltd., 1991), pp. 53–79.

72. United Nations figures cited in Bruno, *Greenwash*, p. 9.

73. Examples can be found throughout the world; see, for instance, Joshua Karliner, "Central America's Other War," *World Policy Journal*, vol. 6, no. 4 (Fall 1989), pp. 789–802.

74. Gore, *Earth in the Balance*, p. 119.

75. Roger Olsson, ed., *The Taiga: A Treasure—Or Timber and Trash?* 4th ed. (Sokkmokk, Sweden: Taiga Rescue Network, 1993), p. 11.

76. Greenpeace, *Fisheries on the Brink: Major Trends in Global Fisheries* (Amsterdam: Greenpeace International, March 1994).

77. UN Food and Agriculture Organization, *The State of World Fisheries and Aquaculture* (Rome: United Nations, Food and Agriculture Organization, Fisheries Department, 1995), p. 6.

78. "World Scientists' Warning to Humanity," released by the Union of Concerned Scientists, Washington, DC, 18 November 1992.

79. The bulk of foreign direct investment (FDI) originates in and is "cross-invested" among the Triad of industrialized nations. Yet a growing proportion of corporate investment is finding its way to the South (with the notable exception of Africa). Whereas during the second half of the 1980s only 16 percent of all FDI flowed from North to South, by 1993 nearly one-third of the world's total went to these so-called developing nations. UNCTAD, *Foreign Direct Investment*, p. 4.

80. UNTCMD, *World Investment Report 1992*, Annex Table 12. The UN defines pollution-intensive industries as chemicals, pulp and paper, metals, and coal and petroleum; these figures do not include investment in the often environmentally problematic agricultural, forestry, automobile manufacturing, electronics and tourism sectors.

81. Kenny Bruno and Jed Greer, "Chlorine Industry Expansion: The New Threat from the North," *Third World Resurgence*, no. 34 (June 1993), pp. 18–22.

82. Yoichi Kuroda, "Historical Overview of the Timber Trade and Forestry Development in East and Tropical Asia and the Pacific Nations" (Japan

Tropical Forest Action Network paper presented at the International Workshop for Forest and Environmental Preservation in Asia-Pacific, Seoul, South Korea, 18–21 February 1994), pp. 1–6.

83. Yuta Harago, "Mitsubishi's Investments in Brazil: A Case Study of Eidai do Brasil Madeiras S.A.," paper prepared for the Rainforest Action Network, Rondonia, Brazil, September 1993.

84. "Weyerhaeuser and APEC," Weyerhaeuser fact sheet, 15 November 1993; Olsson, *Taiga*, pp. 53–55.

85. Yoichi Kuroda, "Asia-Pacific Forests" (Paper presented at the World Rainforest Movement Meeting, New Delhi, April 1994), p. 2.

86. Greenpeace, *Fisheries on the Brink*, pp. 7–8.

87. James F. Smith, "United States–Mexico Agricultural Trade," *U.C. Davis Law Review*, Spring 1990; Mark Ritchie, "Free Trade vs. Sustainable Agriculture," Fair Trade Campaign (Minneapolis), fact sheet, February 1991.

88. See David Barkin, *Distorted Development: Mexico in the World Economy* (Boulder, CO: Westview Press, 1990), pp. 11–40.

89. Barnet and Cavanagh, *Global Dreams*, p. 236.

90. Ibid., pp. 16, 425.

91. United Nations Development Programme, *Human Development Report 1994* (New York: Oxford University Press, 1994), p. 1.

92. Ibid.

93. Ibid., p. 2.

94. Third World Network, "A World In Social Crisis: Basic Facts on Poverty, Unemployment and Social Disintegration," *Third World Resurgence*, no. 52 (1994), pp. 24–26.

95. United Nations Development Programme, *Human Development Report 1994*, p. 35; UNDP, *Human Development Report 1996*, cited in Barbara Crosette, "UN Survey Finds World Rich-Poor Gap Widening," *New York Times*, 15 July 1996.

96. Kothari, *Growing Amnesia*, pp. 87–89.

97. The gap between rich and poor in the United States is growing more rapidly than in any other industrialized nation. One percent of U.S. households own 40 percent of the nation's wealth, and the top 20 percent of U.S. households own 80 percent of all wealth. Meanwhile, the bottom 20 percent of Americans earn less than 6 percent of all after-tax income earned in the country. Keith Bradsher, "Gap in Wealth in U.S. Called Widest in West," *New York Times*, 17 April 1995.

98. Third World Network, "Social Crisis," p. 25.

99. Kothari, *Growing Amnesia*, p. 23.

100. Anthony Simoes, interview with author, Mapusa, Goa, India, 2 April 1994.

101. George Fernandes, interview with author, New Delhi, 8 April 1994.

102. World Resources Institute, in collaboration with UNEP and UNDP, *World Resources 1992–93: A Guide to the Global Environment* (New York: Oxford University Press, 1992), p. 18.

103. Ibid.; Hawken, *Ecology of Commerce*, p. 73.

104. Vandana Shiva, *Monocultures of the Mind: Biodiversity, Biotechnology and the Third World* (Penang, Malaysia: Third World Network, 1993); Rural Advancement Fund International cited in "Ever Increasing Biopiracy by TNCs," Third World Network Features, 1995.

105. The United Nations Development Programme reports that "Total external debt of developing countries grew fifteenfold over the past two decades: in 1970, it was $100 billion, in 1980, around $650 billion and in 1992, more than $1,500 billion." Although the debt service ratio has declined in recent years, it is still substantial. UNDP, *Human Development Report 1994*, p. 63.

106. Robert Goodland and Herman Daly, "Ten Reasons Why Northern Income Growth Is Not the Solution to Southern Poverty," photocopy, World Bank, Environment Department, 25 February 1992.

107. Chakravarthi Rhagavan, *Recolonization: GATT, the Uruguay Round and the Third World* (Penang, Malaysia: Third World Network, 1990).

108. The UNDP divides the beneficiaries into OECD (Organization for Economic Development and Cooperation) countries, described here as the North, and non-OECD countries—the South. UNDP, *Human Development Report 1994*, p. 63.

109. Growing Northern consumption is predicted to occur as a result of the increasingly paper-intensive computerized economy, ongoing waste and the rapid growth of the advertising and magazine industry. Olsson, *Taiga*, pp. 11–14.

110. Mitsubishi, "The Facts About the Tropical Rainforest Issue," Mitsubishi Corporation fact sheet, n.d.

111. Popoff's remarks are cited in *President Clinton's New Beginning: The Complete Text of the Clinton-Gore Economic Conference*, Little Rock, AR, 14–15 December 1992 (New York: Donald I. Fine, 1992), p. 324. For a brief critique of Indira Gandhi's remarks, made at the 1972 Stockholm Conference on the Human Environment, see Kothari, *Growing Amnesia*, p. 105.

112. Jun Ui, ed., *Industrial Pollution in Japan*. (Tokyo: United Nations University, 1992), p. 174.

113. James Nations and Daniel Komer, "Rainforests and the Hamburger Society," *Environment*, April 1983, p. 14.

114. Daniel Faber, *Environment Under Fire: Imperialism and the Ecological Crisis in Central America* (New York: Monthly Review Press, 1993), pp. 117–46; Susana Hecht and Alexander Cockburn, *The Fate of the Forest: Developers, Destroyers and Defenders of the Amazon* (New York: Harper Perennial, 1990), pp. 104–106.

115. Cathi Tactaquin, "Environmentalists and the Anti-Immigrant Agenda," and Hannah Creighton, "Not Thinking Globally: The Sierra Club Immigration Policy Wars," both in *Race, Poverty and the Environment*, vol. 4, no. 2 (Summer 1993), pp. 6–8, 24–29.

116. Many of the crops harvested by migrant laborers are grown by agricultural corporations that benefit from government subsidies that make it profitable for them to waste scarce California water supplies, overburdening the state's resource base. Marc Reisner, *Cadillac Desert: The American West and Its Disappearing Water* (New York: Penguin Books, 1986).

117. Ausencio Avila, interview with author, Kettleman City, CA, 2 October 1993.

118. In addition to Kettleman City and WMX's Emelle, Alabama, dump (the largest in the country and located in an African-American community), the company's three commercial hazardous waste incinerator sites on the southeast side of Chicago, in Sauget, Illinois, and in Port Arthur, Texas, are all located in poor communities of color. See Joshua Karliner et al., *Toxic Empire: The WMX Corporation, Hazardous Waste and Global Strategies for Environmental Justice* (San Francisco: Political Ecology Group, 1994).

119. Luke W. Cole, "Empowerment as the Key to Environmental Protection: The Need for Environmental Poverty Law," *Ecology Law Quarterly* (Boalt Hall School of Law, University of California at Berkeley), vol. 19, no. 4 (1992), p. 627.

120. See United Church of Christ, *Toxic Waste and Race in the United States: A National Report on the Racial and Socio-Economic Characteristics of Communities with Hazardous Waste Sites* (New York: United Church of Christ, Commission for Racial Justice, 1987); General Accounting Office, *Siting of Hazardous Waste Landfills and Their Correlation with Racial and Economic Status of Surrounding Communities* (Washington, DC: General Accounting Office, 1983).

121. Bradley Angel, *The Toxic Threat to Indian Lands* (Washington, DC: Greenpeace USA, June 1991).

122. Marianne Lavelle and Marcia Coyle, "Unequal Protection: The Racial Divide in Environmental Law, a Special Investigation," *National Law Journal*, 21 September 1992.

123. Dr. Robert D. Bullard, ed., *Confronting Environmental Racism: Voices from the Grassroots* (Boston: South End Press, 1993); ——, *Dumping in Dixie: Race, Class and Environmental Quality* (Boulder, CO: Westview Press, 1990); Cole, "Empowerment as the Key," p. 619.

124. "Principles of Environmental Justice" (Manifesto by the First National People of Color Environmental Leadership Summit, Washington, DC: 24 October 1991).

125. Vandana Shiva, "A Common Future or Environmental Apartheid?" *The Observer of Business and Politics* (New Delhi), 20 February 1992.

126. See Richard Falk, "Democratising, Internationalising and Globalising: A Collage of Blurred Images," *Third World Quarterly*, excerpted in *Third World Resurgence*, no. 37 (September 1993), pp. 15–16. Falk, a professor of international law at Princeton University, argues that while not formalized as apartheid was and more complex, in general the structure of the world economy resembles the racial divisions of apartheid.

Chapter Two: The Greening of Global Reach

1. See "A Ten Point Plan to Save the Earth Summit," 1 April 1992, sponsored by Greenpeace International, the Forum of Brazilian NGOs, Friends of the Earth International and the Third World Network and endorsed by hundreds of organizations and networks from around the world; Third World Network, *Earth Summit Briefings* (Penang, Malaysia: Third World Network, 1992); Greenpeace, *Beyond UNCED* (Amsterdam: Greenpeace International, 1992).

2. J. Hugh Faulkner, "Business' Mandate for UNCED," *Network '92* (Geneva: Centre for Our Common Future, September 1991).

3. World Business Council for Sustainable Development, *Annual Review 1996*, p. 3.

4. Ricardo Carrerre, comments made at the World Rainforest Movement Meeting, New Delhi, 4 April 1994.

5. Vandana Shiva, "The Greening of Global Reach," *Third World Resurgence*, no. 14–15 (Oct.–Nov. 1991), p. 58.

6. Hidefumi Imura, "Japan's Efforts in the Environment with Sustained Growth" (Paper presented at "Pacific Rim Environmental Challenge: Directions for the 1990s," Shorenstein Symposium Series, University of California at Berkeley, 1 October 1993).

7. CERCLA stands for Comprehensive Environmental Response Compensation and Liability Act. An overview of U.S. environmental legislation can be found in *Selected Environmental Law Statutes: 1991–92 Educational Edition* (St. Paul, MN: West Publishing Company, 1991).

8. See Joshua Karliner, "The Environment Industry: Profiting from Pollution," *The Ecologist*, vol. 24, no. 2 (Mar.–Apr. 1994), pp. 59–63.

9. See hearings held by the Senate Committee on Public Works, 1974, cited in Andrew Szasz, "In Praise of Policy Luddism: Strategic Lessons from the Hazardous Waste Wars," *Capitalism, Nature and Socialism* (University of California, Santa Cruz), vol. 2, no. 1 (1991), pp. 20–31.

10. The OECD characterized the environment industry as "including firms which produce pollution abatement equipment and a range of goods and services for environmental protection and management," including water and effluent treatment, waste management, air quality control and general services. OECD, *The OECD Environment Industry: Situation, Prospects and Government Policies* (Paris: Organization for Economic Cooperation and Development, 1992), pp. 5–12.

11. The broader IFC definition includes so-called clean technologies, such as cogeneration, "clean" coal and CFC substitutes. IFC, *Investing in the Environment: Business Opportunities in Developing Countries* (Washington, DC: International Finance Corporation, 1992), pp. 1–3. Environmental Business International estimated that 1993's global market for "environmental products and services" had already topped $300 billion and predicted growth to $400 billion by 1998; "Competitive Analysis of U.S.

Environmental Exports and Global Market Update" (San Diego: Environmental Business International, 1995).

12. OECD, *The OECD Environment Industry*, p. 12.

13. Harvey A. Himberg, director of development policy and environmental affairs, Overseas Private Investment Corporation, "International Trade in Environmental Goods, Services and Technologies" (Presentation for National Research Council/Academy Industry Program, Symposium on International Trade and Environment, Washington, DC, 4 May 1993). Other analysts calculate the U.S. industry at almost double the size—$170 billion—in 1994; "The End of the Beginning," *Environmental Business Journal*, vol. 8, no. 4/5 (Apr.–May 1995).

14. The dual structure whereby roughly half of the industry is composed of small firms and the other half of large transnational polluters is also apparent in Europe and Japan, where companies such as Bayer, Ciba-Geigy, Hitachi and Mitsubishi are all part of the so-called environment industry. Despite the existence of small innovative firms, the environment industry is becoming increasingly concentrated in the hands of the large polluting companies. As the OECD explains, "Environmental equipment and services is rapidly becoming an international business, dominated by large multinationals in fields ranging from waste management to catalytic converters." OECD, *The Environment Industry*, pp. 7–12.

15. Information on GE's environmental record can be found in William Greider, *Who Will Tell the People?* (New York: Touchstone Books, 1992), pp. 351–54; information on GE as a producer of air pollution control equipment comes from OECD, *The Environment Industry*, p. 11.

16. Council on Economic Priorities, *DuPont: A Report on the Company's Environmental Policies and Practices* (New York: Council on Economic Priorities, December 1994).

17. K. D. Sadhale, interview with author, Ponda, Goa, India, 3 April 1995.

18. Ed Woolen and Martin Cohn's comments came during and after a press conference held at the Environmental Business Council of the United States founding conference, 8 June 1993; Raytheon information comes from *Raytheon 1992 Annual Report*.

19. "Global 500: The World's Largest Corporations," *Fortune*, 7 August 1995, p. - F-8.

20. Subrata N. Chakravarty, "Dean Buntrock's Green Machine," *Forbes*, 2 August 1993, pp. 96.

21. Grant Ferrier, interview with author, 15 July 1993.

22. Grant Ferrier, "The Age of Uncertainty," *Environmental Business Journal*, vol. 6, no. 4 (Apr. 1993), p. 1.

23. See Joshua Karliner et al., *Toxic Empire: The WMX Corporation, Hazardous Waste and Global Strategies for Environmental Justice* (San Francisco: Political Ecology Group, 1994); Charlie Cray, *Waste Management Inc.: An*

Encyclopedia of Environmental Crimes and Other Misdeeds (Washington, DC: Greenpeace, 1991).

24. Peter Montague, "Why Birth Defects Will Continue to Rise," *Rachel's Environment & Health Weekly* (Environmental Research Foundation), no. 411 (13 October 1994).

25. Pat Costner and Joe Thornton, *Playing with Fire: Hazardous Waste Incineration* (Washington, DC: Greenpeace USA, 1990); Cathy Brown, "Workers at Ensco PCB Prone," *El Dorado News-Times*, 1 August 1987.

26. OECD, *The Environment Industry*, p. 29.

27. See, for example, Ray Reece, *The Sun Betrayed: A Report on the Corporate Seizure of U.S. Solar Energy Development* (Boston: South End Press, 1979).

28. See Paul Hawken, *The Ecology of Commerce: A Declaration of Sustainability* (New York: Harper Business, 1993).

29. See Curtis Moore and Alan Miller, *Green Gold: Japan, Germany, the United States and the Race for Environmental Technology* (Boston: Beacon Press, 1994).

30. Nakamura Yoichi, "The Ecobusiness Logic," *AMPO: Japan-Asia Quarterly Review*, vol. 23, no. 3 (1992), p. 56.

31. Harris Gleckman with Riva Krut, "Transnational Corporations' Strategic Responses to 'Sustainable Development'," in *Green Globe 1995* (New York: Oxford University Press, 1995), p. 3.

32. World Resources Institute, ed., *Corporate Environmental Accounting* (Washington, DC: World Resources Institute, 1995).

33. See, for example, Stephan Schmidheiny, with the Business Council for Sustainable Development, *Changing Course: A Global Business Perspective on Development and the Environment* (Cambridge: MIT Press, 1992), pp. 181–334; Jan-Olaf Willums and Ulrich Goluke, *From Ideas to Action: Business and Sustainable Development—The Greening of Enterprise 1992* (Oslo, Norway: International Environmental Bureau of the International Chamber of Commerce, May 1992); Kurt Fischer and Johan Schot, eds., *Environmental Strategies for Industry: International Perspectives on Research Needs and Policy Implications* (Washington, DC: Island Press, 1993); Charles S. Pearson, ed., *Multinational Corporations, Environment and the Third World* (Durham, NC: World Resources Institute/Duke University Press, 1987); Bruce Smart, ed., *Beyond Compliance: A New Industry View of the Environment* (Washington, DC: World Resources Institute, 1992).

34. World Commission on Environment and Development, *Our Common Future* (New York: World Commission on Environment and Development/Oxford University Press, 1987).

35. United Nations General Assembly, Resolution 44/228, 22 December 1989.

36. Willums and Goluke, *From Ideas to Action*, pp. 87–88.

37. Schmidheiny, *Changing Course;* in *Corporations' Strategic Responses*, Gleckman remarks that *Changing Course* is comparatively enlightened when seen in the context of the ICC and other trade associations' recommendations for

UNCED. Yet it is important to note that it shares the fundamental tenets of corporate environmentalism with these other groups.

38. Schmidheiny, *Changing Course*, pp. 1–178.

39. Ibid., p. xii.

40. Such concerns were expressed, for example, by New York State environmentalists who feared that a trading scheme by the Long Island Lighting Company would generate *more* acid rain in the Adirondack Mountains; James Dao, "A New, Unregulated Market: Selling the Right to Pollute," *New York Times*, 6 February 1993; Matthew L. Wald, "Emissions Sale by LILCO Spurs Acid Rain Fears," *New York Times*, 18 March 1993. Similarly, Communities for a Better Environment charged that a pollution trading scheme in Los Angeles would lead to more smog; Jim Jenal, "Trading Health for More Smog," *CBE Environmental Review* (Communities for a Better Environment), Fall 1994.

41. International Chamber of Commerce, "Business Brief: Summary of the Series Nos. 1–9," prepared for UNCED by the International Chamber of Commerce, June 1992.

42. David C. Korten, "The Global Economy: Is Sustainability Possible?" (Presentation to the Presidio Conference, San Francisco, 25 April 1995).

43. Naomi Roht-Arriaza, *UNCED Undermined: Why Free Trade Won't Save the Planet*, Greenpeace UNCED Reports (Amsterdam: Greenpeace International, March 1992), pp. 9–10.

44. Testimony of Lori Wallach of Public Citizen's Congress Watch on the GATT Uruguay Round Agreement, before the U.S. Senate Commerce Committee, 17 October 1994.

45. Chakravarthi Raghavan, "South Urges More Study on TRIPs/Sustainable Development Interface," *Third World Economics*, 1–15 July 1995; "Correcting Potential Conflicts Between MEAs and GATT," submission by Greenpeace International to the GATT's Commission on Trade and Environment, 1994.

46. Harris Gleckman and Riva Krut, *The Social Benefits of Regulating Transnational Corporations* (Portland, ME: Benchmark Environmental Consulting, 1995), p. 7.

47. The Third World Network writes, "GATT and WTO, because of their narrow trade focus, lack the jurisdiction, competence and capacity to be a coordinating agency to handle these interlinked issues. Moreover, as the closing phase of the Uruguay Round showed, the GATT's decision making is dominated by only two or three major countries or entities . . . rules developed in this asymmetric forum would most likely serve to legitimise the use of trade weapons which the North and the powerful can use against the South and the weak. . . . Thus there is the danger, if not likelihood, that through particular and narrow definitions of the trade-environment link, the powerful nations will try to shift the economic burden of ecological

adjustment to the weaker parties in order to preserve and expand their own unsustainable consumption patterns." "The World Trade Organization, Trade and Environment," position paper of the Third World Network, Penang, Malaysia, March 1994.

48. International Chamber of Commerce, "Business Brief."

49. Richard Grossman, "Growth as Metaphor, Growth as Politics," *The Wrenching Debate Gazette* (Provincetown), July 1985.

50. United Nations Development Programme, *Human Development Report 1994* (New York: United Nations Development Programme/Oxford University Press, 1994), p. 17.

51. See, for instance, Isabel Carvalho and Gabriela Scotto, "A Natureza e Nossa? *Democracia* (IBASE, Rio de Janeiro), July 1995.

52. Rajni Kothari, *Growing Amnesia: An Essay on Poverty and the Human Consciousness* (New Delhi: Viking-Penguin, 1993), pp. 80–81.

53. David C. Korten, *When Corporations Rule the World* (San Francisco: Kumarian Press/Berrett-Koehler, 1995), pp. 37–50.

54. David C. Korten, "The Global Economy."

55. See Schmidheiny, *Changing Course*, pp. 14–34.

56. Paul Hawken, *Ecology of Commerce*; Herman E. Daly and John B. Cobb, Jr., *For the Common Good: Redirecting the Economy Toward Community, the Environment and a Sustainable Future* (Boston: Beacon Press, 1989).

57. Kenneth T. Derr, speech to the American Petroleum Institute's annual meeting, Houston, 13 November 1995.

58. Kristin Dawkins, "Internalizing Environmental Costs: Nice in Theory But . . ." Third World Network Features, 1994.

59. Vandana Shiva, "After 50 Years, Is the World Bank Socially and Environmentally Responsible?" *Third World Resurgence*, no. 49 (Sept. 1994), pp. 23–24.

60. A study prepared for the Intergovernmental Panel on Climate Change valued one North American or European life at $1.5 million and one life in the South at $150,000, leading to significant controversy. Chakravarthi Raghavan, "'Genocidal' Economic Analysis on Climate Change," *Third World Economics*, 1–15 April 1995; ———, "Climate Body Economists Asked to Redo Their Work," *Third World Economics*, 16–31 August 1995.

61. Marlise Simons, "Ecological Plea from Executives: International Group Urges Action at Rio," *New York Times*, 8 May 1992.

62. Gleckman and Krut, *Regulating Transnational Corporations*, p. 9.

63. UNTCMD, *World Investment Report 1992: Transnational Corporations as Engines of Growth* (New York: United Nations, Transnational Corporations and Management Division, Department of Economic and Social Development, 1992), pp. 90–91.

64. The case of the BCSD and climate change illustrates the point. *Changing Course* assiduously avoids endorsing the Climate Convention's efforts to

stabilize and reduce carbon dioxide. Rather, the BCSD presents a mix of market mechanisms and self-regulation designed to promote a "gradual shift" to alternative energy, which the BCSD defines as nuclear power and toxic waste-to-energy incineration schemes, among others. Such a prolonged weaning would, according to the Business Council, avoid destabilizing both the global climate and the global economy. On one level this may be a comforting scenario, yet upon closer inspection *Changing Course* (echoing many in the petroleum industry) makes it crystal clear that "fossil fuels are expected to be the main source of energy well into the next century." The BCSD book notes that coal supplies could last 1,500 years, natural gas up to 240 years and oil up to more than 100 sweltering summers. Ongoing fossil fuel production, it says, will constitute sustainable development because new technology will make it less polluting and more efficient. Schmidheiny, *Changing Course*, pp. 34–53.

65. Environmental audit information from Sanford Lewis, *Feel Good Nations, Corporate Power and the Reinvention of Environmental Law* (Waverly: The Good Neighbor Project, 1997); "A Green Account," *The Economist*, 4 September 1993.

66. Michael Weisskopf and David Maraniss, "Forging an Alliance for Deregulation: Rep. DeLay Makes Companies Full Partners in the Movement," *Washington Post*, 12 March 1995; John H. Cushman, Jr., "Lobbyists Helped the G.O.P. in Revising Clean Water Act," *New York Times*, 22 March 1995; Stephen Engelberg, "Business Leaves the Lobby and Sits at Congress's Table, *New York Times*, 31 March 1995; Stephen Engelberg, "Wood Products Company Helps Write a Law to Derail an EPA Inquiry," *New York Times*, 26 April 1995.

67. Natural Resources Defense Council, "State of Nature," *Legislative Watch*, 27 October 1995.

68. John H. Cushman, Jr., "Spending Bill Would Reverse Nation's Environment Policy," *New York Times*, 22 September 1995.

69. Natural Resources Defense Council, *Stealth Attack: Gutting Environmental Protection Through the Budget Process*, online version (New York: Natural Resources Defense Council, July 1995), sec. 15.

70. Ibid., sec. 1–14.

71. William K. Stevens, "GOP Seeks to Delay Ban on Chemical Harming Ozone," *New York Times*, 21 September 1995.

72. Marian Burros, "Congress Moving to Revamp Rules on Food Safety," *New York Times*, 3 July 1995.

73. Jane Fritsch, "Sometimes, Lobbyists Strive to Keep Public in the Dark," *New York Times*, 19 March 1996; Natural Resources Defense Council, *Stealth Attack*, sec. 3.

74. John H. Cushman, Jr., "Congressional Republicans Take Aim at an Extensive List of Environmental Statutes," *New York Times*, 22 February 1995.

75. Sierra Club, "House Passes Anti-Environmental Bill Amounting to a 'Polluters Bill of Rights'," Sierra Club press release, 3 March 1995.

76. Jay D. Hair, interview with author, San Francisco, 27 April 1995.

77. Shiva, *Greening of Global Reach*, p. 58.

78. Jack Doyle, *Hold the Applause! A Case Study of Corporate Environmentalism as Practiced at DuPont* (Washington, DC: Friends of the Earth, 1991), pp. 37–57.

79. Steve Kretzmann, "Money to Burn: The World Bank, Chemical Companies and Ozone Depletion" (Washington, DC: Greenpeace, September 1994).

80. Shiva, *Greening of Global Reach*, p. 59.

81. Cited in John Passacantando and Andre Carothers, "Crisis? What Crisis? The Ozone Backlash," *The Ecologist*, vol. 25, no. 1 (Jan.–Feb. 1995), p. 7.

82. Ken Derr, "Oil and Its Critics: The Facts and the Future" (Speech delivered to the Cambridge Energy Research Associates Executive Conference, Houston, 8 February 1994).

83. The Global Climate Coalition is a collection of fifty-six oil, coal, car and mining corporations and associations, including BP, Shell, Dow and Kaiser Aluminum. "Lobbyists Blocking Action on Climate Change Negotiations," *Greenpeace Business*, No. 36 (April–May 1997), p. 4.

84. John H. Cushman, Jr., "U.S. Will Seek Pact on Global Warming," *New York Times*, 17 July 1996.

85. The recommendations had five sections: (a) global corporate environmental management; (b) risk and hazard minimization; (c) environmentally sounder consumption patterns; (d) full-cost environmental accounting and (e) environmental conventions, standards and guidelines. See Commission on Transnational Corporations, "Transnational Corporations and Sustainable Development: Recommendations of the Executive Director," E/C.10/1992/2 (New York: United Nations Economic and Social Council, January 1992).

86. In February 1992 the UNCTC was placed under the Department of Social and Economic Development and reconstituted as the Transnationals and Management Division. A year later it was kicked over to the United Nations Conference on Trade and Development, making it more marginal still. See "UNCTAD Gets TNCs and Science/Technology Sectors," *Third World Economics*, 1–15 April 1993.

87. Gleckman with Krut, "Transnational Corporations' Strategic Responses," p. 31.

88. Third World Network, *Earth Summit Briefings*; Greenpeace, *Beyond UNCED*; Greenpeace, "UNCED Undone: Key Issues Agenda 21 Doesn't Address" (Amsterdam: Greenpeace International, March 1992); "Toxic Militarism Should Be on UNCED's Agenda," *Disarmament Times: Special Double Issue, Militarism and the Environment* (NGO Committee on Disarmament), vol 15, no. 1 (March 1992); Angela Harkavy, *The Final Effort: A Progress Report on*

Preparatory Negotiations for UNCED (Washington, DC: National Wildlife Federation/CAPE '92, June 1992).

89. Harris Gleckman, "Transnational Corporations and Sustainable Development: Reflections from Inside the Debate," draft document, 21 August 1992; "Transnational Corporations and Sustainable Development: A Review of Agenda 21" (New York: United Nations, Transnational Corporations and Management Division, Department of Economic and Social Development, 10 October 1992).

90. Willums and Goluke, *From Ideas to Action*, pp. 20–21.

91. William Reilly, "Reflections on the Earth Summit," memorandum to all EPA employees, n.d.; also see Office of the Vice-President, memorandum for Bill Kristol from John Cohressen and David McIntosh, "Major Problems with the Draft Convention on Biological Diversity," 14 April 1992.

92. Cited in Kenny Bruno, "The Corporate Capture of the Earth Summit," *Multinational Monitor*, July–August 1992, p. 17.

93. Jonathan Plaut, prepared statement before the U.S. House of Representatives Committee on Foreign Affairs, 21 July 1992.

94. William Reilly, testimony before the U.S. House of Representatives Committee on Foreign Affairs, 28 July 1992.

95. Jane Rissler and Margaret Mellon, *Perils Amidst the Promise: Ecological Risks of Transgenic Crops in a Global Market* (Cambridge, MA: Union of Concerned Scientists, 1993).

96. "U.S. Interpretive Statement Makes Mockery of Convention," *Biodiversity Coalition*, newsletter no. 7, November 1993.

97. Despite resistance from the United States, the European Union and Japan, as well as hard lobbying from the biotechnology industry, delegates to the Convention on Biological Diversity, led by countries such as Colombia, India, China and Malaysia, agreed in late 1995 to establish a protocol on biosafety. Gurdial Singh Nijar, "The South Finally Secures a Biosafety Protocol," *Third World Resurgence*, no. 65–66 (Jan.–Feb. 1996).

98. Gurdial Singh Nijar, "CSD Staves Off U.S. Assault on Balanced Approach to Biotech" and "UN Accused of Industry Bias on Biotech," both in *Third World Resurgence*, no. 58 (June 1995).

99. Joshua Karliner Alba Morales and Dora O'Rourke, *The Bromide Barons: Methyl Bromide, Corporate Power and Environmental Justice.* (San Francisco: Political Ecology Group and Transnational Resource and Action Center, June 1997).

Chapter Three: Surfing the Pipeline

1. The refinery processes nearly a quarter of a million barrels of gasoline a day. Chevron, *Supplement to Chevron Corporation 1992 Annual Report* (San Francisco: Chevron Corporation), p. 32.

2. In addition to Los Angeles having the worst smog problem in the country, it

is estimated that nearly one-third of all cancer deaths in that city come from breathing its lethal air. Presentation of Pat Laden, staff director, Los Angeles Air Quality Management District, AQMD Board Hearing, 9 July 1993; Eric Mann, *LA's Lethal Air: New Strategies for Policy, Organizing and Action* (Los Angeles: Labor/Community Strategy Center, 1991), pp. 5–15.

3. Self-reported industry data compiled by Citizens for a Better Environment and cited in Mann, *LA's Lethal Air*, pp. 42–45.

4. Jack Doyle, *Crude Awakening: The Oil Mess in America, Wasting Energy, Jobs and the Environment* (Washington, DC: Friends of the Earth, 1993), pp. 17, 48.

5. While El Segundo is located beside a quite affluent neighborhood, LA's other polluting refineries and factories, owned by Texaco, Arco, Mobil and Shell, are located in poor African-American communities such as Wilmington and Carson. Mann, *LA's Lethal Air*, pp. 42–43.

6. Marc Gold, Heal the Bay, interview with author, 1 July 1993.

7. Young Hutchinson, South Bay Chapter, Surfrider Foundation, interview with author, 7 June 1993.

8. For an excellent overview of oil in the twentieth century see Daniel Yergin, *The Prize: The Epic Quest for Oil, Money and Power* (New York: Touchstone Books, 1991) and Anthony Sampson, *The Seven Sisters: The Great Oil Companies and the World They Shaped*, 3rd ed. (New York: Bantam Books, 1983).

9. Yergin, *The Prize*, p. 15.

10. "Global 500: The World's Largest Corporations," *Fortune,* 7 August 1995, p. F-2; "The *Fortune* 500: Largest U.S. Corporations," *Fortune,* 15 May 1995, p. F-1.

11. Chevron, *Chevron Corporation Annual Report 1996: Dimensions of Growth* (San Francisco: Chevron Corporation), p. 3.

12. Chevron, *1995 Form 10-K* (Washington, DC: United States Securities and Exchange Commission, 1995), p. 1; Chevron, *Supplement to 1992 Annual Report*, p. 1.

13. "Global 500," p. F-2.

14. GDP figures from the World Bank, *World Development Report 1995* (New York: Oxford University Press, 1995), pp. 166-67.

15. Standard Oil Company of California, *1879–1979: One Hundred Years Helping to Create the Future* (San Francisco: Standard Oil Company of California, 1979), p. 16.

16. Gerald T. White, *Formative Years in the Far West: A History of Standard Oil Company of California and Predecessors Through 1919* (New York: Appleton-Century-Crofts, 1962).

17. Yergin, *The Prize*, pp. 35–55.

18. Ibid., p. 54.

19. Ibid., pp. 106–13.

20. See Ida M. Tarbell, *The History of the Standard Oil Company* (New York: W. W. Norton and Company, 1969) (first published in 1904).

21. Such agencies included the Interstate Commerce Commission, the Federal

Trade Commission and the now defunct Bureau of Corporations. Ralph Nader, Mark Green and Joel Seligman, *Constitutionalizing the Corporation* (c. 1976), cited in Jonathan Rowe, "Reinventing the Corporation," *Washington Monthly*, April 1996, pp. 17–19.

22. The Supreme Court decision came despite Standard Oil's pioneering efforts to curry favor with politicians through timely and large campaign contributions, despite the fact that it helped establish the tradition of hiring the best and most expensive corporate lawyers to defend it, and despite some public relations efforts to project a new "antitrust" corporate image. Sampson, *The Seven Sisters,* pp. 32–34; Yergin, *The Prize,* pp. 100–109.

23. Yergin, *The Prize*, p. 110.

24. Ibid., p. 82.

25. White, *Formative Years*, pp. 249–83.

26. "Starting on World's Greatest Refinery," *Los Angeles Times*, 12 July 1911.

27. White, *Formative Years*; Yergin, *The Prize*, pp. 110–11; Sampson, *Seven Sisters*, p. 43.

28. White, *Formative Years*, p. 512.

29. Douglas G. McPhee, *The Story of the Standard Oil Company of California* (San Francisco: Standard Oil Company of California, 1937), p. 15.

30. See Bradford C. Snell, *American Ground Transport: A Proposal for Restructuring the Automobile, Truck, Bus and Rail Industries*, report prepared for the Subcommittee on Antitrust and Monopoly, Committee on the Judiciary (Washington, DC: U.S. Government Printing Office, U.S. Senate, 26 February 1974.

31. General Motors Corporation, "The Truth About 'American Ground Transport': A Reply by General Motors," submitted to the Subcommittee on Antitrust and Monopoly, Committee on the Judiciary, U.S. Senate, April 1974.

32. Snell, *American Ground Transport*, pp. 30–31.

33. Ibid., p. 31.

34. By 1949 GM had been involved in the replacement of more than 100 electric transit systems with buses in forty-five cities, including Philadelphia, Baltimore, St. Louis, Oakland, Salt Lake City and Los Angeles. In New York City the world's largest electric street car system was converted to buses in only eighteen months. Snell, *American Ground Transport*, p. 32.

35. Ibid., p. 32.

36. In addition to the local air pollution problems created by this transformation, the United States' automobile-based transportation system continues to make a significant contribution to the potential for global climate change today. According to the United Nations, the United States contributes one-third of the total carbon dioxide emitted by the transport sector worldwide. Arjun Makhijani et al., *Climate Change and Transnational Cor-*

porations: Analysis and Trends (New York: United Nations Centre on Transnational Corporations, 1992), p. 55.

37. Snell, *American Ground Transport*, p. 1.

38. For instance, GM acquired Germany's largest automobile company, Adam Opel, A.G., in 1929. By 1935 GM was building a heavy truck facility in Brandenburg, Germany, designed to be invulnerable to air attack. For this and other contributions to Nazi wartime preparations, GM's chief executive for overseas operations was awarded the Order of the German Eagle by Chancellor Adolf Hitler in 1938. Ford's chief executive received a similar award from Hitler in the same year for producing troop transport vehicles. Meanwhile, Exxon helped produce synthetic fuel. In response to questions about patriotism that emerged on the eve of the Nazis' 1939 invasion of Poland, GM's chairman, Alfred P. Sloan, is reported to have remarked that his company was "too big" to be affected by "petty international squabbles." The new global corporations had already begun to view themselves as stateless. Snell, *American Ground Transport*, pp. 16–23.

39. Chevron provided, for example, the specialized aviation fuel that Charles Lindbergh used in his pioneering flight across the Atlantic. Standard Oil Company of California, *One Hundred Years*, pp. 24–25.

40. Yergin, *The Prize*, pp. 410–19; SoCAL, *One Hundred Years*, pp. 27–30.

41. See Irvine H. Anderson, *Aramco, the United States, and Saudi Arabia: A Study of the Dynamics of Foreign Oil Policy 1933–1950* (Princeton, NJ: Princeton University Press, 1981).

42. Chevron, *Supplement to 1992 Annual Report*, p. 1.

43. Carl Deal, *The Greenpeace Guide to Anti-Environmental Organizations* (Berkeley, CA: Odonian Press, 1993), p. 59.

44. Philip Mattera, "Chevron: The Big Oil Boys," *Multinational Monitor*, April 1992, p. 29.

45. In addition to complaints that female employees had received pornographic material from managers in interoffice mail, employees charged Chevron with discriminating against women in promotions, pay, job assignments and performance evaluations. Harriet Chiang, "Chevron Settles Harass Suit," *San Francisco Chronicle*, 22 February 1995.

46. Ironically, when Chevron bought Gulf, it came under fire from U.S. conservatives for maintaining Gulf's investments in Angola; thus the company was able to walk the line between its left- and right-wing critics. Mattera, "Big Oil Boys," p. 30.

47. Chevron, *Chevron Corporation 1996 Annual Report* (San Francisco: Chevron Corporation), p. 1.

48. Chevron, *Chevron Corporation 1995 Annual Report: New Prospects, New Perspectives* (San Francisco: Chevron Corporation), pp. 10–16.

49. José Goncalves, economist, Universidade del Cabo of Angola, interview with author, Buenos Aires, 25 July 1995.

50. Jeff Pelline, "Chevron Signs $20 Billion Tengiz Oil Deal," *San Francisco Chronicle*, 7 April 1993; Chevron, *1996 Annual Report*, p. 1.

51. Chevron, *Chevron Corporation 1994 Annual Report* (San Francisco: Chevron Corporation), p. 6.

52. Chevron, *1995 Form 10-K*, pp. 17–21.

53. Ibid., pp. 21–22.

54. Chevron, *1994 Annual Report*, pp. 6–7.

55. Richard J. Samuels, *The Business of the Japanese State: Energy Markets in Comparative and Historical Perspective* (Ithaca, NY: Cornell University Press, 1987), p. 190.

56. Chevron, *1994 Annual Report*, pp. 18–19.

57. For instance, the IRS found that from 1979 to 1981 Aramco conducted "transfer pricing," routing oil through third-country subsidiaries in order to mark up the price on cheap oil acquired in Saudi Arabia and avoid paying U.S. taxes. Mattera, "Big Oil Boys," p. 29.

58. Interoffice memo from Arthur E. Wiese to William F. O'Keefe and Phil G. Goulding regarding "Initial Report and Recommendations of the API Staff Task Force on the Aftermath of the Alaskan Oil Spill," 20 April 1989.

59. William Mulligan, manager of federal relations, Chevron Corporation, interview with author, Washington, DC, 25 October 1994.

60. Ibid.

61. Friends of the Earth et al., *Indictment: The Case Against the Reagan Environmental Record* (San Francisco: Friends of the Earth, March 1982).

62. "Chevron Sued for Ocean Dumping," United Press International, 21 March 1985.

63. "Chevron Plant Says It Violated State Water Quality Rules 250 Times in Eight Years," Associated Press, 24 April 1985.

64. U.S. attorney Robert Bonner, quoted in "Government Sues Chevron Over Pollutants," United Press International, 27 August 1986.

65. "Chevron Responds to Pollution Suit," United Press International, 27 August 1986.

66. "Chevron to Pay Fine for Dumping Pollutants," Associated Press, 22 January 1988. Chevron later settled with the Sierra Club for $100,000 which was used for land conservation in the Los Angeles area; "Sierra Club and Chevron Move to Settle Lawsuit," Business Wire, Inc., 15 April 1988.

67. The effluent load contains more than 1,000 pounds of oil and grease and nearly 3,000 pounds of ammonia and heavy metals every day, "Chevron Plant Says."

68. Doyle, *Crude Awakening*, pp. 48–49. Adding to its problems, in 1989 the refinery was listed as the seventh-largest toxic air polluter in Los Angeles County, producing ammonia, toluene, 1,3-butadiene and m-Xylene and distinguishing itself as the top generator of nitrogen oxide, the number-two producer of reactive hydrocarbons and the third-largest LA generator of benzene. Mann, *LA's Lethal Air*, pp. 17, 42–45.

69. In 1988 the EPA filed suit for nineteen alleged air pollution violations at Chevron's refinery in Philadelphia; "EPA Sues Chevron, Charging Benzene Leaks," United Press International, 30 August 1988. A year later the company's Port Arthur, Texas, refinery leaked hydrogen sulfide from a ruptured storage tank, forcing the evacuation of 7,000 people; UPI Regional News, 13 September 1989. Also in 1989, a Chevron pipeline broke in Beaumont, Texas, spilling 231,000 gallons of crude into Hildebrandt Bayou. In Washington State nine Chevron storage sites were found to be leaking into soil and groundwater in the late 1980s and early 1990s. In 1992 the company pled guilty to sixty-five violations of the Clean Water Act that occurred in the 1980s at Platform Grace in the Santa Barbara Channel; it was fined $8 million by the EPA. Doyle, *Crude Awakening*, pp. 18, 82, 123.

At Chevron's Richmond, California, refinery, the largest emitter of toxic chemicals in the San Francisco Bay Area, contaminated water was found seeping onto property that Chevron had donated to the YMCA. Its pesticide plant adjacent to the refinery was producing hazardous waste that Chevron burned on site in an incinerator that was out of compliance with pollution control laws; Council on Economic Priorities, *Chevron: A Report on the Company's Environmental Performance* (New York: Council on Economic Priorities, 1991), pp. 16–17. In 1989 the state also ordered Chevron to clean up a thirty-five-year-old, three-acre acid sludge pit at the Richmond refinery. Between 1984 and 1989 more than seventy fires were reported in just one unit at the refinery, and in 1989 five workers were seriously burned in a fire that raged for more than four days. Following the latter incident OSHA alleged that Chevron had committed 109 willful and five "serious" legal violations of health and safety laws at Richmond; Doyle, *Crude Awakening*, pp. 107, 166. Moreover, residents of the mostly African-American working-class Richmond community accused Chevron of environmental racism for allowing the fire to burn, thus subjecting them to the potentially toxic smoke; Milton Moskowitz, Robert Levering and Michael Katz, *Everybody's Business: A Field Guide to the 400 Leading Companies in America* (New York: Doubleday, 1990), p. 477; Citizens for a Better Environment, "Chevron's Record," fact sheet from Citizens for a Better Environment, San Francisco, June 1992.

70. Council on Economic Priorities, *Chevron: A Report*, p. 24; Roger Moody, *The Gulliver File: Mines, People and Land: A Global Battleground* (London: Minewatch, 1992), pp. 192–93.

71. Council on Economic Priorities, *Chevron: A Report*, pp. 22–23; "Indians Oppose Drilling on Montana Land," *San Francisco Examiner*, 11 November 1990.

72. Also in 1989, Exxon, Chevron, ARCO, Phillips, Sun and Texaco took more than $3 billion in write-downs in direct response to environmental issues. Bob Williams, *U.S. Petroleum Strategies in the Decade of the Environment* (Tulsa: Penwell Books, 1991), pp. 107–108.

73. Chevron, *1991 Annual Report* (San Francisco: Chevron Corporation), p. 38.

74. William Mulligan, interview with author.

75. Keith Schneider, "Exxon Is Ordered to Pay $5 Billion for Alaska Spill," *New York Times*, 17 September 1994.

76. William Mulligan, interview with author.

77. Ironically, around the time of the report's release the Persian Gulf was covered in oil spills, while the area's atmosphere was choked with smoke and flames from oil fires produced by the United States–Iraq war.

78. Chevron, *1990 Report on the Environment: A Commitment to Excellence* (San Francisco: Chevron Corporation, 1990), p. 1.

79. Chevron, *1994 Annual Report*, p. 27.

80. "API Statement," American Petroleum Institute press release, Washington, DC, 17 May 1993.

81. Greg Karras, personal communication with author, 29 June 1996.

82. Chevron, *Measuring Progress: A Report on Chevron's Environmental Performance* (San Francisco: Chevron Corporation, 1994), p. 13; Karras, in a personal communication with the author, charges that the industry's "most expensive 'clean fuels' expenditures are for nonenvironmental purposes, mainly . . . to make higher-value products from poor-quality crude."

83. Additionally, in a voluntary program with the EPA, it curtailed its production of seventeen highly toxic chemicals by 35 percent—a reduction of 1 million pounds; Chevron, *Measuring Progress*, pp. 4–5. Also in the 1980s the company's Tank Integrity Program removed or replaced more than 90 percent of its underground storage tanks in U.S. service stations; Chevron, *1990 Report on the Environment*, p. 6.

84. Chevron, *Measuring Progress*, p. 5.

85. Emissions at Richmond dropped from 80,000 pounds in 1982 to 7,000 pounds in 1988; Council on Economic Priorities, *Chevron: A Report*, p. 18.

86. Letter from Rodney K. Spackman, public affairs manager, the Chevron Companies, to Dr. Scott Jenkins, Surfrider Foundation, 25 January 1993; "Evaluation of Potential Health Risks Resulting from Exposure to Ocean Water Near the Chevron El Segundo Refinery Outfall," prepared for Chevron by Radian Corporation, 2 October 1992.

87. Tina Barseghian, "Chevron Agrees to Remove Outfall," *El Segundo Herald*, 11 February 1993.

88. Maria L. LaGanga, "Chevron to Stop Dumping Waste Near Shoreline," *Los Angeles Times*, 4 February 1993.

89. Mary Hernandez, interview with author, East Austin, 29 July 1993; Doyle, *Crude Awakening*, pp. 22–27.

90. Doyle, *Crude Awakening*, pp. 23–27.

91. Susana Almanza, interview with author, Austin, 29 July 1993.

92. Mike Ward, "Escaping the Shadows of the Tanks: Citizens Use Voice for Change," *Austin American-Statesman*, 14 February 1993.

93. Roberto Suro, "Pollution-Weary Minorities Try Civil Rights Tack," *New York Times*, 11 January 1993.

94. For example, in a letter to U.S. Congressman Jay Pickle (D-TX) that was made public, Chevron's Miller attempted to portray those calling for closure of the tank farm as fringe elements. Miller stated that trouble at the tank farms was being stirred up by a small minority of "activists who cannot be satisfied under any circumstances." Ultimately, Miller's efforts did more to hurt his cause than help it. Mike Ward, "Activists Say Letter Belittles Contamination Worries," *Austin American-Statesman*, 14 March 1992.

95. Susana Almanza, interview with author.

96. Mike Ward and Scott W. Wright, "Exxon to Move Terminal," *Austin American-Statesman*, 19 February 1993.

97. William Mulligan, interview with author.

98. The coalition, called Get Oil Out (GOO), advocated sending the oil through existing land-based pipelines and charged that "there is no justification except their desire for enhanced cash flow to justify any tanker permit"; Jana Zimmer, special counsel, American Oceans Campaign, memorandum to Thomas Gwyn, chair, California Coastal Commission, 26 April 1993.

99. Linda Krop, interview with author, Santa Barbara, 8 July 1993; also, Zimmer, memorandum to Thomas Gwyn, and Linda Krop, memorandum to Thomas Gwyn, California Coastal Commission, 21 September 1993, pp. 14–17.

100. Kenneth J. Garcia, "Coastal Agency OKs Oil Shipping: Chevron Gets Go-Ahead to Use Tankers Off Santa Barbara Coast," *San Francisco Chronicle*, 13 May 1993.

101. All told, Chevron listed $1.4 million in donations to 288 "environmental and natural resource protection groups" around the world in 1993. Chevron, *Measuring Progress*, p. 14.

102. "Who Funds 'Wise Use' Groups? Chevron Does!" *Earth Island Journal*, Spring 1994, p. 20; Deal, *Greenpeace Guide*, pp. 23–101. Chevron also contributed nearly $1 million for advertisements to help defeat the "Big Green," a 1990 California ballot initiative (Proposition 128) that included provisions to phase out the use of carcinogenic pesticides, severely limit offshore oil exploration and drilling, and ban logging in old-growth forests; Council on Economic Priorities, *Chevron: A Report*, p. 7.

103. Chevron, *Report on the Environment*, p. 20.

104. Glen Martin, "Green and Proud to Be Black and Blue: Environmental Movement in Despair," *San Francisco Chronicle*, 2 June 1995.

105. Michael Weisskopf and David Maraniss, "Forging an Alliance for Deregulation: Rep. DeLay Makes Companies Full Partners in the Movement," *Washington Post*, 12 March 1995; "How a Bill Becomes a Law: The New Approach," *Harper's*, July 1995, p. 9.

106. Susan Sward, "SF Fears Chevron Pipe May Threaten Reservoir," *San Francisco*

Chronicle, 12 March 1996; ———, "Chevron Talks Nice, Sues SF," *San Francisco Chronicle,* 14 March 1996; ———, "Judge Says Chevron Can Keep Using Pipeline," *San Francisco Chronicle,* 20 March 1996.

107. Chevron's Richmond refinery suffered an explosion in late 1991 that released a forty-ton cloud of toxic catalyst dust. The nickel-laden dust fell in a sixteen-mile radius, blanketing the largely African-American community adjacent to the refinery. This was just one in an ongoing series of leaks and explosions at Richmond; "Chevron's Record," fact sheet from Citizens for a Better Environment, June 1992; Seth Rosenfeld, "Chevron Negligent on Toxics, Jury Says," *San Francisco Examiner,* 2 February 1997. In 1994 the company's other refineries suffered a series of accidents, including the release of 770,000 pounds of ethylene and propylene into the atmosphere at one unspecified plant; Edward R. Spaulding, Chevron Corporation, personal communication with author, 21 February 1995.

In 1990–91 Chevron was cited twenty-six times for exceeding maximum daily discharge limits at its drilling operations in the Gulf of Mexico; Doyle, *Crude Awakening,* pp. 123–24. In 1990 a Chevron tanker unloading asphalt at the company's refinery near Seattle spilled 2,600 barrels of oil onto the beach and into Puget Sound. While Chevron claims it was able to clean up all but 100 barrels (4,200 gallons), the state government fined the company $35,000, charging it with negligence, pollution of state waters and failure to notify officials promptly; Doyle, *Crude Awakening,* p. 120.

While it boasts of improvements, overall Chevron continues to generate nearly as much hazardous waste and toxic emissions as ever—its total releases and transfers of toxic chemicals range from 13.7 million to 15.9 million pounds per year between 1988 and 1993; Edward R. Spaulding, personal communication with author. The company speaks proudly of reducing toxics released directly into U.S. air, water and land by 18 percent between 1988 and 1993 (it still discharged more than 10 million pounds of chemicals in 1993). At the same time, transfers of toxic waste for incineration, landfill or "treatment" nearly doubled over the same period; Chevron, *Measuring Progress,* pp. 3–6.

In 1991 the company was also a potentially responsible party at 140 Superfund sites and was listed by the EPA as having the highest number of potential sites among all the oil companies. That number rose to more than 200 by the end of 1993 and 251 at the end of 1995. Chevron, *1995 10K,* p. 24. Some of these toxic sites have been created by leaking underground storage tanks (LUSTS) at Chevron service stations. Despite Chevron's tank replacement program, it is still plagued by leaks that contaminate groundwater and wells. In 1992, for example, the company was the leader in Washington State's Northwest region in terms of LUSTS, with eighty-one stations listed as leaky. In California between 1988 and 1992, more than 50,000 gallons of fuel leaked from at least fifteen gas stations. Doyle, *Crude Awakening,* pp. 98–100.

108. Chevron, *Measuring Progress*, p. 10.

109. Doyle, *Crude Awakening*, p. 3.

110. The Asian region, for example, has accounted for half of all the world's new oil demand in the 1990s. Kim Coghill, "Asia Rapidly Becoming World's Top Air Polluter," Reuters News Service, 21 May 1993.

111. Chevron, *1996 Annual Report*, p. 11. The oil majors increased their foreign spending by 30 percent in the late 1980s and early 1990s; Doyle, *Crude Awakening*, pp. 3–5.

112. Chevron, *Supplement to 1992 Annual Report*, p. 11.

113. Agis Salpukas, "Chevron Plans Cuts in U.S. to Finance Growth Abroad," *New York Times*, 28 May 1993.

114. William Mulligan, interview with author.

115. Chevron, *1994 Annual Report*, pp. 18–19.

116. In 1973 U.S. oil imports totaled 35 percent of total consumption. While demand has remained more or less constant, imports now account for roughly half of demand; Doyle, *Crude Awakening*, p. 5.

117. Ibid., pp. 1–7. Overall, at least 100 U.S. oil refineries have closed since 1981. This trend has reduced employment in the U.S. oil industry by more than half between 1982 and 1994. "OPEC Rivals Curb Cartel Impact," *New York Times*, 27 December 1994.

118. William Mulligan, interview with author.

119. Carol Alexander and Ken Stump, *The North American Free Trade Agreement and Energy Trade* (Washington, DC: Greenpeace Inc., 1992).

120. Greenpeace goes on to report that "the remoteness of the region and abundant oil and gas reserves, together with cheap labour and lax or no environmental standards, have clearly made Russia attractive for investment by the Western oil industry. Added to these are tax exemptions, credit systems and contracts negotiated specifically to exclude responsibility for oil spills." Greenpeace, *Black Ice: The Behavior of Multinational Oil Companies in Russia* (Amsterdam: Greenpeace International, November 1994).

121. Edward R. Spaulding, personal communication with author.

122. Edward R. Spaulding, personal communication with author.

123. Chevron Corporation, *1994 Form 10-K* (Washington, DC: United States Securities and Exchange Commission, 1994), p. C-4.

124. Chevron, *1994 Annual Report*, p. 46.

125. Chevron, *Measuring Progress*, p. 3.

126. Robin Broad and John Cavanagh, *Plundering Paradise: The Struggle for the Environment in the Philippines* (Berkeley: University of California Press, 1993), p. 82.

127. Caltex has denied the charges. Robert Weissman, "Caltex's Corporate Colony: How an Oil Consortium Pollutes Indonesia," *Multinational Monitor*, November 1993.

128. Caltex bases its claim to the land on a fifty-year-old agreement with a single indigenous leader. The Sakai deny the legitimacy of this claim, chal-

lenging the right of the individual leader to transfer ownership of their land without their knowledge. Robert Weissman, "Deforestation on Indigenous Lands," *Multinational Monitor*, April 1994.

129. Andrew Rowell and Andrea Goodall, *Shell-Shocked: The Environmental and Social Costs of Living with Shell in Nigeria* (Amsterdam: Greenpeace International, July 1994), p. 5.

130. Geraldine Brooks, "Shell's Nigerian Fields Produce Few Benefits for Region's Villagers," *Wall Street Journal*, 6 May 1994; Kenneth R. Noble, "Atop a Sea of Oil, Nothing but Misery," *New York Times*, 9 September 1993.

131. Chevron, *1996 Annual Report*, pp. 11–12.

132. Chevron, *Measuring Progress*, p. 9; Edward R. Spaulding, personal communication with author.

133. Ken Saro-Wiwa, *Genocide in Nigeria: The Ogoni Tragedy* (London: Saros International Publishers, 1992), p. 83.

134. Howard W. French, "Nigeria Executes Critic of Regime; Nations Protest," *New York Times*, 11 November 1995.

135. Bob Herbert, "Unholy Alliance in Nigeria," *New York Times*, 26 January 1996, op-ed.

136. Joshua Hammer, "Nigeria Crude: A Hanged Man and an Oil-Fouled Landscape," *Harper's*, June 1996, p. 68.

137. Ibid., p. 59.

138. Joe Kane, "With Spears from All Sides," *New Yorker*, 27 September 1993; Judith Kimmerling et al., *Amazon Crude* (New York: Natural Resources Defense Council, 1991), pp. 55–84.

139. Valerio Grefa, president, Coordinadora Indigena de la Cuenca Amazonica, interview with author, San Francisco, 19 February 1993.

140. Cited in Conrad B. MacKerron, *Business in the Rainforests: Corporations, Deforestation and Sustainability* (Washington, DC: Investor Responsibility Research Center, 1993), p. 102. In Nigeria, Shell's response is nearly identical: "We have operated within the guidelines set out by Government," says spokesman Stephen Lawson-Jack; Noble, "A Sea of Oil."

141. See, for example, Julius Tahija, "Swapping Business Skills for Oil," *Harvard Business Review*, September–October 1993, pp. 64–77.

142. "Kutubu Project Puts PNG on World Oil Map," *Petroleum Gazette* (Australian Institute of Petroleum), vol. 28, no. 2 (1993).

143. Chevron, "Kutubu Project," Kutubu Joint Venture promotional video produced by Frank Mills and Associates, Port Moresby, 1993.

144. Gai Pobe, interview with author, Lake Kutubu, Papua New Guinea, 13 March 1994.

145. Jim Price, interview with author, Lake Kutubu, Papua New Guinea, 14 March 1994.

146. Gai Pobe, interview with author.

147. "PNG on World Oil Map"; Jim Price, interview with author.

148. George Marshall, interview with author, Port Moresby, Papua New Guinea, 5 March 1994.

149. Danny Kennedy, "Drilling Papua New Guinea: Chevron Comes to Lake Kutubu," *Multinational Monitor*, March 1996, pp. 10–14. Also Chris Angus, Chevron's manager of legal and government relations, interview with author, Port Moresby, 5 March 1994; Jim Price, interview with author.

150. Danny Kennedy, "Development Is Not Sustainability: A Case Study of the Kutubu Petroleum Development Project, Papua New Guinea" (honors thesis, Macquarie University, Australia, 17 June 1994), app. 1.

151. Gary Hartshorn, report to World Wildlife Fund on trip to Indonesia, Malaysia and Papua New Guinea, 27 July to 28 August 1993.

152. Paul Chatterton, South Pacific Program, World Wide Fund for Nature, telephone interview with author, 27 June 1995. When it built the pipeline, Chevron did not cut a wide road into the rainforest that would have opened it to logging and colonization; rather it cut a small swath and then replanted.

153. The refinery was one of two that the PNG government committed to build. Abby Yadi, "Kopi Refinery Agreement Signed Against Department's Advice," *Saturday Independent* (Port Moresby, PNG), 3 June 1995; Paul Chatterton, interview with author.

154. Abby Yadi, "Ombudsmen Urged to Probe Turama Deal," *Saturday Independent* (PNG), 10 June 1995.

155. Paul Chatterton, interview with author.

156. An independent assessment of the plan undertaken by academics from the University of California and Humboldt State University concludes, "We are particularly concerned about potential impacts of catastrophic oil spills from pipeline breakage. . . . Given the proximity to active faulting and subduction, and given the nature of deltaic sediments, pipeline failure at multiple points can be expected due to seismic shaking and liquefaction"; M. Kondolf and R. Chaney quoted in Kennedy, "Development Is Not," app. 1.

157. Lafcadio Cortesi, personal communication with author, 26 April 1993.

158. Kimmerling et al., in *Amazon Crude*, pp. 79–80, write, "With each step into the wage economy, subsistence activities are neglected and a spiral of economic dependency begins or quickens. . . . According to regional medical personnel, the health and nutrition of indigenous people decline as they are integrated into a predominantly cash economy. As they abandon traditional subsistence activities, they change their diet. . . . The result can be malnutrition and lowered resistance to disease."

159. Nadeem Anwar, interview with author, Kutubu, 13 March 1994.

160. Kennedy, "Development Is Not," app. 1.

161. Makhijani, *Climate Change*, pp. 41–45.

162. Greenpeace, *Fossil Fuels in a Changing Climate: How to Protect the World's*

Climate by Ending the Use of Coal, Oil and Gas (Amsterdam: Greenpeace International, 1993), p. 45.

163. "The New Order of Oil," part 7 of *The Prize*, an Invision Production for Majestic Films and Transpacific Films in association with BBC Television and WGBH in Boston, 1992.

164. Coghill, "Asia Rapidly Becoming."

165. See Anil Agarwal and Sunita Narain, *Global Warming in an Unequal World: A Case of Environmental Colonialism* (New Delhi: Centre for Science and Environment, 1991).

166. Makhijani, *Climate Change*, pp. 45–53.

167. Kenneth T. Derr, "Oil and Its Critics: The Facts and the Future" (Remarks delivered to the Cambridge Energy Research Associates Executive Conference, Houston, 8 February 1994).

168. See Sharon L. Roan, *Ozone Crisis: The 15 Year Evolution of a Sudden Global Emergency* (New York: John Wiley & Sons, 1989).

169. Derr, "Oil and Its Critics."

170. Greenpeace, *Fossil Fuels*, pp. 45–48.

171. William Mulligan, interview with author.

172. Derr, "Oil and Its Critics."

173. Makhijani, *Climate Change*, pp. 38, 45.

Chapter Four: Island of Dreams

1. François Nectoux and Yoichi Kuroda, *Timber from the South Seas: An Analysis of Japan's Tropical Timber Trade and Its Environmental Impact* (Geneva: World Wildlife Fund International, 1989), p 34; JATAN, *Asia-Pacific Forests* (Tokyo: Japan Tropical Forest Action Network, November 1993), p. 1.

2. There are more than 600 companies—most of them small—operating in Shin Kiba. Just one operation, the Tokyo Timber Terminal, processes well over 3.3 million cubic feet of wood every year, 20 percent of which comes from one corporation—the Canadian giant MacMillan Bloedel. Other corporations, such as Itochu and Mitsubishi, have their own docks at another port, but sooner or later much of their wood passes through Shin Kiba, where it is processed and distributed by these smaller companies. Japanese timber industry analyst who wished to remain anonymous, interview with author, Shin Kiba, 23 January 1994.

3. Nectoux and Kuroda, *Timber from the South Seas*, pp. 46–60.

4. "Yumenoshima Tropical Plant Dome," brochure produced by the Tokyo Metropolitan Park Association.

5. Hidefumi Imura, Institute of Environmental Systems, Faculty of Engineering, Kyushu University, interview with author, Tokyo, 22 January 1994.

6. Maruyama Yoshinari, "The Big Six Horizontal Keiretsu," *Japan Quarterly*, April–June 1992, pp. 186–99; Sumiya Toshio, "The Structure and Operation of Monopoly Capital in Japan," in Tessa Morris-Suzuki and

Takuro Seiyama, eds., *Japanese Capitalism Since 1945* (New York: M. E. Sharpe, 1989), pp. 105–30; Max Eli, *Japan Inc.: Global Strategies of Japanese Trading Corporations*, (Chicago: Probus Publishing Company, 1991); Michael Gerlach, *The Keiretsu: A Primer* (New York: The Japan Society, 1992); ———, *Alliance Capitalism: The Social Organization of Japanese Business* (Berkeley: University of California Press, 1992).

7. "Global 500: The World's Largest Corporations," *Fortune*, 7 August 1995, p. F-1.

8. Patrick J. Spain and James R. Talbot, *Hoover's Handbook of World Business 1995–1996* (Austin, TX: The Reference Press, 1995), p. 44.

9. Yoshinari, "The Big Six," pp. 190–94; Eli, *Japan Inc.*, pp. 8–18; Gerlach, *The Keiretsu*, pp. 8–20.

10. Gerlach, *The Keiretsu*, pp. 9–10; Toshio, "Monopoly Capital," p. 120.

11. Yoichi Kuroda, interview with author, San Francisco, November 1993.

12. Eli, *Japan Inc.*, pp. 19–23.

13. "The Global 500," p. F-1.

14. Sheryl WuDunn, "Merger to Create New Japan Bank, World's Largest," *New York Times*, 29 March 1995.

15. "The Global 500," pp. F-15–26.

16. Figures are for the 1994 sales of Mitsubishi Corporation, Mitsubishi Electric, Mitsubishi Motors, Mitsubishi Heavy Industries, Mitsubishi Bank, Tokio Marine, Mitsubishi Chemical, Mitsubishi Materials, Mitsubishi Trust and Banking, Mitsubishi Oil, Asahi Glass and Kirin Brewery, which add up to more than $373 billion; "Global 500," pp. F-1–10. The GDP is from World Bank, *World Development Report 1995* (New York: Oxford University Press, 1995), pp. 166–67.

17. Robert Neff et al., "Mighty Mitsubishi Is on the Move," *Business Week*, 24 September 1990.

18. "Global 500," pp. F-1–10; World Bank, *World Development Report 1995*, pp. 166–67.

19. "Additional LNG Contracts," *MC Now* (Mitsubishi Corporation), vol. 2, no. 1 (December 1991); "An Alternative Fuel for the New Age—Orimulsion: Exporting Natural Tar from the Orinoco Belt," *MC Now*, vol. 1, no. 3 (April 1991).

20. Neff et al., "Mighty Mitsubishi"; "Loan to Large-Scale Platinum Mining Company in South Africa: First Japanese Loan After Economic Sanctions Lifted," *MC Now*, no. 16 (June 1993); "Escondida Copper Mine Begins Operation: Largest Private Investment in Chile to Date," *MC Now*, vol. 1, no. 4 (June 1991).

21. Japan has the third-largest navy in the world. It is also a major weapons component supplier to Southeast Asia and the U.S. military, providing the U.S. Department of Defense with ninety-two types of semiconductors used in U.S. weapons systems, including key chips for the cruise missile's naviga-

tional system. Walden Bello, *People and Power in the Pacific* (San Francisco: Institute for Food and Development Policy, 1993), pp. 104–107.

22. Mitsubishi Kasei, "Global Ten: Toward the Year 2000," video viewed by author in January 1994 at Tokyo Stock Exchange. Milton Moskowitz, *The Global Marketplace* (New York: Macmillan, 1987), p. 366.

23. Eli, *Japan Inc.*, p. 19.

24. Moskowitz, *The Global Marketplace*, p. 366.

25. Competition may flourish—for example, if the price is right, Mitsubishi Electric might buy a generator from Toshiba, a member of the Mitsui group, instead of Mitsubishi Heavy—yet reciprocal trade makes up a significant share of each group's transactions. For example, Mitsubishi Corporation handles more than 80 percent of Mitsubishi Heavy Industries' sales. Yoshinari, "The Big Six," p. 194; also see Michael L. Gerlach, "Twilight of the *Keiretsu?* A Critical Assessment," *Journal of Japanese Studies* (Society for Japanese Studies), vol. 18, no. 1 (1992), pp. 83–87.

26. William J. Holstein et al., "Hands Across America: The Rise of Mitsubishi," *Business Week*, 24 September 1990.

27. Nectoux and Kuroda, *Timber from the South Seas*, pp. 61–94.

28. Hidefumi Imura, interview with author.

29. Mitsubishi, *A Brief History of Mitsubishi* (Tokyo: Mitsubishi Corporation, July 1988), p. 5.

30. Eli, *Japan Inc.*, pp. 3–4.

31. Joel Kotkin and Yoriko Kishimoto, *The Third Century: America's Resurgence in the Asian Era* (New York: Ivy Books, 1988), p. 46.

32. Kotkin and Kishimoto, *The Third Century*, pp. 58–59; Toshio, "Monopoly Capital," pp. 112–13.

33. Bello, *People and Power*, p. 33; Toshio, "Monopoly Capital," p. 114.

34. Kotkin and Kishimoto, *The Third Century*, p. 59.

35. Tim Weiner et al., "CIA Spent Millions to Support Japanese Right in 50s and 60s," *New York Times*, 9 October 1994.

36. Kotkin and Kishimoto, *The Third Century*, p. 58.

37. Today the twenty-eight core members of the Mitsubishi Group hold more than 26 percent of Mitsubishi Bank's and 32 percent of Mitsubishi Corporation's stock. Overall, an average of 24 percent of each of the core Mitsubishi companies is owned by its fellow core members. While the other Big Six have somewhat lower ownership percentages, the structure and its effect are similar. The percentage of member company stock held by the entire group amounts to 17.24 percent for Mitsui, 23.81 percent for Sumitomo, 15.31 percent for Fuyo, 16.24 percent for Sanwa and 12.03 percent for Dai Ichi Kangyo. Yoshinari, "The Big Six," p. 192; Neff et al., "Mighty Mitsubishi."

In addition to cross-shareholding, the *keiretsu* were able to form coherent groups through such mechanisms as informal presidents' councils, interlocking directorates, joint projects, reciprocal trade arrangements, the cultural attributes of group mentality and loyalty, and financing from group banks. Eli, *Japan Inc.*, pp. 4–6.

38. Yoshinari, "The Big Six," p. 190.

39. Jonathan Friedland, "Survival of the Fit: Mitsubishi Heavy Beats the Odds of Ageing Industry," *Far Eastern Economic Review*, 13 January 1994, p. 74.

40. Toshio, "Monopoly Capital," p. 114.

41. Bello, *People and Power*; Fujiwara Sadao, "Foreign Trade and Industrial Imperialism," in Morris-Suzuki and Seiyama, eds., *Japanese Capitalism*.

42. Richard J. Samuels, *The Business of the Japanese State* (Ithaca, NY: Cornell University Press, 1987), p. 234.

43. Gerlach, *The Keiretsu*, p. 14.

44. Jinzaburo Takagi, executive director, Citizens' Nuclear Information Center, interview with author, Tokyo, 22 January 1994.

45. Jinzaburo Takagi, interview with author.

46. Jean McSorley, "The Nuke Frontier in Indonesia," *Multinational Monitor*, September 1995, pp. 14–16.

47. Fuel, food and fishery products are the top three, followed by forest products and then minerals. Nectoux and Kuroda, *Timber from the South Seas*, p. 27.

48. Yoichi Kuroda, "Historical Overview of the Timber Trade and Forestry Development in East and Tropical Asia and the Pacific Nations" (Japan Tropical Forest Action Network paper presented at the International Workshop for Forest and Environmental Preservation in Asia-Pacific, Seoul, South Korea, 18–21 February 1994, pp. 1–6.

49. U.S. Forest Service, "Validation Report on Alaska Pulp Company, Ltd.," 1982, p. 6.

50. Fujiwara Sadao, "Foreign Trade, Investment, and Industrial Imperialism in Postwar Japan," in Morris-Suzuki and Seiyama, eds., *Japanese Capitalism*, p. 202.

51. JATAN, *Asia-Pacific Forests*, pp. 3–4.

52. U.S. Forest Service, "Validation Report," p. 6.

53. Mitsubishi Corporation entered the project with 8.73 percent ownership. Other members of the Group, such as Mitsubishi Bank, bought in later, increasing Mitsubishi's overall ownership. Mitsubishi, "Facts About Mitsubishi Corporation's Timber Business (vs. RAN's Claims)," correspondence from the Mitsubishi Corporation to the Rainforest Action Network, 12 January 1995; Rainforest Action Newtwork, "Facts About Mitsubishi Corporation's Timber Business (vs. RAN's Claims)," reply to Mitsubishi Corporation by the Rainforest Action Network, 15 June 1995.

54. Hal Bernton, "Alaska Pulp Strives to Keep Its Log Contract," *Anchorage Daily News*, 18 July 1993.

55. JATAN, *Asia-Pacific Forests*, pp. 3–4.

56. U.S. Department of Commerce, *National Trade Data Bank*, CD-ROM, 1994.

57. Bello, *People and Power*, pp. 38, 53.

58. Yoichi Kuroda, "The Tropical Forest Crisis and the Future Course of Japanese Society," Japan Tropical Forest Action Network booklet (Tokyo, 1991), p. 2.

59. Between 1986 and 1991 alone, the APC was fined more than $700,000 for violating its water pollution permit. Andy Romanoff, "The Legacy of APC's Contract," *Ravencall* (Southeast Alaska Conservation Council), Spring 1994.

60. "APC to Pay $223,000 for Air Emission Costs," *Sitka Sentinel*, 29 April 1991; Dave Hardy, chairman, Air and Water Quality Committee, final report to Sitka Assembly, 8 May 1991; "Victory in Temperate Rainforest," Alert #97, Rainforest Action Network, June 1994.

61. Buck Lindekugel, "It's Over! Forest Service Ends APC's Timber Monopoly," *Ravencall* (Southeast Alaska Conservation Council), Spring 1994.

62. Ruling of U.S. District Court Judge Barbara Rothstein reprinted in the *Sitka Sentinel*, 9 July 1981.

63. Jane Fritsch, "Senate Aide Uses Budget Threat to Intervene in a Pollution Case," *New York Times*, 24 August 1995.

64. On April 14, 1994, the Forest Service terminated APC's contract, but an APC sawmill continues operating under a similar but separate concession. Lindekugel, "It's Over"; Bernton, "Alaska Pulp."

65. Fritsch, "Senate Aide Uses."

66. Samuels, *Business of the Japanese State*, pp. 186–92.

67. Per capita income went from $123 in 1950 to $1,658 in 1970. Between 1958 and 1972 the percentage of households owning television sets rose from 15 to 75 percent and washing machines from 29 to 96 percent. Norie Huddle and Michael Reich, *Island of Dreams: Environmental Crisis in Japan* (Rochester, VT: Schenkman Books, 1975), pp. 90, 212.

68. Jun Ui, *Industrial Pollution in Japan* (Tokyo: United Nations University, 1992), p. 1.

69. Takuya Negami, interview with author, Tokyo, 25 January 1994.

70. Yoshiro Sawai, interview with author, Yokkaichi, 24 January 1994.

71. Huddle and Reich, *Island of Dreams*, pp. 51–77.

72. Ibid.; Yoshiro Sawai, "Summer of 1972, Yokkaichi," *Ronin* (Hong Kong), vol. 1, no. 12 (August 1973).

73. *The Yokkaichi Air Pollution Photograph Album: 20th Anniversary of the Victorious Decision* (Yokkaichi: Editing Committee of the Yokkaichi Air Pollution Photograph Album, 1992).

74. Huddle and Reich, *Island of Dreams*, pp. 66, 72.

75. *Air Pollution Photograph Album*, p. 17.

76. Huddle and Reich, *Island of Dreams*, p. 95.

77. *Air Pollution Photograph Album*, p. 35.

78. Ui, *Industrial Pollution*, pp. 112–30; Sawai, "Summer of 1972."

79. Hidefumi Imura, "Air Pollution Control Policies and the Changing Attitudes

of the Public and Industry," in *Environmental Pollution Control: The Japanese Experience* (Papers presented at the UNU International Symposium on Eco-Restructuring) (Tokyo: United Nations University, 1993), pp. 55–70.

80. OECD, *The OECD Environment Industry: Situation, Prospects and Government Policies* (Paris: Organization for Economic Cooperation and Development, 1992), p. 11.

81. Yoshiro Sawai, interview with author.

82. Yokkaichi refinery brochure (1993).

83. Current sulfur dioxide emissions in Yokkaichi are one-thirtieth of what they were in the 1960s. Imura, "Air Pollution Control" p. 65.

84. Ui, *Industrial Pollution*, p. 180.

85. Half the nitrogen oxide in Yokkaichi comes from industry; the other half is from cars. A similar breakdown exists in Osaka. In Tokyo more than 70 percent of nitrogen oxide comes from cars. Kenzo Matsubu, chairman of the Environmental Association of Mie Prefecture, interview with author, Yokkaichi, 24 January 1994.

86. Ui, *Industrial Pollution*, p. 179. The number of motor vehicles grew from 3.4 million in 1960 to 57.6 million in 1990; Imura, "Air Pollution Control," p. 74.

87. Kazuki Kumamoto, "The Politics of Garbage," *AMPO: Japan-Asia Quarterly Review*, vol. 25, no. 2 (1994), pp. 15–19.

88. Nearly 40 percent of this waste is incinerated and another 15 percent is sent to landfills. The lack of space and local resistance to the siting of hazardous waste facilities have led to an increase of illegal waste dumping in Japan's mountains, forests and agricultural land. Masaru Tanaka, "Waste Management in Japan," in *Environmental Pollution Control*, p. 94. A number of cases of waste export have also been documented; Kumamoto, *Politics of Garbage*, p. 18.

89. Walden Bello and Stephanie Rosenfeld, *Dragons in Distress: Asia's Miracle Economies in Crisis* (San Francisco: Institute for Food and Development Policy, 1990), pp. 98–99; ESCAP/UNCTC, *Environmental Aspects of Transnational Corporation Activities in Pollution-Intensive Industries in Selected Asian and Pacific Developing Countries*, ESCAP/UNCTC Pub. Ser. B, no. 15 (New York: United Nations, Economic and Social Commission for Asia and the Pacific, 1990), pp. 293, 297–98.

90. Takasada Hirayama, "Exporting Pollution," *Kogai: The Newsletter from Polluted Japan* (Tokyo), no. 2 (Winter 1974), pp. 2–10.

91. Yoshiwara Toshiyuki, "The Kawasaki Steel Corporation: A Case Study of Japanese Pollution Export," *Kogai: The Newsletter from Polluted Japan* (Tokyo) vol. 5, no. 3 (Summer 1977), pp. 12–24.

92. Nobuo Kojima, "Japanese ODA and Corporate Expansion" (Paper presented to the Second Conference of Lawyers of Asia and the Pacific, Tokyo, 26–28 September 1991).

93. Walter Russell Mead, "From Bretton Woods to the Bush Team," *World Policy Journal* (New York), Winter 1988–89.

94. Prepared statement of Richard P. Cronin, Foreign Affairs and National Defense Division, Congressional Research Service, at the Joint Economic Committee Hearing on Japan and the Asia-Pacific Region, 22 July 1992.

95. Philip Shenon, "Missing Out on a Glittering Market," *New York Times*, 12 September 1993, sec. 3.

96. Prepared statement of Richard P. Cronin.

97. Bello, *People and Power*, p. 88.

98. Hisahiko Okazaki, "New Strategies Toward 'Super Asian Bloc'," *This Is* (Tokyo), August 1992, translated by FBIS, 7 October 1992.

99. Mitsubishi Kasei, "Global Ten: Toward the Year 2000," video; Bob Lyons, "Notes on the Environment Record of Mitsubishi" (Unpublished report prepared for Greenpeace International, 11 January 1992).

100. "Building China's Largest Ethylene Facility," *MC Now*, no. 13 (December 1992).

101. Indian Investment Centre, "List of Foreign Collaborations Approved During the Year 1992" (New Delhi Indian Investment Centre, 1993); Ashish Kothari, "Environment," in *Alternative Economic Survey 1993–1994* (New Delhi: Public Interest Research Group, 1994), p. 163.

102. Bello and Rosenfeld, *Dragons in Distress*, p. 12.

103. ESCAP/UNCTC, *Environmental Aspects*; Chee Yoke Ling, "The Environmental and Social Costs of South-East Asia's Economic Success," *Third World Resurgence*, January 1994.

104. Bello, *People and Power*, pp. 50–65.

105. Peh Swee Chin, *Judgment in Civil Suit No. 185 of 1985*, High Court of Malaya at Ipoh, 11 July 1992; Mitsubishi Kasei, "Lawsuit in Malaysia Against Asian Rare Earth Sendirian Berhad (ARE), Fact versus Fiction," n.d.; Mitsue Aizawa and Nobuo Kojima, "Pollution Export by Japanese Companies Doing Business in Asia: The Impact in Japan of the ARE Case," New Tokyo Sogoh and Bukyo-Sogoh law offices, n.d.

106. Nobuo Kojima, "Exporting Dirty Industry," *AMPO: Japan-Asia Quarterly Review*, vol. 25, no. 2, p. 21.

107. Testimonies of Dr. Rosalie Bertell, Dr. Jayabalan, Dr. Edward Radford and Professor Ichikawa, cited in Peh Swee Chin, *Judgment*.

108. "Japan Firms Abroad Must Monitor Local Sensibilities," *Nikkei Weekly*, 25 July 1992; Nobuo Kojima, interview with author, Tokyo, 12 January 1994.

109. "Mitsubishi Reports to Government on Malaysia Ruling," *Jiji Press*, 14 July 1992.

110. Meenakshi Raman, interview with author, Penang, Malaysia, 6 March 1993.

111. Nobuo Kojima, interview with author.

112. Keidanren, *Towards Preservation of the Global Environment: Results of a Follow-up Survey on the Subject of the Keidanren Global Environment Charter* (Tokyo:

Keidanren, 27 May 1993); Hajime Ohta, director, Industry and Telecommunications Department, Keidanren, 14 January 1994.

113. Nobuo Kojima, interview with author.

114. Kenzo Tamura, interview with author, Tokyo, 20 January 1994.

115. Ibid.

116. Rainforest Action Network, *Mitsubishi's Forestry Operations: A Global Summary* (San Francisco: Rainforest Action Network, 1995).

117. Yuta Harago, "Mitsubishi's Investments in Brazil: A Case Study of Eidai do Brasil Madeiras S.A.," paper prepared for the Rainforest Action Network, Rondonia, Brazil, September 1993.

118. JATAN, *Report on Eucalyptus Plantation Schemes in Brazil and Chile by Japanese Companies* (Tokyo: Japan Tropical Forest Action Network, May 1993).

119. Mitsubishi Corporation imports the following wood into the United States: mahogany from Brazil, Bolivia, Belize and Guatemala; meranti from Indonesia and Malaysia; luan from the Philippines; teak (possibly from Burma) originating in Thailand or brokered through Singapore. "Mitsubishi Giving Northwest a Raw Deal," *Boycott Mitsubishi Campaign Update*, Rainforest Action Network, January 1995.

120. Ibid.

121. Roger Olsson, ed., *The Taiga: A Treasure—Or Timber and Trash?* 4th ed. (Sokkmokk, Sweden: Taiga Rescue Network, 1993), pp. 53–54.

122. *Easy Money: The Most Heavily Subsidized Mill in History* (Edmonton: Western Canada Wilderness Committee, 1994). Mitsubishi, "Sustainable Development: Seeking to Meet the Challenge," Mitsubishi Corporation brochure, 1993.

123. "Japan NKK to Supply 350 Km of Piping for Burma Pipeline," AP-Dow Jones, 25 April 1996.

124. Rainforest Action Network, "Facts About Mitsubishi"; "Mitsubishi/Burma Connection," *Boycott Mitsubishi Corporation*, February 1997; Communities Occupy Bishimetals Mining Installations," Action Alert, Acción Ecologia, Quito, 16 May 1997.

125. Ibid.

126. South Korea's domestic roundwood log demand, for example, doubled between 1970 and 1990. Together South Korea and Taiwan's demand for tropical timber has reached 60 percent of Japan's (although some of this is processed and re-exported to Japan). When all three are combined, they make up the majority of the world's trade in tropical logs. Yoichi Kuroda, "Historical Overview of the Timber Trade."

127. Norman Myers, *Deforestation Rates in Tropical Forests and Their Climatic Implications* (London: Friends of the Earth, 1989).

128. Rowan Callick, "Fighting the Rush to Chop Down the Trees," *Islands Business Pacific*, July 1993.

129. T. E. Barnett, "Commission of Inquiry into Aspects of Papua New Guinea

Forestry Industry," Interim Report No. 6, June 1989, and Appendix 4 (unpublished).

130. Barnett Report, cited in George Marshall, *The Barnett Report: A Summary of the Report of the Commission of Inquiry into Aspects of the Timber Industry in Papua New Guinea* (Sandy Bay, Tasmania: Asia Pacific Action Group, 1990), p. 5.

131. Max Henderson, *Ol Draipela Diwai I Lus Pinis (All the Big Trees Have Gone): A Discussion on Various Financial, Environmental, and Social Aspects of the Current Export Logging Explosion* (Rabaul, Papua New Guinea: Pacific Heritage Foundation, 1993).

132. Henderson, *Ol Draipela Diwai*; Callick, "Fighting the Rush."

133. Eric Wakker, *No Time for Criticism: An Evaluation of Mitsubishi Corporation's Tropical Forest Policy and Practise* (Amsterdam: Milieu Defensie, May 1992), p. 13.

134. Evelyne Hong, *Natives of Sarawak: Survival in Borneo's Vanishing Forests* (Pulau Pinang, Malaysia: Institut Masyarakat, 1987); Raphael Pura, "In Sarawak, a Clash Over Land and Power," *Wall Street Journal*, 7 February 1990.

135. Wakker, *No Time for Criticism*, p. 13.

136. Herb Thompson, "Environment and Development: Deforestation in Papua New Guinea" (Paper presented at the Pacific Islands Political Studies Association, Fifth Conference, Rarotonga, Cook Islands, December 1993). Marcus Colchester, "The New Sultans: Asian Loggers Move in on Guyana's Forests," *The Ecologist*, vol. 24, no. 2 (Mar.–Apr. 1994).

137. Despite Rimbunan Hijau's virtual monopoly control of PNG's timber resources, the company declared no profit between 1989 and 1992, echoing the patterns of Japanese transnationals that the Barnett Commission condemned for transfer-pricing. Clement Miria, "PNG Is Logging at an Unsustainable Rate," *Times of Papua New Guinea*, 3 March 1994; Philip Shenon, "Isolated Papua New Guineans Fall Prey to Foreign Bulldozers," *New York Times*, 5 June 1994.

138. While in 1993 $500 million worth of trees were exported, tribal groups who legally own PNG's forests received only $15 million; Shenon, "Prey to Foreign Bulldozers."

139. Villagers often end up trading their inheritance for the promise of "development," free junkets to PNG's capital, relatively small amounts of cash and consumer items such as televisions, radios and even automobiles—the modern-day equivalent of beads and trinkets. Simon Pasingan, East New Britain Social Action Committee, interview with author, 8 March 1994.

140. Wakker, *No Time for Criticism*, p. i.

141. Kyosuke Mori, general manager, Environmental Affairs Department, Mitsubishi Corporation, letter to Ulf Rasmusson, World Wildlife Fund–Sweden, 28 June 1991.

142. Ibid.

143. Ibid.; Wakker, *No Time for Criticism*, p. 6.
144. Mitsubishi, "Sustainable Development."
145. Michael Marx, interview with author, San Francisco, 9 November 1995.
146. Wakker, *No Time for Criticism*, pp. 6–8.
147. Ibid.
148. Mitsubishi, *For Gaia* (Tokyo: Mitsubishi Corporation, Environmental Affairs Department, n.d.).
149. Elaine Kurtenbach, "Education Ministry Raps Mitsubishi Logging Comic," *Asahi Evening News*, 3 April 1992.
150. Mitsubishi Group manager who wished to remain anonymous, interview with author, Tokyo, January 1994.
151. Wakker, *No Time for Criticism*, pp. 1–3; Michael Marx, interview with author, 9 November 1995.
152. Michael Marx, interview with author, San Francisco, 28 June 1995.
153. Yoichi Kuroda, interview with author, San Francisco, 29 June 1995.
154. Michael Marx, interview with author, 28 June 1995.
155. Mitsubishi, "Sustainable Development"; "How Does Mitsubishi Corporation Ride the Waves of Change?" Mitsubishi Corporation brochure, n.d.
156. Official from Mitsubishi Corporation Nuclear Fuel Department who wished to remain anonymous, interview with author, Tokyo, January 1994.

Chapter Five: Toxic Empire

1. World Bank figures presented at the NGO Technical Seminar and Strategy Meeting on Private Sector Development and the Role of the World Bank Group, Washington, DC, 3–6 June 1996.
2. Bruce Rich, "Public International Financial Institutions: Environmental Performance and Management," statement before the Subcommittee on International Economic Policy, Trade, Oceans and Environment, U.S. Senate Committee on Foreign Relations, 3 March 1994, p. 1.
3. Bruce Rich, *Mortgaging the Earth: The World Bank, Environmental Impoverishment, and the Crisis of Development* (Boston: Beacon Press, 1994); Walden Bello with Shea Cunningham and Bill Rau, *Dark Victory: The United States, Structural Adjustment and Global Poverty* (San Francisco: Institute for Food and Development Policy, 1994).
4. Rich, *Mortgaging the Earth*, p. 25.
5. Cheryl Payer, *The World Bank: A Critical Analysis* (New York: Monthly Review Press, 1982), pp. 19–22.
6. Ibid., p. 20.
7. Lloyd Bentsen, U.S. Secretary of the Treasury, statement before the Foreign Operations Subcommittee of the U.S. Senate Appropriations Committee, 27 April 1993; contract recipients included Bechtel, Cargill, Chevron, Dow Chemical, General Motors, General Electric and Westinghouse. U.S. Treasury Department, *Multilateral Development Banks: Increasing U.S.*

Exports and Creating U.S. Jobs (Washington, DC: U.S. Government Printing Office, 19 May 1994).

8. World Bank figures from Rich, "International Financial Institutions," p. 16.

9. Yoichi Kuroda, "Vested Interests: Japan and the World Bank," *AMPO: Japan-Asia Quarterly Review*, vol. 23, no. 3 (1992), p. 38.

10. Nobuo Kojima, "Japanese ODA and Corporate Expansion: Problem Areas and Lawyers' Responses" (Paper presented at the Second Conference of Lawyers of Asia and the Pacific, Tokyo, 26–28 September 1991).

11. PEAN, "Government Resorts to Forcible Taking of Masinloc Property!" and "Campaign Against Mitsubishi: Defending the Commons in Masinloc," Philippine Environmental Action Network Alerts, n.d.; "Priests Hit Napocor Tactics on Masinloc Coal Plant," *Nation* (Philippines), 27 June 1994; Roby Alampay, "Ramos to Officiate in Groundbreaking of Coal-Fired Plant," *Today* (Philippines), 22 June 1994.

12. Kojima, "Japanese ODA"; Kanda Hiroshi, "A Big Lie: Japan's ODA and Environmental Policy," *AMPO: Japan-Asia Quarterly Review*, vol. 23, no. 3 (1992), p. 44.

13. During the 1960s and 1970s, Honduras and Nicaragua led the world in per capita pesticide poisonings; Daniel Faber, *Environment Under Fire: Imperialism and the Ecological Crisis in Central America* (New York: Monthly Review Press, 1993), pp. 83–115.

14. Joshua Karliner, "Central America's Other War," *World Policy Journal*, vol. 6, no. 4 (Fall 1989), pp. 787–94.

15. Payer, *The World Bank*, p. 99.

16. "No Dollars for Destruction: Bankfacts," Greenpeace International World Bank Fact Sheet #1, September 1994.

17. Payer, *The World Bank*, p. 99.

18. Patrick E. Tyler, "Awe-Struck U.S. Executives Survey the China Market," *New York Times*, 2 September 1994, p. C1; Jeff Pelline, "U.S. Businesses Pour into China," *San Francisco Chronicle*, 17 May 1994; UNCTAD, *Transnational Corporations in the World Economy and Trends in Foreign Direct Investment*, E/C.10/1994/2 (Geneva: United Nations Economic and Social Council, 11 March 1994), p. 7.

19. "The World Bank and Climate Change," Greenpeace International World Bank Fact Sheet #5, September 1994.

20. Marcus Colchester and Larry Lohmann, *Tropical Forestry Action Plan: What Progress?* (Penang, Malaysia: World Rainforest Movement, 1990); Rich, *Mortgaging the Earth*, pp. 160–64.

21. Rich, *Mortgaging the Earth*, pp. 164–65.

22. Korinna Horta, comments at the meeting of the World Rainforest Movement, New Delhi, 4 April 1994; also Vandana Shiva, "After 50 Years: Is the World Bank Socially and Environmentally Responsible?" Third World Network Features, December 1994.

23. See Tom Athanasiou, *Divided Planet: The Ecology of Rich and Poor* (New York: Little, Brown, 1996), pp. 277–87.

24. Rich, *Mortgaging the Earth*, pp. 175–81.

25. Ibid.

26. Global Environment Facility, "GEF FY 93 Investment Projects—Fourth Tranche," project briefs, p. 33; GEF, "Nigeria: Escravos-Flared Gas Reduction Project," project documentation.

27. Kenneth T. Derr, "Oil and Its Critics: The Facts and the Future" (Remarks delivered to the Cambridge Energy Research Associates Executive Conference, Houston, 8 February 1994).

28. "Nigeria: Flared Gas Utilization (Reduction) Project (Investment)," (U.S. Government comments to the Global Environment Facility, n.d.).

29. Angela Wood and Alex Wilks, *Recent World Bank Assessment of Structural Adjustment's Social Impacts* (London: Bretton Woods Project, 1996), p. 1.

30. Bello with Cunningham and Rau, *Dark Victory*.

31. UNCTAD, *Transnational Corporations*, p. 4.

32. Bello with Cunningham and Rau, *Dark Victory*, pp. 51–65; Dominic Hogg, *The SAP in the Forest: The Environmental and Social Impacts of Structural Adjustment Programmes in the Philippines, Ghana and Guyana* (London: Friends of the Earth, 1993).

33. Bello with Cunningham and Rau, *Dark Victory*, p. 58.

34. Michelle Chan, *The Anatomy of a Deal* (Washington, DC: Friends of the Earth, 1996), p. 4.

35. International Finance Corporation, *Annual Report 1995* (Washington, DC: International Finance Corporation, 1995), pp. 3–8.

36. Bob Miller, consultant with the International Finance Corporation, Economics Department, presentation to NGO Technical Seminar and Strategy Meeting on Private Sector Development and the Role of the World Bank Group, Washington, DC, 3 June 1996.

37. *World Bank Annual Report 1995* (Washington, DC: World Bank), p. 30.

38. Jeff Gerth, "In Post-Cold-War Washington, Development Is a Hot Business," *New York Times*, 25 May 1996.

39. Peter Bosshard, *The Private Sector Lending of the World Bank Group: Issues and Challenges* (Geneva: Berne Declaration, January 1996), pp. 17–18.

40. International Finance Corporation, *Annual Report 1995*, p. 7.

41. Sarah Anderson, John Cavanagh and Sandra Gross, *NAFTA's Corporate Cadre: An Analysis of the USA*NAFTA State Captains* (Washington, DC: Institute for Policy Studies, 1993).

42. Tom Hilliard, *Trade Advisory Committees: Privileged Access for Polluters* (Washington, DC: Public Citizen, 1991). Only after pressure from groups such as Public Citizen were these committees, which are given preferential access and input to trade negotiations (in effect, helping to design the agreements), opened to token representation from environmental and consumer groups.

43. UNTCMD, *World Investment Report 1992: Transnational Corporations as Engines of Growth* (New York: United Nations, Transnational Corporations and Management Division, Department of Economic and Social Development, 1992), pp. 2–5, 32–35.

44. Martin Khor, *The Uruguay Round and Third World Sovereignty* (Penang, Malaysia: Third World Network, 1990), p. 6.

45. China, which is increasingly opening its doors to foreign investment, has an even larger consumer market, estimated at nearly 350 million people. Andrew Tanzer, "This Time It's for Real," *Forbes*, 2 August 1993.

46. Public Interest Research Group, *The State of India's Economy 1994–1995* (New Delhi: Public Interest Research Group, 1995), p. 10.

47. Pratip K. Chatterjee, general manager, Corporate Planning, ICI India, interview with author, New Dehli, 13 April 1994; John S. Hamilton, managing director, Cargill Seeds India, interview with author, Bangalore, India, 21 March 1994.

48. Cited in Ashish Kothari, "Environment," *Alternative Economic Survey 1993–94*, (New Delhi: Public Interest Research Group, 1994), p. 163.

49. National Fishworkers Forum, *A Dossier on the All India Fisheries Bandh* (New Delhi: National Fishworkers Forum, 26 February 1994); John Kurien, "Joint Action Against Joint Ventures: Resistance to Multinationals in Indian Waters," *The Ecologist*, vol. 25, no. 2/3 (Mar.–Apr. 1995).

50. Ashish Kothari, interview with author, New Delhi, 13 April 1994.

51. Some evidence does exist that environmental deregulation has been instigated by transnational corporations. For instance, in its efforts to set up a refinery on the Kutch Coast of India, the Japanese corporation C. Itoh insisted that part of the Marine National Park in the Gulf of Kutch be "denotified" before it moved in. Kothari, "Environment," p. 162.

52. M. D. Nanjundaswamy, interview with author, Bangalore, India, 19 March 1994.

53. Martin Khor, "500,000 Indian Farmers Rally Against GATT and Patenting of Seeds," *Third World Resurgence*, no. 39 (November 1993).

54. Tom Kochery, interview with author, New Delhi, 8 April 1994.

55. Girish Sant, Shantu Dixit and Subodh Wagle, *The Enron Controversy: Techno-Economic Analysis and Policy Implications* (Pune, India: Prayas, 1995); "Enron Power Project Scrapped," *Indian Express*, 4 August 1995; John F. Burns, "India Project in the Balance," *New York Times*, 6 September 1995.

56. Lawrence H. Summers, World Bank office memorandum, 12 December 1991.

57. Death and injury compensation figures from *Times of India*, 1 October 1994. The Indian Government's Council for Medical Research believes that the number of permanent injuries exceeds 150,000. Wil Lepkowski, "The Restructuring of Union Carbide," in Sheila Jasanoff ed., *Learning from Disaster: Risk Management After Bhopal* (Philadelphia: University of Pennsylvania Press, 1995).

58. ESCAP/UNCTC, *Environmental Aspects of Transnational Corporation Activities in Pollution-Intensive Industries in Selected Asian and Pacific Developing Countries*, ESCAP/UNCTC Publ. Ser. B, no. 15 (New York: United Nations, Economic and Social Commission for Asia and the Pacific, 1990), p. 62; Larry Everest, *Behind the Poison Cloud: Union Carbide's Bhopal Massacre* (Chicago: Banner Press, 1986), pp. 17–64; David Weir, *The Bhopal Syndrome* (San Francisco: Sierra Club Books, 1987), p. 59; David Dembo, Ward Morehouse and Lucinda Wykle, *Abuse of Power: Social Performance of Multinational Corporations: The Case of Union Carbide* (New York: New Horizons Press, 1990), pp. 88–91.

59. ESCAP/UNCTC, *Environmental Aspects*, p. 61.

60. ESCAP/UNCTC, *Environmental Aspects*, p. 59.

61. ESCAP/UNCTC, *Environmental Aspects*, pp. 240–67.

62. Tekla S. Perry, "Cleaning Up," *IEEE Spectrum* (International Association of Electric and Electronic Engineers), February 1993, p. 25.

63. ESCAP/UNCTC, *Environmental Aspects*, p. 12.

64. Dr. Jerome Nriagu, cited in Kenny Bruno and Jed Greer, "Chlorine Industry Expansion: The New Threat from the North," *Third World Resurgence*, no. 34 (June 1993), p. 19.

65. Everest, *Behind the Poison Cloud*, pp. 58–59.

66. UNCTC, *World Investment Report 1992*, p. 237.

67. As the critics commented, "There are no orchards in or around Richmond which provide the only means of sustenance to communities. Neither . . . does the pollution-infested James River provide fresh fish to the surrounding localities." Claude Alvares, ed., *Unwanted Guest: Goans vs. DuPont* (Goa: The Other India Press, 1994), p. 61.

68. Jane Rissler and Margaret Mellon, *Perils Amidst the Promise: Ecological Risks of Transgenic Crops in a Global Market* (Cambridge, MA: Union of Concerned Scientists, 1993), pp. 72–73.

69. ESCAP/UNCTC, *Environmental Aspects*, p. 3.

70. In one case of many, British-owned Thor Chemicals imported thousands of pounds of mercury waste from European and U.S. corporations such as American Cyanamid and burned them in its mercury reprocessing plant in South Africa under conditions that would not have been allowed in the United States or Europe. Numbers of workers suffered mercury poisoning, and mercury effluent from the plant contaminated the Mngeweni River, used by Zulu villagers, livestock and game for drinking water. Greenpeace, *The Gods Must Be Crazy: Mercury Wastes Dumped by Thor in South Africa* (Amsterdam: Greenpeace International, 1990).

71. Jim Puckett and Cathy Fogel, "A Victory for Environment and Justice: The Basel Ban and How It Happened," *Toxic Trade Update* (Greenpeace International), no. 7.1 (1994), pp. 2–13.

72. U.S. Government Accounting Office figures cited in Sandra Marquardt, Laura

Glassman and Elizabeth Sheldon, *Never Registered Pesticides: Rejected Toxics Join the "Circle of Poison"* (Washington, DC: Greenpeace, December 1991), p. 1.

73. Kenny Bruno, *Greenpeace Book on Greenwash* (Washington, DC: Greenpeace International, 1992), pp. 20–21.

74. The pesticide industry is also generally expanding its production and markets in countries such as Brazil, Mexico, India, China, Indonesia and South Korea. National manufacturers make up a significant part of the market share in those nations. Angus Wright, "Where Does the Circle Begin? The Global Dangers of Pesticide Plants," *Global Pesticide Campaigner* (Pesticide Action Network), vol. 4, no. 4 (December 1994); Jed Greer, "Pesticide Manufacturers Proliferate," *Third World Resurgence*, no. 52 (December 1994), pp. 5–7.

75. World Health Organization, *Public Health Impact of Pesticides Used in Agriculture* (Geneva: World Health Organization, 1990), p. 85.

76. J. Jeyaratnam, "Acute Pesticide Poisoning: A Major Global Health Problem," *World Health Statistic Quarterly*, 43 (1990), pp. 139–43.

77. Bruno and Greer, "Chlorine Industry," p. 19; Barry I. Castleman, "The Double Standard in Industrial Hazards," *International Journal of Health Services*, vol. 13, no. 1 (1983), pp. 6–8.

78. Control Risks Group, *Business Security Outlook 1996* (Washington, DC: Control Risks Group, 1996), p. 8.

79. Kenny Bruno, "Poison Petrol: Leaded Gas Exports to the Third World," *Multinational Monitor*, July–August 1991; Jack Doyle, *Hold the Applause! A Case Study of Corporate Environmentalism as Practiced at DuPont* (Washington, DC: Friends of the Earth, 1991), pp. 34–36.

80. Walden Bello, *People and Power in the Pacific: The Struggle for the Post-Cold War Order* (San Francisco: Institute for Food and Development Policy, 1992), p. 60.

81. Bruno, *Greenwash*, pp. 20–21.

82. Walden Bello and Stephanie Rosenfeld, *Dragons in Distress: Asia's Miracle Economies in Crisis* (San Francisco: Institute for Food and Development Policy, 1990), p. 214.

83. Cited in John Ross, "Treasure of the Costa Grande," *Sierra*, July–August 1996, p. 22.

84. Barbara Rose Johnston and Gregory Button, "Human Environmental Rights Issues and the Multinational Corporation: Industrial Development in the Free Trade Zone," in Barbara Rose Johnston, ed., *Who Pays the Price? The Sociocultural Context of the Environmental Crisis* (Washington, DC: Island Press, 1994), pp. 206–15.

85. Robert A. Sanchez, "Health and Environmental Risks of the Maquiladora in Mexicali," *Natural Resources Journal*, vol. 30 (Winter 1990), pp. 163–70.

86. Proceedings of Interdenominational Hearings on Toxics in Minority

Communities, Southwest Organizing Project, National Council of Churches, cited in Johnston, "Human Environmental Rights," p. 209.

87. Johnston, "Human Environmental Rights," p. 210.

88. Sanford J. Lewis, Marco Kaltofen and Gregory Ormsby, *Border Trouble: Rivers in Peril—A Report on Water Pollution Due to Industrial Development in Northern Mexico* (Boston: National Toxics Campaign Fund, May 1991), p. vii.

89. Molly Moore, "Toxic Cleanup Along Border a Huge Flop, GAO Study Says," *San Francisco Examiner*, 4 August 1996.

90. Faced with rising wages and growing environmental problems at home, Taiwanese corporations are also migrating throughout Southeast Asia. In fact, Taiwan has replaced Japan as the largest foreign investor in the Philippines, Malaysia, Thailand and Indonesia. It is also the leading investor in Vietnam. Bello, *People and Power*, p. 89.

91. Richard J. Barnet and John Cavanagh, *Global Dreams: Imperial Corporations and the New World Order* (New York: Simon & Schuster, 1994), pp. 184–204.

92. In order to expand its market, the industry is vigorously promoting PVC use in the South. Already, PVC accounts for more than 25 percent of the world's chlorine production, and that percentage appears to be growing. Bruno and Greer, "Chlorine Industry Expansion," pp. 20–21.

93. Mitsubishi Corporation official who wished to remain anonymous, interview with author, Tokyo, January 1994.

94. Philip Shenon, "Energy-Hungry, Asia Embraces Nuclear Power," *New York Times*, 23 April 1995.

95. Don Mathew and Andrew Rowell, *The Environmental Impact of the Car* (Washington, DC: Greenpeace, 1992), p. 6.

96. Patrick E. Tyler, "China Planning People's Car to Put Masses Behind Wheel," *New York Times*, 22 September 1994.

97. Alejandro Calvillo Unna, "La Contribución del Transporte a la Contaminación Atmosférica," in *El Transporte y la Contaminación*, Proceedings of the Atmosphere and Energy Campaign Seminar (Mexico City: Greenpeace Mexico, March 1993).

98. Whereas the United States has 1.6 people per car, the countries of the former USSR average 21 people per auto, India has 455 per vehicle and China more than 1,000 (in 1994 China had fewer autos than Belgium), providing plenty of opportunities for the expansion of sales and production in countries whose economies are growing rapidly. Mathew and Rowell, *Impact of the Car*, p. 6.

99. The other three heavy industries are telecommunications, computers and petrochemicals. Tyler, "China Planning."

100. Automobiles are already the single largest source of atmospheric pollution. Their exhaust fumes cause cancer, lead poisoning, acid air pollution and a variety of respiratory illnesses. And cars consume one-third of the world's

oil, the drilling, transportation and refining of which cause other serious environmental problems. Mathew and Rowell, *Impact of the Car*, pp. 14–44.

101. "Cars: The Hidden Costs of Four Extra Wheels," Third World Network Features, 1994.

102. Abdul Jabbar Khan, interview with author, Bhopal, 13 April 1994.

103. While taking "moral responsibility" for the disaster, Carbide employed numerous tactics in its effort to avoid liability. It designated India as a codefendant, accusing it of contributory negligence. It put forth a sabotage theory. It denied responsibility for its Indian subsidiary. It deceptively touted an "excellent" health and safety record. It employed a legal strategy to delay the case as much as possible. It co-opted Indian professionals. It launched a PR campaign that downplayed the nature of the substance leaked, blamed the victims and gave a positive spin to its relief and settlement offers. David Dembo, Clarence J. Dias, Ayesha Kadwani and Ward Morehouse, *Nothing to Lose But Our Lives: Empowerment to Oppose Industrial Hazards in a Transnational World* (New York: New Horizons Press, 1988), pp. 27–46.

104. Lepkowski, "Restructuring of Union Carbide."

105. Cited in Ibid.

106. Pratip K. Chatterjee, interview with author.

107. ICI is the single largest water polluter in the United Kingdom, violating its water pollution permits there more than 1,200 times between 1985 and 1992. The company is the largest dumper of industrial waste into the North Sea and the largest discharger of mercury into the Irish Sea. What's more, as one of the ten largest chemical corporations on the planet and the second-largest pesticide manufacturer, ICI/Zeneca continues to be the world's leading producer of paraquat, aggressively marketing it in more than 130 nations. Environmental advocates estimate that paraquat causes at least 1,000 deaths annually, or the equivalent of the official Bhopal toll every six years. Pesticide Action Network, Greenpeace International and International Organization of Consumers Unions, "Review of the Pesticide Paraquat for Submission to the World Bank Pesticide Advisory Panel," Washington, DC, 6–7 December 1989, p. 13; Castleman and Navarro, p. 618.

108. DuPont official Rita Heckrote, cited in Alvares, ed., *Unwanted Guest*, p. 19.

109. The clause states that DuPont and its representatives will be "harmless from any claims made in the Republic of India against representatives of DuPont or its assignees alleging bodily harm or death sustained as a direct result of, or in direct connection with, the performance of this Agreement." Mark Schapiro, "DuPont's Post-Bhopal Blues," *The Nation*, 2 November 1992, p. 500.

110. Control Risks Group, *Business Security Outlook*, p. 8.

111. The 1993 environmental market totaled $4 billion in Latin America, $10 billion in Asia and $5 billion in Eastern Europe. Projections for 1998 were $7 billion, $13 billion and $10 billion respectively. Environmental Business International, "Competitive Analysis of U.S. Environmental Exports and Global Market Update," Environmental Business International, San Diego, 1995, pp. 6, 15, 21.

112. Levi Richardson, US-ASEAN Business Council, interview with author, Washington, DC, 10 June 1993.

113. International Center for Environmental Technology Transfer brochure, Yokkaichi, Japan.

114. *Environment Watch: Latin America*, Cutter Information Corp. brochure, November 1992, p. 6.

115. Rust International, *Annual Report 1993* (Birmingham: Rust International).

116. Thomas G. Smith, vice-president for Asia, Waste Management International, interview with author, Hong Kong, 31 January 1994.

117. World Resources Institute, *World Resources: A Guide to the Global Environment* (New York: Oxford University Press, 1992), p. 52.

118. Gary Lee, "World Bank, Mexico Agree on Pollution Cleanup Loan," *Washington Post*, 29 September 1993.

119. Alejandro Salmon A., "La Basura, Desecho Que Se Convierte en Polemica," *Diario de Chihuahua*, 23 February 1995.

120. Connie Murtagh, "As the World Burns," *Toxic Trade Update* (Greenpeace International), no. 6.2 (second quarter 1993).

121. Sobhana William, interview with author, Penang, Malaysia, 3 March 1994.

122. Thomas G. Smith, interview with author.

123. Veronica Odriozla, Greenpeace Argentina, interview with author, Buenos Aires, 11 July 1995.

124. Nobuo Kojima, interview with author, Tokyo, 12 January 1994.

125. Satinath Sarangi, Bhopal Group for Information and Action, interview with author, Bhopal, 11 April 1994.

126. Woolard quoted in Schapiro, "Post-Bhopal Blues," p. 501.

127. Sabra Bi, interview with author, Bhopal, India, 11 April 1994.

Chapter Six: The Emerald City

1. Kenny Bruno, *The Greenpeace Book on Greenwash* (Washington, DC: Greenpeace International, 1992), p. 1.

2. Paul Hawken, *The Ecology of Commerce: A Declaration of Sustainability* (San Francisco: Harper Business, 1993), p. 130.

3. John C. Stauber and Sheldon Rampton, *Toxic Sludge Is Good for You: Lies, Damn Lies and the Public Relations Industry* (Monroe, ME: Common Courage Press, 1995), pp. 18–24.

4. Rachel Carson, *Silent Spring* (New York: Fawcett Crest, 1962).

5. E. Bruce Harrison, *Going Green: How to Communicate Your Company's*

Environmental Commitment (New York: Irwin Professional Publishing, 1993), pp. xiv–xv.

6. John C. Stauber, "Going . . . Going . . . Green!" *PR Watch*, vol. 1, no. 3 (1994), p. 2.

7. David R. Brower, *For Earth's Sake: The Life and Times of David Brower* (Salt Lake City: Peregrine Smith Books, 1990), pp. 214–17.

8. Stauber, "Going . . . Going . . . Green!" p. 2.

9. Jerry Mander, interview with author, San Francisco, 7 February 1995.

10. Jerry Mander, "Ecopornography: One Year and Nearly a Billion Dollars Later, Advertising Owns Ecology," *Communication Arts*, vol. 14, no. 2 (1972), pp. 45–56; Thomas Turner, "Eco-Pornography or How to Spot an Ecological Phony," in Garrett de Bell, ed., *The Environmental Handbook: Prepared for the First National Environmental Teach-In* (New York: Ballantine/Friends of the Earth, 1970), pp. 263–67.

11. Mander, "Ecopornography," p. 47.

12. Jack Doyle, "'Enviro Imaging' for Market Share: Corporations Take to the Ad Pages to Brush Up Their Images," *Not Man Apart* (Friends of the Earth), no. 2 (1990).

13. Jack Doyle, *Hold the Applause! A Case Study of Corporate Environmentalism as Practiced at DuPont*, (Washington, DC: Friends of the Earth, 1991), p. iii.

14. Alan Thein Durning, "Can't Live Without It," *World Watch*, May–June 1993, p. 18.

15. Narrator's comment in *The Prize*, part 7, "The New Order of Oil," an Invision Production for Majestic Films and Transpacific Films in association with BBC-TV and WGBH Boston, 1992.

16. "What on Earth Is Dow Doing?" Dow Chemical Company advertisement.

17. Nakamura Yoichi, "The Ecobusiness Logic," *AMPO: Japan-Asia Quarterly Review*, vol. 23, no. 3 (1992), p. 56.

18. Joshua Karliner, "God's Little Chopsticks," *Mother Jones*, September–October 1994, p. 16.

19. Bruno, *Greenwash*, p. 20.

20. Doyle, "Enviro Imaging."

21. ICI advertisement, *Malay Mail*, 5 April 1993.

22. Kenny Bruno and Jed Greer, "Imperial Chemical Industries," Greenwash Snapshot #10 (Greenpeace International), 1993; Walden Bello, *People and Power in the Pacific: The Struggle for the Post-Cold-War Order* (San Francisco: Institute for Food and Development Policy, 1992), p. 57.

23. K. D. Sadhale, interview with author, Ponda, Goa, India, 3 April 1994.

24. "Preserving Nature Is a Good Deal," Aracruz Cellulosa advertisement; Christina Lamb, "Chopping Down Rainforest Myths," *Financial Times* (London), 8 January 1992.

25. Exxon "Hay Un Tigre Que Cuida de los Ciervos" advertisement in *Gerencia Ambiental* (Buenos Aires), May 1994.

26. Justin Lowe, "Chevron's Fish Stories," *San Francisco Bay Guardian*, 18 July 1990, p. 26.

27. Other Eco-Fund donors included Volkswagen, Swatch and 3M; Thomas Harding, Danny Kennedy and Pratap Chatterjee, *Whose Summit Is It Anyway? An Investigative Report on the Corporate Sponsorship of the Earth Summit* (Rio de Janeiro: ASEED-International Youth Network, June 1992).

28. Lewis C. Winters, "Does It Pay to Advertise to Hostile Audiences with Corporate Advertising?" *Journal of Advertising Research*, June–July 1988, pp. 11–18.

29. Ralph C. Wooton, Communications and Advertising, Chevron Corporation, personal communication with author, 19 December 1994.

30. Lowe, "Chevron's Fish Stories," p. 45; Chevron justifies the campaign by citing the $1.5 billion total the company spends complying with environmental laws. William Mulligan, Chevron Federal Relations, interview with author, 25 October 1994.

31. Greg Lyon, *Target Four Investigation of Chevron Advertisements*, KRON-TV news video, San Francisco, n.d.

32. Justin Lowe and Hillary Hansen, "A Look Behind the Advertising," *Earth Island Journal*, Winter 1990, p. 27.

33. Lyon, *Target Four Investigation*.

34. Winters, "Does It Pay?" p. 11.

35. Jerry Mander, interview with author.

36. Durning, "Can't Live Without It," p. 17.

37. Consumers' Association of Penang, *Selling Dreams: How Advertising Misleads Us* (Penang, Malaysia: Consumers' Association of Penang, 1986), pp. 134–42.

38. Michael C. Lasky, "Earth-Friendly PR Claims Must Meet FTC's 'Green' Guidelines," *O'Dwyer's PR Services Report*, February 1995.

39. Doyle, *Hold the Applause!* p. 53.

40. Ben Bagdikian, *The Media Monopoly*, 4th ed. (Boston: Beacon Press, 1992), cited in Stauber and Rampton, *Toxic Sludge*, p. 181; N. John, "The Global Media: Caught in a Whirlpool of Bad Logic," Third World Network Features, 1994.

41. Ronald K. L. Collins, *Dictating Content: How Advertising Pressure Can Corrupt a Free Press* (Washington, DC: Center for the Study of Commercialism, 1992), pp. 27–30; William Greider, *Who Will Tell the People? The Betrayal of American Democracy* (New York: Simon & Schuster, 1992), p. 329.

42. Collins, *Dictating Content*, pp. 9–12; $3 billion figure from "Corporate Advertising Expenditures 1988–1992 in Nine Media," Leading National Advertisers/Arbitron Multi-Media Services, Publishers Information Bureau, 1993.

43. Karel van Wolferen, *The Enigma of Japanese Power: People and Politics in a Stateless Nation* (London: Macmillan, 1989), pp. 230–37.

44. Ibid., p. 234.

45. Durning, "Can't Live Without It," p. 13.

46. Chin Saik Yoon, "New Global Trends Worsen N-S Information Imbalance," *Third World Resurgence*, no. 58 (June 1995), pp. 17–19; Inez Hedges, "Transnational Corporate Culture and Cultural Resistance," *Socialism and Democracy*, vol. 9, no. 1 (Spring 1995), pp. 151–64.

47. Ricardo Zisis, "El Joint Venture de las Américas," and Ted Bardacke, "Comprar Mucho, Vender Más," both in *América Economía, Número Especial*, 1993–1994.

48. Marcus W. Brauchli, "A Satellite TV System Is Quickly Moving Asia into the Global Village," *Wall Street Journal*, 10 May 1993.

49. Anthony Simoes, interview with author, Mapusa, Goa, India, 2 April 1994.

50. James Petras, "Cultural Imperialism in the Late 20th Century," *Third World Resurgence*, no. 37 (September 1993), p. 30.

51. Durning, "Can't Live Without It," p. 13.

52. Takuya Negami, interview with author, Tokyo, 25 January 1994.

53. Consumers' Association of Penang, *Selling Dreams*, pp. 7–8, 104.

54. Rajni Kothari, *Growing Amnesia: An Essay on Poverty and the Human Consciousness* (New Delhi: Viking-Penguin, 1993), p. 107.

55. John Berger, *Ways of Seeing* (London: Penguin Books, 1972), pp. 131, 149.

56. Stauber and Rampton, *Toxic Sludge*, pp. 17–19.

57. Ibid.

58. Buddy Menton, general manager, Marine Department, Exxon Company USA, correspondence to Terry A. Kirkley, Exxon Corporation, 12 January 1977.

59. Ibid.

60. "Action Plan to Prepare for 1977 Legislative Session," Exxon, Alaska, n.d.

61. Greider, *Who Will Tell the People?*

62. The lawsuit came in response to an Exxon suit seeking compensation from the insurance companies for its clean-up and other spill-related costs. "Insurers Sue Exxon Over Alaska Spill," Associated Press, 1 September 1993.

63. Caleb Solomon, "Exxon Attacks Scientific Views of Valdez Spill," *Wall Street Journal*, 15 April 1993.

64. Agis Salpukas, "Exxon Is Accused of 'Astonishing Ruse' in Oil-Spill Trial," *New York Times*, 14 June 1996.

65. Stauber and Rampton, *Toxic Sludge*, p. 125.

66. Kevin McCauley, interview with author, 22 February 1995.

67. Alan Chai, Alta Campbell and Patrick J. Spain, *Hoover's Handbook of World Business 1993* (Austin, TX: Reference Press, 1993), p. 85.

68. Stauber and Rampton, *Toxic Sludge*, pp. 13, 125.

69. Chevron, for example, has its own internal public affairs group, which employs forty professionals who are constantly busy handling media relations, writing speeches, producing publications, developing advertising,

conducting opinion research, coordinating lobbying, managing investor
relations and administering grants and programs. All of this is overseen
by a manager of corporate communications and a vice-president in charge
of public affairs. *O'Dwyer's Directory of Public Relations Firms 1993* (New
York: J. R. O'Dwyer Co., 1993), p. 49.

70. Stauber and Rampton, *Toxic Sludge*, p. 2.

71. "Young and Rubicam, 1994 Facts and Figures," Young and Rubicam brochure.

72. *O'Dwyer's Directory of PR Firms 1993*, cited in *PR Watch*, vol. 1, no. 3 (1994),
p. 8.

73. Bruno, *Greenwash*, pp. 6–7.

74. Joyce Nelson, *Sultans of Sleaze* (Toronto: Between the Lines, 1989), pp. 21–42.

75. Joyce Nelson, "Great Global Greenwash: Burson-Marsteller, Pax Trilateral,
and the Brundtland Gang vs. the Environment," *Covert Action*, no. 44
(Spring 1993), p. 27.

76. Bob Davis, "Mexico Mounts a Massive Lobbying Campaign to Sell North
American Trade Accord in U.S.," *Wall Street Journal*, 20 May 1993.

77. Burson-Marsteller, "Public Relations/Public Affairs Worldwide," brochure,
cited in Bruno, *Greenwash*, pp. 6–7; Joyce Nelson, "On the Road to Rio:
Burson-Marsteller, Global Power-Brokers" (unpublished).

78. John Dillon, "Poisoning the Grassroots: PR Giant Burson-Marsteller Thinks
Global, Acts Local," *Covert Action*, no. 44 (Spring 1993), pp. 34–38; Nelson,
"Great Global Greenwash," p. 58.

79. David Corn, "Bad Air Day," *Nation*, 24 March 1997, p. 18.

80. Naomi Roht-Arriaza, "Shifting the Point of Regulation: The International
Organization for Standardization and Global Law Making on Trade and
the Environment," *Ecology Law Quarterly*, vol. 22 (1995), pp. 479–539;
Naomi Roht-Arriaza, interview with author, 18 June 1996.

81. Harrison, *Going Green*, p. 257.

82. Council on Economic Priorities, "America's Least Wanted: The 1994
Campaign for Cleaner Corporations," *Research Report* (Council on
Economic Priorities), November–December 1994.

83. Chris Bedford et al., *Just Cause: Bhopal 10 Year Commemoration* (New York:
Communities Concerned about Corporations, November 1994).

84. Peter Simmons and Brian Wynne, "Responsible Care: Trust, Credibility and
Environmental Management," in Kurt Fischer and Johan Schot, eds.,
*Environmental Strategies for Industry: International Perspectives on Research
Needs and Policy Implications* (Washington, DC: Island Press, 1993), pp.
201–26. Ironically, while Bhopal catalyzed the creation of Responsible
Care, the voluntary code does not apply to foreign subsidiaries of member
companies. There are also a number of other fundamental problems with
the program. For instance, while it operates under the motto "Don't trust
us, track us," Responsible Care hasn't provided the public with any more
information to track chemical companies than was available before.

While it calls for the development of "safe" products, the program doesn't present criteria for what "safe" means, allowing member companies to define banned pesticides and ozone-destroying chemicals as "safe." Furthermore, Responsible Care's definition of "pollution prevention" dwells on "solutions" such as waste management and source reduction, rather than clean production; thus methods of waste disposal, such as incineration, are legitimized as "pollution prevention" by Responsible Care. Bruno, *Greenwash*, pp. 4–5.

85. Harrison, *Going Green*, p. 260.

86. Ibid., p. 105.

87. Ibid., p. 106

88. Suzanne Alexander Ryan, "Companies Teach All Sorts of Lessons with Educational Tools They Give Away," *Wall Street Journal*, 19 April 1994; Jodi Mailander and Cyril T. Zanesky, "Big Business and the Classroom," *Miami Herald*, 17 April 1994; Stewart Allen, "Exxon's School Spill," *San Francisco Weekly*, 9 December 1992; Keith Schneider, "Exxon Is Ordered to Pay $5 Billion for Alaska Spill," *New York Times*, 17 September 1994.

89. John J. Fried, "Firms Gain Hold in Environmental Education," *Philadelphia Inquirer*, 27 March 1994.

90. David Lapp, "Private Gain, Public Loss," *Environmental Action*, Spring 1994; Ryan, "Companies Teach."

91. Angela Gennino, "Pulling the Plug on Channel One," *Detroit News*, 29 September 1994.

92. Jay Mathews, "The Entrepreneur's Grade Expectations," *Washington Post*, 29 July 1994; Margaret Spillane, "Unplug It!" *The Nation*, 21 November 1994.

93. "Links with Activist Groups Get Results in Environmental PR," *O'Dwyer's PR Services Report*, vol. 8, no. 2 (February 1994), pp. 1, 20–22.

94. Jonathan Lash, remarks made during a PCSD press briefing, Washington, DC, 26 October 1994.

95. Lois Gibbs, phone interview with author, 21 March 1995.

96. Laura Nader, "From Legal Process to Mind Processing," *Family and Conciliation Courts Review*, vol. 30, no. 4 (October 1992), pp. 468–73.

97. "Links with Activist Groups" pp. 1, 20–22.

98. Craig Smith, "The New Corporate Philanthropy," *Harvard Business Review*, May–June 1994, p. 106.

99. Ronald A. Duchin quoted in "MBD's Divide-and-Conquer Strategy to Defeat Activists," *PR Watch*, October–December 1993, p. 6.

100. Nina Kogan, phone interview with author, 14 March 1995; "Corporate Relations Program," World Resources Institute brochure, 1995.

101. Kimberlee A. McDonald, director of foundation relations, National Audubon Society, phone interview with author, 14 March 1995; National Audubon Society, *Annual Report 1994*, p. 13.

102. Mark Dowie, *Losing Ground: American Environmentalism at the Close of the Twentieth Century* (Cambridge: MIT Press, 1995), p. 57.

103. Dowie, *Losing Ground*, pp. 53–59, 115; Margaret Morgan-Hubbard, "Money and Environmental Groups: How Clean Is Green?" *Environmental Action*, Winter 1996, pp. 20–23.

104. Nature Conservancy, *Annual Report 1994*, p. 58.

105. This makes up about 6 percent of all corporate philanthropy; Dowie, *Losing Ground*, p. 54. While it maintains its political independence, the Sierra Club Foundation has received small grants from a number of corporations. Despite a strong set of guidelines stipulating that gifts will not be accepted from recognized major polluters, consistent violators of environmental laws or major antagonists of environmental organizations, the Sierra Club has accepted small grants (often through its local chapters) from the IBM Corporation, National Semiconductor and Nissan of North America. The Sierra Club Foundation, along with many other environmental groups, also accepts donations made by individual employees of corporations such as ARCO and Exxon and automatically (and blindly) matched by their employers. *In Service to Grassroots Environmentalism: Annual Report 1993* (San Francisco: Sierra Club Foundation); "Sierra Club Policy on Corporate Fundraising," 1 July 1993; William H. Meadows, Centennial Campaign director, Sierra Club, interview with author, San Francisco, 6 November 1995.

106. For a more in-depth analysis of the environmental movement's role in the NAFTA debate, see Dowie, *Losing Ground*, pp. 184–88.

107. David T. Buzzelli, remarks made during a PCSD press briefing, Washington, DC, 26 October 1994.

108. "Links with Activist Groups," p. 20.

109. Dowie, *Losing Ground*, pp. 139–40.

110. Lois Gibbs, interview with author.

111. Joe Kane, "With Spears from All Sides," *The New Yorker*, 27 September 1993; Dowie, *Losing Ground*, pp. 119–21.

112. Cited in Dowie, *Losing Ground*, p. 58.

113. For the best account of Wise Use, see David Helvarg, *The War Against the Greens* (San Francisco: Sierra Club Books, 1994).

114. Carl Deal, *The Greenpeace Guide to Anti-Environmental Organizations* (Berkeley, CA: Odonian Press, 1993), pp. 19–22; Dowie, *Losing Ground*, pp. 93–98.

115. Stauber and Rampton, *Toxic Sludge*, pp. 75–98.

116. Michael Weisskopf and David Maraniss, "Forging an Alliance for Deregulation: Rep. DeLay Makes Companies Full Partners in the Movement," *Washington Post*, 12 March 1995; John H. Cushman, Jr., "Lobbyists Helped the G.O.P. in Revising Clean Water Act," *New York Times*, 22 March 1995.

117. A partial list of the PCSD member in 1994: Dick Barth, Ciba-Geigy; Dick Clarke, PG&E; Pete Correll, Georgia-Pacific; Ken Derr, Chevron; William Hoglund, General Motors; Sam Johnson, S. C. Johnson & Son; Ken Lay, Enron; Dave Buzzelli, Dow Chemical; William Ruckelshaus, Browning-Ferris; John Adams, NRDC; Jay Hair, NWF; Fred Krupp, EDF; Jonathan Lash, WRI; Michelle Perrault, Sierra Club; John Sawhill, Nature Conservancy; Bruce Babbitt, Interior; Ron Brown, Commerce; Carol Browner, EPA; Mike Espy, Agriculture; Madeline Kunin, Education.

118. Audubon receives money from Chevron, Dow, Enron and Georgia-Pacific; Audubon, *Annual Report 1994*, p. 13. The WRI receives money from Chevron, BFI, Dow, Ciba-Geigy and S. C. Johnson; WRI, *World Resources Institute at a Glance* (Washington, DC: World Resources Institute, 1995), pp. 23–24. The NWF receives money for its Corporate Conservation Council from CCC members General Motors, BFI, Ciba-Geigy and S. C. Johnson; National Wildlife Federation, "Corporate Conservation Council" fact sheet, November 1995. The Nature Conservancy receives money from Chevron, Enron and Dow; Nature Conservancy, *Annual Report*, 1994, p. 58.

119. Chevron has funded the National Wetlands Coalition, Citizens for the Environment, People for the West, the Heritage Foundation, Project Relief and the Mountain States Legal Foundation. Dow has given to the Alliance for Responsible CFC Policy, the Global Climate Coalition, the Heritage Foundation and Keep America Beautiful. Browning-Ferris has helped underwrite Keep America Beautiful. Enron's money has gone to the National Wetlands Coalition and the Global Climate Coalition. Ciba-Geigy has funded Accuracy in Media. Georgia-Pacific has given to the Center for the Defense of Free Enterprise, Citizens for the Environment (a subsidiary of Citizens for a Sound Economy) and the Pacific Legal Foundation. General Motors' philanthropy has included Citizens for the Environment. The Motor Vehicle Manufacturers Association, of which GM is a member, has supported the Global Climate Coalition and Coalition for Vehicle Choice. Information on these groups and some of their corporate supporters is found in Deal, *Guide to Anti-Environmental Organizations*, pp. 23–101; information on the Clean Water Task Force comes from "Memorandum from Patricia Law, re: Clean Water Task Force," Committee on Transportation and Infrastructure, U.S. House of Representatives, 2 March 1995.

120. John Adams, interview with author, San Francisco, 26 April 1995.

121. John H. Cushman, Jr., "Adversaries Back Pollution Rules Now on the Books," *New York Times*, 12 February 1996.

122. James Gerstenzang, "The Exxon Valdez Is Back: Should Polluters be Paid?" *San Francisco Examiner*, 5 May 1996.

123. Natural Resources Defense Council, "State of Nature," *Legislative Watch*, 20 September 1996.

124. Natural Resources Defense Council, "Environment and the 105th Congress," *Legislative Watch—Special Edition*, 10 January 1997.

Chapter Seven: Grassroots Globalization

1. "La BMV Suspendió Operaciones por 2 Horas," *La Jornada*, online edition, 6 June 1995.

2. Ibid.

3. "From Global Pillage to Global Village: A Perspective from Working People and People of Color on the Unregulated Internationalization of the Economy and the North American Free Trade Agreement (NAFTA)," declaration, October 1993.

4. Roberto Bissio, "Cyberspace and the Disabled of the Global Village," *Third World Guide 1995–96* (Montevideo, Uruguay: Third World Institute, 1995), p. 71.

5. See http://www.corpwatch.org. Although some of its strongest boosters point to the Internet as the great technological leveler, progressive "nodes" such as IGC/APC comprise only a tiny segment of the activities in cyberspace— a vast global communications realm that plays a central role in integrating the world economy. The same technology that allows RAN to bombard Mitsubishi with faxes allows Mitsubishi to coordinate its activities more efficiently on a global level, including keeping abreast of activist organizing. Moreover, the mid-1990s frenzy of mergers, acquisitions and new alliances in the communications, entertainment and computer industries is leading to ever greater corporate concentration and control. See Jerry Mander, "Technologies of Globalization," in Jerry Mander and Edward Goldsmith, eds., *The Case Against the Global Economy: And for a Turn Toward the Local* (San Francisco: Sierra Club Books, 1996) pp. 353–58.

6. The International Baby Food Action Network (IBFAN) stigmatized Nestlé in the public eye and succeeded in building an international boycott of Nestle's products. Finally, after a seven-year global organizing effort, IBFAN forced the corporation to the negotiating table, where it agreed to a number of demands, including adhering to a new World Health Organization Code of Conduct on baby food. Having achieved this success, IBFAN ended the boycott. Soon thereafter, however, the campaign's limitations became clear. Nestlé began to violate and exploit loopholes in the Code of Conduct. While it has curtailed its worst excesses, Nestlé continues to expand its marketing of a mother's milk substitute in the Third World. The boycott, albeit in a much weaker form than before, has been renewed. Ellen Sokol, "A Formula for Disaster," *Multinational Monitor*, March 1992, pp. 9–13; Annelies Allain, "Breastfeeding Is Politics: A Personal View of the International Baby Milk Campaign," *The Ecologist*, vol. 21, no. 5 (Sept.–Oct. 1991), pp. 206–13.

7. Jeremy Leggett, *Climate Change and the Insurance Industry: Solidarity Among the Risk Community?* (Amsterdam: Greenpeace International, 1993).

8. "Insurers Confront Carbon Club at Berlin Climate Summit," *Greenpeace Business* (London), April 1995; for an interesting perspective, see Stephan Schmidheiny, "Insuring Our Common Future," a speech given to insurance industry leaders (www. wbcsd.ch/Speeches/speechhp.html), September 1996.

9. Generally, the U.S. paper industry continues to fiercely resist a transition to chlorine-free production. "Industries Can Benefit from Regulation," *Rachel's Hazardous Waste News* (Environmental Research Foundation), no. 344 (1 July 1993).

10. Greenpeace, *The Greenfreeze Story* (London: Greenpeace, September 1994), p. 11.

11. "Chinese Factories Win Greenfreeze Funding," *Greenpeace Business* (London), August–September 1995; Emeliano Ezcurra, Greenpeace Argentina Greenfreeze campaigner, interview with author, Buenos Aires, 21 July 1995.

12. Greenpeace, *The Greenfreeze Story*, p. 1.

13. Divestment helped trigger the peaceful revolution that ended apartheid; yet like almost every other country today, South Africa has economic options that are severely limited by the pressures and rules of the global economy. Patrick Bond, "Neoliberalism Comes to South Africa," *Multinational Monitor*, May 1996, pp. 8–14.

14. Ralph Nader, plenary speech at the International Forum on Globalization's Teach-In on the Social, Ecological, Cultural, and Political Costs of Economic Globalization, Riverside Church, New York, 10 November 1995.

15. Jeremy Brecher, "Global Village or Global Pillage?" *The Nation*, 6 December 1993, p. 685.

16. Letter to the prime minister of Canada and the presidents of the United States, Mexico and Chile, 7 June 1995.

17. Investment figures from "Evolución de la Inversión Extranjera en México," SECOFI, January 1994; poverty indicators include the fact that the infant mortality rate in Mexico tripled between 1980 and 1992. Carlos Heredia and Mary Purcell, "The Polarization of Mexican Society," cited in "World Bank Report Shows Poor Record in Mexico," *Bank Check Quarterly*, no. 11 (May 1995).

18. Subcomandante Marcos, "La Larga Travesia del Dolor a la Esperanza: Un Texto del Subcomandante Marcos," *La Jornada*, 22 September 1994.

19. Ken Silverstein and Alexander Cockburn, "Major U.S. Bank Urges Zapatista Wipe-Out: 'A Litmus Test for Mexico's Stability,'" *CounterPunch*, 1 February 1995.

20. Riordan Roett, "Mexico Political Update: Chase Manhattan's Emerging Markets Group Memo," Chase Manhattan Bank, 13 January 1995.

21. See, for example, "Reverberations from Mexico Crisis Continue," *Third World Economics*, 16 February 1995.

22. Tom Barry, *Zapata's Revenge: Free Trade and the Farm Crisis in Mexico* (Boston: South End Press, 1995), pp. 1–3, 156–59.

23. George Fernandes, interview with author, New Delhi, 8 April 1994.

24. M. D. Nanjundaswamy, interview with author, Bangalore, India, 19 March 1994.

25. Public Interest Research Group, *Cargill's Bitter Salt* (New Delhi: Public Interest Research Group, August 1993).

26. Public Interest Research Group, "Cargill Thrown Out," Action Alert, November 1993; "Cargill: The New East India Company," dossier compiled by the Research Foundation for Science, Technology and Natural Resource Policy, Dehra Dun, India.

27. Public Interest Research Group, *Cargill's Bitter Salt*, p. 28.

28. Rajni Bakshi, "From Harvard to Charkha," *Sunday Times of India*, 3 April 1994.

29. Richard L. Grossman and Frank T. Adams, *Taking Care of Business: Citizenship and the Charter of Incorporation* (Cambridge, MA: Charter Ink., January 1993), pp. 6–10.

30. Ibid., pp. 10–21.

31. Richard Grossman, interview with author, 27 June 1995.

32. The certificate of dissolution states that the Weyerhaeuser companies are "one of the major causes in the irretrievable and impending extinction of numerous salmon runs, are responsible for repeated releases of carcinogens and toxic pollutants, have violated Native sovereignty claims, treaty rights, and destroyed numerous Native sacred sites, illegally obtained much of their lands through fraudulent railroad land grant schemes, have played a dominant role in the corporate control and corruption of Congress and the American political systems through corporate financing/buying politicians, have consistently deceived the public . . . to hide the fact that they have clear cut over 4 million acres and continue to profit from the exportation of the ecological heritage of the Northwest while mills and communities suffer the economic consequences, are one of the responsible parties for the continuing decline and imperilment of the spotted owl, marbled murrelet, goshawk, pine marten fisher, bull trout, rainbow trout, steelhead, salmon and numerous other wildlife and aquatic species." Earth First! "Certificate of Dissolution: Revocation of Corporate Charter," 18 April 1995.

33. Peter Kellman, "A Goal. A Framework. A Myth." Distributed to the Corporations Group electronic mail list, 26 July 1996.

34. Ethel Klein and Guy Molyneux, *Corporate Irresponsibility: There Ought to Be Some Laws: A Study of the Political and Policy Implications of Public Attitudes Toward Corporate America* (New York: EDK Associates, 29 July 1996), p. 1.

35. Zafar Agha, "Damning Dunkel," *India Today*, 15 April 1994.

36. "Swadeshi Jagran Manch Welcomes Decision," *Times of India*, 4 August 1995; "Beginning of Swadeshi Says Advani," *Telegraph* (India), 4 August 1995.

37. Jeremy Brecher and Tim Costello, *Global Village or Global Pillage: Economic Reconstruction from the Bottom Up* (Boston: South End Press, 1994), pp. 7, 76–77.

38. Vandana Shiva, "The Greening of Global Reach," *Third World Resurgence* (Penang, Malaysia), no. 14–15 (1992), p. 58.

39. Rajni Kothari, *Growing Amnesia: An Essay on Poverty and the Human Consciousness* (New Delhi: Viking-Penguin, 1993), pp. 9–10.

40. Ibid.

41. Jorge Castaneda, *Utopia Unarmed: The Latin American Left After the Cold War* (New York: Vintage Books, 1993), p. 374.

42. This figure is from the 1970s; Jonathan Rowe, "Reinventing the Corporation," *Washington Monthly*, April 1996, p. 19.

43. "Understanding the Conflict Between Jobs and the Environment: A Preliminary Discussion of the Superfund for Workers Concept," Oil, Chemical and Atomic Workers International Union pamphlet, 1991.

44. See Kenny Bruno, *Screening Foreign Investments: An Environmental Guide for Policy Makers and NGOs* (Penang, Malaysia: Third World Network, 1994).

45. Sherle R. Schwenninger writes that "a modest levy of 0.1 percent would be so small as to have virtually no effect on capital flows but large enough . . . to yield $300 billion." "How to Save the World: The Case for a Global Flat Tax," *The Nation*, 13 May 1996, p. 17.

46. UNTCMD, *International Environmental Law: Emerging Trends and Implications for Transnational Corporations* (New York: United Nations, Transnational Corporations and Management Division, Department of Economic and Social Development, 1993), p. xv.

47. Harris Gleckman with Riva Krut, "Transnational Corporations' Strategic Responses to 'Sustainable Development,'" in *Green Globe 1995* (New York: Oxford University Press, 1995).

48. Thomas W. Lippman, "The Fight Against POPS Proves Another Tough Sell," *Washington Post*, 20 April 1995; Greenpeace International, "Global Ban on Persistent Toxic Chemicals" (Briefing paper for UNEP Inter-governmental Conference on Protection of the Marine Environment from Land-Based Activities, Washington, DC, 23 October–3 November, 1995).

49. Tony Clarke, *Dismantling Corporate Rule: Toward a New Form of Politics in an Age of Globalization* (San Francisco: International Forum on Globalization, 1996), p. 22.

50. Candido Grzybowski, "Civil Society's Responses to Globalization," Third World Network Features, posted on the Internet 2 October 1996.

Index